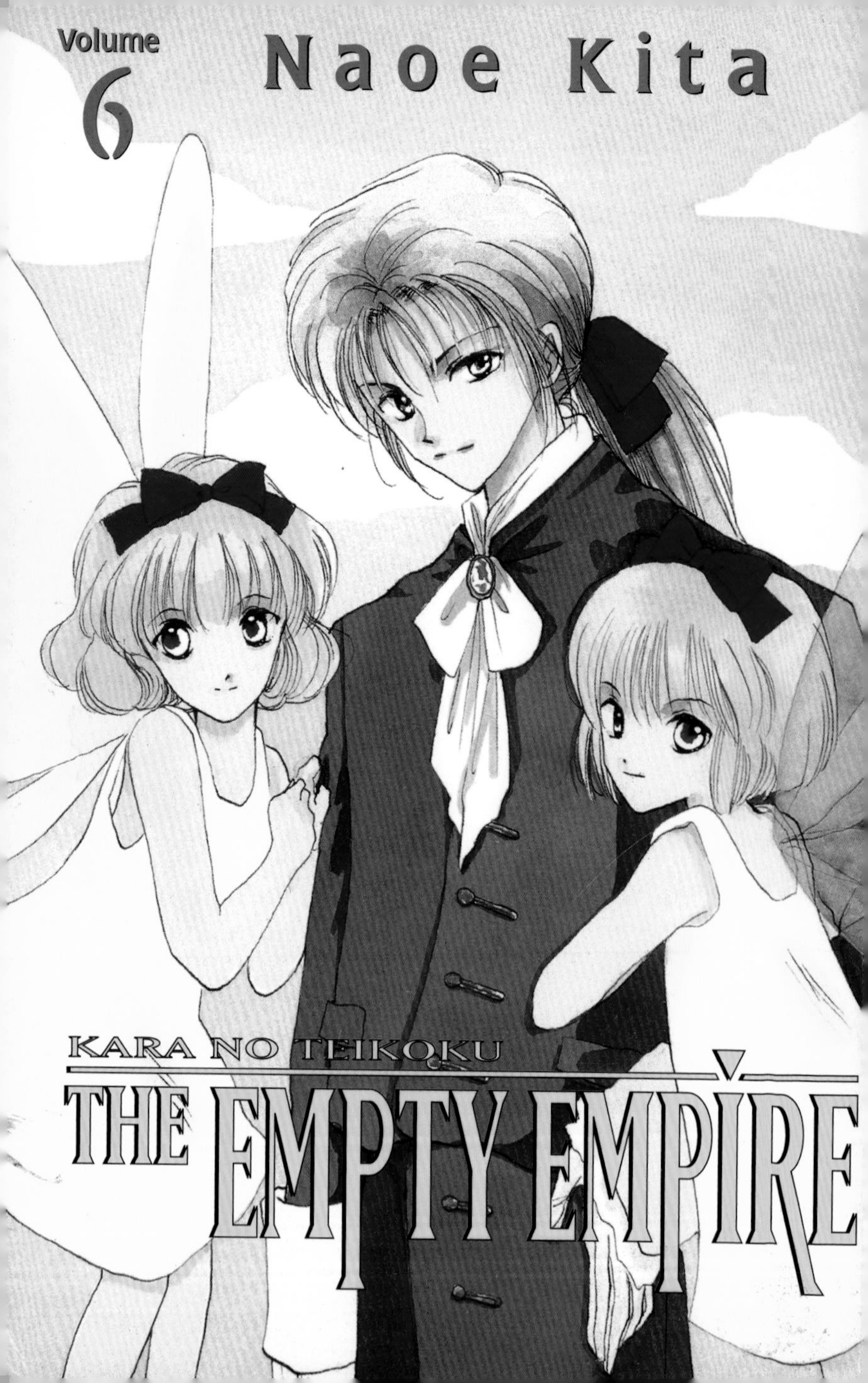
Volume
6
Naoe Kita
KARA NO TEIKOKU
THE EMPTY EMPIRE

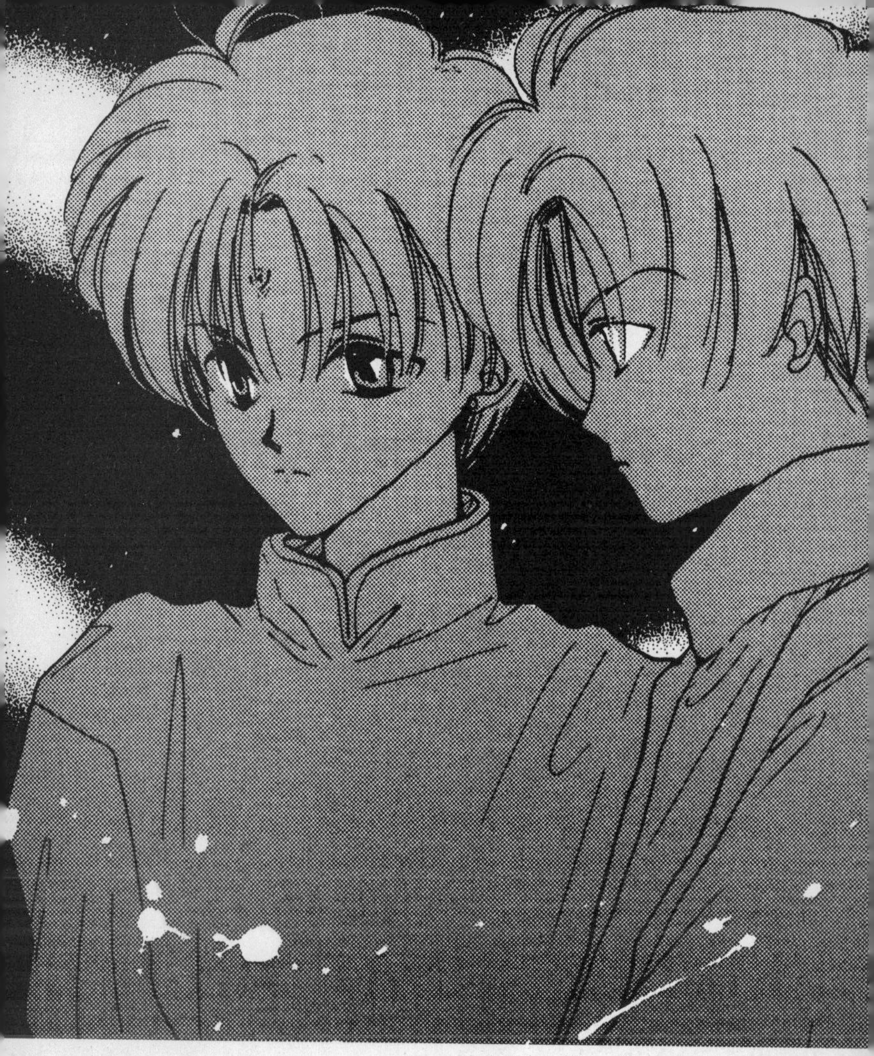

KARA NO TEIKOKU

THE EMPTY EMPIRE

By Naoe Kita

Volume 6

CONTENTS

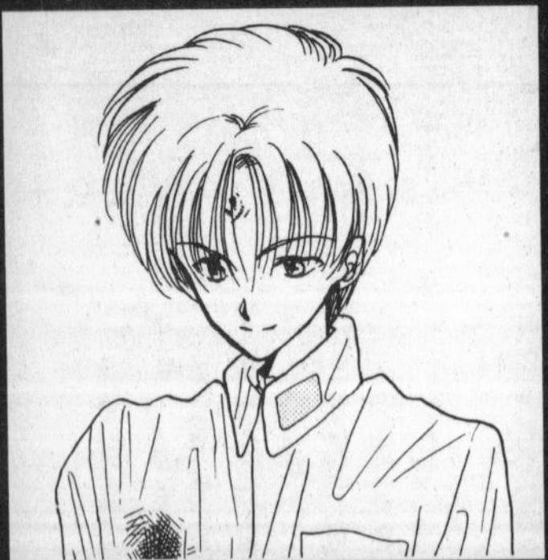

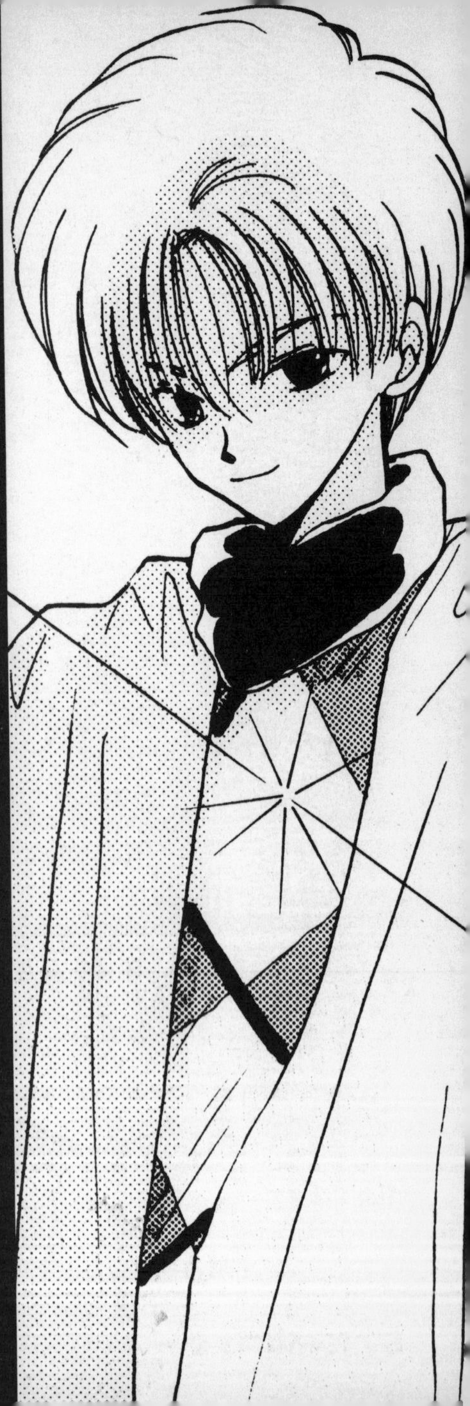

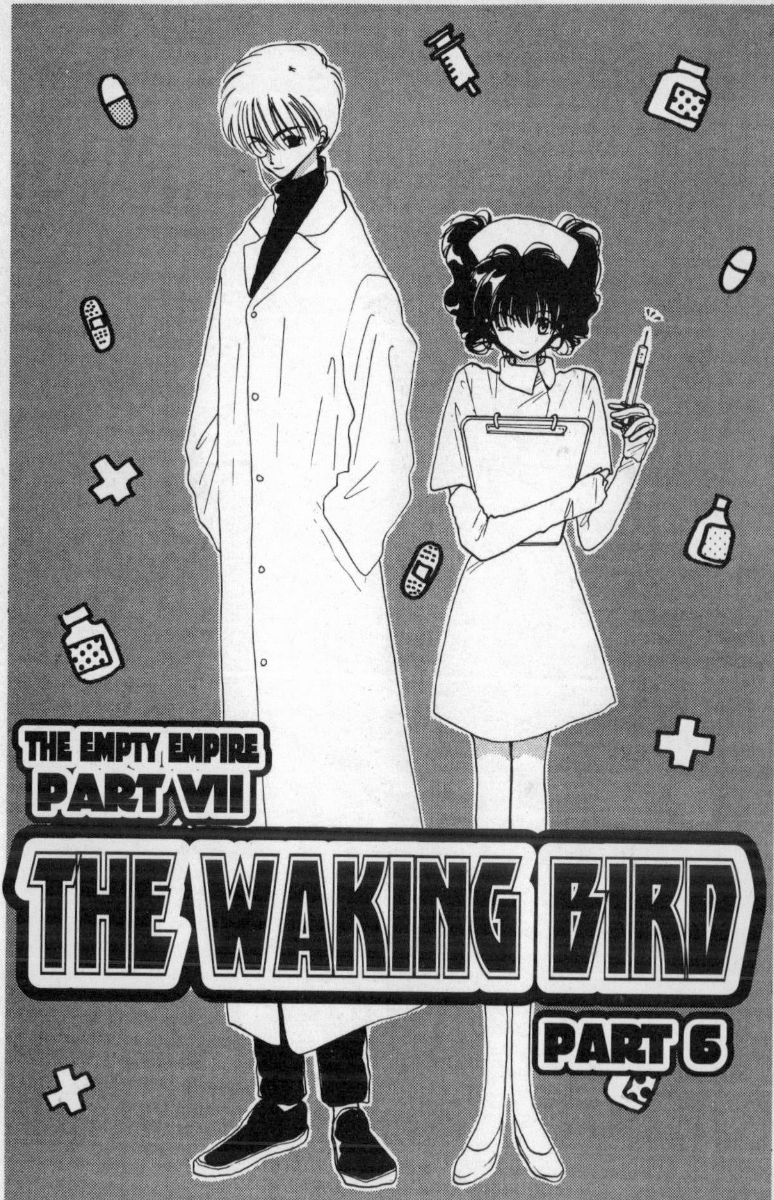
THE EMPTY EMPIRE
PART VII
THE WAKING BIRD
PART 6

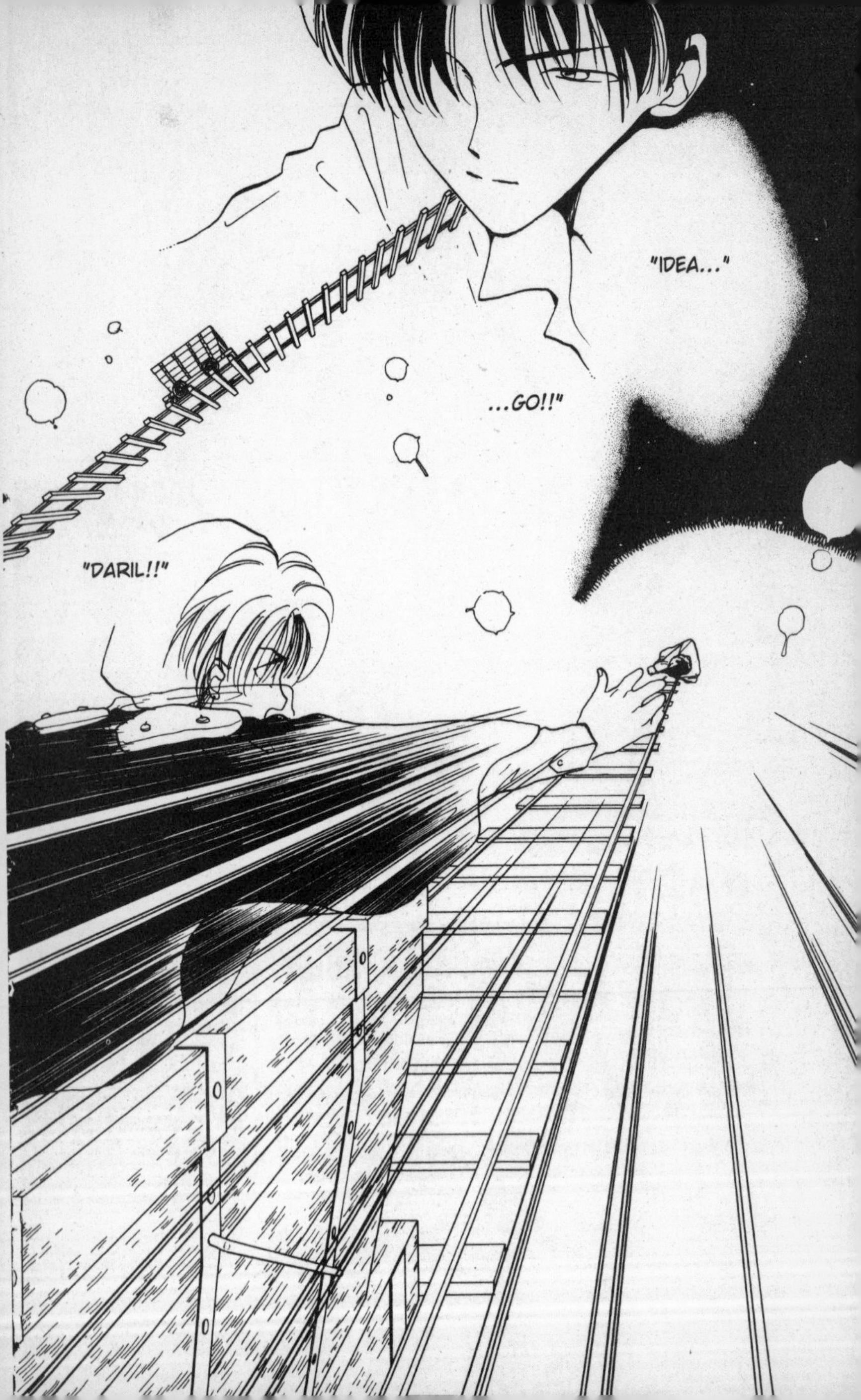
"IDEA..."
...GO!!"
"DARIL!!"

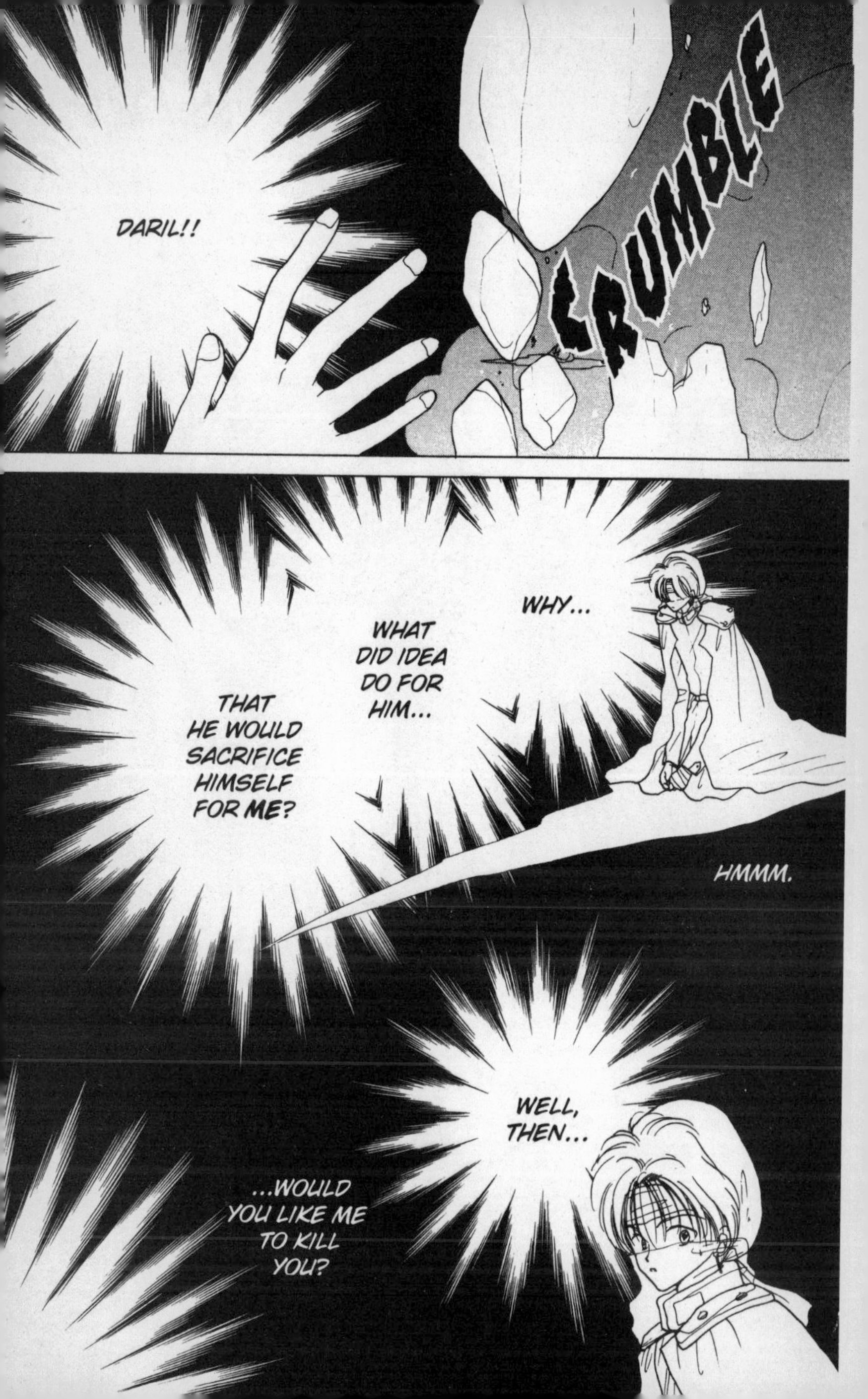
CRUMBLE
DARIL!!
WHY...
WHAT DID IDEA DO FOR HIM...
THAT HE WOULD SACRIFICE HIMSELF FOR ME?
HMMM.
WELL, THEN...
...WOULD YOU LIKE ME TO KILL YOU?

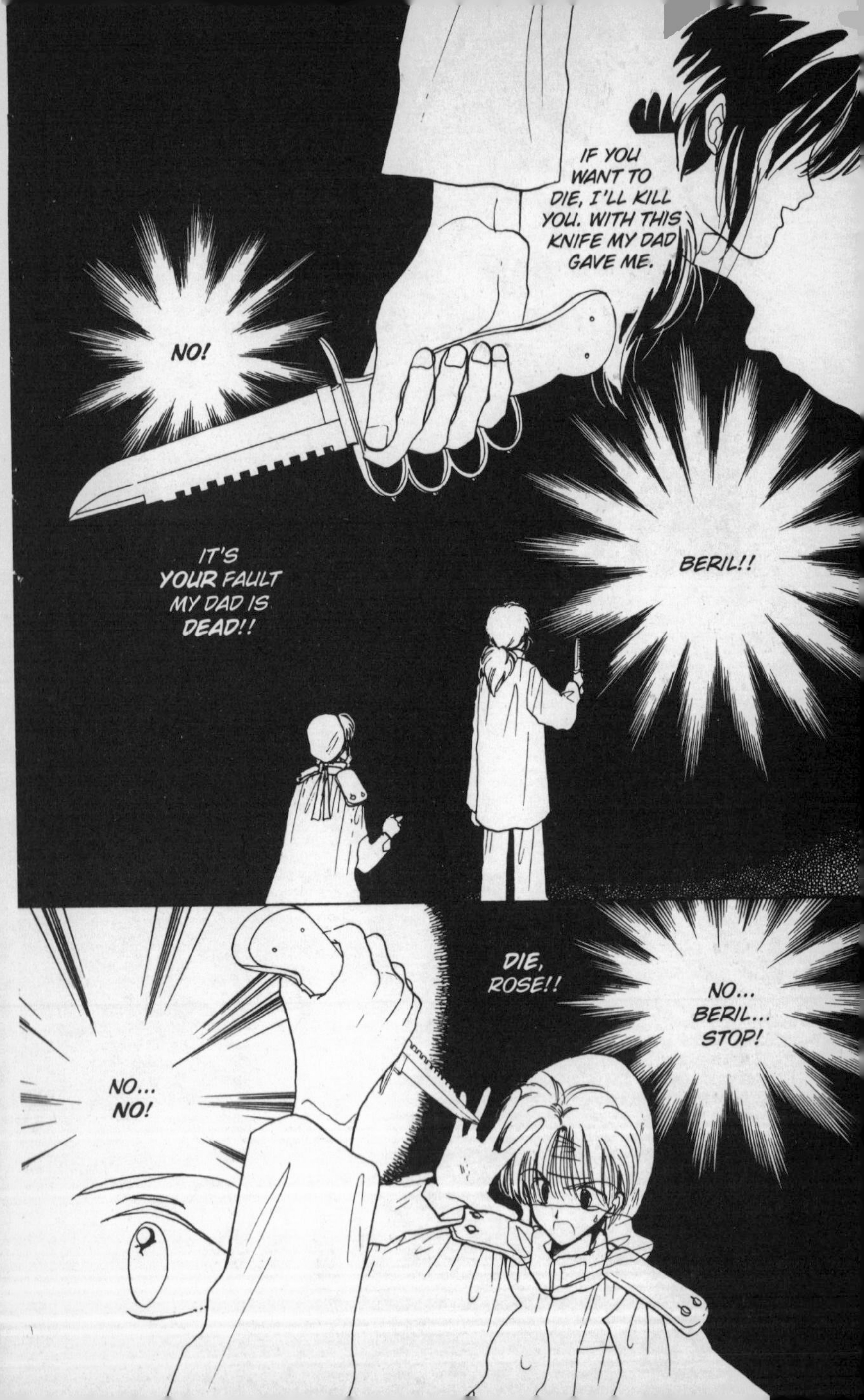
IF YOU WANT TO DIE, I'LL KILL YOU. WITH THIS KNIFE MY DAD GAVE ME.
NO!
BERIL!!
IT'S YOUR FAULT MY DAD IS DEAD!!
NO... BERIL... STOP!
DIE, ROSE!!
NO... NO!

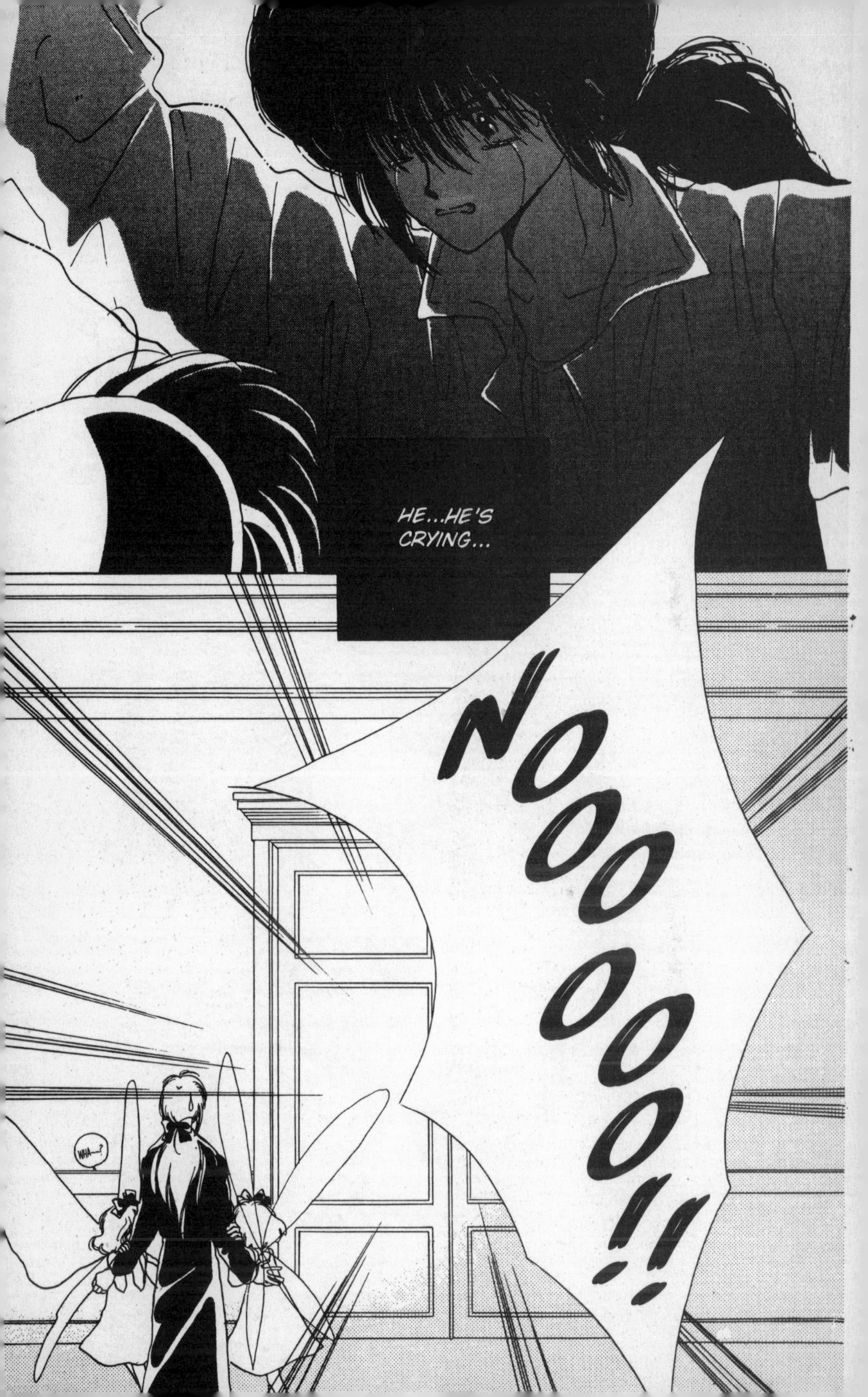
HE...HE'S CRYING...
NOOOOO!!!
WHA--?

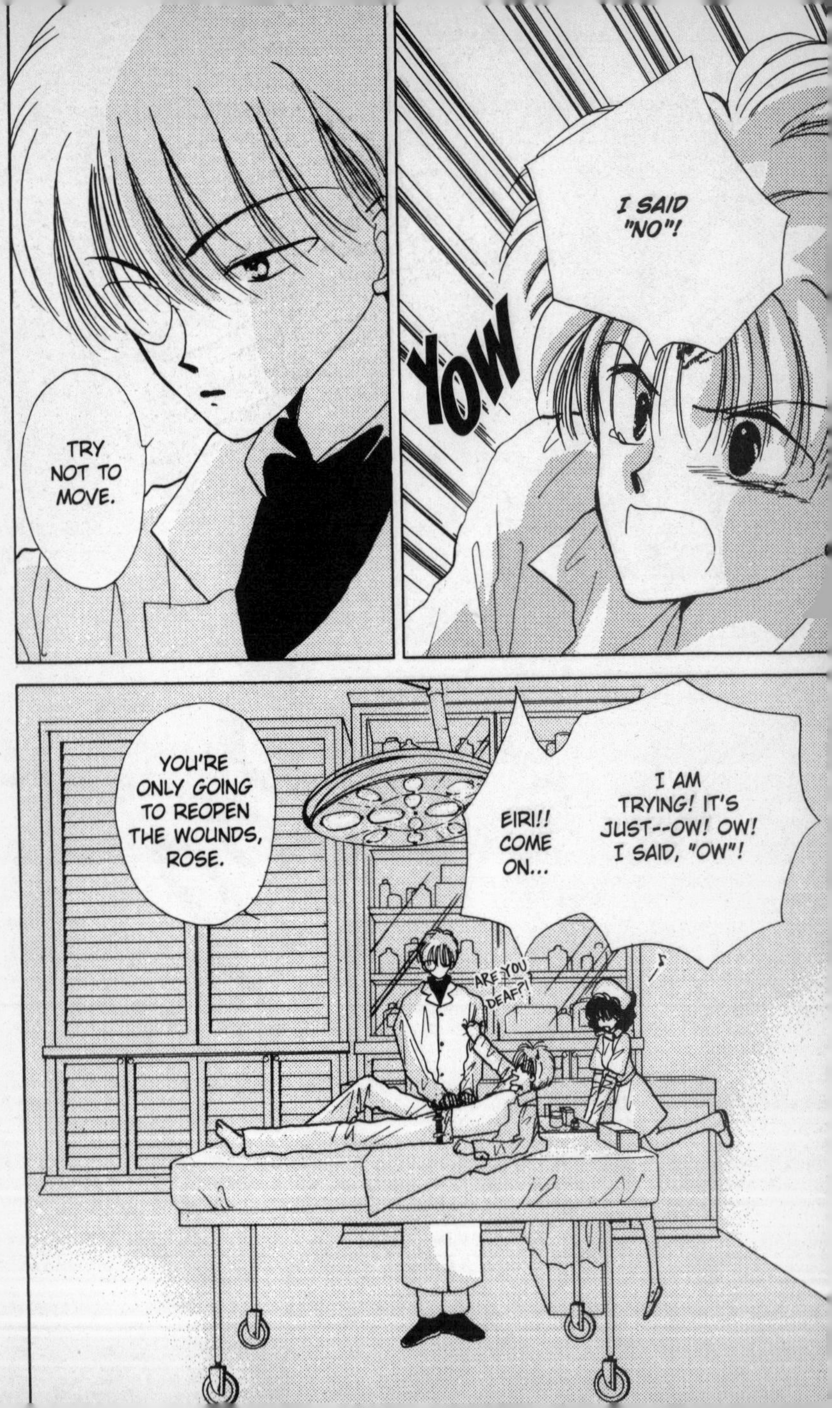
I SAID "NO"!
YOW
TRY NOT TO MOVE.
I AM TRYING! IT'S JUST--OW! OW! I SAID, "OW"!
EIRI!! COME ON...
YOU'RE ONLY GOING TO REOPEN THE WOUNDS, ROSE.
ARE YOU DEAF?!

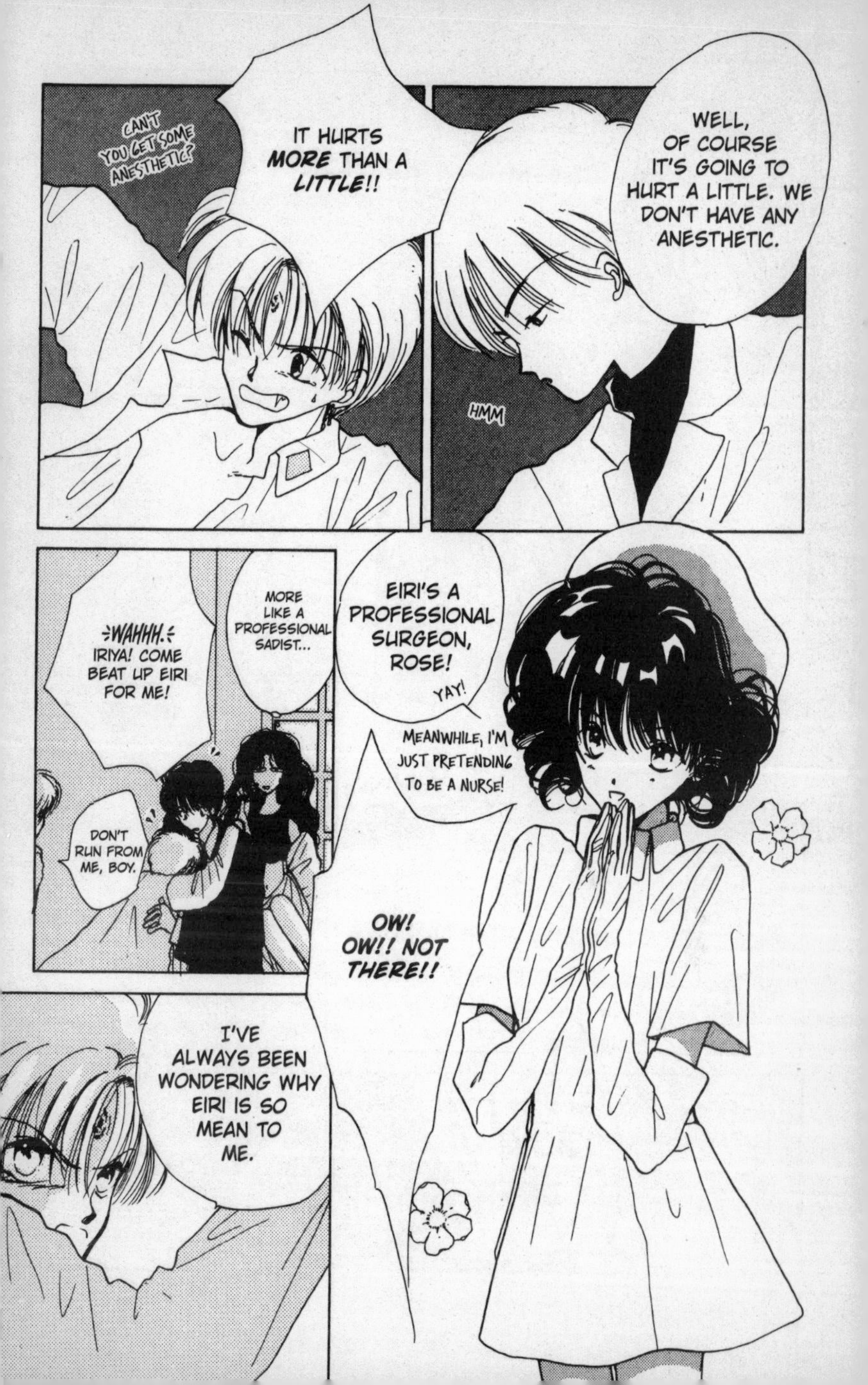
WELL, OF COURSE IT'S GOING TO HURT A LITTLE. WE DON'T HAVE ANY ANESTHETIC.
HMM
IT HURTS MORE THAN A LITTLE!!
CAN'T YOU GET SOME ANESTHETIC?
EIRI'S A PROFESSIONAL SURGEON, ROSE!
YAY!
MEANWHILE, I'M JUST PRETENDING TO BE A NURSE!
OW! OW!! NOT THERE!!
MORE LIKE A PROFESSIONAL SADIST...
WAHHH. IRIYA! COME BEAT UP EIRI FOR ME!
DON'T RUN FROM ME, BOY.
I'VE ALWAYS BEEN WONDERING WHY EIRI IS SO MEAN TO ME.

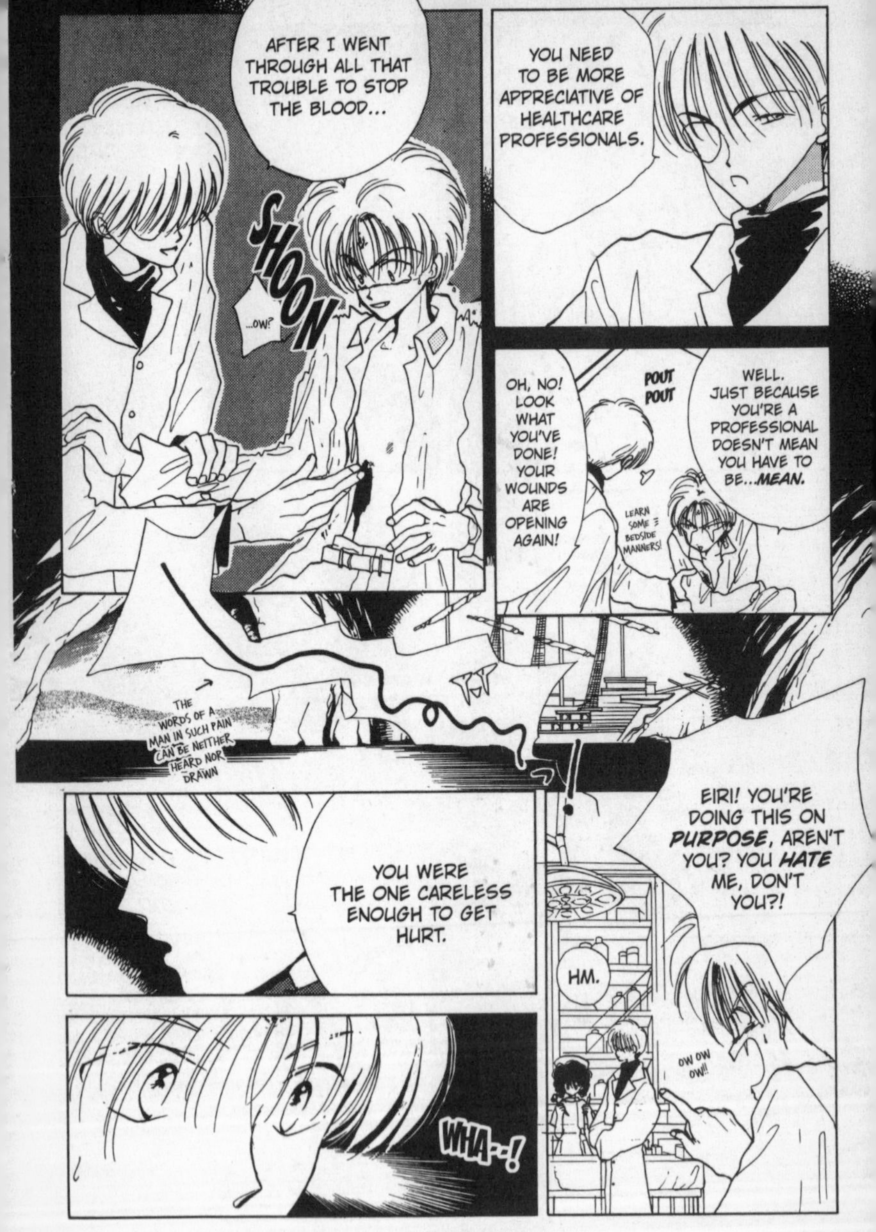
YOU NEED TO BE MORE APPRECIATIVE OF HEALTHCARE PROFESSIONALS.
WELL. JUST BECAUSE YOU'RE A PROFESSIONAL DOESN'T MEAN YOU HAVE TO BE...MEAN.
POUT POUT
OH, NO! LOOK WHAT YOU'VE DONE! YOUR WOUNDS ARE OPENING AGAIN!
LEARN SOME BEDSIDE MANNERS!
AFTER I WENT THROUGH ALL THAT TROUBLE TO STOP THE BLOOD...
SHOON
...OW?
THE WORDS OF A MAN IN SUCH PAIN CAN BE NEITHER HEARD NOR DRAWN
!
EIRI! YOU'RE DOING THIS ON PURPOSE, AREN'T YOU? YOU HATE ME, DON'T YOU?!
HM.
OW OW OW!!
YOU WERE THE ONE CARELESS ENOUGH TO GET HURT.
WHA--!

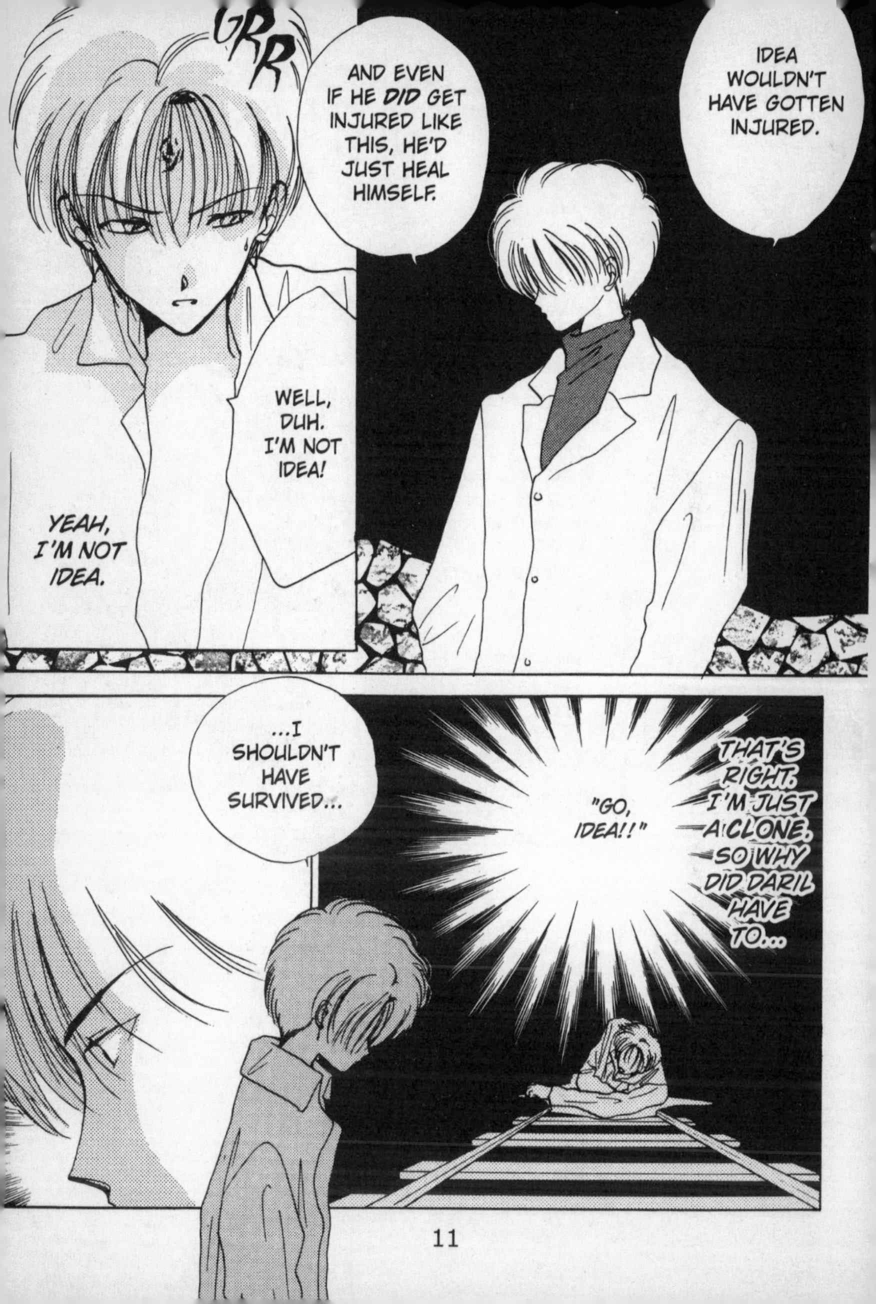

IDEA WOULDN'T HAVE GOTTEN INJURED.
AND EVEN IF HE *DID* GET INJURED LIKE THIS, HE'D JUST HEAL HIMSELF.
GRR
WELL, DUH. I'M NOT IDEA!
YEAH, I'M NOT IDEA.
THAT'S RIGHT. I'M JUST A CLONE. SO WHY DID DARIL HAVE TO...
"GO, IDEA!!"
...I SHOULDN'T HAVE SURVIVED...

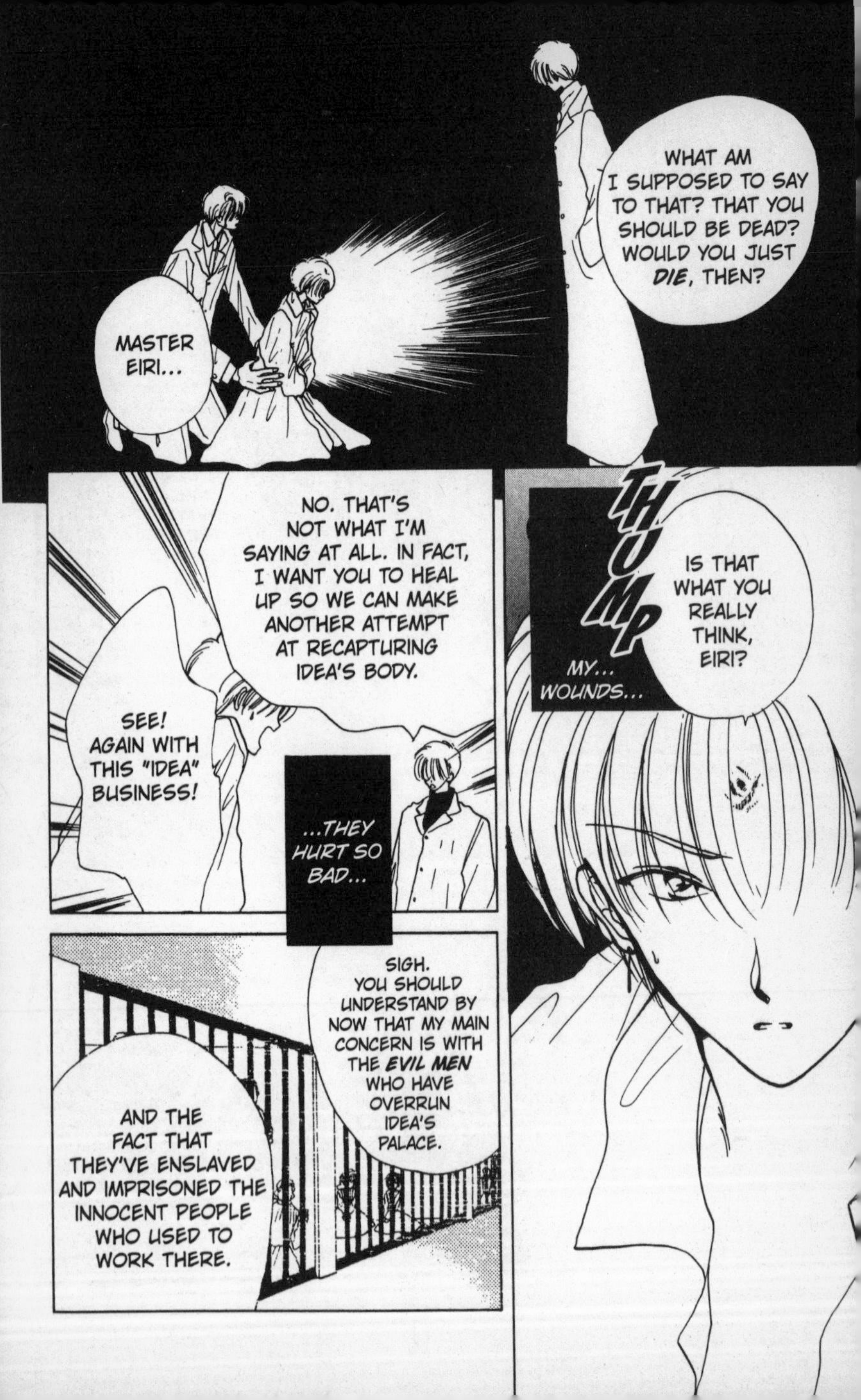
WHAT AM I SUPPOSED TO SAY TO THAT? THAT YOU SHOULD BE DEAD? WOULD YOU JUST *DIE*, THEN?
MASTER EIRI...
THUMP
IS THAT WHAT YOU REALLY THINK, EIRI?
MY... WOUNDS...
NO. THAT'S NOT WHAT I'M SAYING AT ALL. IN FACT, I WANT YOU TO HEAL UP SO WE CAN MAKE ANOTHER ATTEMPT AT RECAPTURING IDEA'S BODY.
SEE! AGAIN WITH THIS "IDEA" BUSINESS!
...THEY HURT SO BAD...
SIGH. YOU SHOULD UNDERSTAND BY NOW THAT MY MAIN CONCERN IS WITH THE *EVIL MEN* WHO HAVE OVERRUN IDEA'S PALACE.
AND THE FACT THAT THEY'VE ENSLAVED AND IMPRISONED THE INNOCENT PEOPLE WHO USED TO WORK THERE.

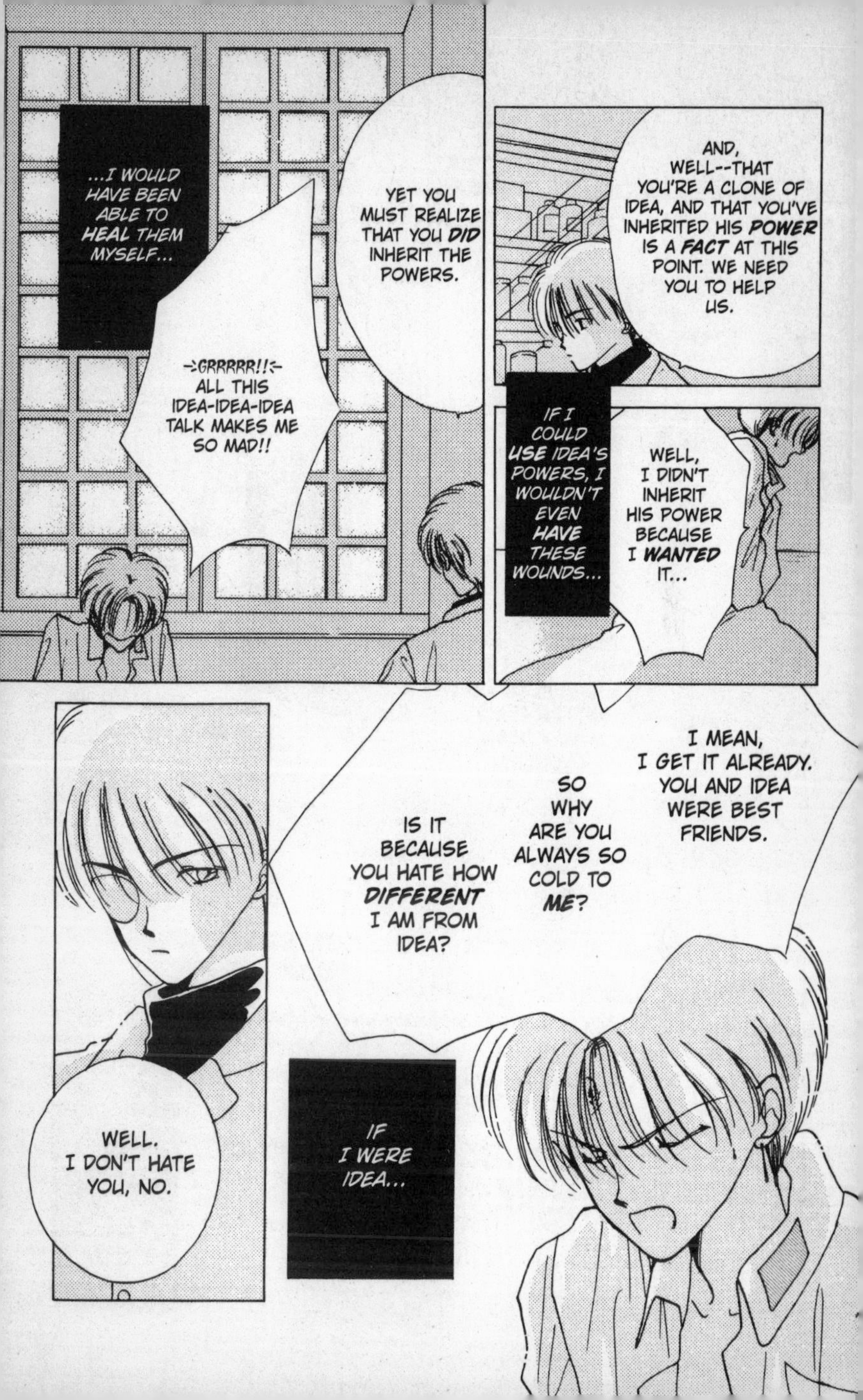
AND, WELL--THAT YOU'RE A CLONE OF IDEA, AND THAT YOU'VE INHERITED HIS POWER IS A FACT AT THIS POINT. WE NEED YOU TO HELP US.
WELL, I DIDN'T INHERIT HIS POWER BECAUSE I WANTED IT...
IF I COULD USE IDEA'S POWERS, I WOULDN'T EVEN HAVE THESE WOUNDS...
YET YOU MUST REALIZE THAT YOU DID INHERIT THE POWERS.
-GRRRRR!!- ALL THIS IDEA-IDEA-IDEA TALK MAKES ME SO MAD!!
...I WOULD HAVE BEEN ABLE TO HEAL THEM MYSELF...
I MEAN, I GET IT ALREADY. YOU AND IDEA WERE BEST FRIENDS.
SO WHY ARE YOU ALWAYS SO COLD TO ME?
IS IT BECAUSE YOU HATE HOW DIFFERENT I AM FROM IDEA?
IF I WERE IDEA...
WELL. I DON'T HATE YOU, NO.

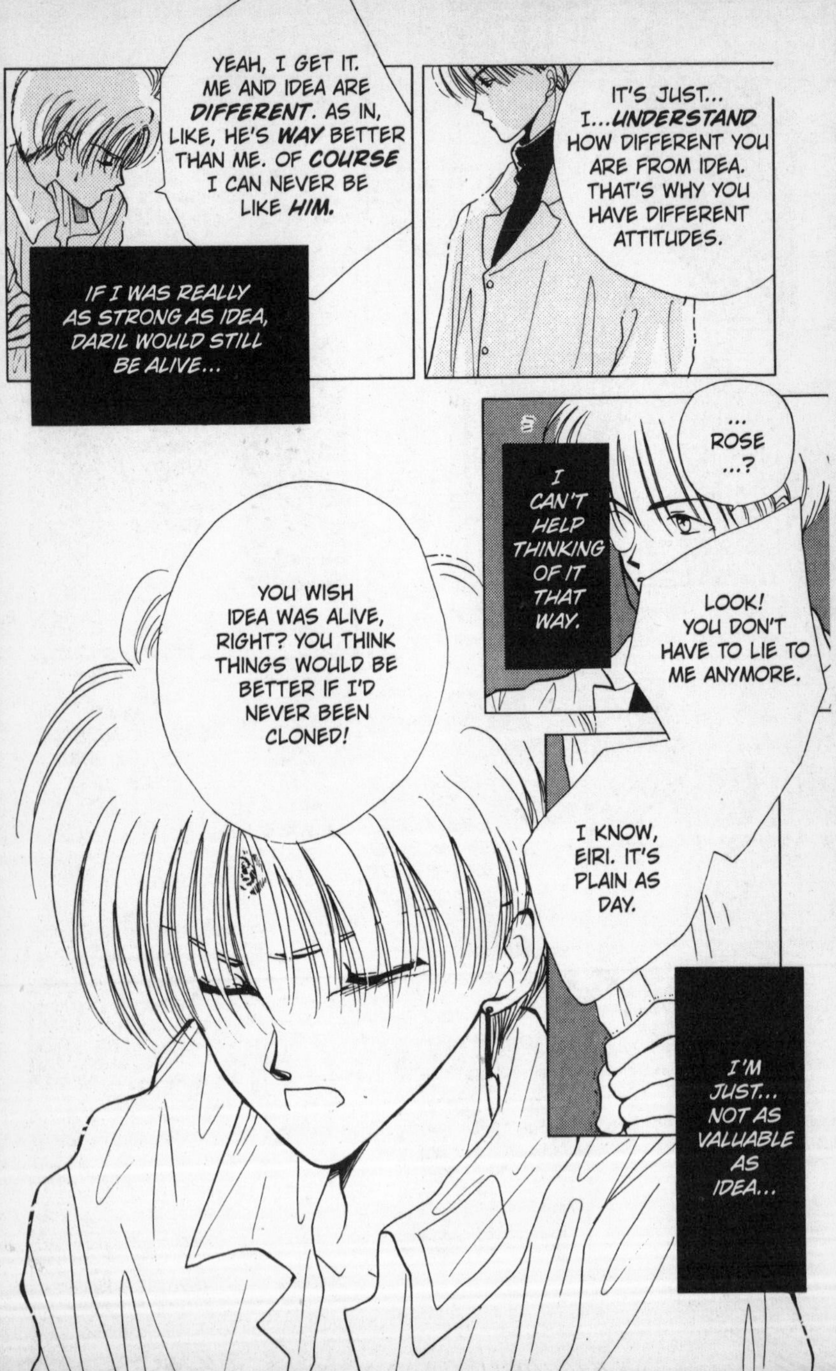
IT'S JUST... I...UNDERSTAND HOW DIFFERENT YOU ARE FROM IDEA. THAT'S WHY YOU HAVE DIFFERENT ATTITUDES.
YEAH, I GET IT. ME AND IDEA ARE DIFFERENT. AS IN, LIKE, HE'S WAY BETTER THAN ME. OF COURSE I CAN NEVER BE LIKE HIM.
IF I WAS REALLY AS STRONG AS IDEA, DARIL WOULD STILL BE ALIVE...
YOU WISH IDEA WAS ALIVE, RIGHT? YOU THINK THINGS WOULD BE BETTER IF I'D NEVER BEEN CLONED!
... ROSE ...?
I CAN'T HELP THINKING OF IT THAT WAY.
LOOK! YOU DON'T HAVE TO LIE TO ME ANYMORE.
I KNOW, EIRI. IT'S PLAIN AS DAY.
I'M JUST... NOT AS VALUABLE AS IDEA...

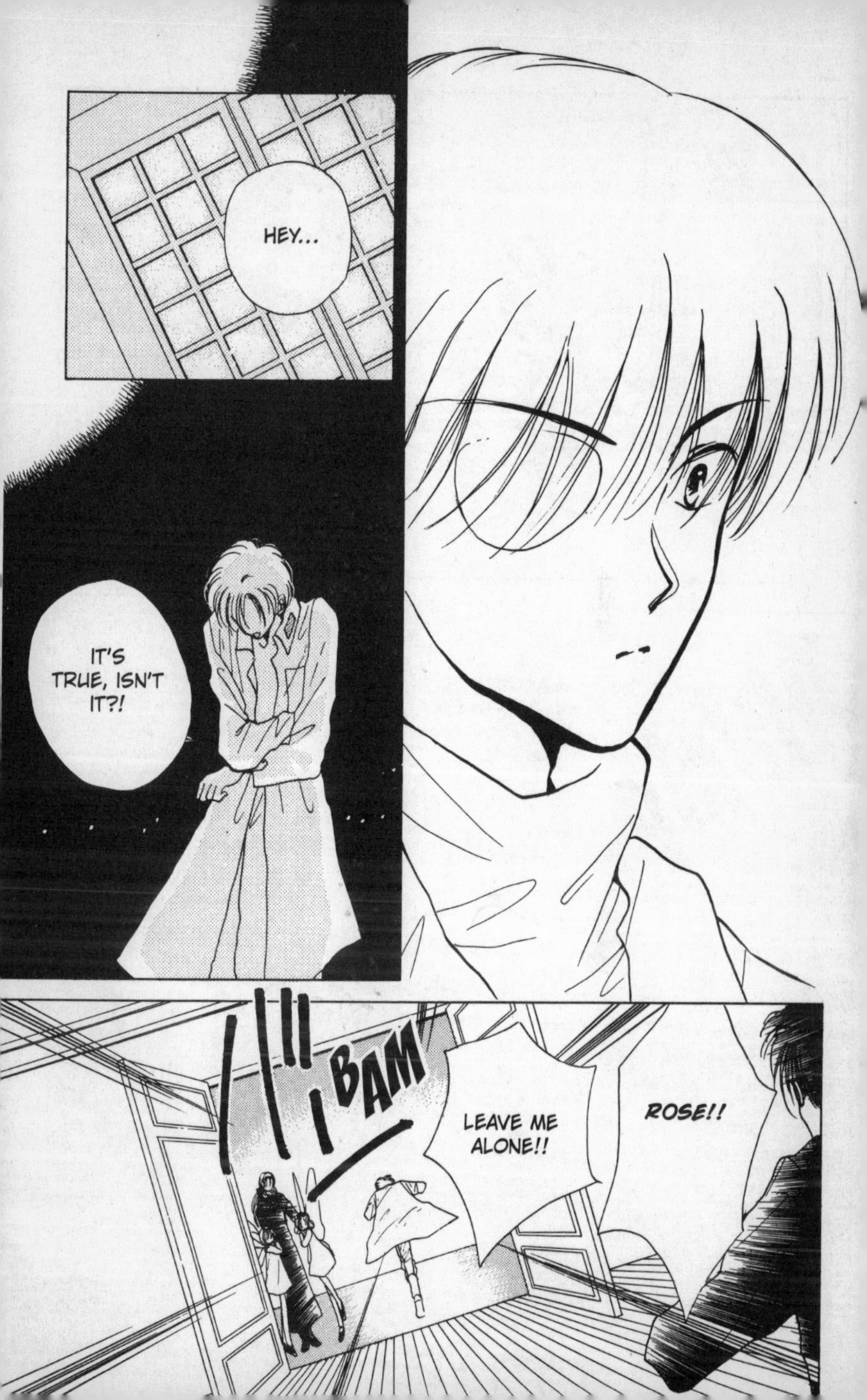
HEY...
IT'S TRUE, ISN'T IT?!
ROSE!!
LEAVE ME ALONE!!
BAM

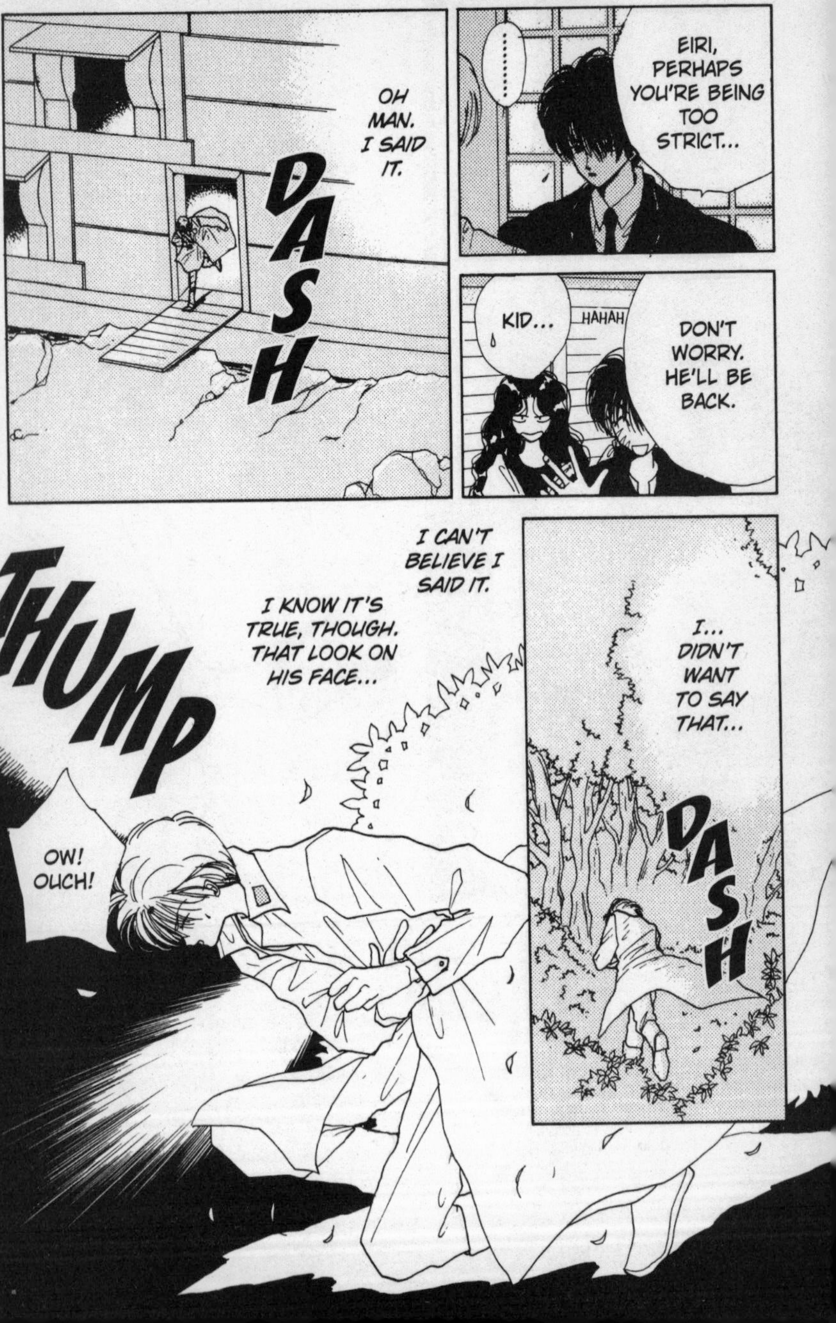
EIRI, PERHAPS YOU'RE BEING TOO STRICT...
......
DON'T WORRY. HE'LL BE BACK.
HAHAH
KID...
OH MAN. I SAID IT.
DASH
I... DIDN'T WANT TO SAY THAT...
DASH
I CAN'T BELIEVE I SAID IT.
I KNOW IT'S TRUE, THOUGH. THAT LOOK ON HIS FACE...
THUMP
OW! OUCH!

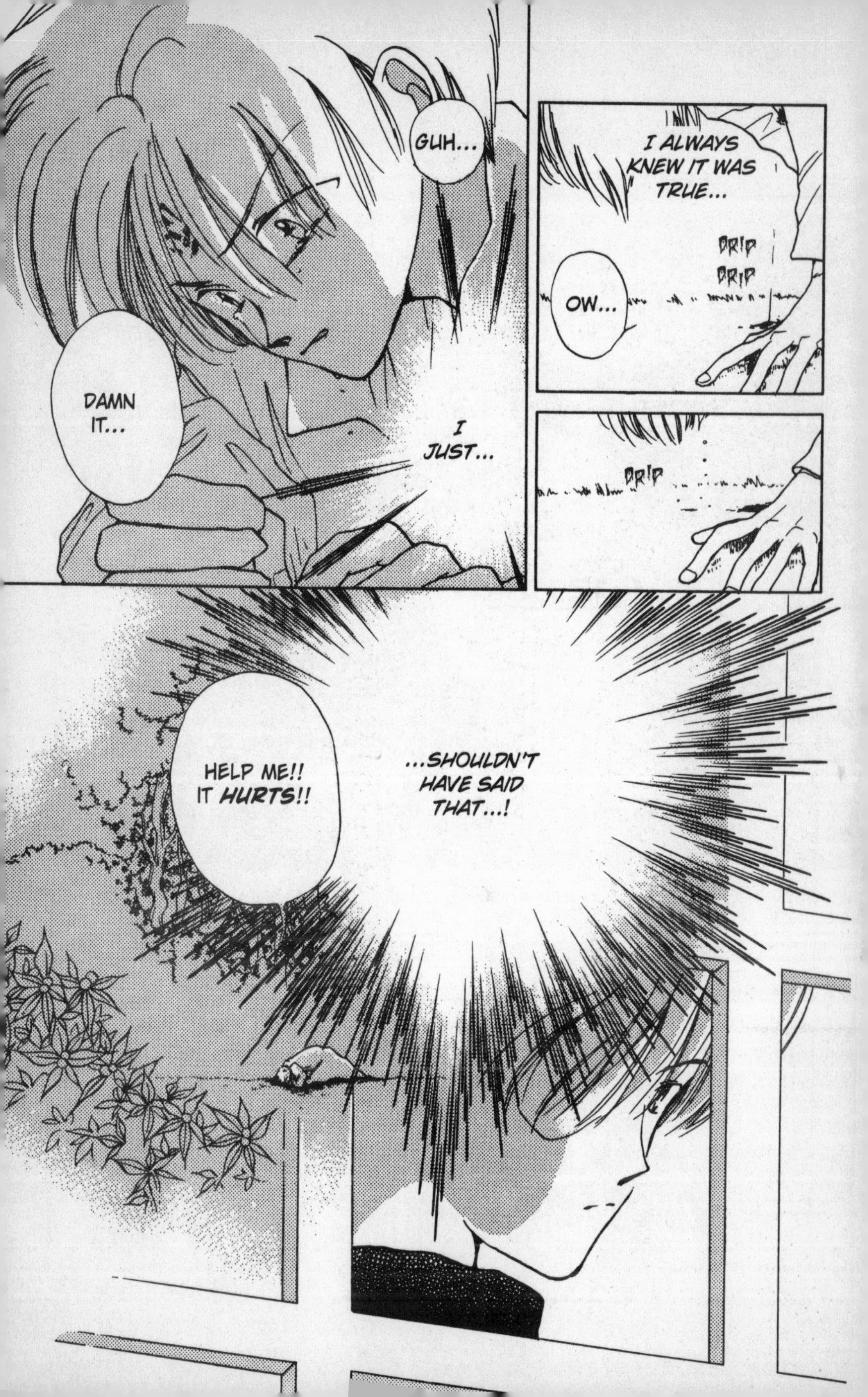
I ALWAYS KNEW IT WAS TRUE...
DRIP
DRIP
OW...
DRIP
GUH...
DAMN IT...
I JUST...
...SHOULDN'T HAVE SAID THAT...!
HELP ME!! IT *HURTS*!!

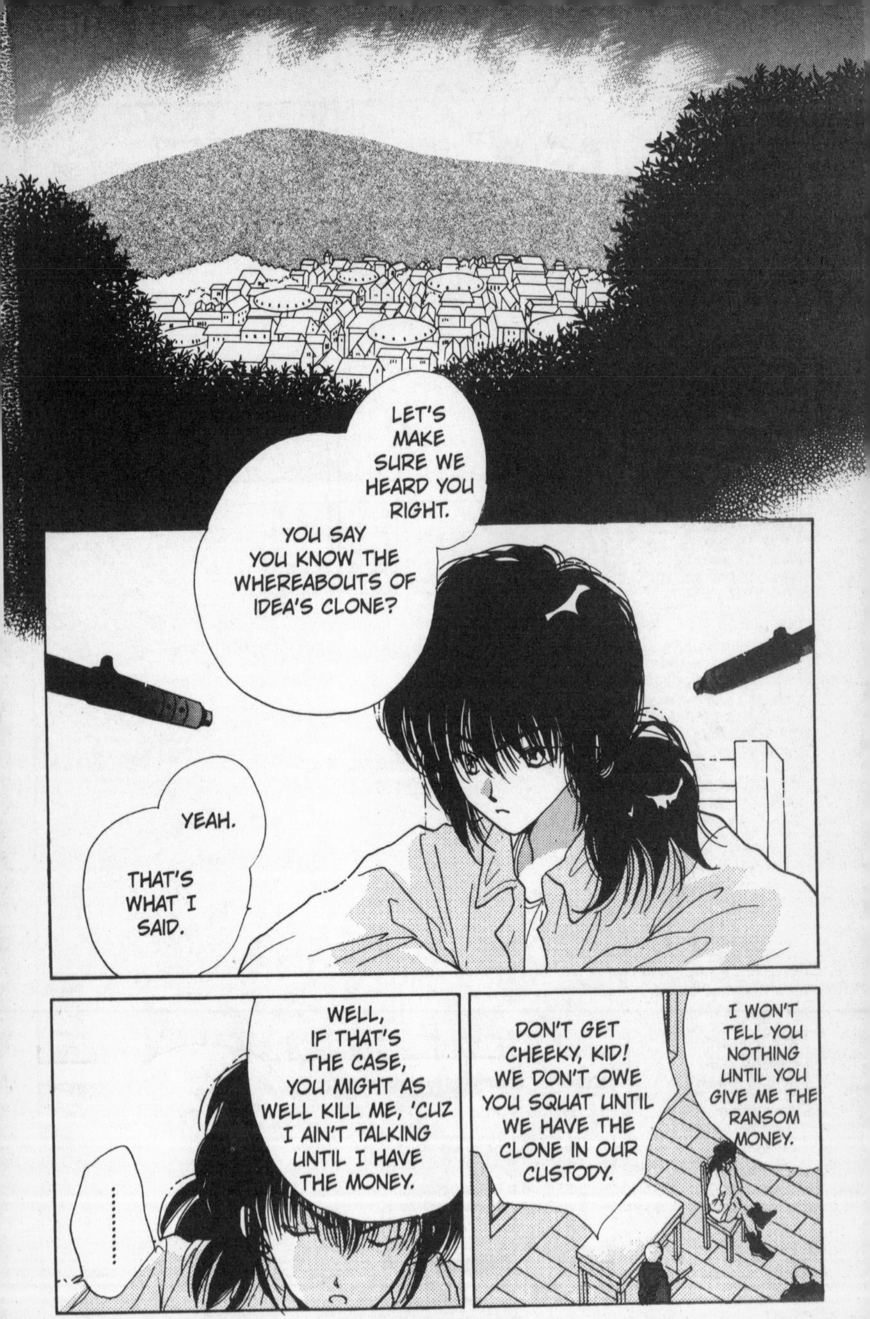
LET'S MAKE SURE WE HEARD YOU RIGHT.
YOU SAY YOU KNOW THE WHEREABOUTS OF IDEA'S CLONE?
YEAH.
THAT'S WHAT I SAID.
I WON'T TELL YOU NOTHING UNTIL YOU GIVE ME THE RANSOM MONEY.
DON'T GET CHEEKY, KID! WE DON'T OWE YOU SQUAT UNTIL WE HAVE THE CLONE IN OUR CUSTODY.
WELL, IF THAT'S THE CASE, YOU MIGHT AS WELL KILL ME, 'CUZ I AIN'T TALKING UNTIL I HAVE THE MONEY.
......

FINE. GIVE HIM THE MONEY, THEN.
SIR?
HERE IT IS.
TELL US QUICKLY.
DEEP AT THE BOTTOM OF THE VALLEY, THERE'S A CREVASSE.
THEY'VE LANDED A SHIP IN THERE SOMEWHERE. IT'S KINDA TOUGH TO NAVIGATE.
SO YOU'RE GONNA VOLUNTEER TO GUIDE US.

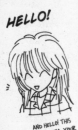

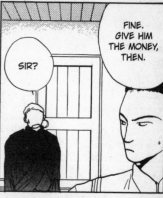

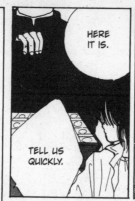

HELLO!
AND HELLO! THIS IS NAOE KITA, YOUR AUTHOR, SPEAKING.

I GOT A DIFFERENT HAIRSTYLE FOR THE FIRST TIME IN ***YEARS***. I NOW HAVE THIS... THING GOING ON WITH MY BANGS. THEY'RE KIND OF... JAGGY, AND BOUNCY. I GUESS THIS IS SUPPOSED TO BE FASHIONABLE? I DECIDED TO GET MY HAIRCUT BECAUSE, WELL, SEE, I WEAR GLASSES. AND THESE GLASSES I'D BEEN WEARING FOR, UHMM... LET'S JUST SAY "QUITE A LONG TIME"-- THEY BROKE. SO I DECIDED TO GET NEW GLASSES. I GOT SOME REALLY HIP YOHJI YAMAMOTO GLASSES, AND THEY JUST DIDN'T LOOK RIGHT WITH THAT OLD HAIRSTYLE OF MINE. SO I GOT IT CUT. IT'S KIND OF SHORT, NOW. I FEEL LIKE A NEW HUMAN BEING! IT'S KIND OF FUN TO CHANGE YOUR LOOK EVERY ONCE IN A WHILE, HUH? ANYWAY, YES, THIS IS VOLUME 6. IT'S THE CONTINUATION OF VOLUME 5, AND THE LEAD-IN TO VOLUME 7. IN CASE YOU DIDN'T KNOW THAT. I NEED TO REMIND MYSELF, SOMETIMES, SERIOUSLY.

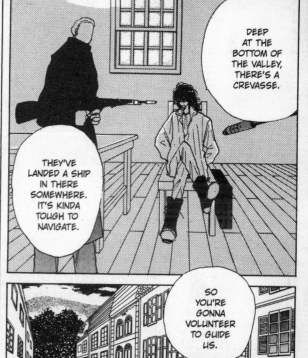

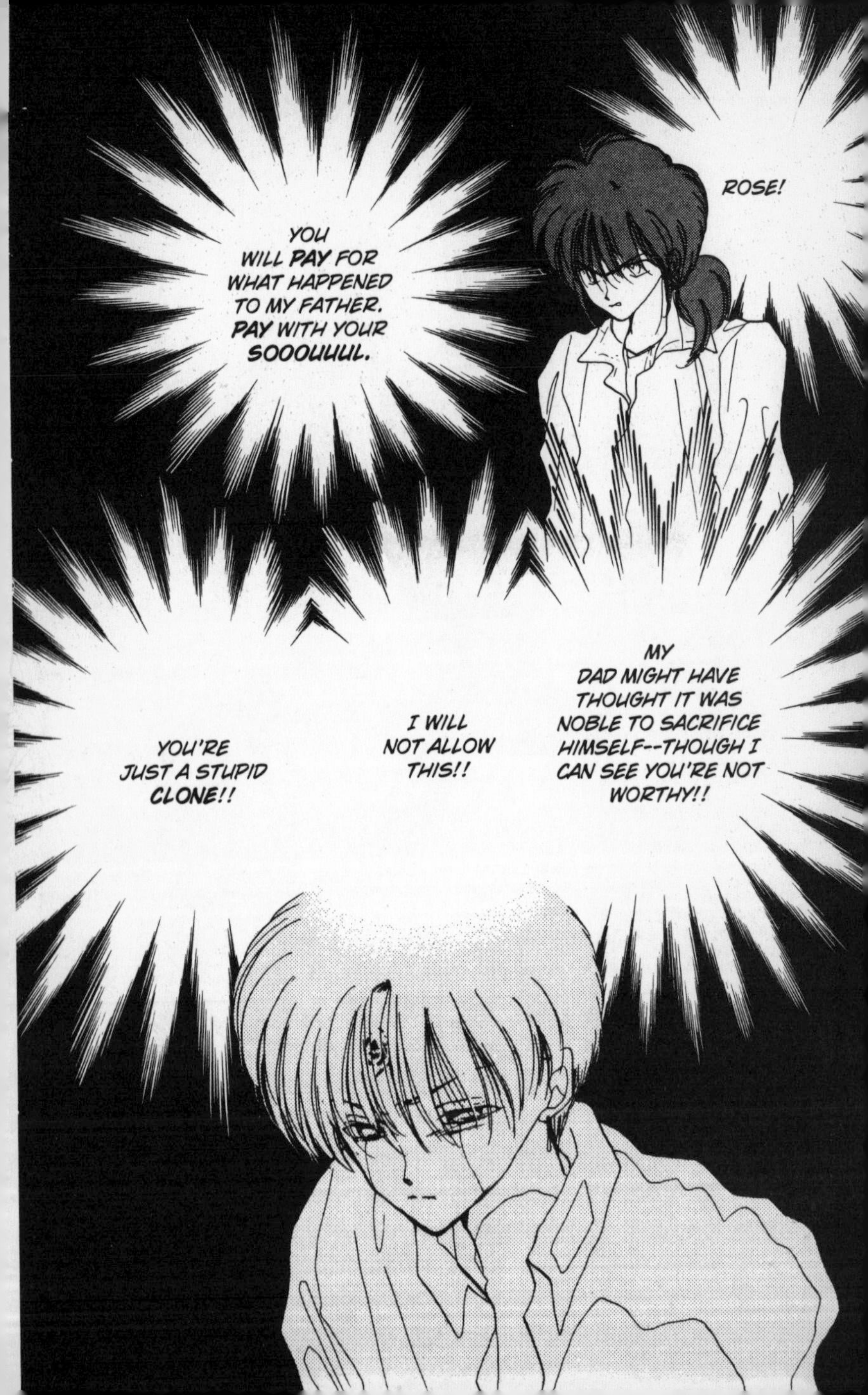
ROSE!
YOU WILL PAY FOR WHAT HAPPENED TO MY FATHER. PAY WITH YOUR SOOOUUUL.
MY DAD MIGHT HAVE THOUGHT IT WAS NOBLE TO SACRIFICE HIMSELF--THOUGH I CAN SEE YOU'RE NOT WORTHY!!
I WILL NOT ALLOW THIS!!
YOU'RE JUST A STUPID CLONE!!

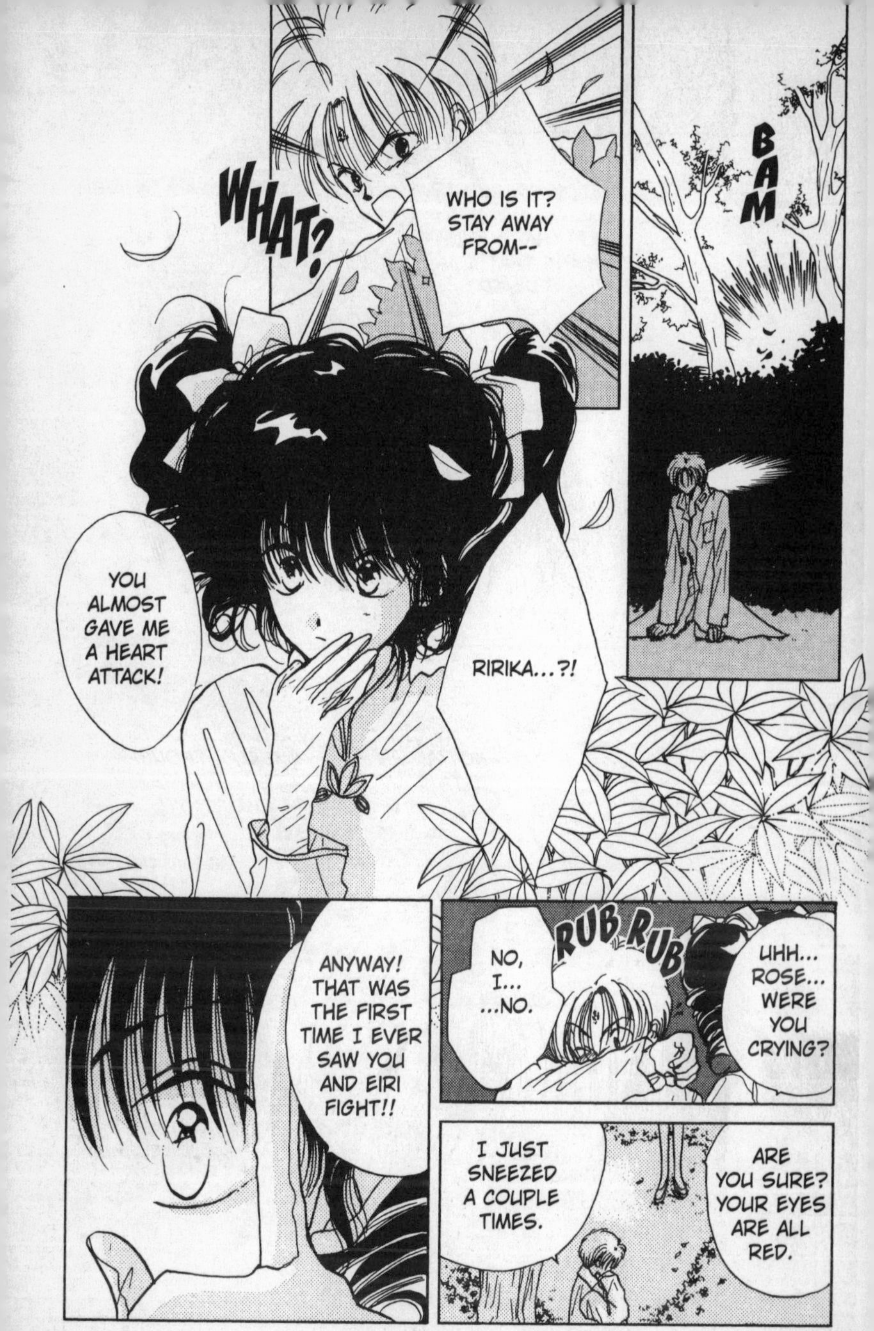
BAM
WHAT?
WHO IS IT? STAY AWAY FROM--
RIRIKA...?!
YOU ALMOST GAVE ME A HEART ATTACK!
UHH... ROSE... WERE YOU CRYING?
RUB RUB
NO, I... ...NO.
ARE YOU SURE? YOUR EYES ARE ALL RED.
I JUST SNEEZED A COUPLE TIMES.
ANYWAY! THAT WAS THE FIRST TIME I EVER SAW YOU AND EIRI FIGHT!!

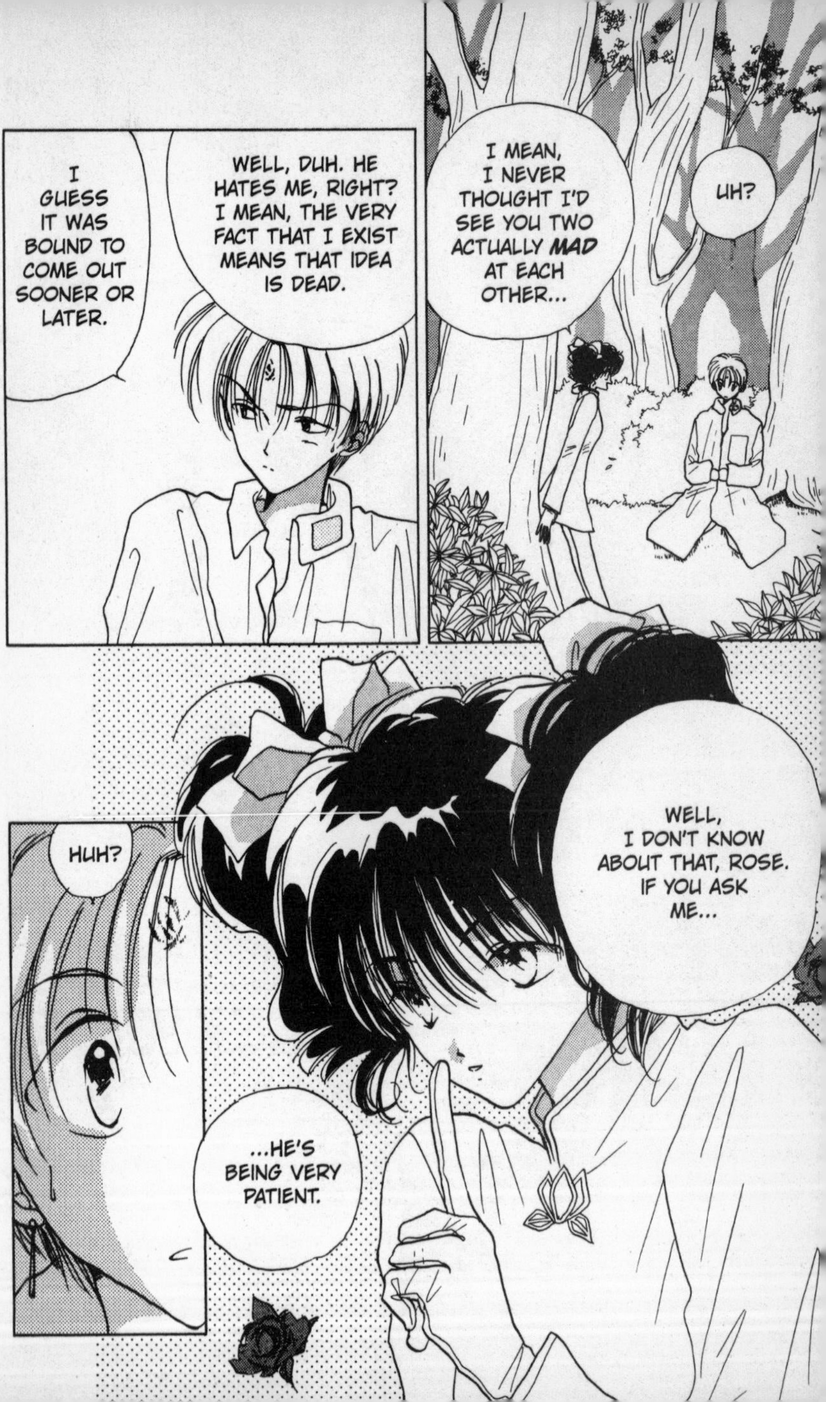
I MEAN, I NEVER THOUGHT I'D SEE YOU TWO ACTUALLY **MAD** AT EACH OTHER...
UH?
WELL, DUH. HE HATES ME, RIGHT? I MEAN, THE VERY FACT THAT I EXIST MEANS THAT IDEA IS DEAD.
I GUESS IT WAS BOUND TO COME OUT SOONER OR LATER.
WELL, I DON'T KNOW ABOUT THAT, ROSE. IF YOU ASK ME...
...HE'S BEING VERY PATIENT.
HUH?

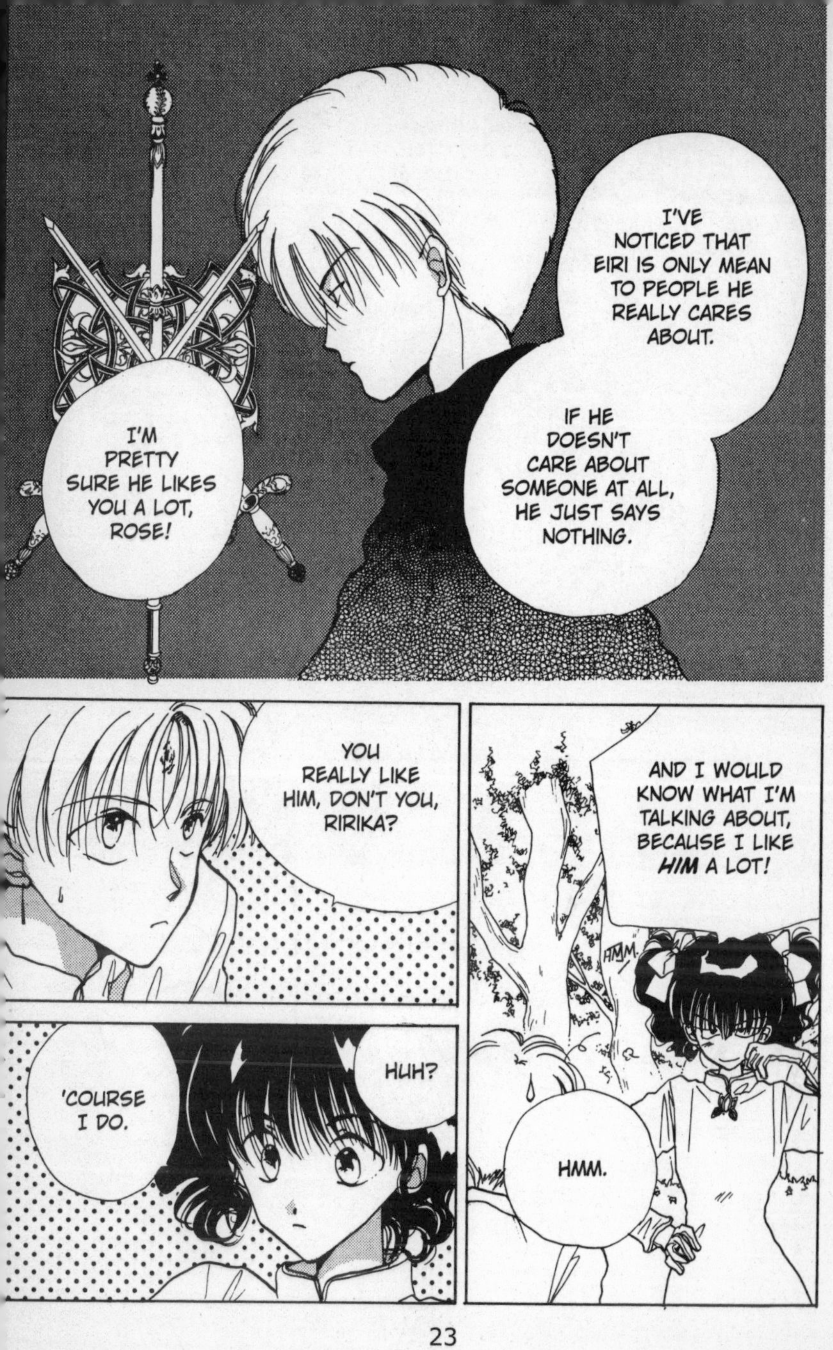
I'VE NOTICED THAT EIRI IS ONLY MEAN TO PEOPLE HE REALLY CARES ABOUT.
IF HE DOESN'T CARE ABOUT SOMEONE AT ALL, HE JUST SAYS NOTHING.
I'M PRETTY SURE HE LIKES YOU A LOT, ROSE!
AND I WOULD KNOW WHAT I'M TALKING ABOUT, BECAUSE I LIKE *HIM* A LOT!
HMM.
HMM.
YOU REALLY LIKE HIM, DON'T YOU, RIRIKA?
HUH?
'COURSE I DO.

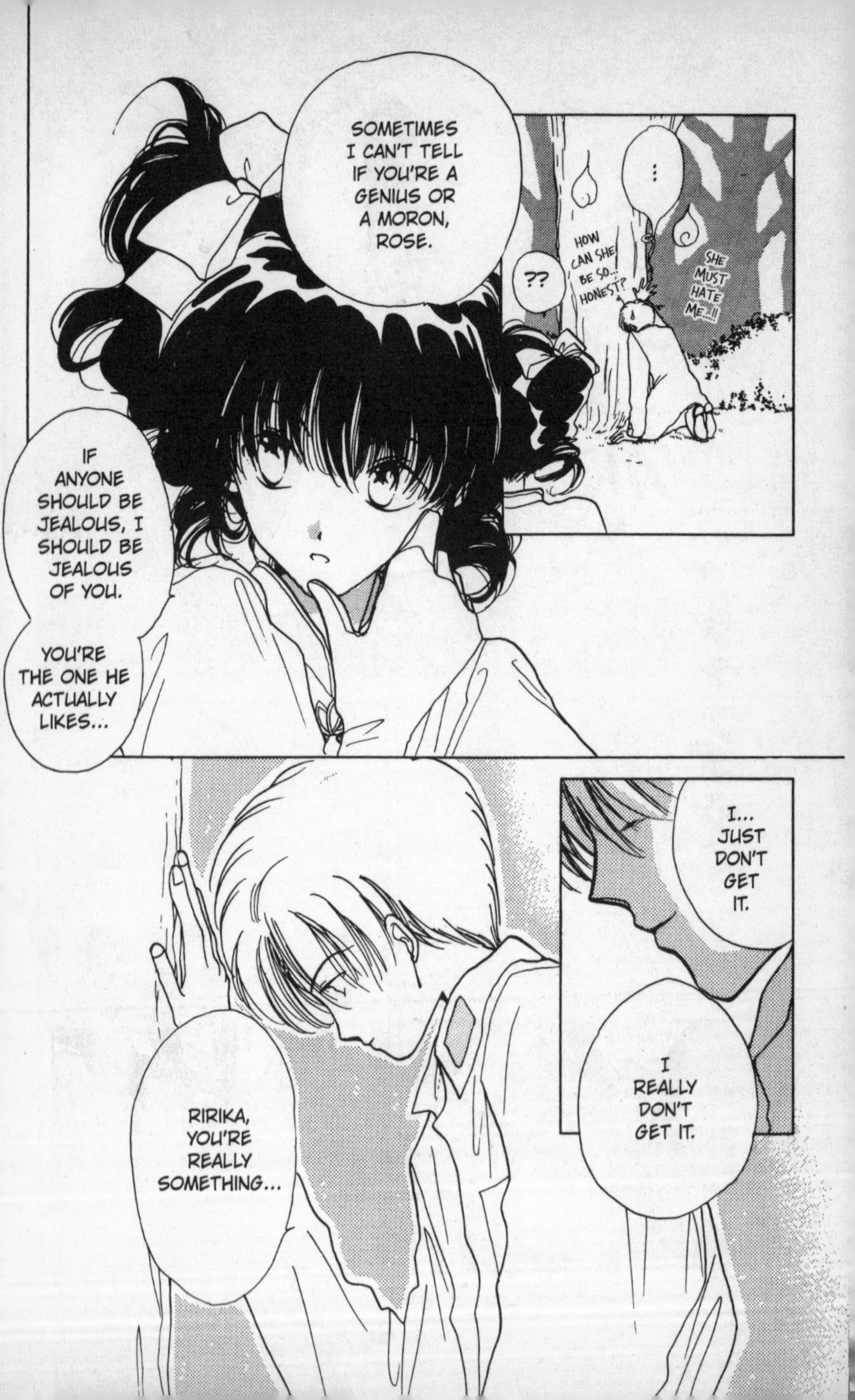
SOMETIMES I CAN'T TELL IF YOU'RE A GENIUS OR A MORON, ROSE.
...
HOW CAN SHE BE SO... HONEST?
SHE MUST HATE ME...!!
??
IF ANYONE SHOULD BE JEALOUS, I SHOULD BE JEALOUS OF YOU.
YOU'RE THE ONE HE ACTUALLY LIKES...
I... JUST DON'T GET IT.
I REALLY DON'T GET IT.
RIRIKA, YOU'RE REALLY SOMETHING...

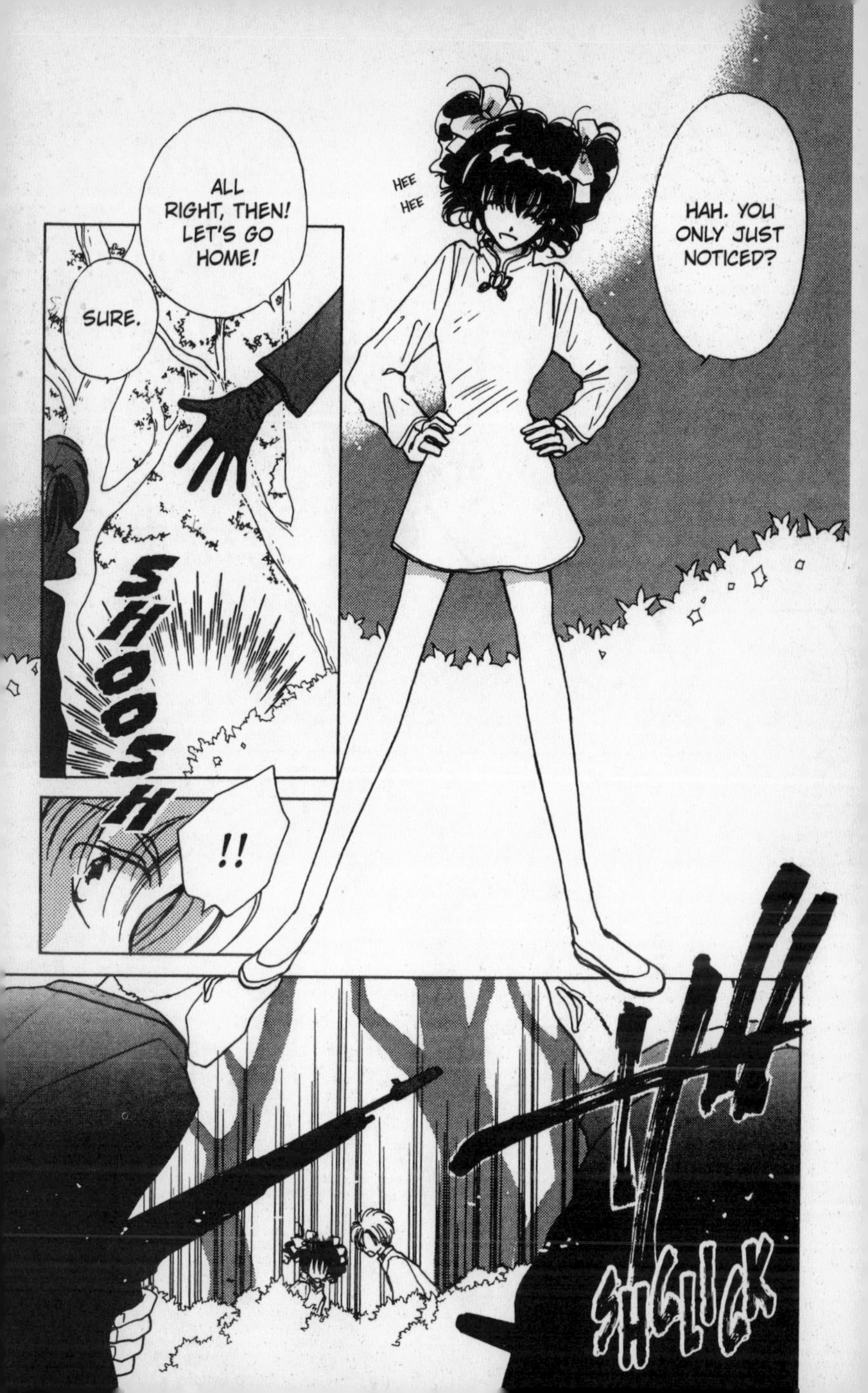
HAH. YOU ONLY JUST NOTICED?
HEE HEE
ALL RIGHT, THEN! LET'S GO HOME!
SURE.
SHOOSH
!!
SHLICK

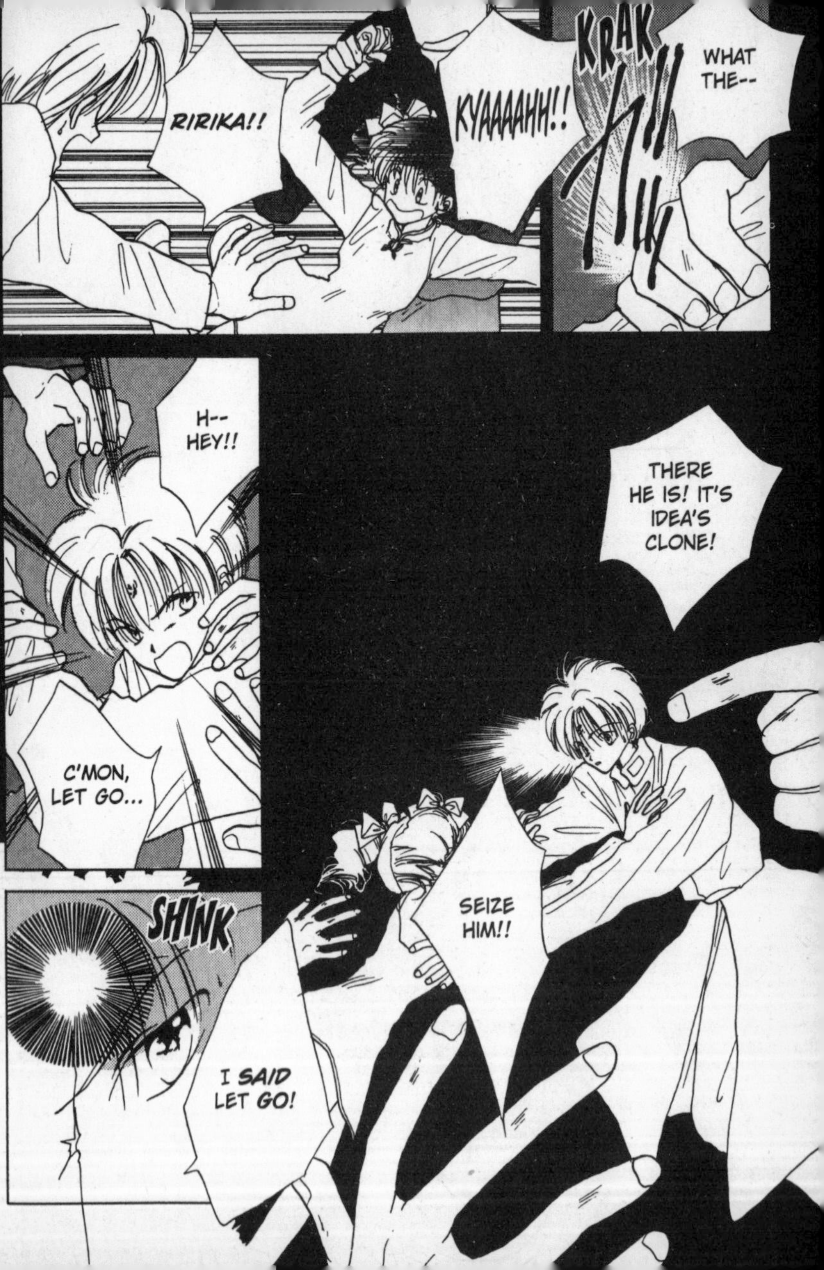
KRAK
WHAT THE--
KYAAAAHH!!
RIRIKA!!
THERE HE IS! IT'S IDEA'S CLONE!
SEIZE HIM!!
H-- HEY!!
C'MON, LET GO...
SHINK
I SAID LET GO!

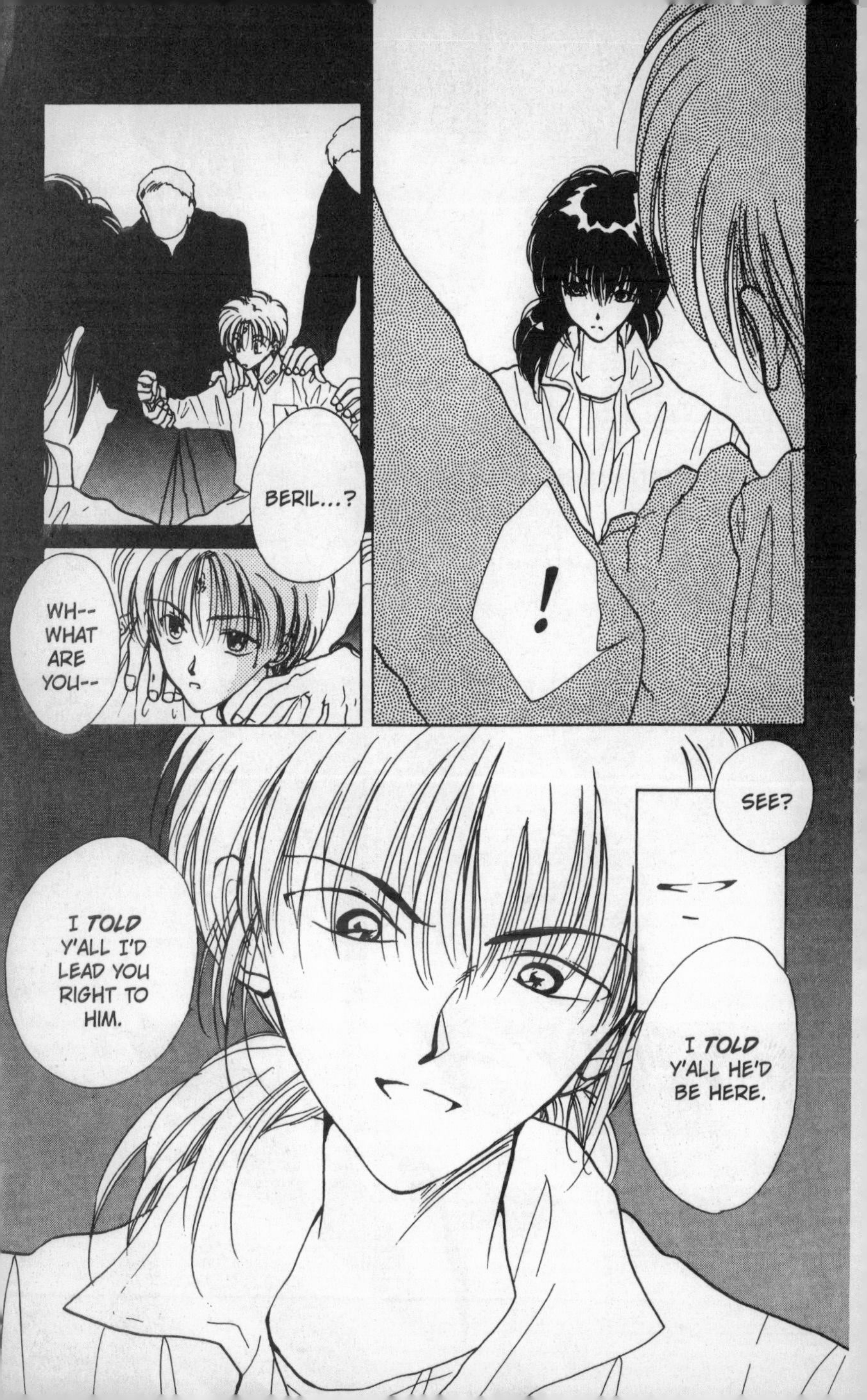
!
BERIL...?
WH-- WHAT ARE YOU--
SEE?
I *TOLD* Y'ALL HE'D BE HERE.
I *TOLD* Y'ALL I'D LEAD YOU RIGHT TO HIM.

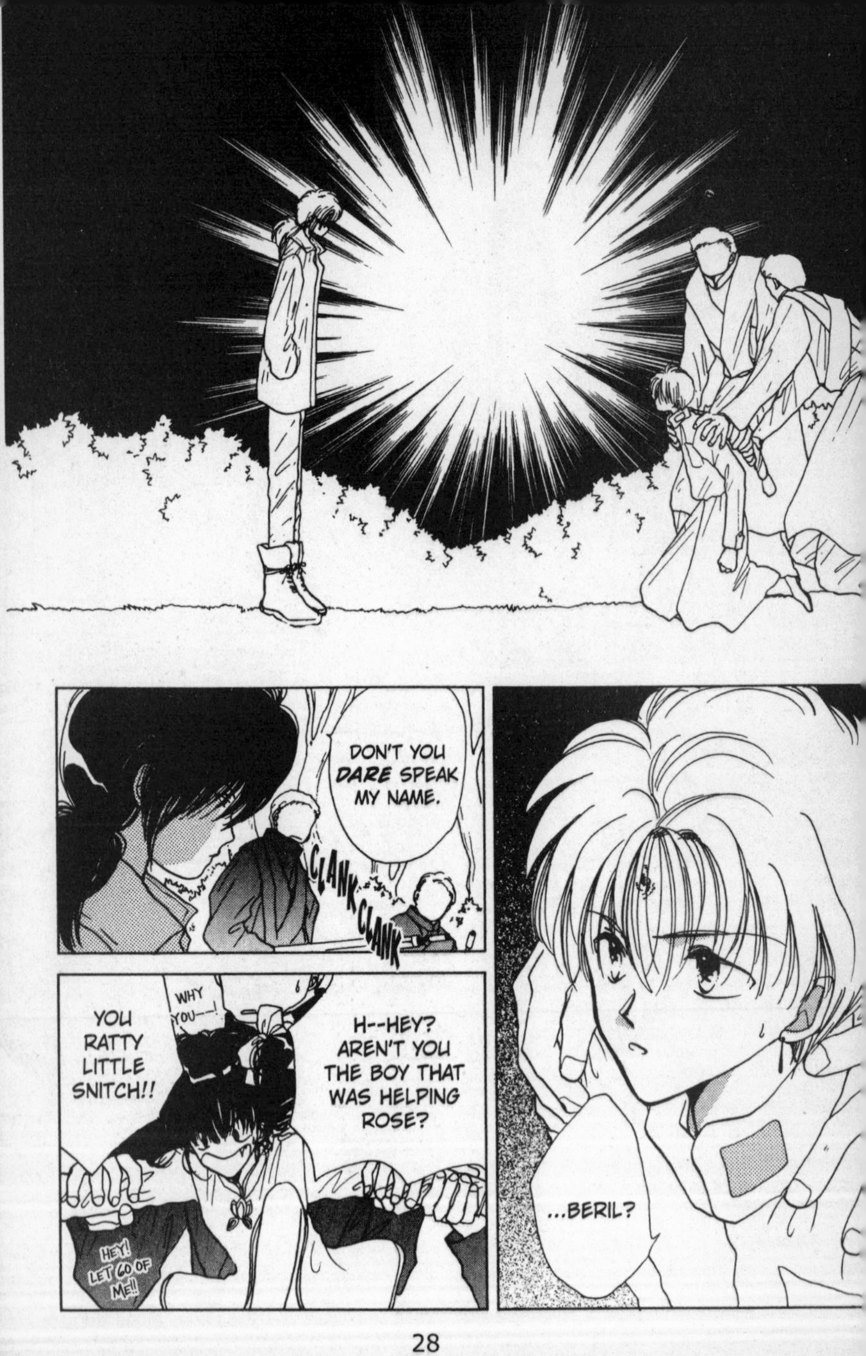
...BERIL?
DON'T YOU DARE SPEAK MY NAME.
CLANK CLANK
H--HEY? AREN'T YOU THE BOY THAT WAS HELPING ROSE?
WHY YOU--!
YOU RATTY LITTLE SNITCH!!
HEY! LET GO OF ME!!

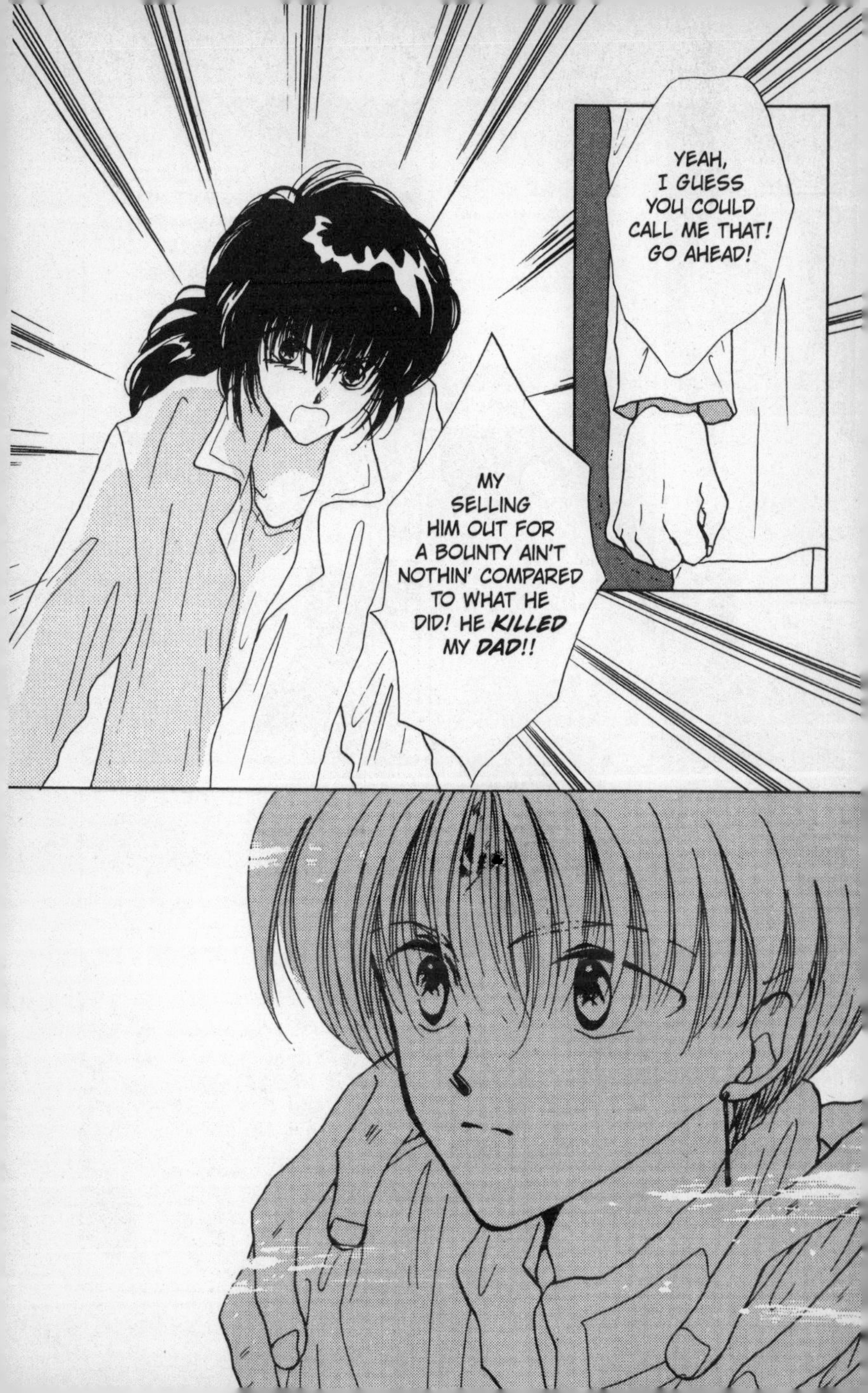
YEAH, I GUESS YOU COULD CALL ME THAT! GO AHEAD!
MY SELLING HIM OUT FOR A BOUNTY AIN'T NOTHIN' COMPARED TO WHAT HE DID! HE *KILLED* MY *DAD*!!

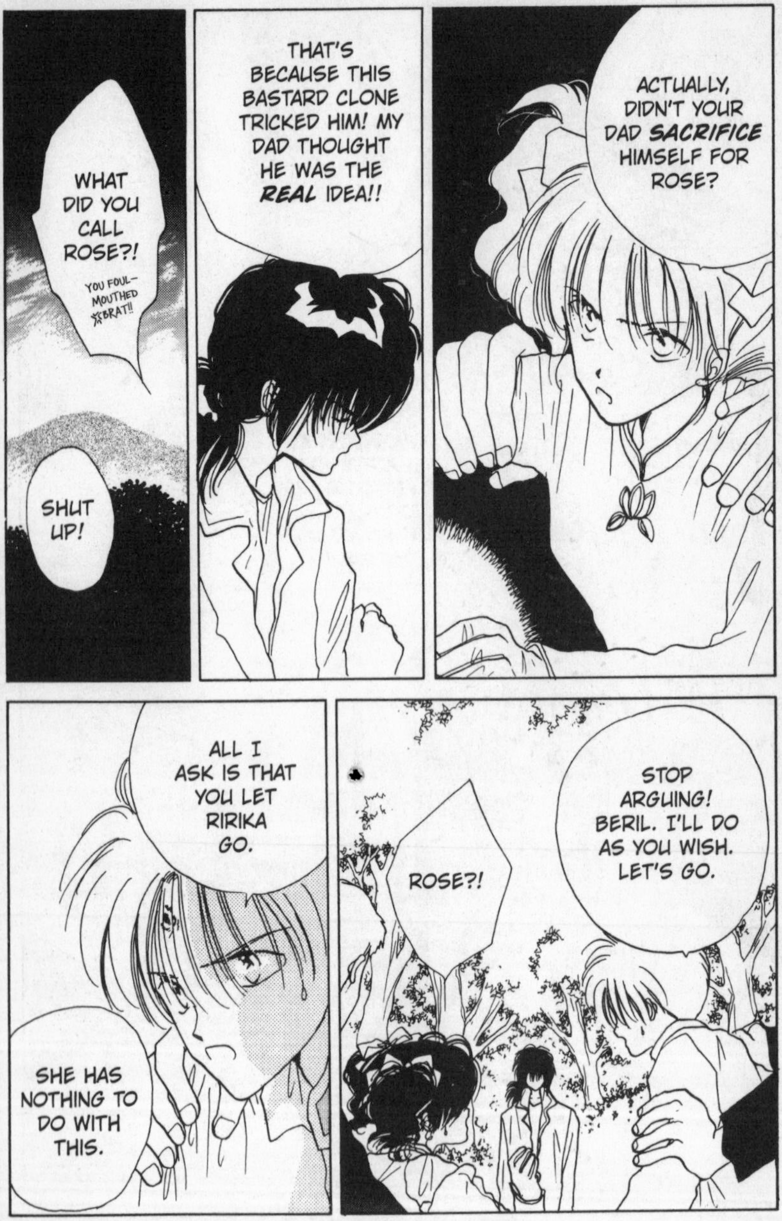
ACTUALLY, DIDN'T YOUR DAD **SACRIFICE** HIMSELF FOR ROSE?
THAT'S BECAUSE THIS BASTARD CLONE TRICKED HIM! MY DAD THOUGHT HE WAS THE **REAL** IDEA!!
WHAT DID YOU CALL ROSE?!
YOU FOUL-MOUTHED BRAT!!
SHUT UP!
STOP ARGUING! BERIL. I'LL DO AS YOU WISH. LET'S GO.
ROSE?!
ALL I ASK IS THAT YOU LET RIRIKA GO.
SHE HAS NOTHING TO DO WITH THIS.

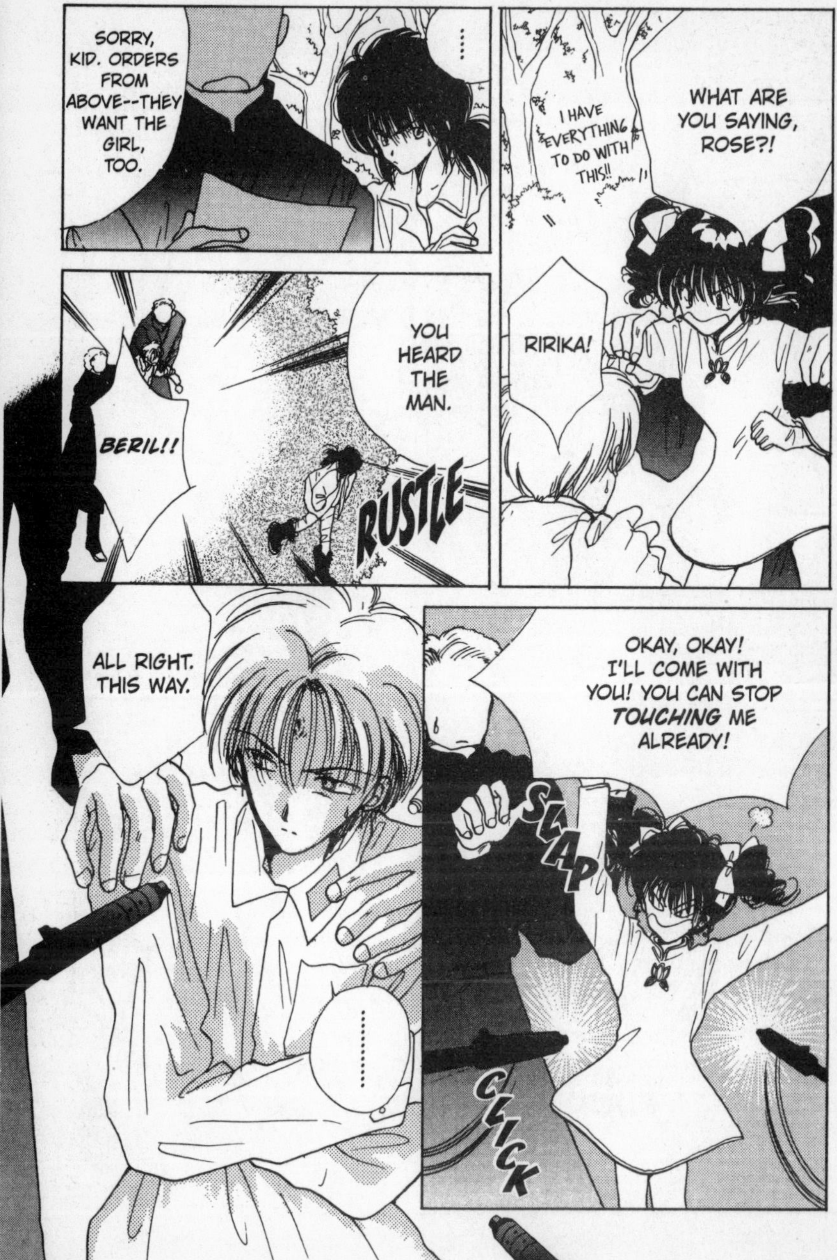
WHAT ARE YOU SAYING, ROSE?!
I HAVE EVERYTHING TO DO WITH THIS!!
RIRIKA!
SORRY, KID. ORDERS FROM ABOVE--THEY WANT THE GIRL, TOO.
.....
YOU HEARD THE MAN.
BERIL!!
RUSTLE
OKAY, OKAY! I'LL COME WITH YOU! YOU CAN STOP TOUCHING ME ALREADY!
SLAP
CLICK
ALL RIGHT. THIS WAY.
......

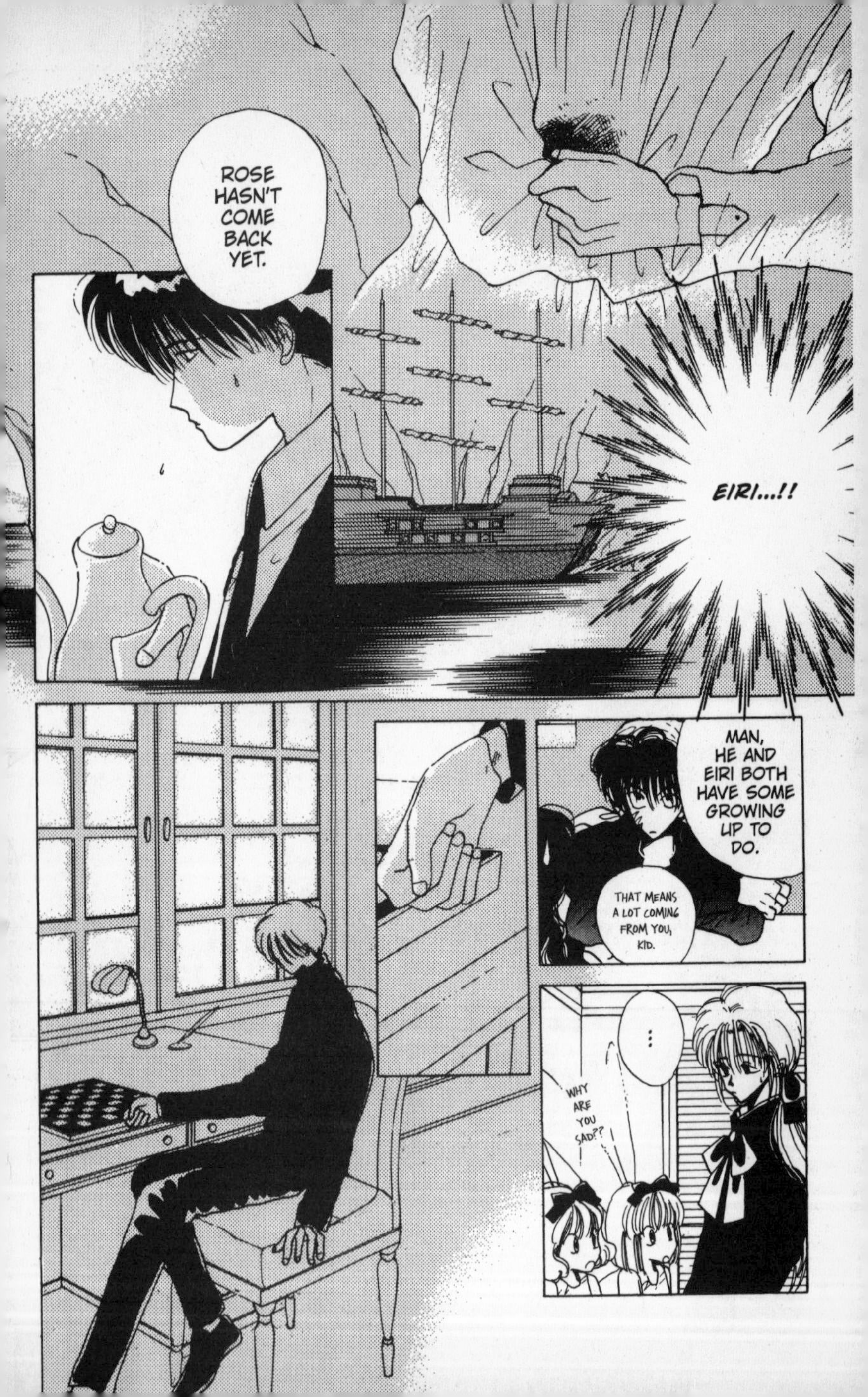

EIRI...!!
ROSE HASN'T COME BACK YET.
MAN, HE AND EIRI BOTH HAVE SOME GROWING UP TO DO.
THAT MEANS A LOT COMING FROM YOU, KID.
...
WHY ARE YOU SAD??

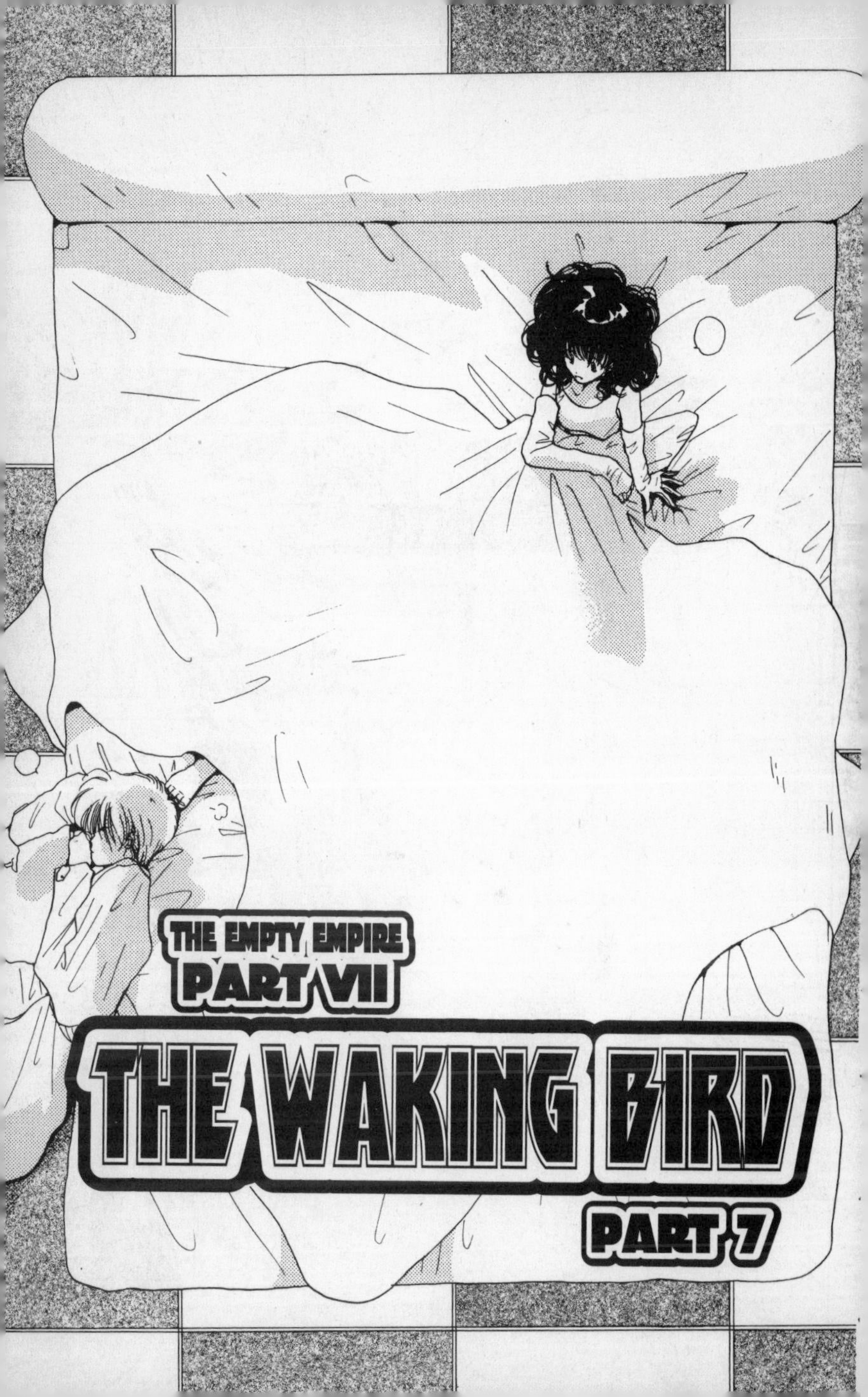
THE EMPTY EMPIRE
PART VII
THE WAKING BIRD
PART 7

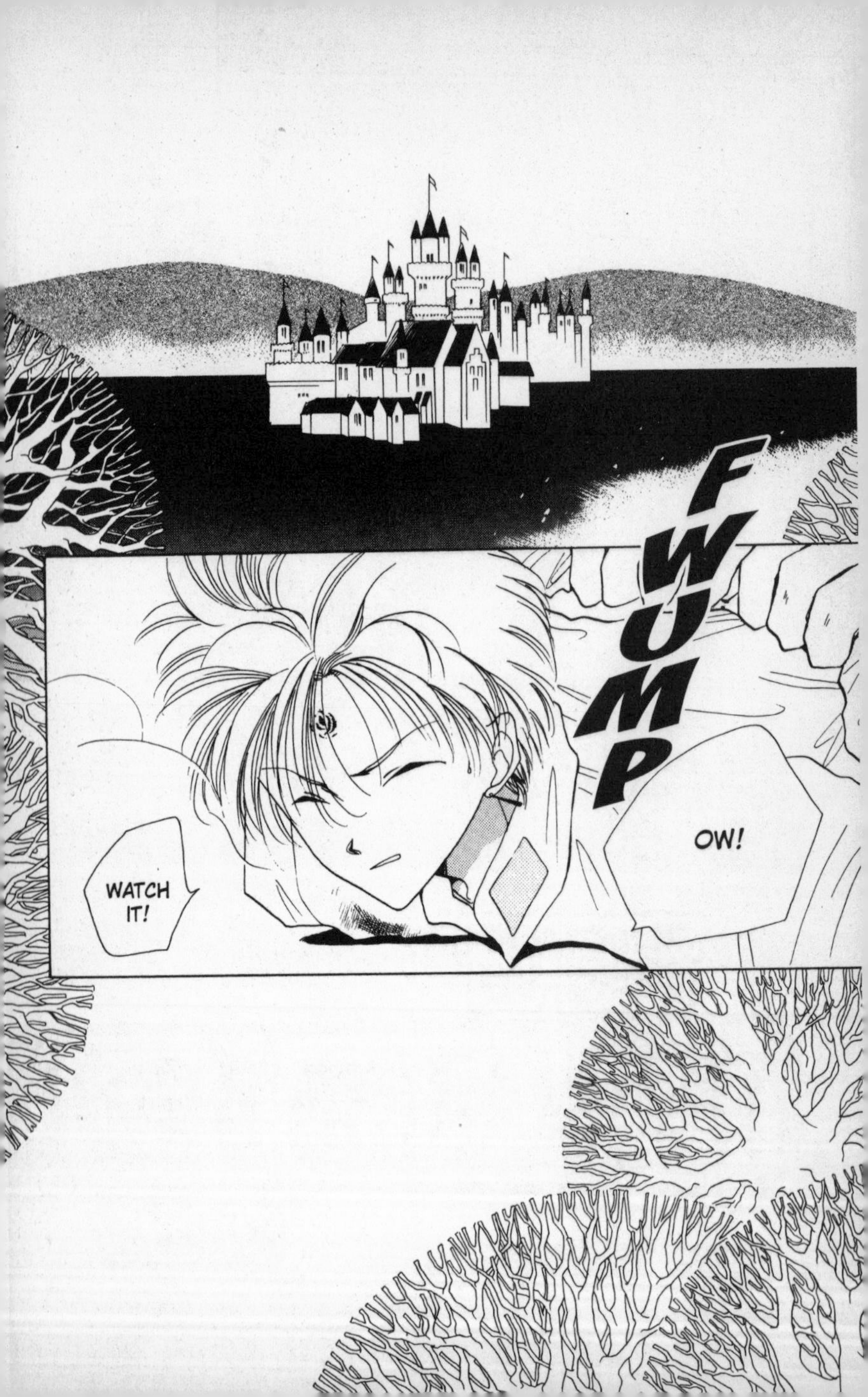
FWUMP
OW!
WATCH IT!

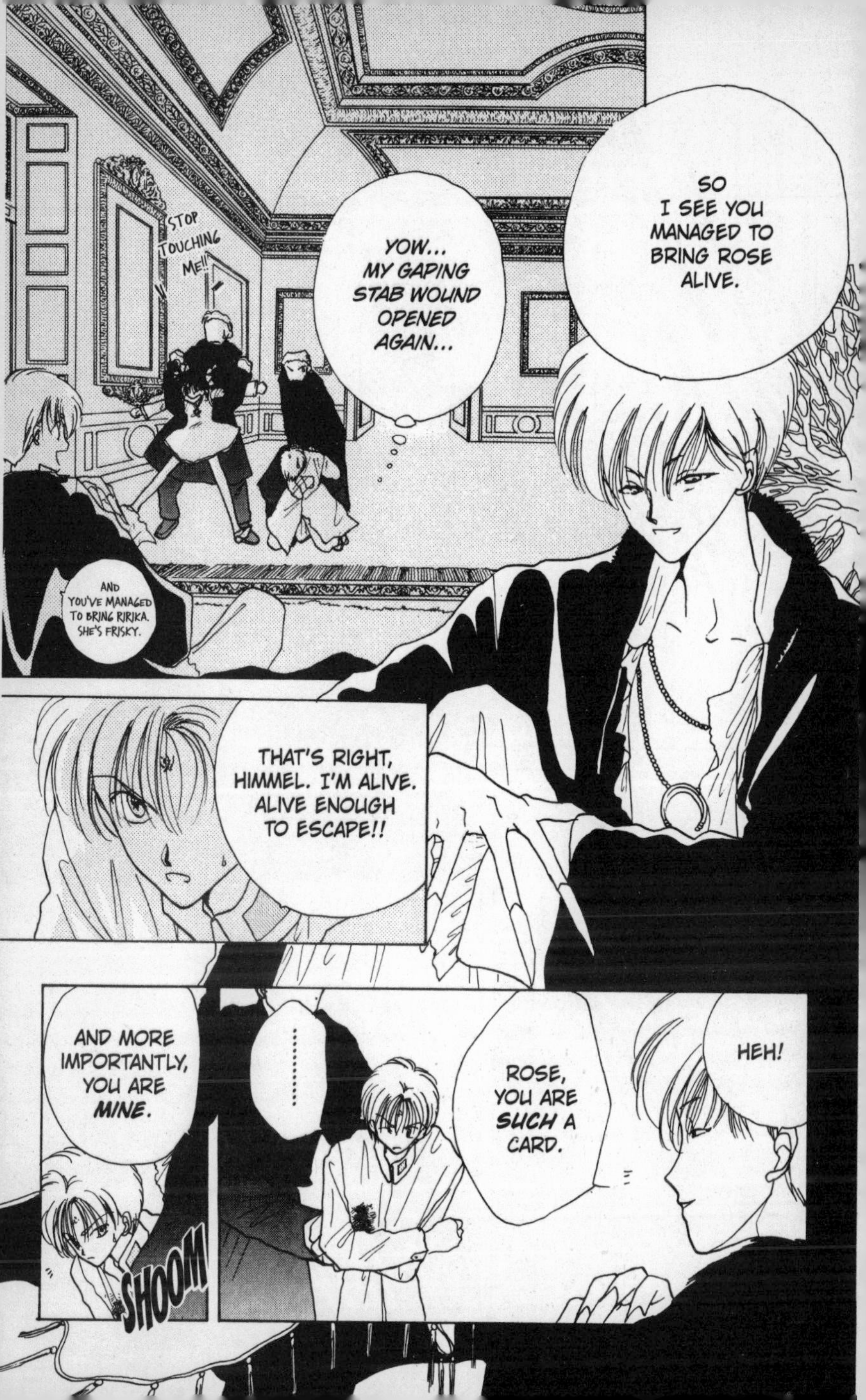
SO I SEE YOU MANAGED TO BRING ROSE ALIVE.
YOW... MY GAPING STAB WOUND OPENED AGAIN...
STOP TOUCHING ME!!
AND YOU'VE MANAGED TO BRING RIRIKA. SHE'S FRISKY.
THAT'S RIGHT, HIMMEL. I'M ALIVE. ALIVE ENOUGH TO ESCAPE!!
HEH!
ROSE, YOU ARE *SUCH* A CARD.
....
AND MORE IMPORTANTLY, YOU ARE *MINE*.
SHOOM

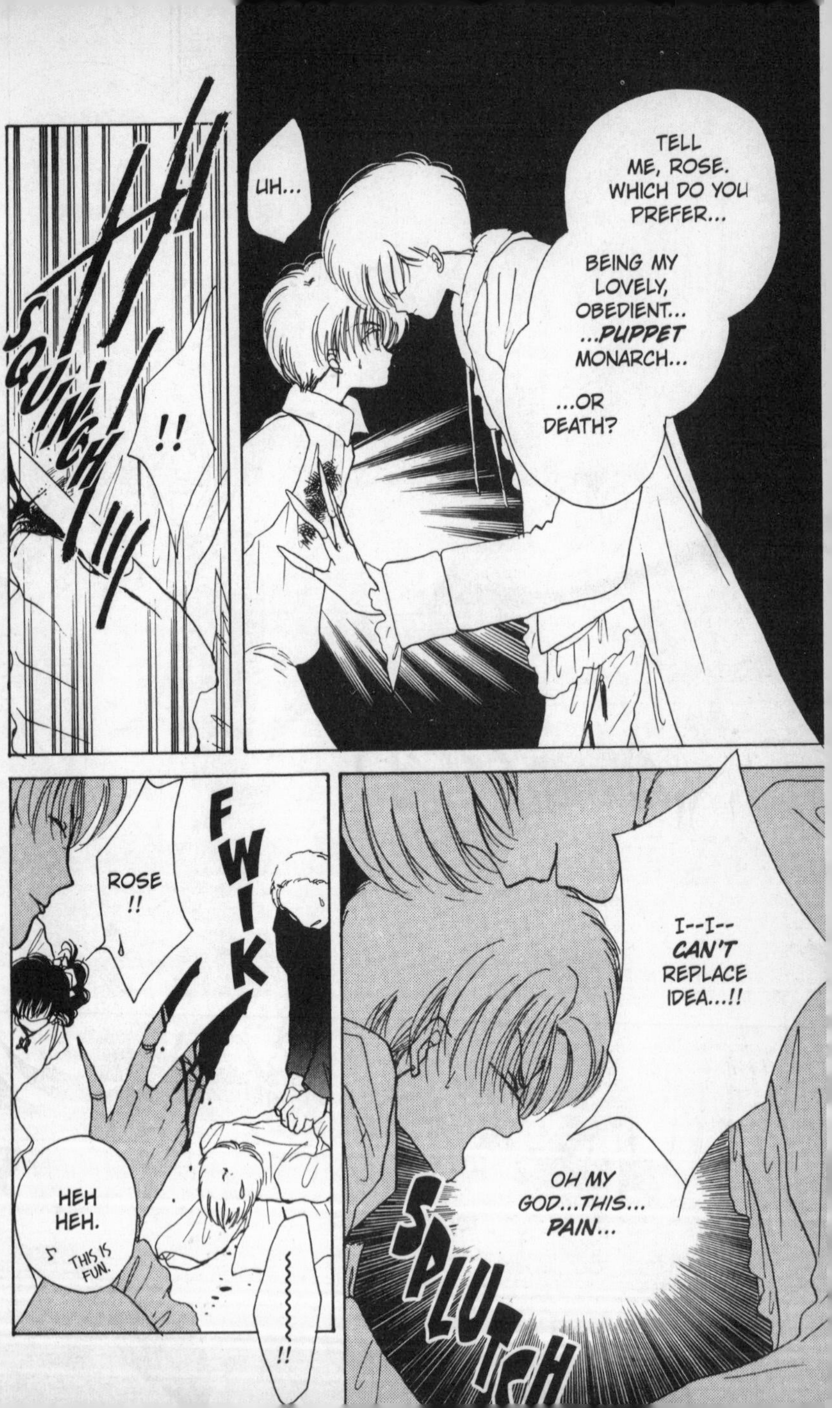
TELL ME, ROSE. WHICH DO YOU PREFER...
BEING MY LOVELY, OBEDIENT... ...*PUPPET* MONARCH...
...OR DEATH?
UH...
SQUINCH!!!
!!
I--I-- *CAN'T* REPLACE IDEA...!!
OH MY GOD...THIS... *PAIN*...
SPLUTCH
FWIK
ROSE !!
HEH HEH.
THIS IS FUN.
~~~~~~ !!
~~~~~~

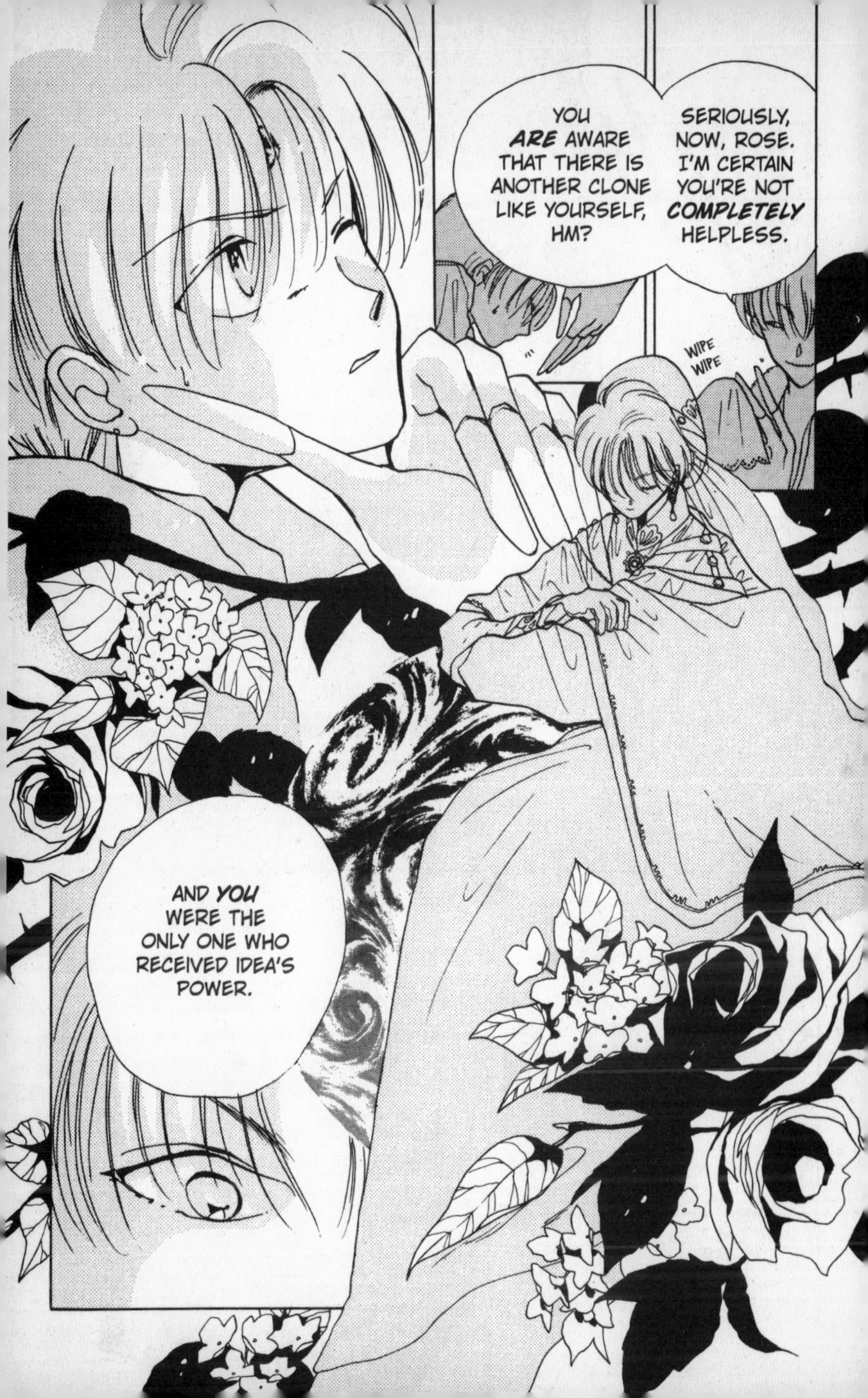
SERIOUSLY, NOW, ROSE. I'M CERTAIN YOU'RE NOT COMPLETELY HELPLESS.
YOU ARE AWARE THAT THERE IS ANOTHER CLONE LIKE YOURSELF, HM?
WIPE WIPE
AND YOU WERE THE ONLY ONE WHO RECEIVED IDEA'S POWER.

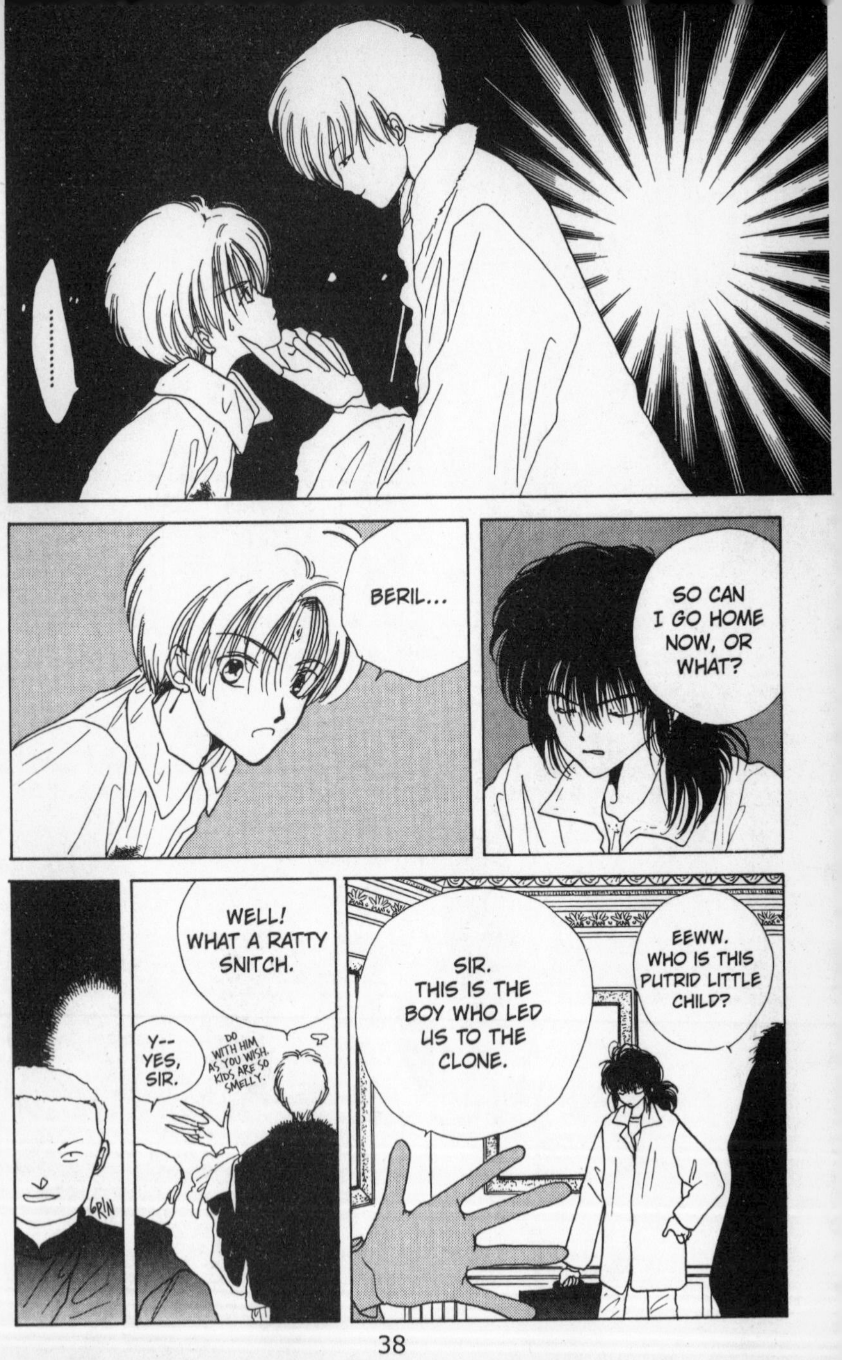
......
SO CAN I GO HOME NOW, OR WHAT?
BERIL...
EEWW. WHO IS THIS PUTRID LITTLE CHILD?
SIR. THIS IS THE BOY WHO LED US TO THE CLONE.
WELL! WHAT A RATTY SNITCH.
DO WITH HIM AS YOU WISH. KIDS ARE SO SMELLY.
Y-- YES, SIR.
GRIN

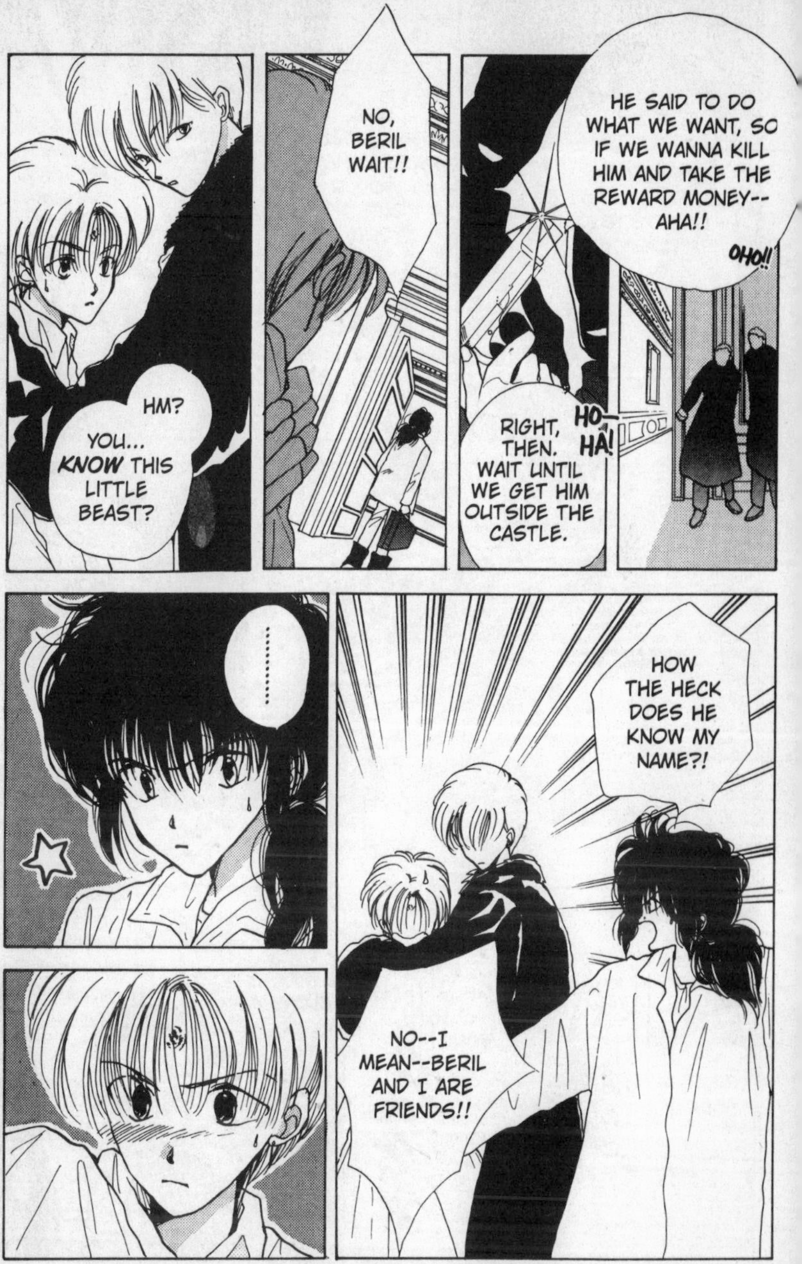
HE SAID TO DO WHAT WE WANT, SO IF WE WANNA KILL HIM AND TAKE THE REWARD MONEY-- AHA!!
OHO!!
RIGHT, THEN. WAIT UNTIL WE GET HIM OUTSIDE THE CASTLE.
HO-HA!
NO, BERIL WAIT!!
HM?
YOU... KNOW THIS LITTLE BEAST?
HOW THE HECK DOES HE KNOW MY NAME?!
NO--I MEAN--BERIL AND I ARE FRIENDS!!
......

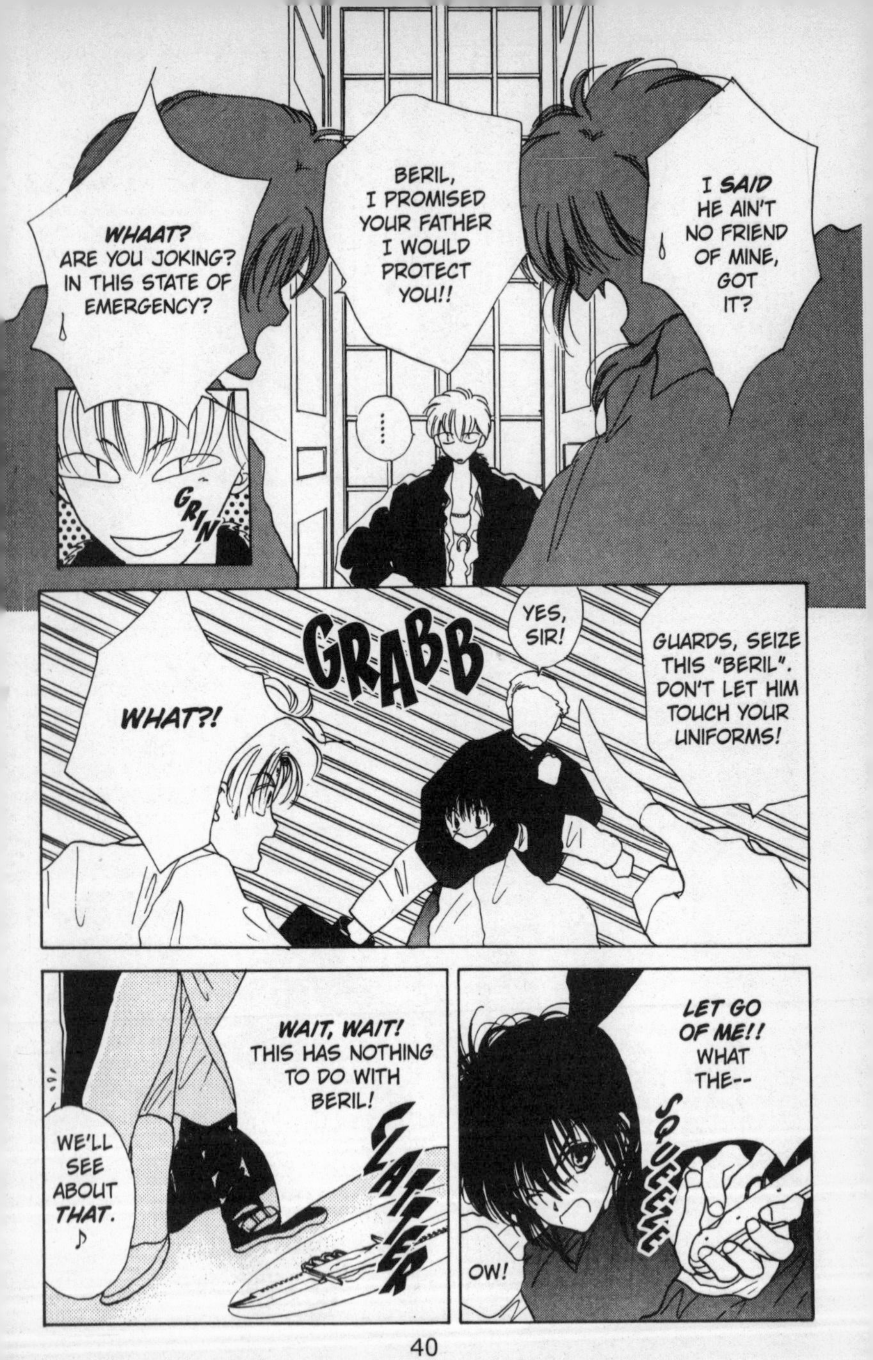

I SAID HE AIN'T NO FRIEND OF MINE, GOT IT?
BERIL, I PROMISED YOUR FATHER I WOULD PROTECT YOU!!
WHAAT? ARE YOU JOKING? IN THIS STATE OF EMERGENCY?
......
GRIN
GUARDS, SEIZE THIS "BERIL". DON'T LET HIM TOUCH YOUR UNIFORMS!
YES, SIR!
GRABB
WHAT?!
LET GO OF ME!! WHAT THE--
SQUEEZE
OW!
WAIT, WAIT! THIS HAS NOTHING TO DO WITH BERIL!
CLATTER
WE'LL SEE ABOUT THAT. ♪

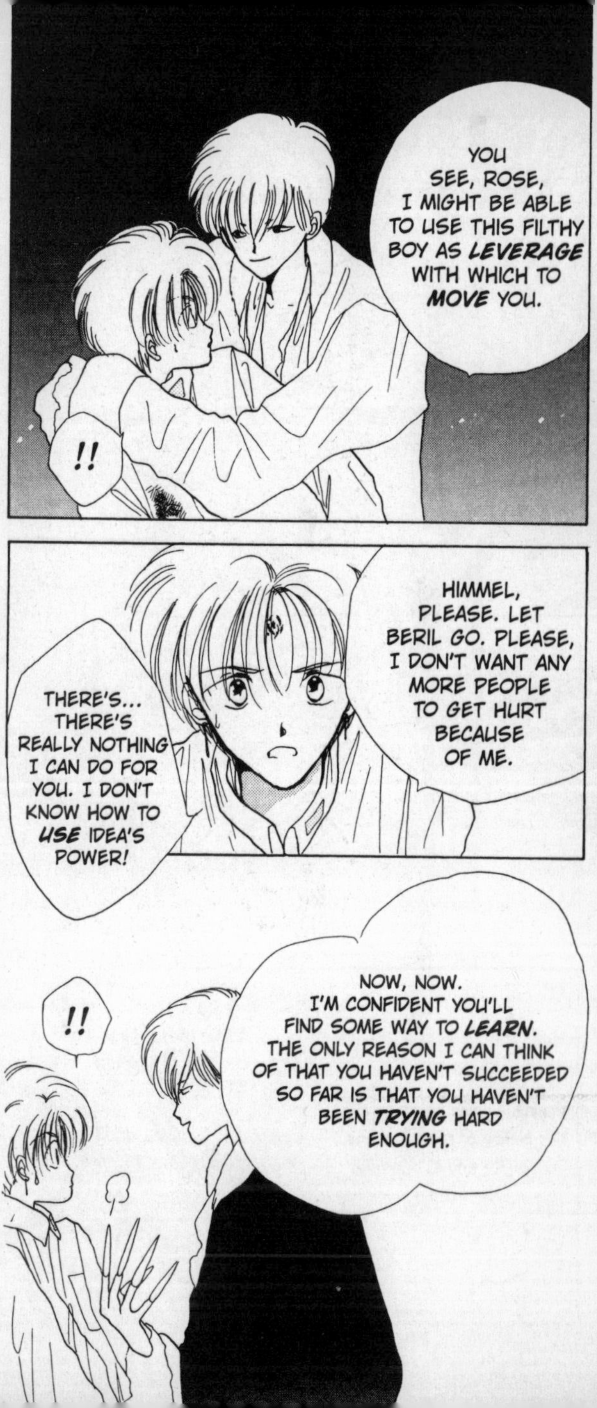
YOU SEE, ROSE, I MIGHT BE ABLE TO USE THIS FILTHY BOY AS ***LEVERAGE*** WITH WHICH TO ***MOVE*** YOU.
!!
HIMMEL, PLEASE. LET BERIL GO. PLEASE, I DON'T WANT ANY MORE PEOPLE TO GET HURT BECAUSE OF ME.
THERE'S... THERE'S REALLY NOTHING I CAN DO FOR YOU. I DON'T KNOW HOW TO ***USE*** IDEA'S POWER!
NOW, NOW. I'M CONFIDENT YOU'LL FIND SOME WAY TO ***LEARN***. THE ONLY REASON I CAN THINK OF THAT YOU HAVEN'T SUCCEEDED SO FAR IS THAT YOU HAVEN'T BEEN ***TRYING*** HARD ENOUGH.
!!

SO, UMMM...IN THE PAST VOLUMES, I WROTE CHARACTER PROFILES. THOUGH NOW, I'VE KIND OF RUN OUT OF CHARACTERS TO PROFILE. SO MAYBE I SHOULD JUST WRITE ABOUT-- I DON'T KNOW-- STUFF THAT'S BEEN HAPPENING IN MY LIFE LATELY? SURE.

I TOOK THE SHINKANSEN (BULLET TRAIN) UP TO NAGOYA RECENTLY, TO DO SOME SHOPPING, EAT SOME GOOD FOOD, AND DO SOME OTHER TOURISTY STUFF.
WE'D HEARD THERE WAS GOING TO BE A TYPHOON IN TOKYO IN THE NEXT FEW DAYS, THOUGH THE WEATHER REPORTS SAID IT WOULDN'T AFFECT THE KANSAI (WESTERN) PART OF JAPAN, SO WE FIGURED WE'D HAVE NO TROUBLE ON THE BULLET TRAIN. AND THEN, THE TRAIN SUDDENLY STOPPED, JUST OUTSIDE OF ONE STATION BEFORE NAGOYA. MY FRIEND AND I STARTED TALKING ABOUT WHAT WE THOUGHT WAS WRONG. WHY HAD THE TRAIN STOPPED? IT COULDN'T HAVE BEEN BECAUSE OF WEATHER, RIGHT?

AFTER A WHOLE HOUR, THE TRAIN STILL HADN'T MOVED. AND THAT WAS WHEN...

(CONTINUED)

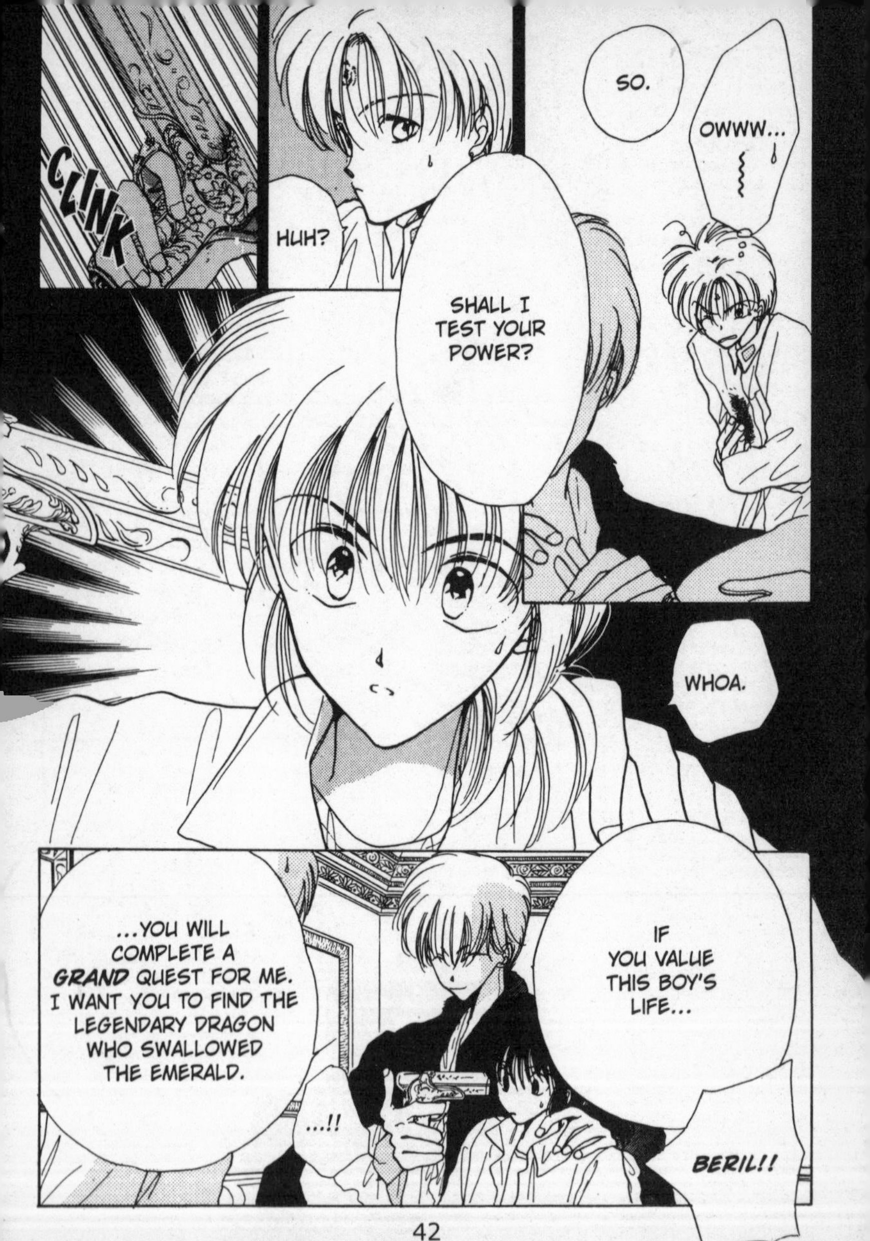
OWWW...
SO.
HUH?
CLINK
SHALL I TEST YOUR POWER?
WHOA.
IF YOU VALUE THIS BOY'S LIFE...
BERIL!!
...!!
...YOU WILL COMPLETE A GRAND QUEST FOR ME. I WANT YOU TO FIND THE LEGENDARY DRAGON WHO SWALLOWED THE EMERALD.

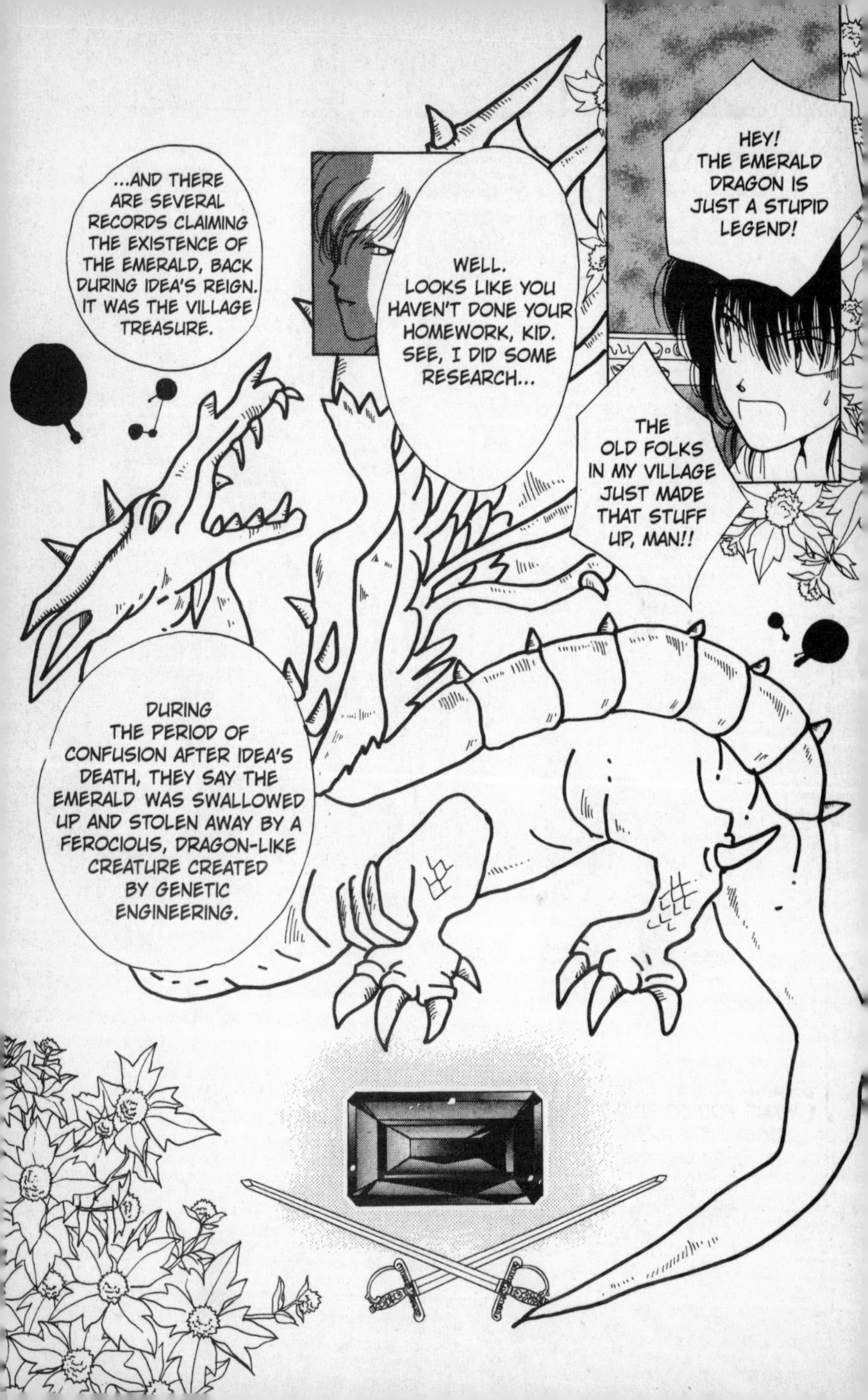
HEY! THE EMERALD DRAGON IS JUST A STUPID LEGEND!
THE OLD FOLKS IN MY VILLAGE JUST MADE THAT STUFF UP, MAN!!
WELL. LOOKS LIKE YOU HAVEN'T DONE YOUR HOMEWORK, KID. SEE, I DID SOME RESEARCH...
...AND THERE ARE SEVERAL RECORDS CLAIMING THE EXISTENCE OF THE EMERALD, BACK DURING IDEA'S REIGN. IT WAS THE VILLAGE TREASURE.
DURING THE PERIOD OF CONFUSION AFTER IDEA'S DEATH, THEY SAY THE EMERALD WAS SWALLOWED UP AND STOLEN AWAY BY A FEROCIOUS, DRAGON-LIKE CREATURE CREATED BY GENETIC ENGINEERING.

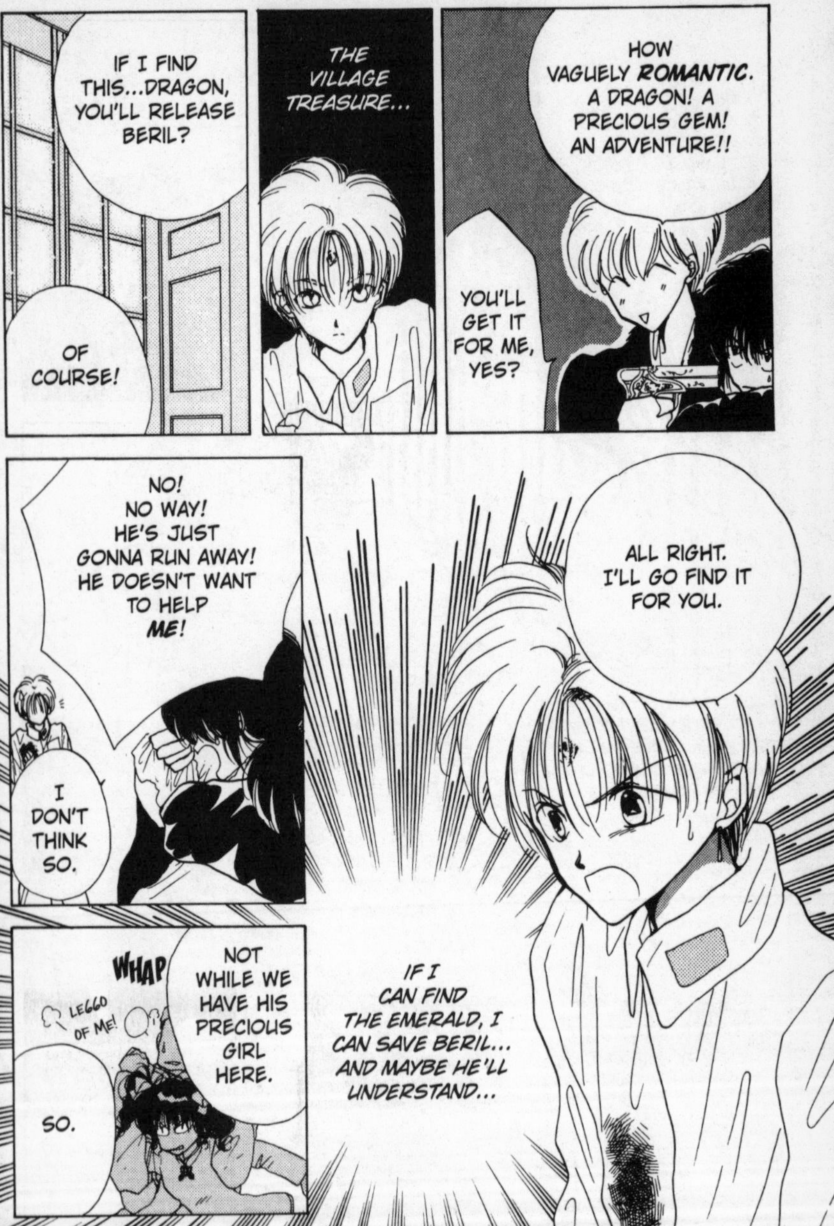
HOW VAGUELY ROMANTIC. A DRAGON! A PRECIOUS GEM! AN ADVENTURE!!
YOU'LL GET IT FOR ME, YES?
THE VILLAGE TREASURE...
IF I FIND THIS...DRAGON, YOU'LL RELEASE BERIL?
OF COURSE!
ALL RIGHT. I'LL GO FIND IT FOR YOU.
IF I CAN FIND THE EMERALD, I CAN SAVE BERIL... AND MAYBE HE'LL UNDERSTAND...
NO! NO WAY! HE'S JUST GONNA RUN AWAY! HE DOESN'T WANT TO HELP ME!
I DON'T THINK SO.
WHAP
NOT WHILE WE HAVE HIS PRECIOUS GIRL HERE.
LEGGO OF ME!
SO.

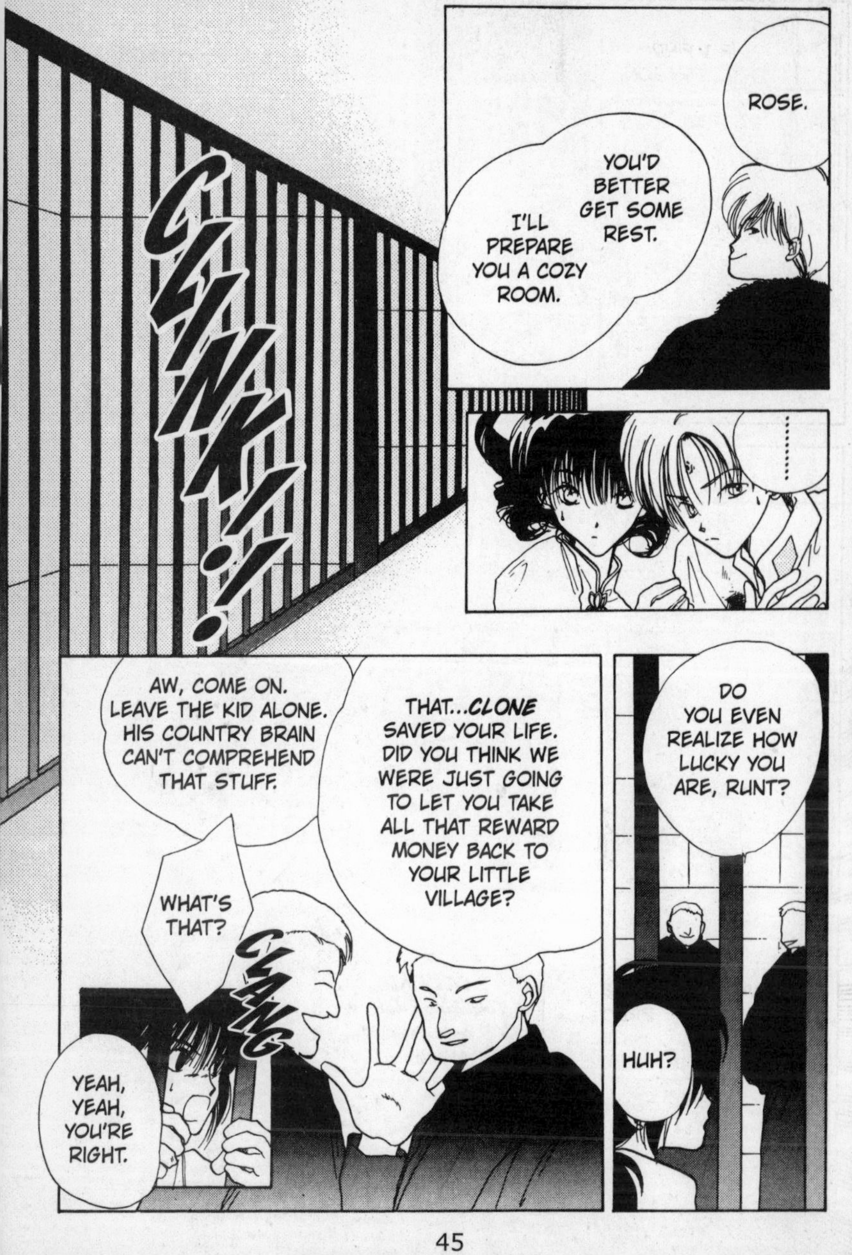

ROSE.
YOU'D BETTER GET SOME REST.
I'LL PREPARE YOU A COZY ROOM.
......
CLINK!!
DO YOU EVEN REALIZE HOW LUCKY YOU ARE, RUNT?
HUH?
THAT...*CLONE* SAVED YOUR LIFE. DID YOU THINK WE WERE JUST GOING TO LET YOU TAKE ALL THAT REWARD MONEY BACK TO YOUR LITTLE VILLAGE?
AW, COME ON. LEAVE THE KID ALONE. HIS COUNTRY BRAIN CAN'T COMPREHEND THAT STUFF.
WHAT'S THAT?
CLANG
YEAH, YEAH, YOU'RE RIGHT.

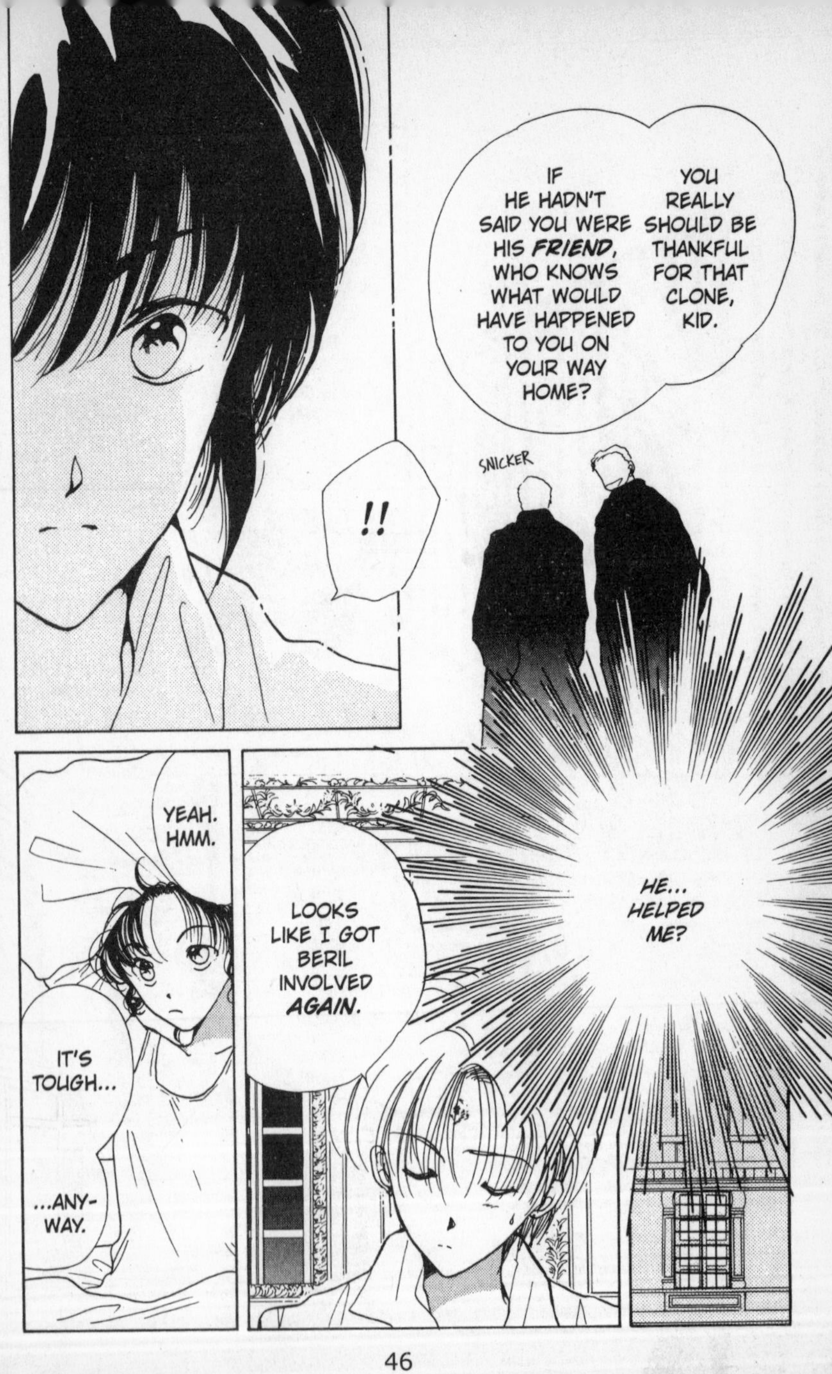
YOU REALLY SHOULD BE THANKFUL FOR THAT CLONE, KID.
IF HE HADN'T SAID YOU WERE HIS ***FRIEND***, WHO KNOWS WHAT WOULD HAVE HAPPENED TO YOU ON YOUR WAY HOME?
SNICKER
!!
HE... HELPED ME?
LOOKS LIKE I GOT BERIL INVOLVED ***AGAIN***.
YEAH. HMM.
IT'S TOUGH...
...ANY-WAY.

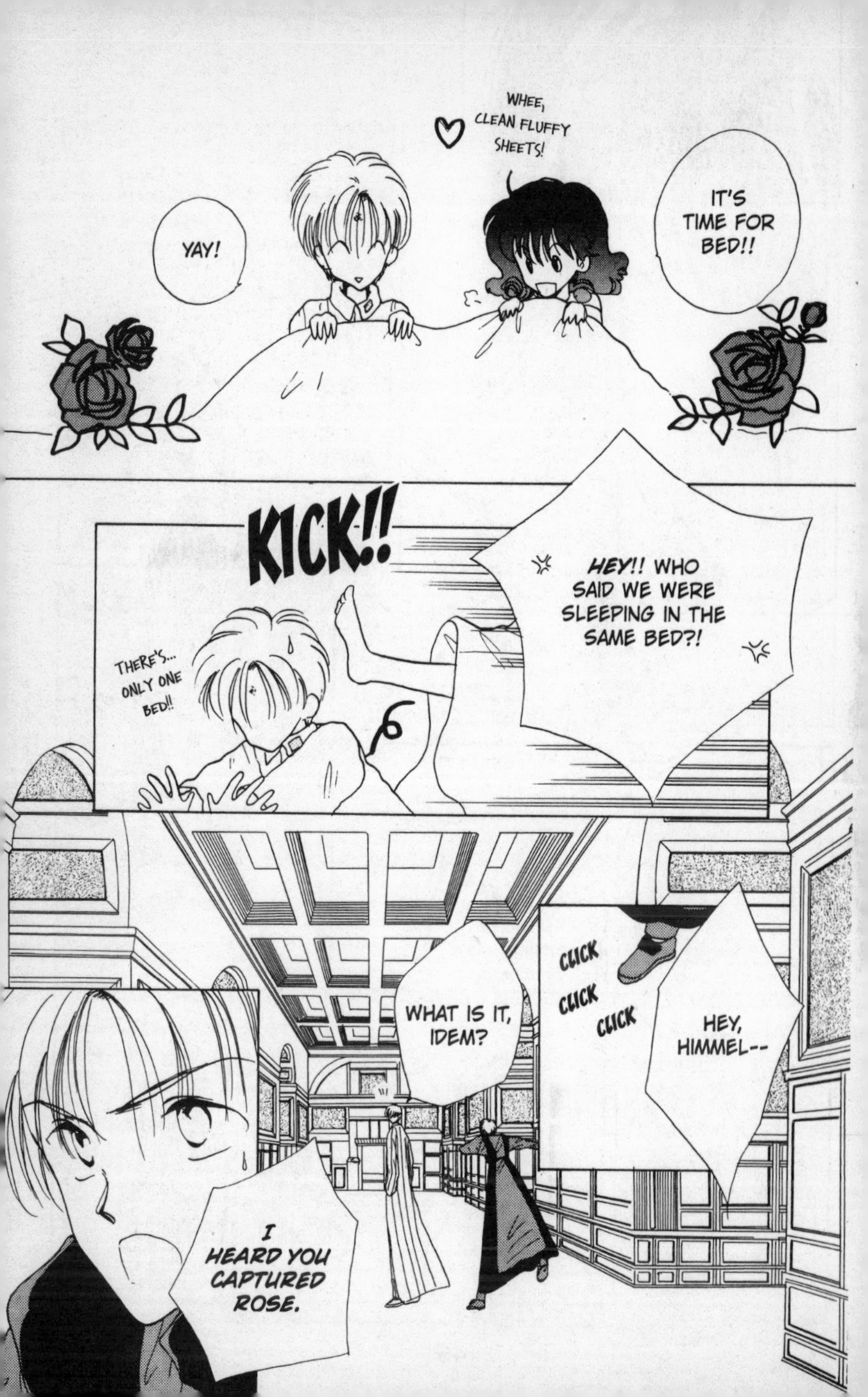
IT'S TIME FOR BED!!
WHEE, CLEAN FLUFFY SHEETS!
YAY!
HEY!! WHO SAID WE WERE SLEEPING IN THE SAME BED?!
KICK!!
THERE'S... ONLY ONE BED!!
HEY, HIMMEL--
CLICK
CLICK
CLICK
WHAT IS IT, IDEM?
I HEARD YOU CAPTURED ROSE.

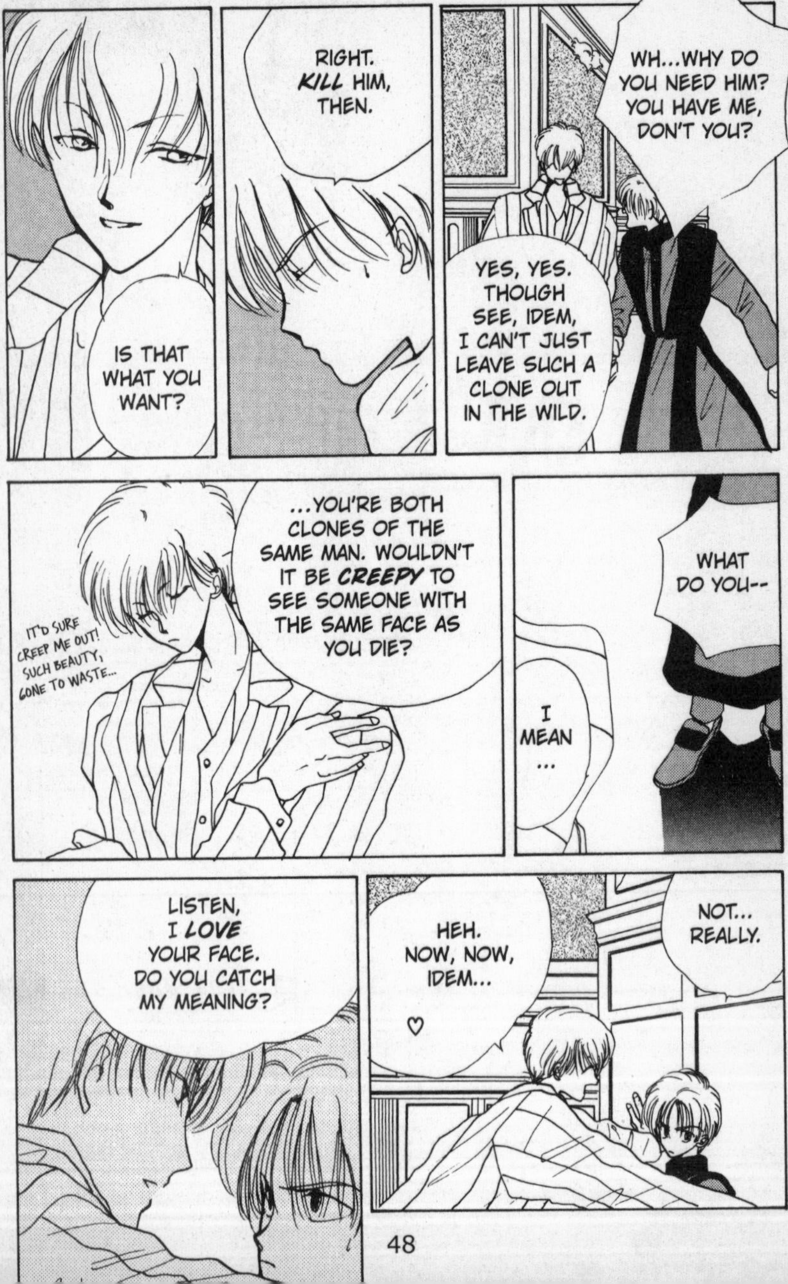
WH...WHY DO YOU NEED HIM? YOU HAVE ME, DON'T YOU?
YES, YES. THOUGH SEE, IDEM, I CAN'T JUST LEAVE SUCH A CLONE OUT IN THE WILD.
RIGHT. *KILL* HIM, THEN.
IS THAT WHAT YOU WANT?
WHAT DO YOU--
I MEAN ...
...YOU'RE BOTH CLONES OF THE SAME MAN. WOULDN'T IT BE *CREEPY* TO SEE SOMEONE WITH THE SAME FACE AS YOU DIE?
IT'D SURE CREEP ME OUT! SUCH BEAUTY, GONE TO WASTE...
NOT... REALLY.
HEH. NOW, NOW, IDEM... ♡
LISTEN, I *LOVE* YOUR FACE. DO YOU CATCH MY MEANING?

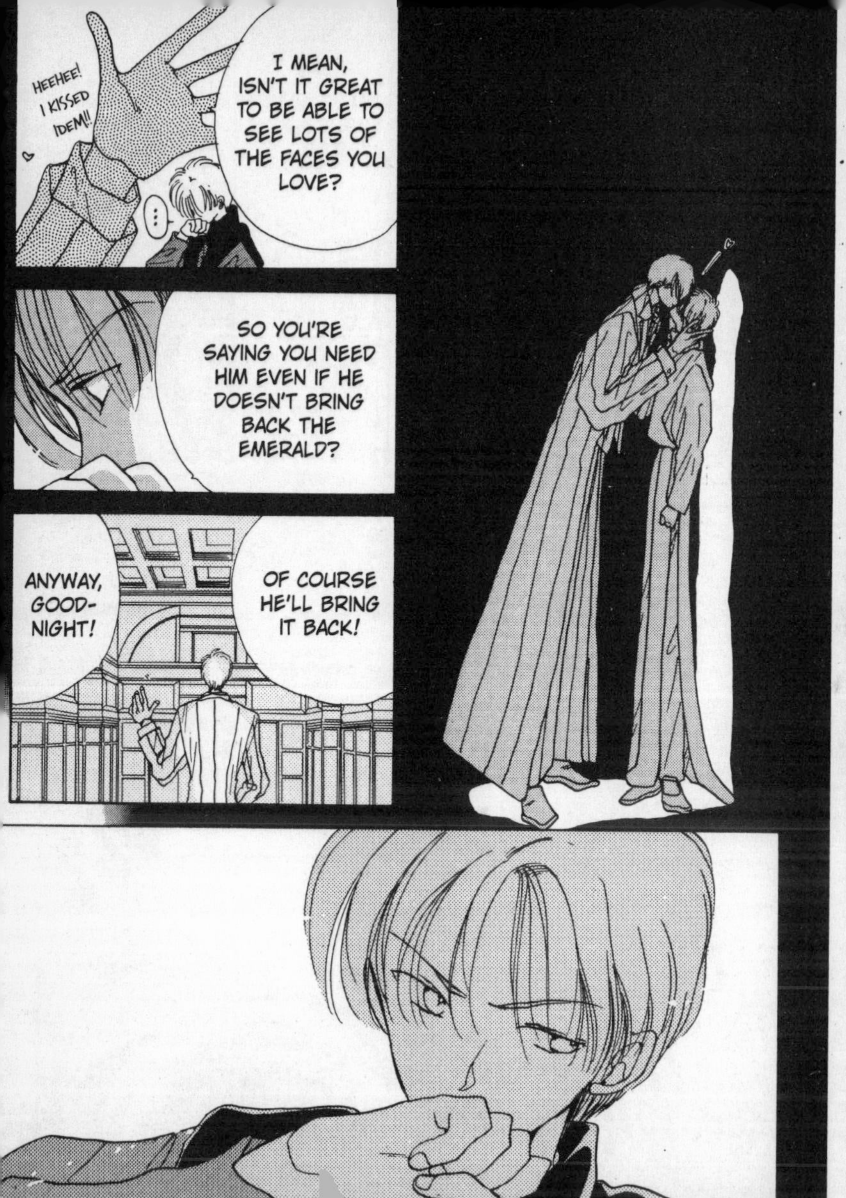
I MEAN, ISN'T IT GREAT TO BE ABLE TO SEE LOTS OF THE FACES YOU LOVE?
HEEHEE! I KISSED IDEM!!
...
SO YOU'RE SAYING YOU NEED HIM EVEN IF HE DOESN'T BRING BACK THE EMERALD?
OF COURSE HE'LL BRING IT BACK!
ANYWAY, GOOD-NIGHT!

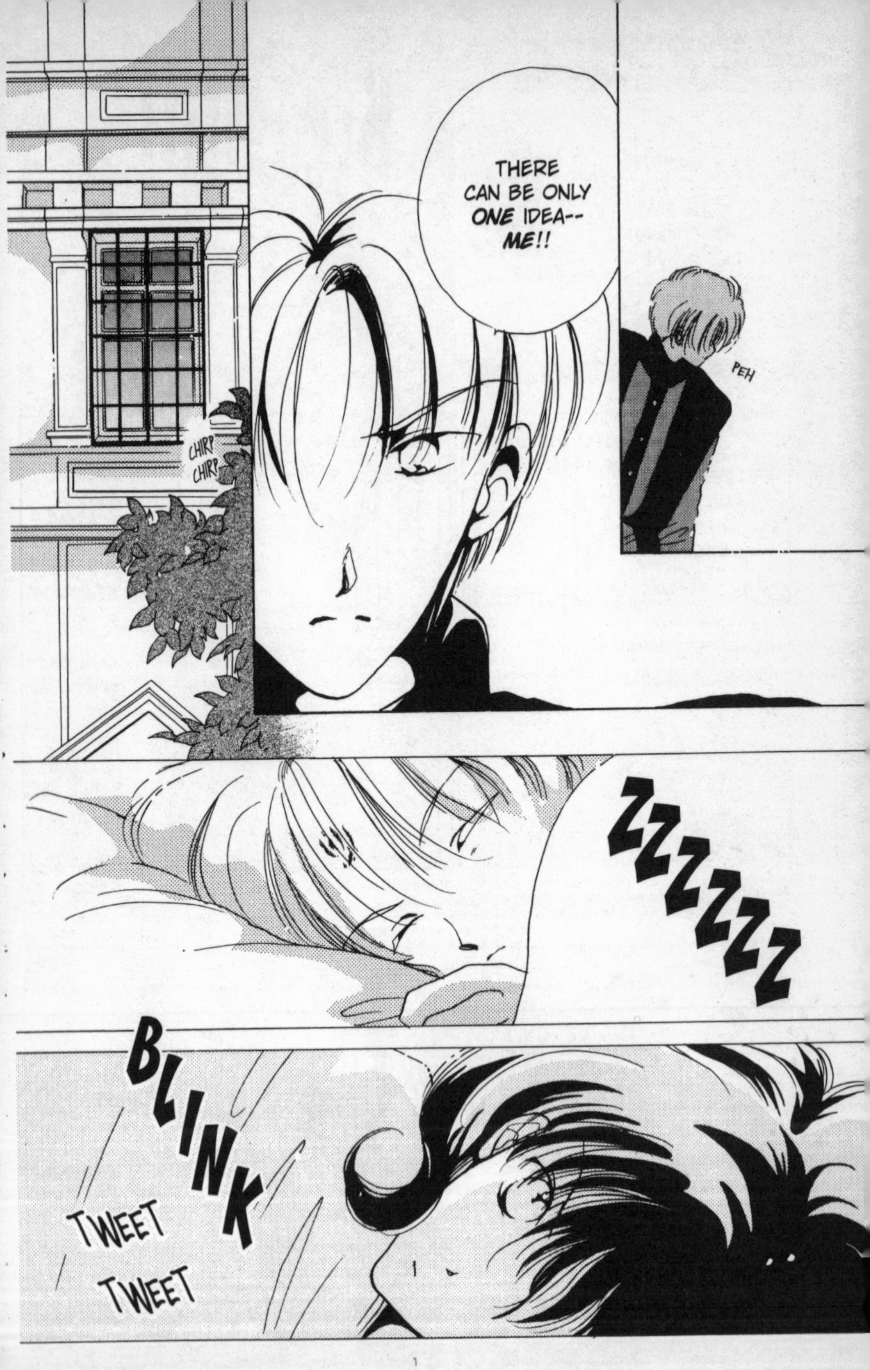
THERE CAN BE ONLY ONE IDEA-- ME!!
PEH
CHIRP CHIRP
ZZZZZZZ
BLINK
TWEET TWEET

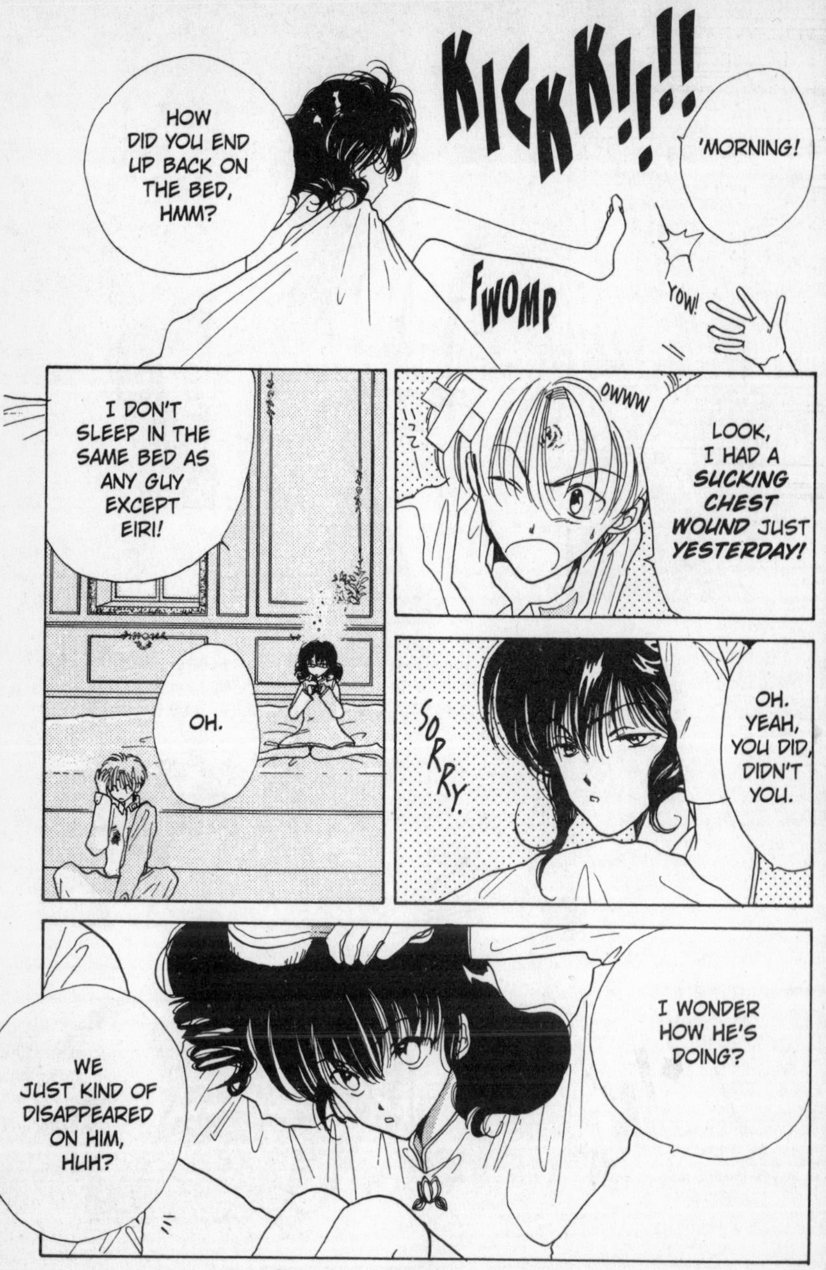

'MORNING!
KICKK!!!!
HOW DID YOU END UP BACK ON THE BED, HMM?
YOW!
FWOMP
OWWW
LOOK, I HAD A SUCKING CHEST WOUND JUST YESTERDAY!
OH. YEAH, YOU DID, DIDN'T YOU.
SORRY.
I DON'T SLEEP IN THE SAME BED AS ANY GUY EXCEPT EIRI!
OH.
I WONDER HOW HE'S DOING?
WE JUST KIND OF DISAPPEARED ON HIM, HUH?

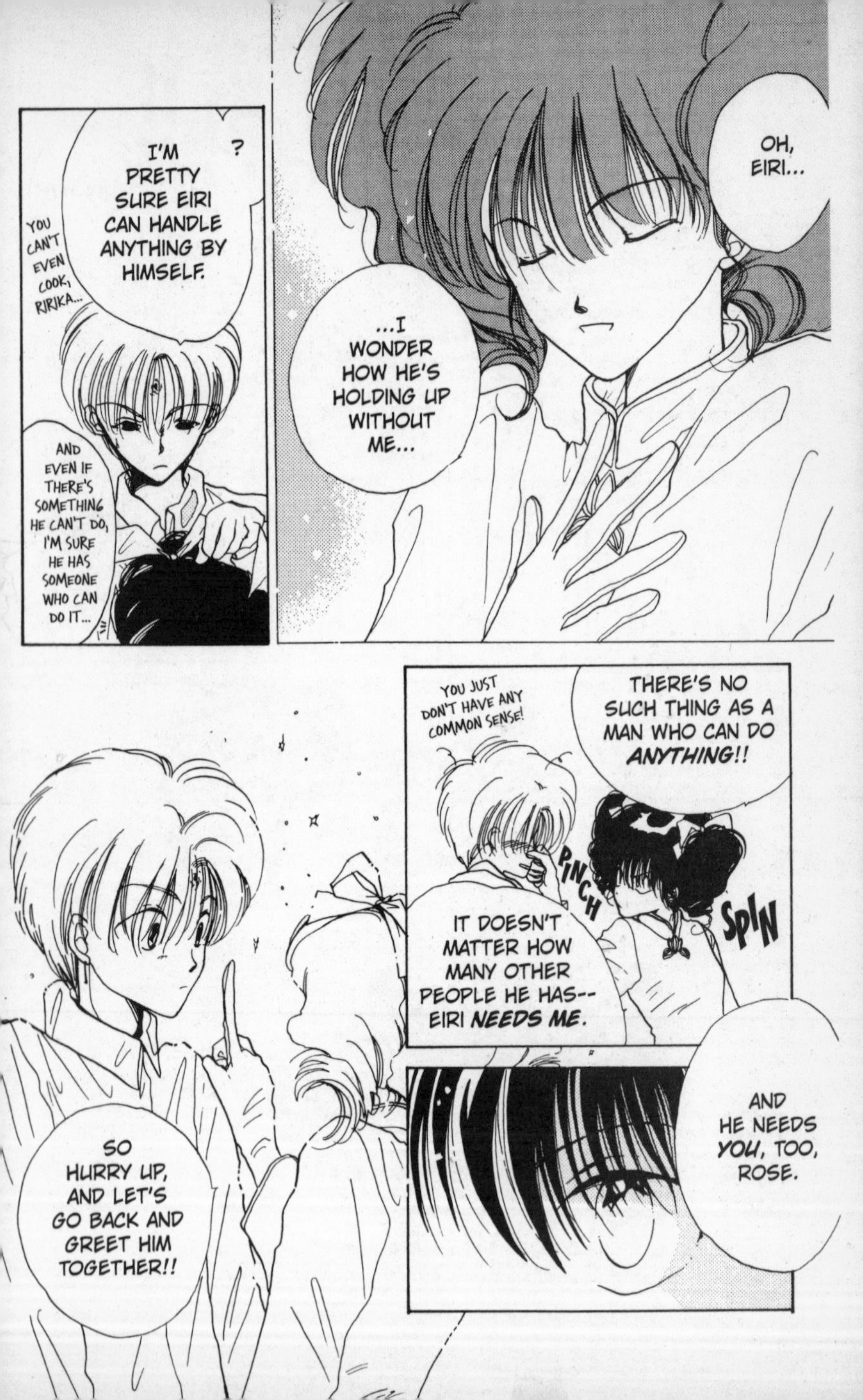
OH, EIRI...
...I WONDER HOW HE'S HOLDING UP WITHOUT ME...
I'M PRETTY SURE EIRI CAN HANDLE ANYTHING BY HIMSELF.
?
YOU CAN'T EVEN COOK, RIRIKA...
AND EVEN IF THERE'S SOMETHING HE CAN'T DO, I'M SURE HE HAS SOMEONE WHO CAN DO IT...
THERE'S NO SUCH THING AS A MAN WHO CAN DO ANYTHING!!
YOU JUST DON'T HAVE ANY COMMON SENSE!
SPIN
PINCH
IT DOESN'T MATTER HOW MANY OTHER PEOPLE HE HAS-- EIRI NEEDS ME.
AND HE NEEDS YOU, TOO, ROSE.
SO HURRY UP, AND LET'S GO BACK AND GREET HIM TOGETHER!!

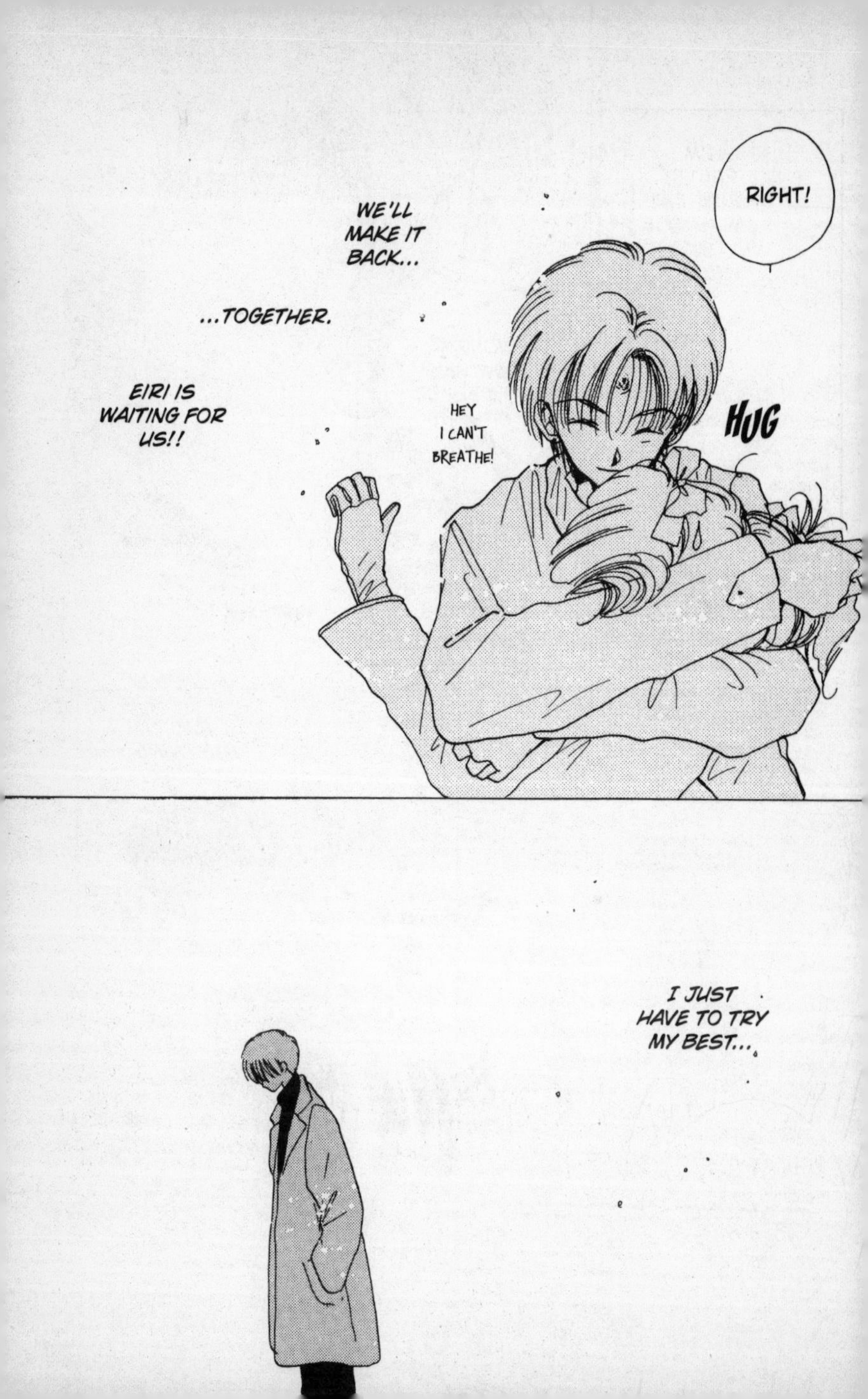
RIGHT!
HUG
HEY I CAN'T BREATHE!
WE'LL MAKE IT BACK...
...TOGETHER.
EIRI IS WAITING FOR US!!
I JUST HAVE TO TRY MY BEST...

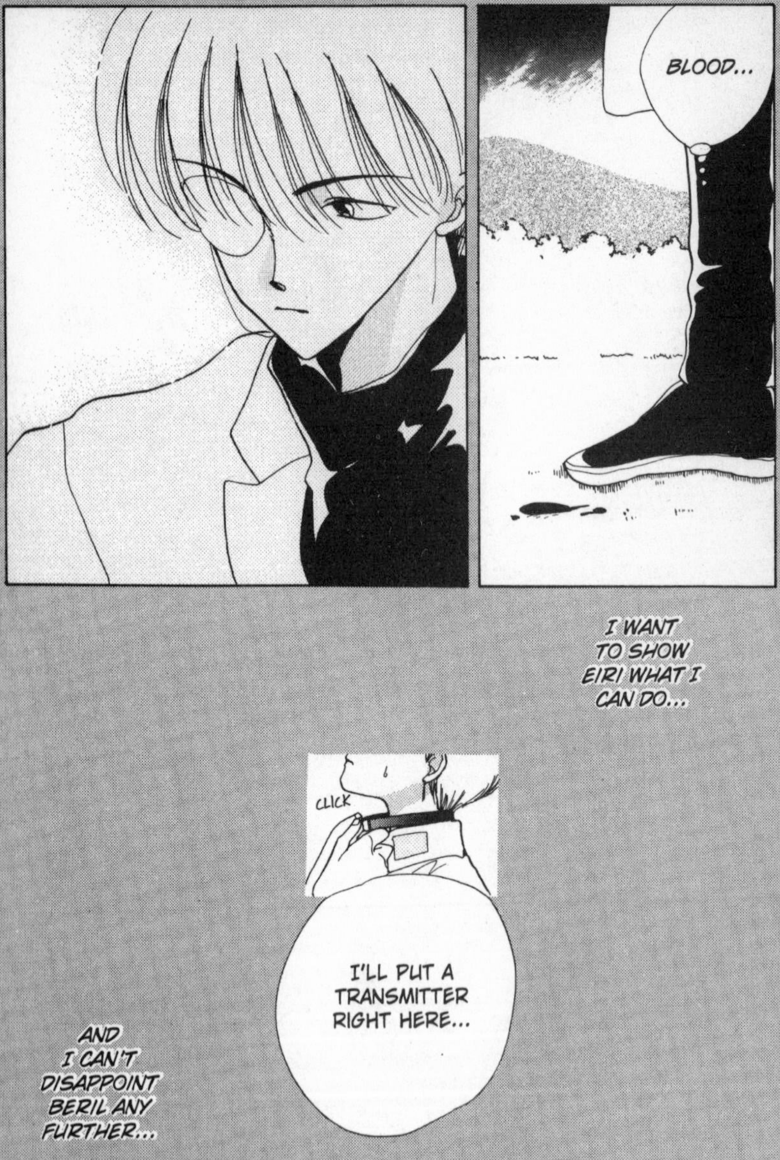
BLOOD...
I WANT TO SHOW EIRI WHAT I CAN DO...
CLICK
I'LL PUT A TRANSMITTER RIGHT HERE...
AND I CAN'T DISAPPOINT BERIL ANY FURTHER...

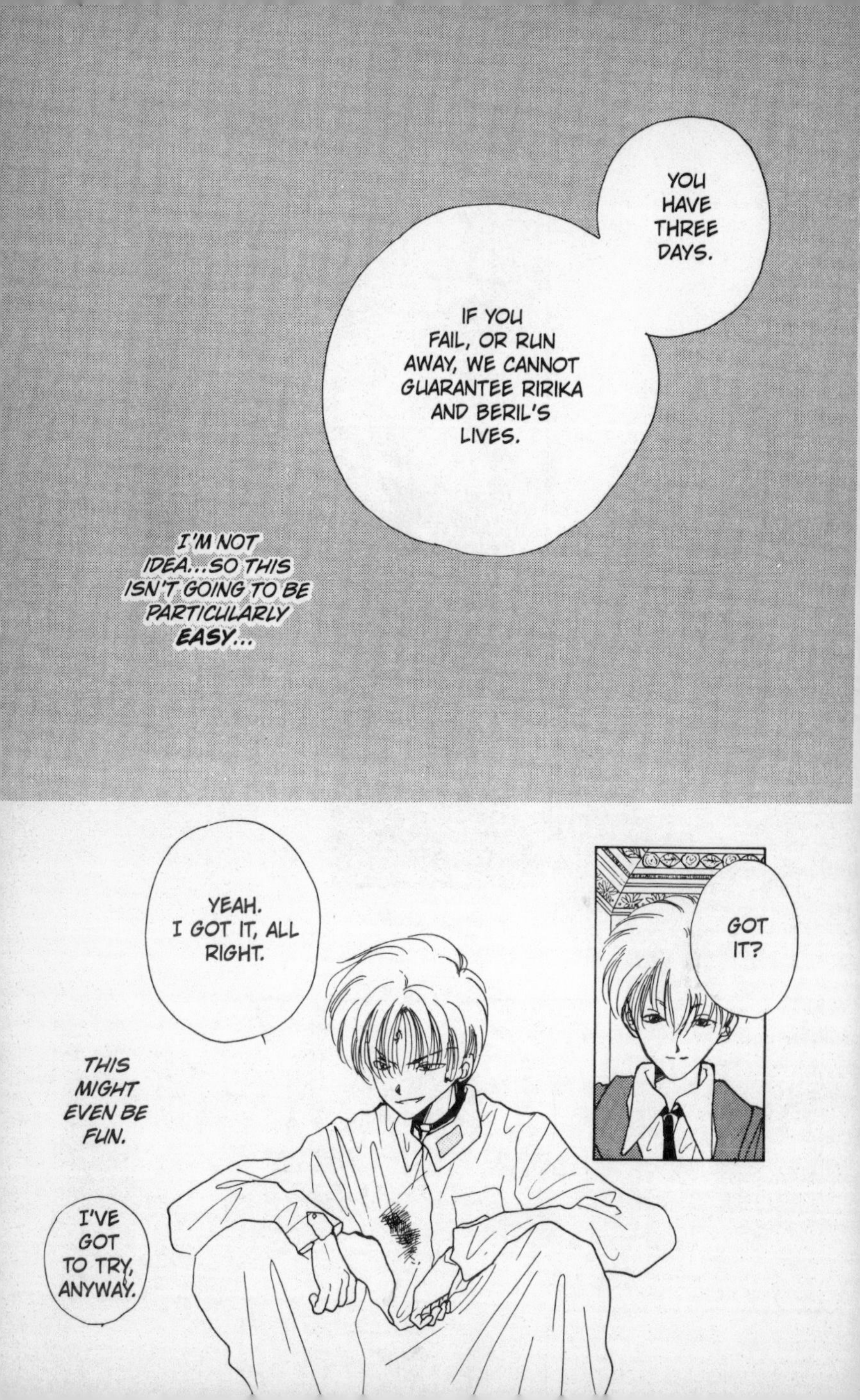
YOU HAVE THREE DAYS.
IF YOU FAIL, OR RUN AWAY, WE CANNOT GUARANTEE RIRIKA AND BERIL'S LIVES.
I'M NOT IDEA...SO THIS ISN'T GOING TO BE PARTICULARLY EASY...
GOT IT?
YEAH. I GOT IT, ALL RIGHT.
THIS MIGHT EVEN BE FUN.
I'VE GOT TO TRY, ANYWAY.

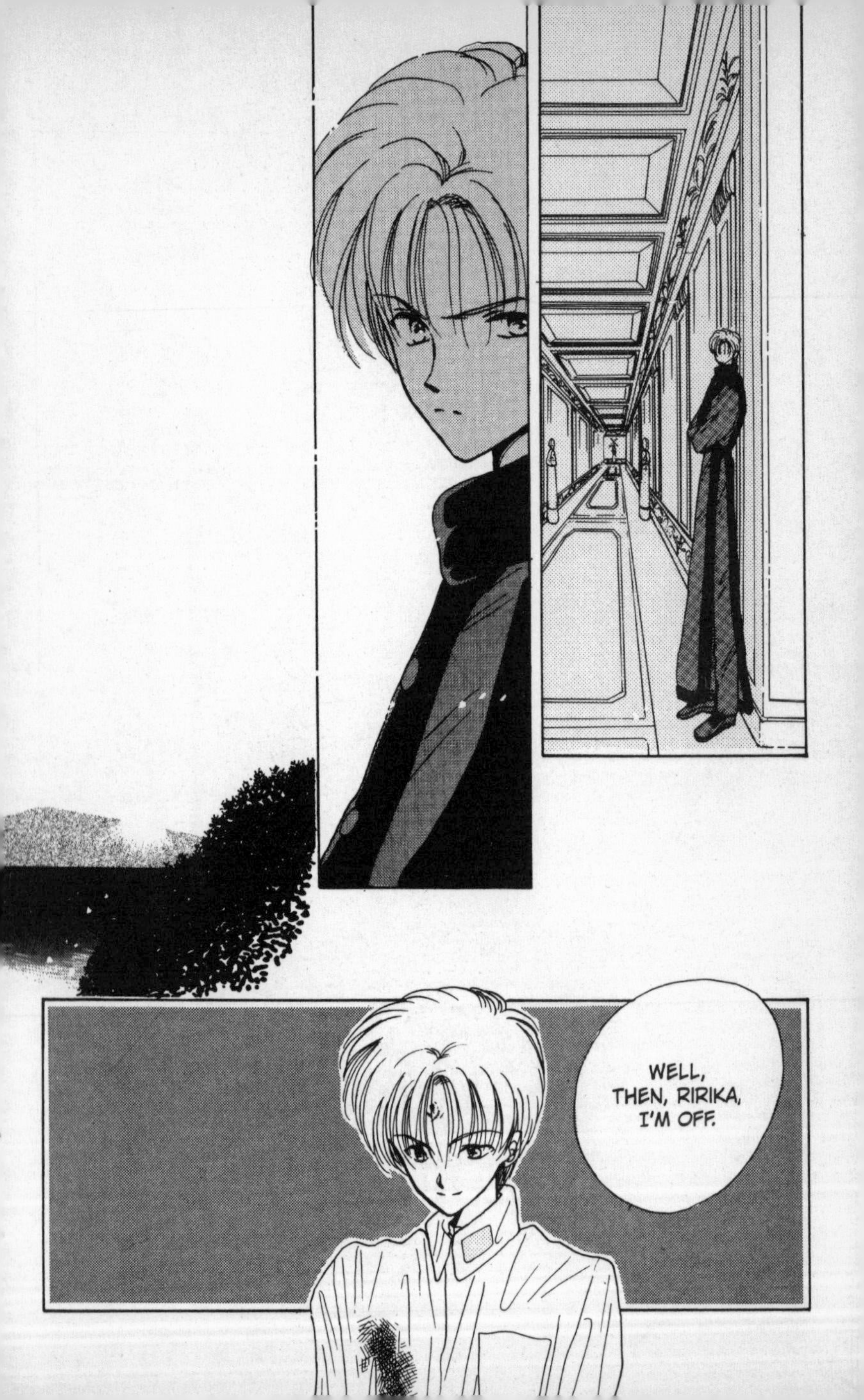
WELL, THEN, RIRIKA, I'M OFF.

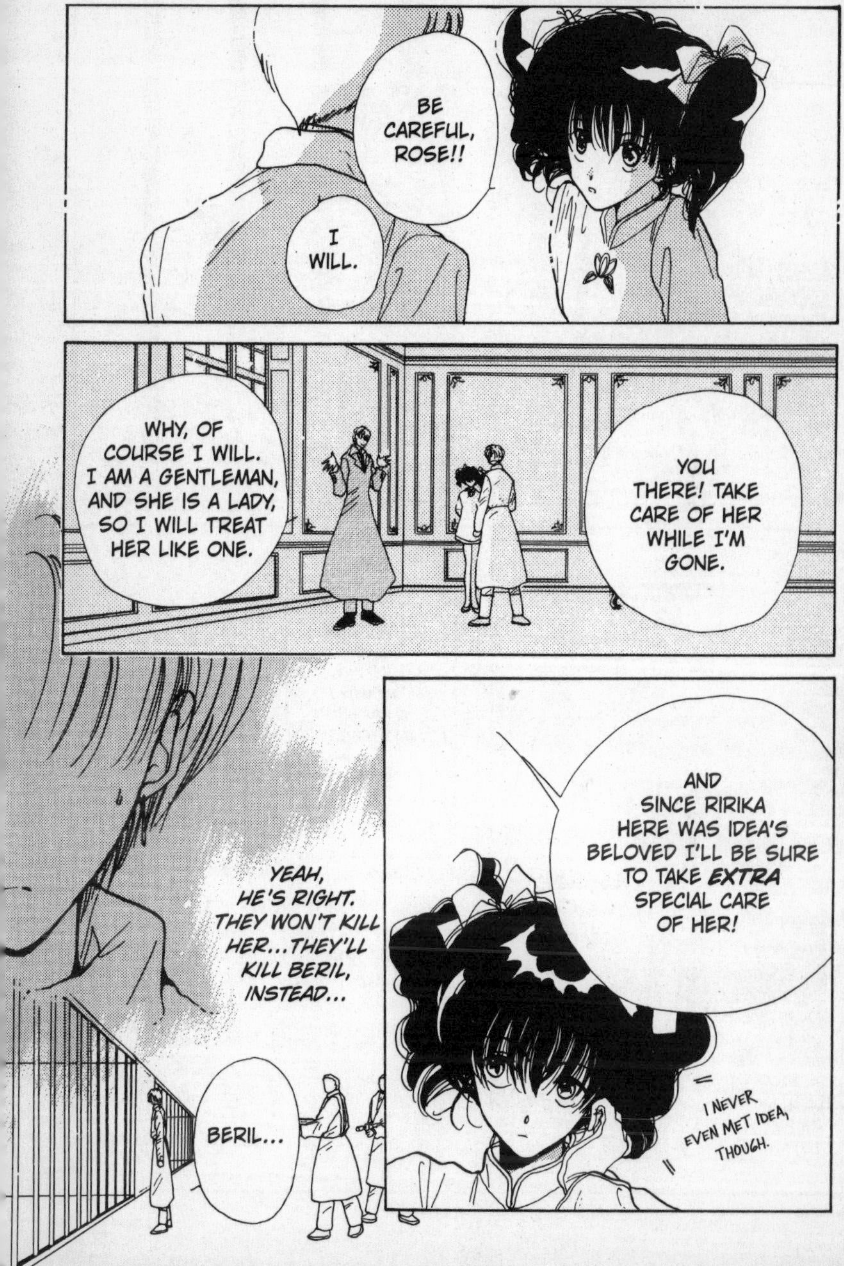
BE CAREFUL, ROSE!!
I WILL.
YOU THERE! TAKE CARE OF HER WHILE I'M GONE.
WHY, OF COURSE I WILL. I AM A GENTLEMAN, AND SHE IS A LADY, SO I WILL TREAT HER LIKE ONE.
AND SINCE RIRIKA HERE WAS IDEA'S BELOVED I'LL BE SURE TO TAKE *EXTRA* SPECIAL CARE OF HER!
I NEVER EVEN MET IDEA, THOUGH.
YEAH, HE'S RIGHT. THEY WON'T KILL HER...THEY'LL KILL BERIL, INSTEAD...
BERIL...

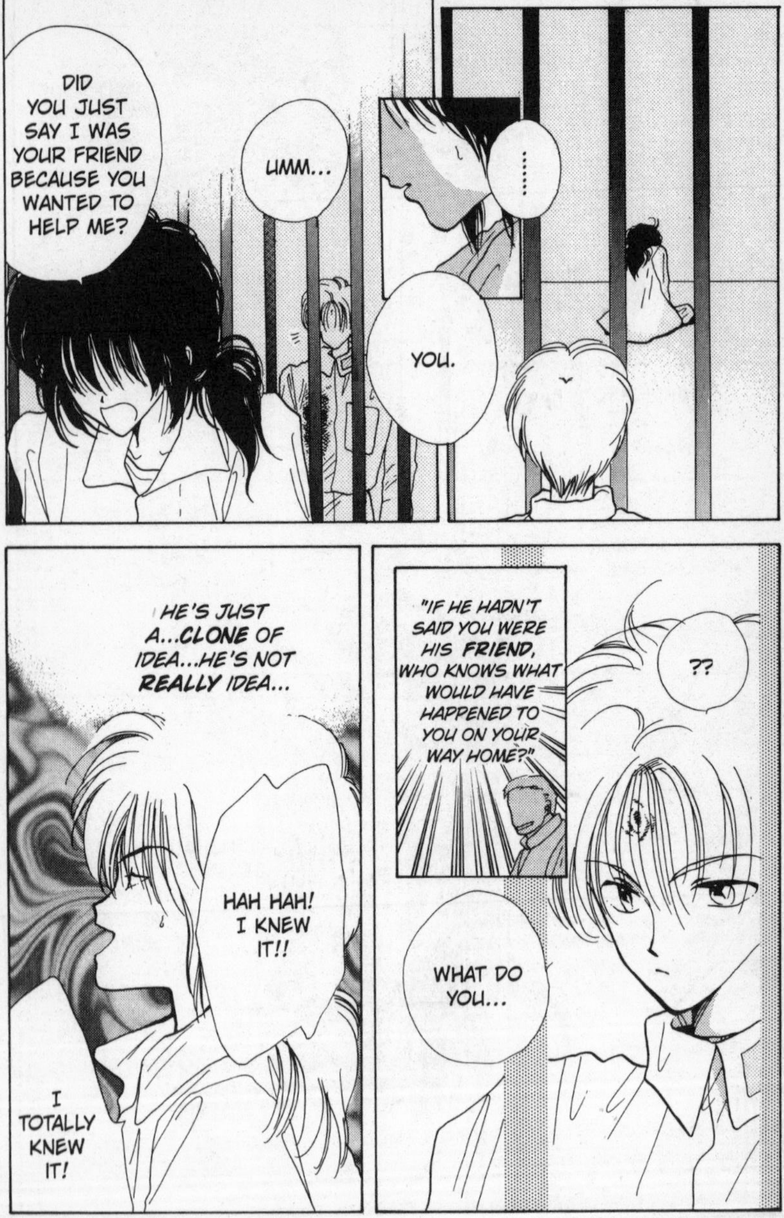
......
DID YOU JUST SAY I WAS YOUR FRIEND BECAUSE YOU WANTED TO HELP ME?
UMM...
YOU.
"IF HE HADN'T SAID YOU WERE HIS FRIEND, WHO KNOWS WHAT WOULD HAVE HAPPENED TO YOU ON YOUR WAY HOME?"
??
WHAT DO YOU...
HE'S JUST A...CLONE OF IDEA...HE'S NOT REALLY IDEA...
HAH HAH! I KNEW IT!!
I TOTALLY KNEW IT!

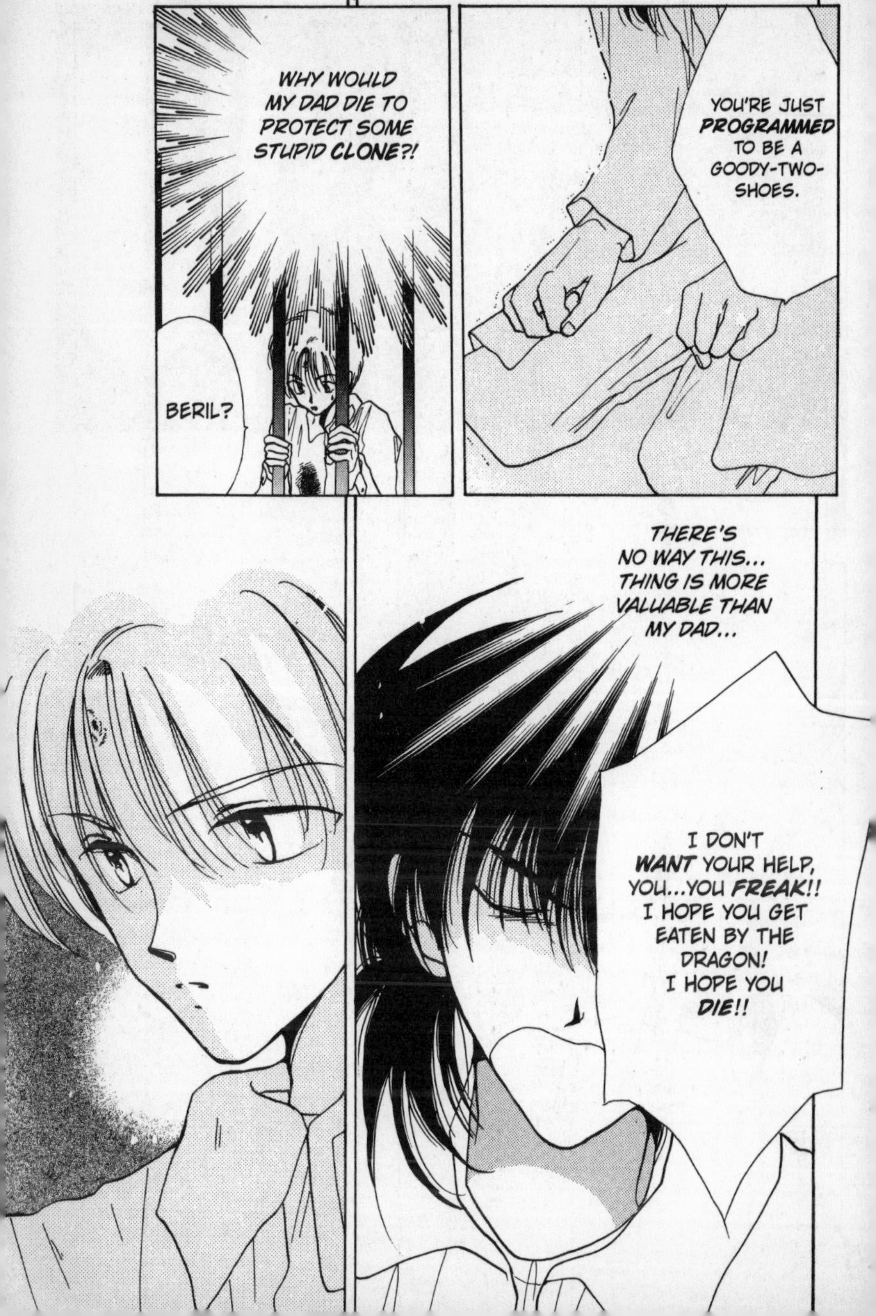
YOU'RE JUST **PROGRAMMED** TO BE A GOODY-TWO-SHOES.
WHY WOULD MY DAD DIE TO PROTECT SOME STUPID **CLONE**?!
BERIL?
THERE'S NO WAY THIS... THING IS MORE VALUABLE THAN MY DAD...
I DON'T **WANT** YOUR HELP, YOU...YOU **FREAK**!! I HOPE YOU GET EATEN BY THE DRAGON! I HOPE YOU **DIE**!!

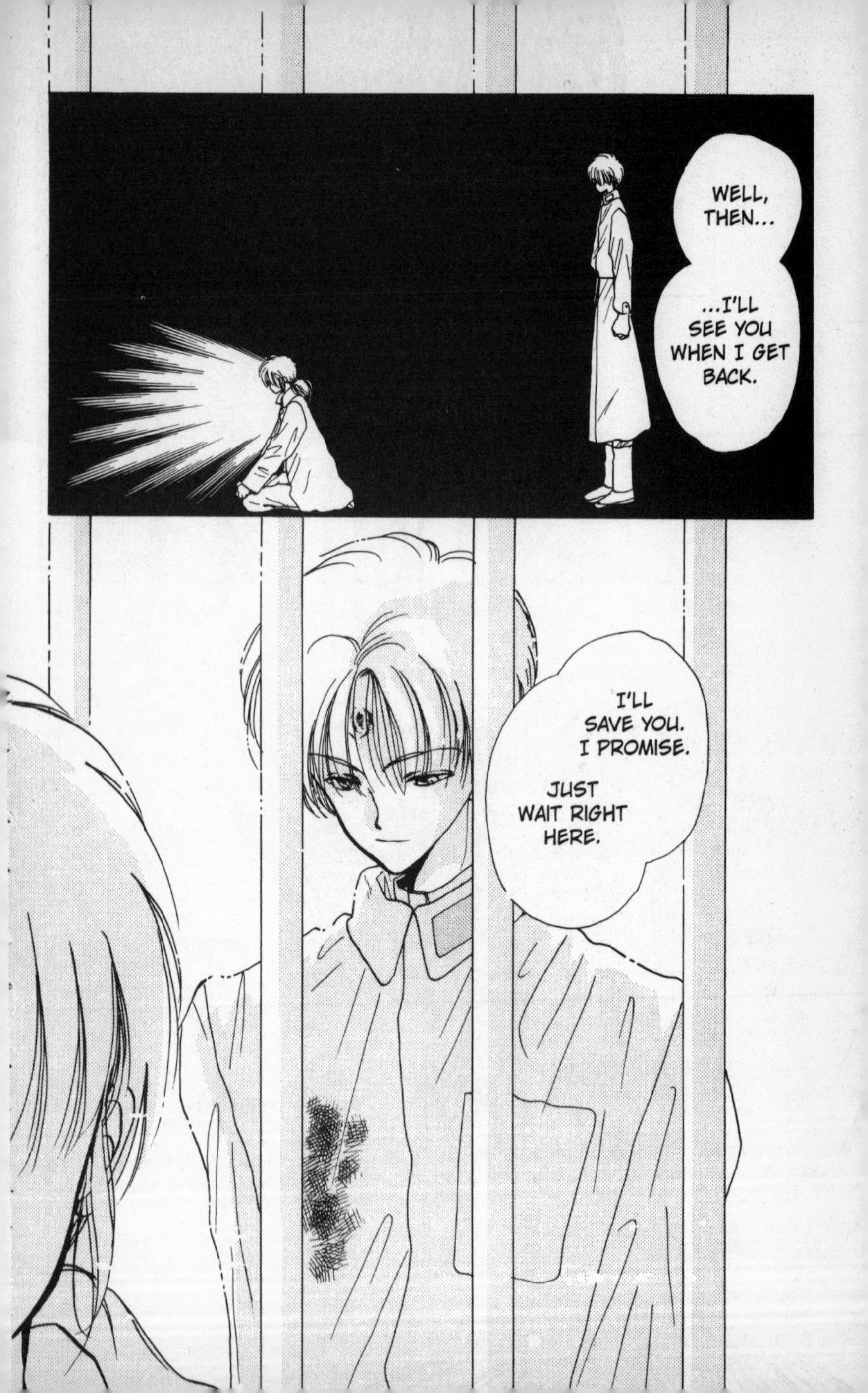
WELL, THEN...
...I'LL SEE YOU WHEN I GET BACK.
I'LL SAVE YOU. I PROMISE.
JUST WAIT RIGHT HERE.

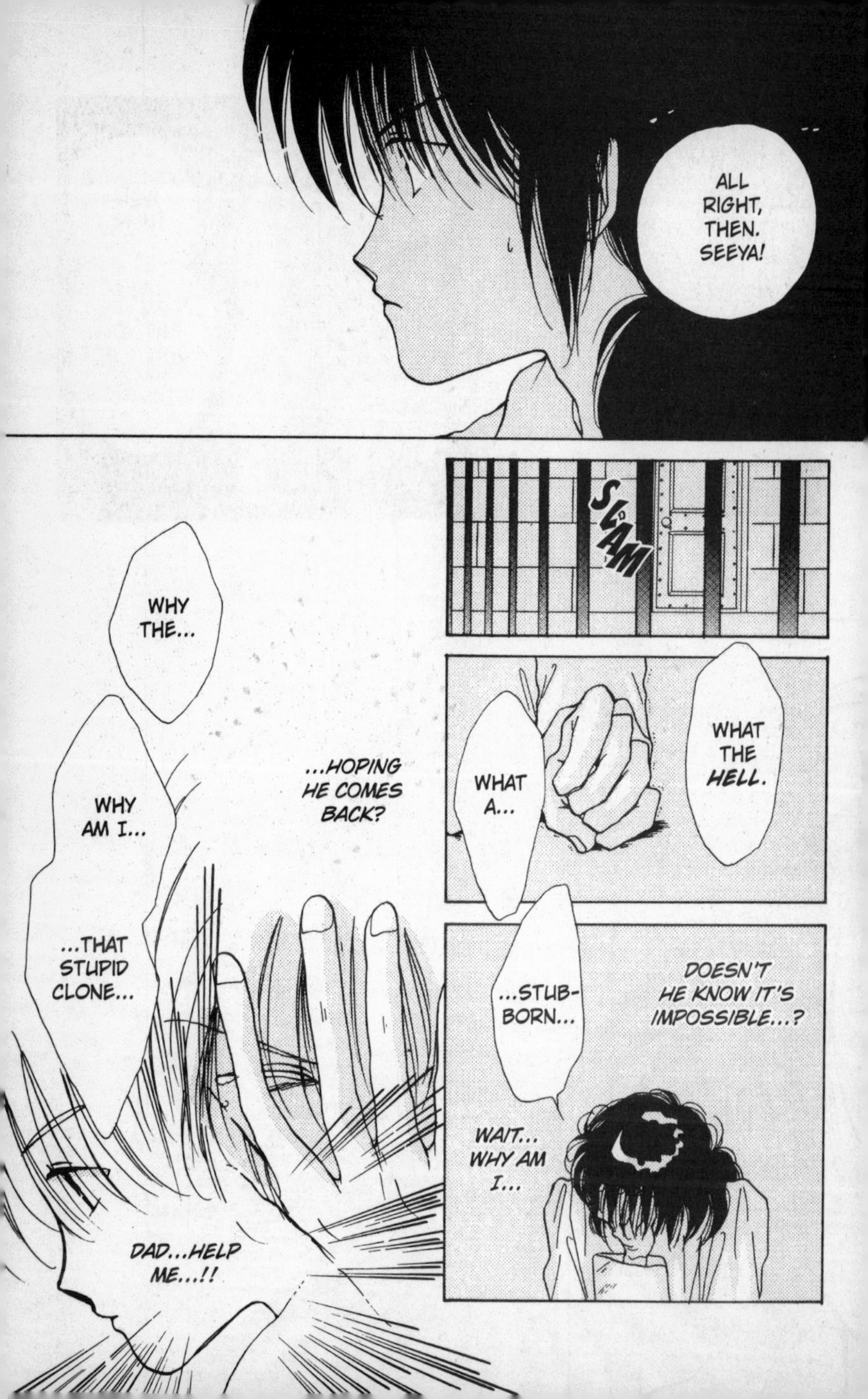
ALL RIGHT, THEN. SEEYA!
SLAM
WHAT THE HELL.
WHAT A...
...STUB-BORN...
DOESN'T HE KNOW IT'S IMPOSSIBLE...?
WAIT... WHY AM I...
WHY THE...
...HOPING HE COMES BACK?
WHY AM I...
...THAT STUPID CLONE...
DAD...HELP ME...!!

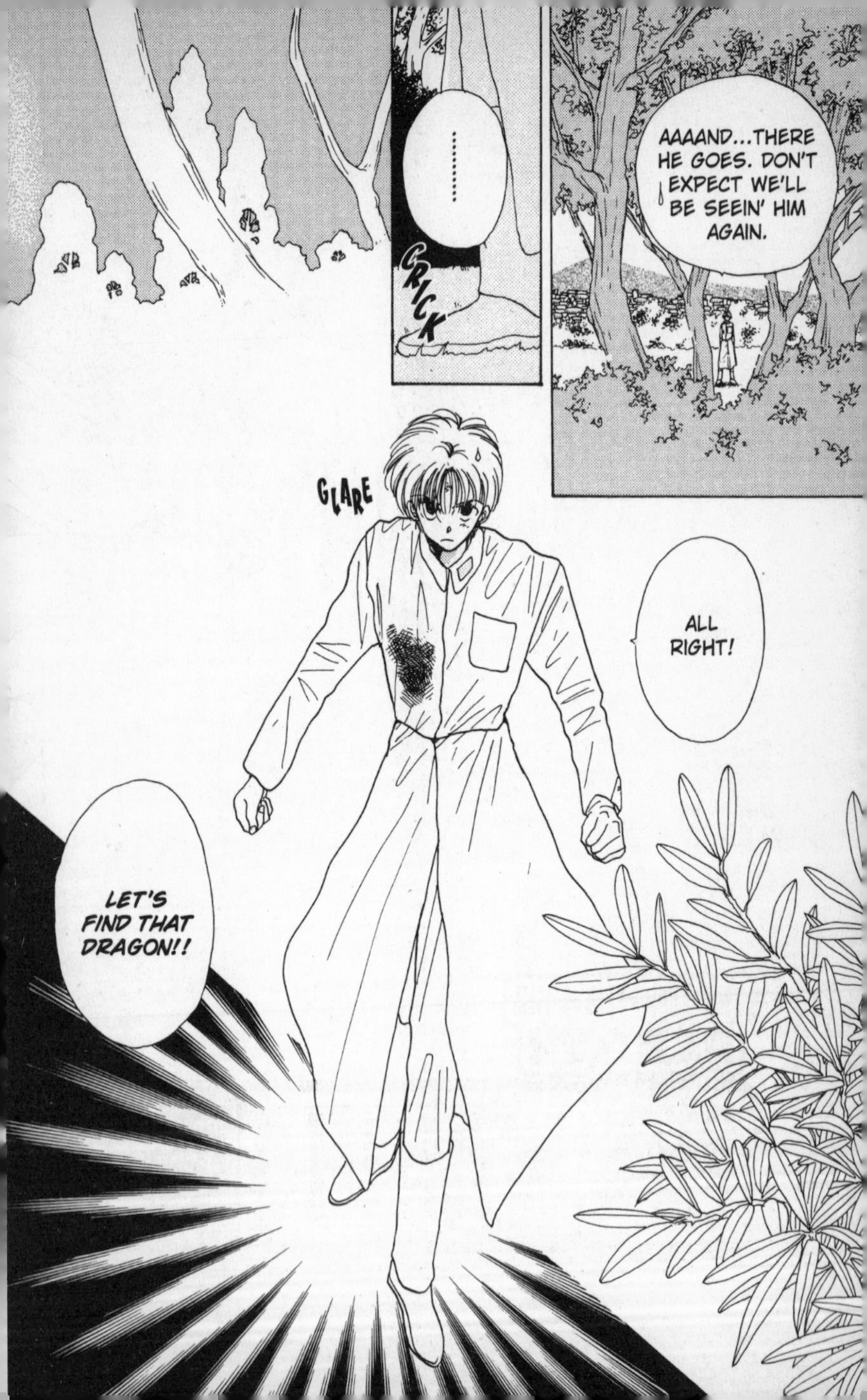
AAAAND...THERE HE GOES. DON'T EXPECT WE'LL BE SEEIN' HIM AGAIN.
......
CRICK
ALL RIGHT!
GLARE
LET'S FIND THAT DRAGON!!

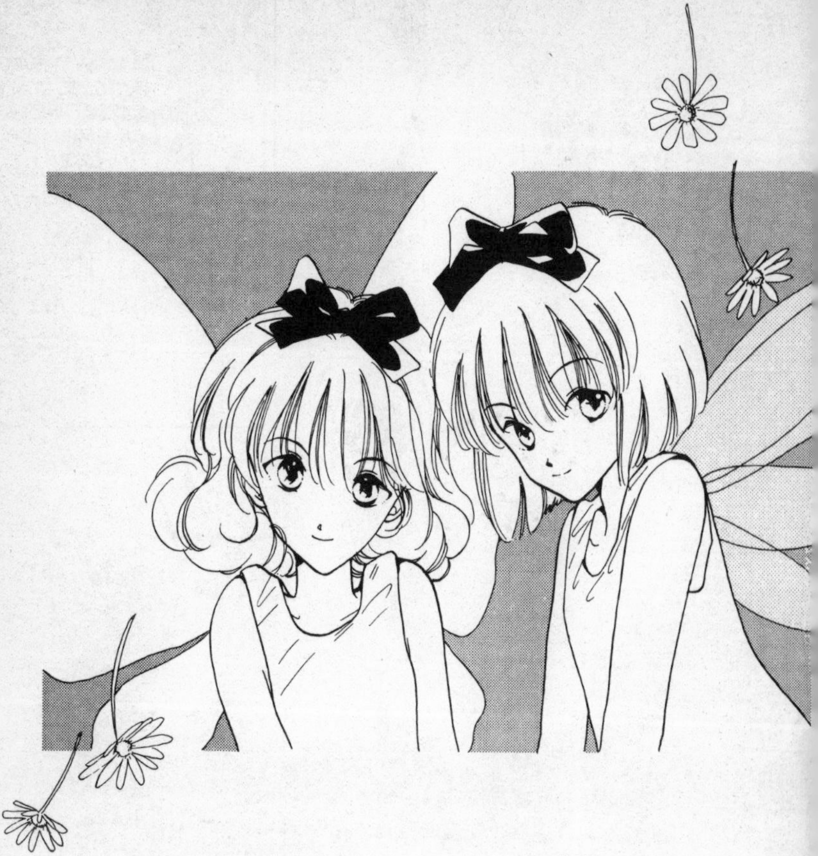

THE EMPTY EMPIRE
PART VII

THE WAKING BIRD

PART 8

MANNN...
CAW
CAW
CHIRP
CHIRP

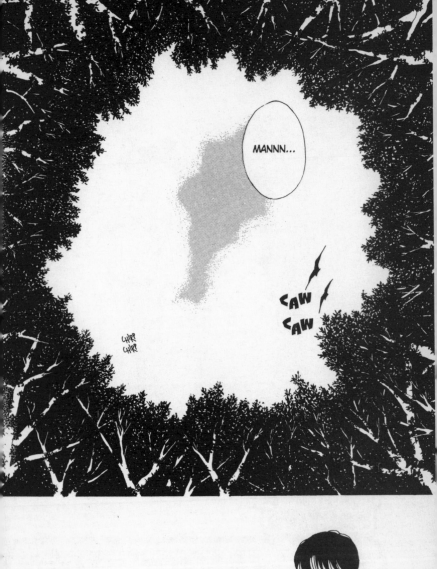

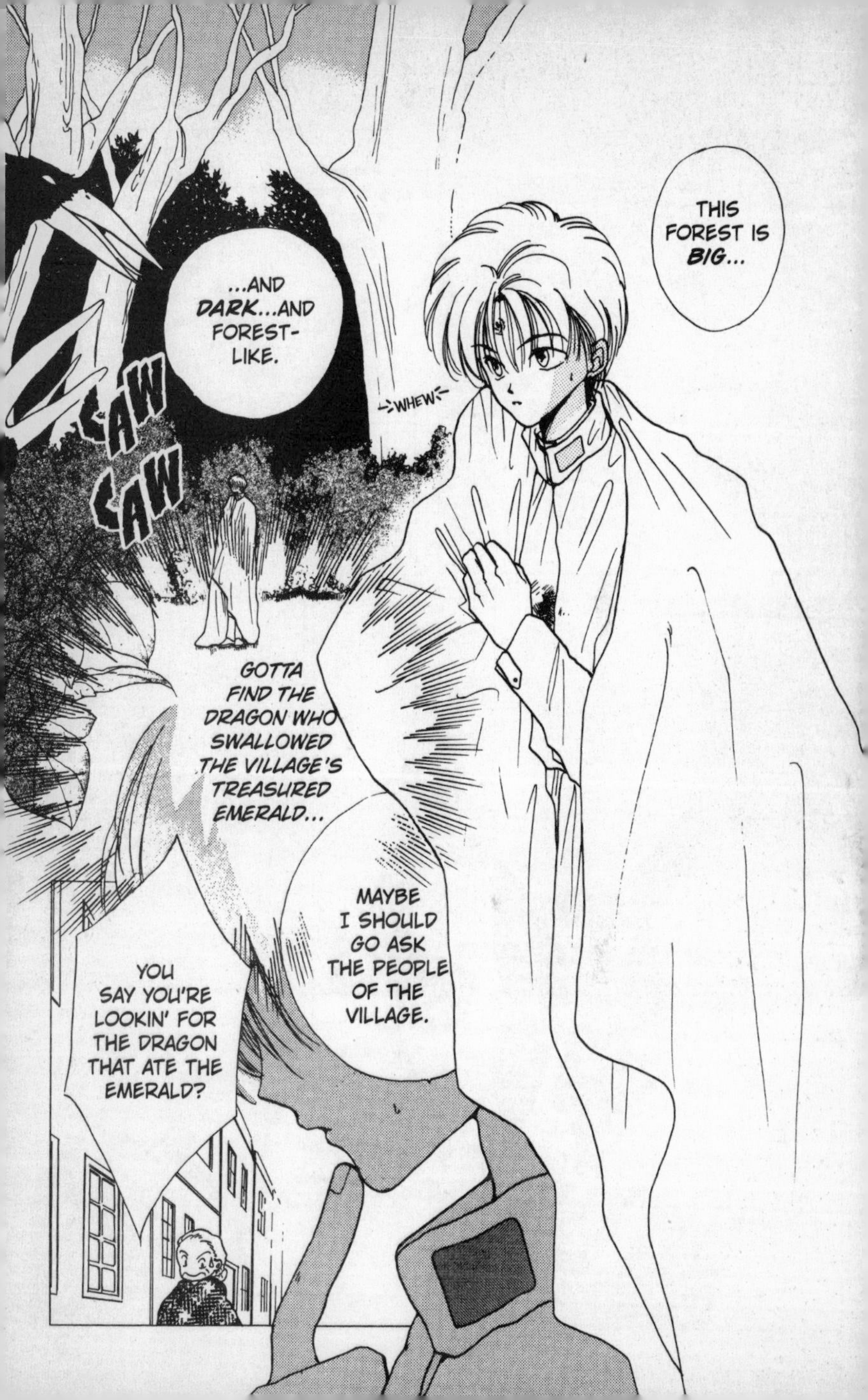
THIS FOREST IS BIG...
...AND DARK...AND FOREST-LIKE.
WHEW
CAW CAW
GOTTA FIND THE DRAGON WHO SWALLOWED THE VILLAGE'S TREASURED EMERALD...
MAYBE I SHOULD GO ASK THE PEOPLE OF THE VILLAGE.
YOU SAY YOU'RE LOOKIN' FOR THE DRAGON THAT ATE THE EMERALD?

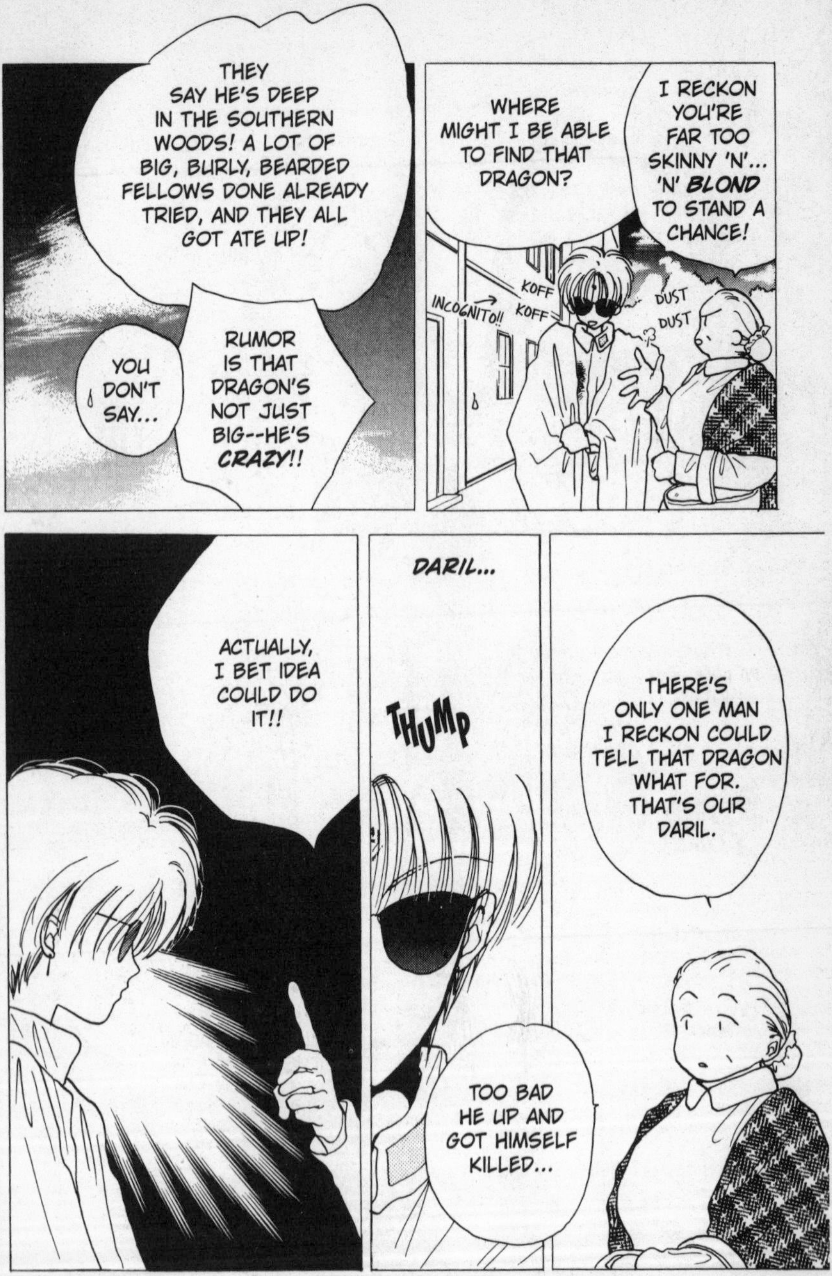
I RECKON YOU'RE FAR TOO SKINNY 'N'... 'N' BLOND TO STAND A CHANCE!
WHERE MIGHT I BE ABLE TO FIND THAT DRAGON?
KOFF KOFF
INCOGNITO!!
DUST DUST
THEY SAY HE'S DEEP IN THE SOUTHERN WOODS! A LOT OF BIG, BURLY, BEARDED FELLOWS DONE ALREADY TRIED, AND THEY ALL GOT ATE UP!
RUMOR IS THAT DRAGON'S NOT JUST BIG--HE'S CRAZY!!
YOU DON'T SAY...
THERE'S ONLY ONE MAN I RECKON COULD TELL THAT DRAGON WHAT FOR. THAT'S OUR DARIL.
DARIL...
THUMP
TOO BAD HE UP AND GOT HIMSELF KILLED...
ACTUALLY, I BET IDEA COULD DO IT!!

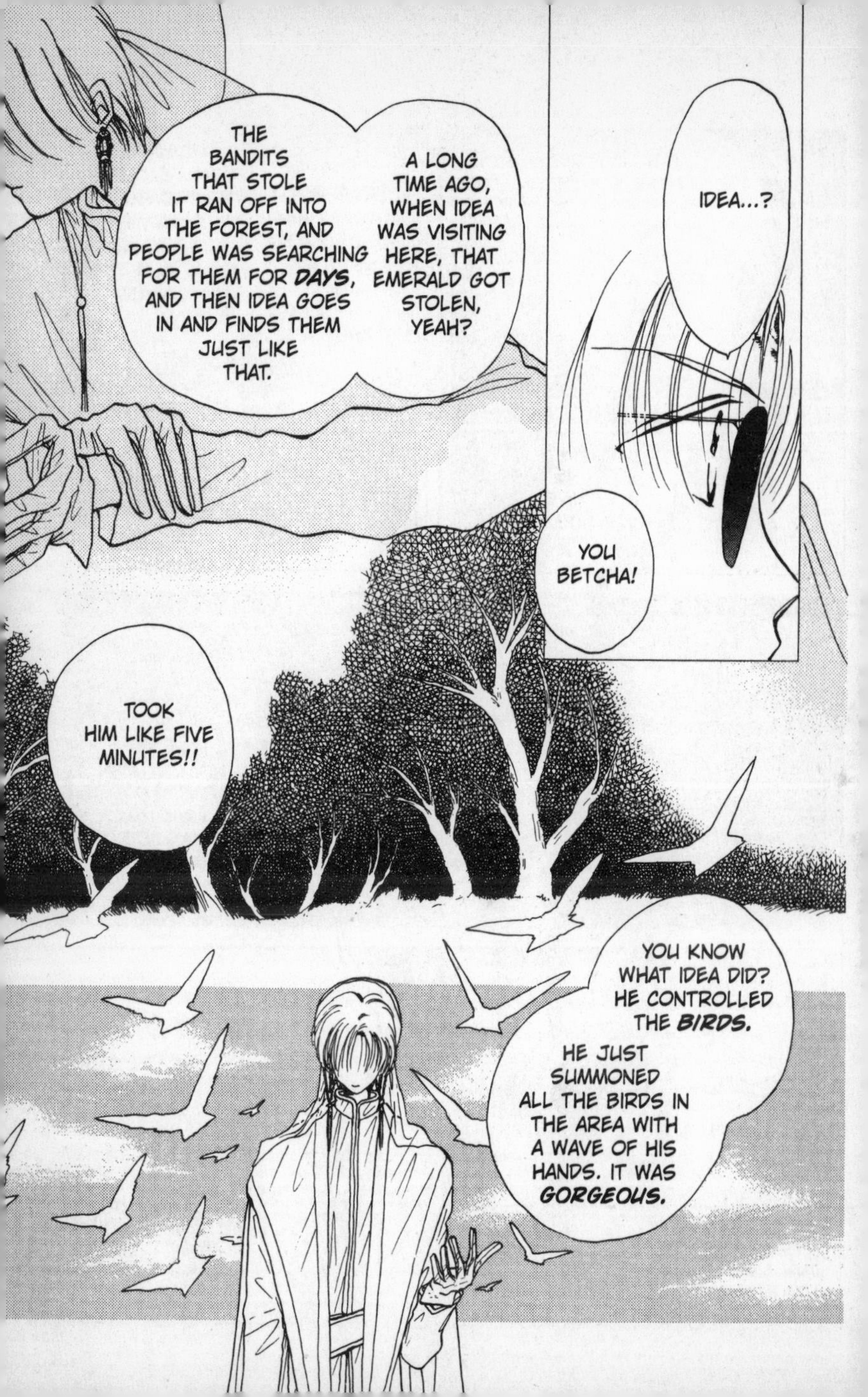

IDEA...?
YOU BETCHA!
A LONG TIME AGO, WHEN IDEA WAS VISITING HERE, THAT EMERALD GOT STOLEN, YEAH?
THE BANDITS THAT STOLE IT RAN OFF INTO THE FOREST, AND PEOPLE WAS SEARCHING FOR THEM FOR *DAYS*, AND THEN IDEA GOES IN AND FINDS THEM JUST LIKE THAT.
TOOK HIM LIKE FIVE MINUTES!!
YOU KNOW WHAT IDEA DID? HE CONTROLLED THE *BIRDS*.
HE JUST SUMMONED ALL THE BIRDS IN THE AREA WITH A WAVE OF HIS HANDS. IT WAS *GORGEOUS*.

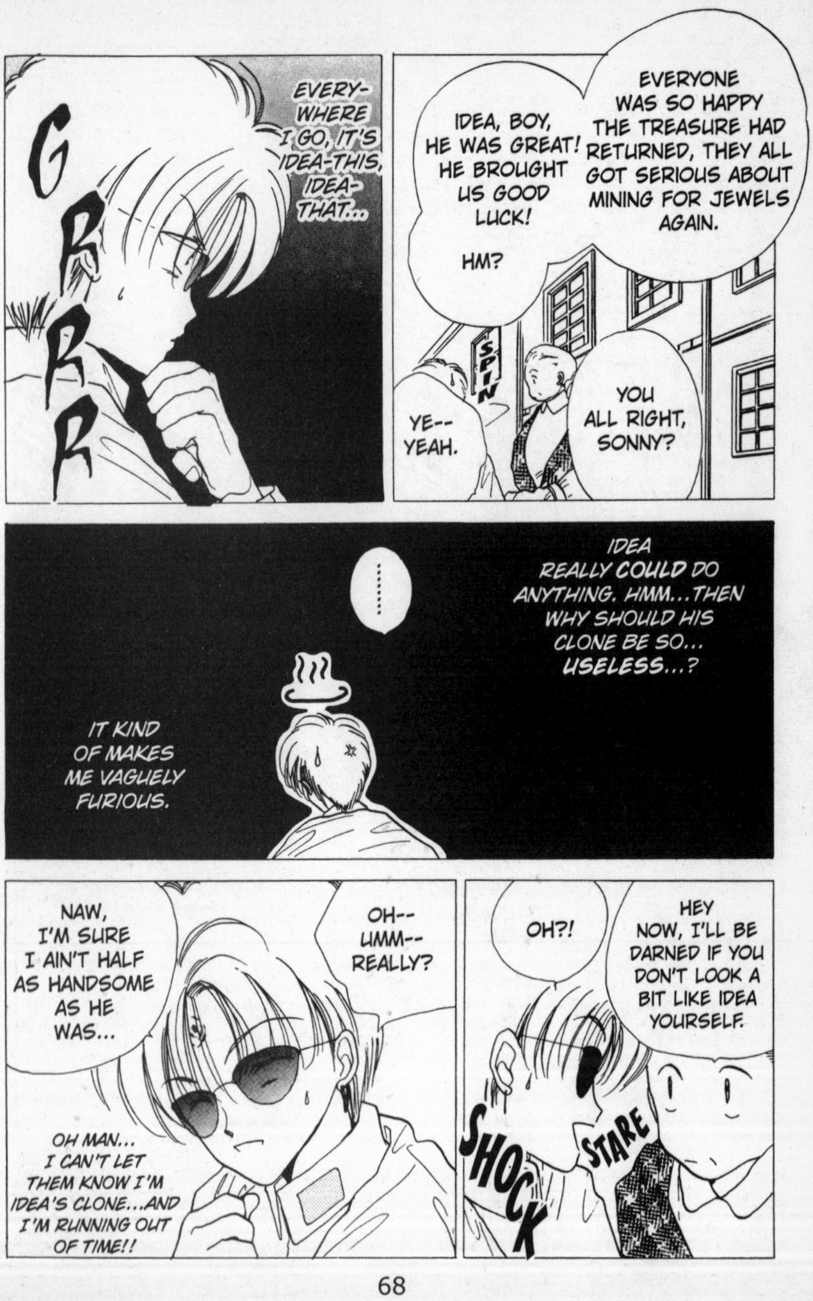
EVERYONE WAS SO HAPPY THE TREASURE HAD RETURNED, THEY ALL GOT SERIOUS ABOUT MINING FOR JEWELS AGAIN.
IDEA, BOY, HE WAS GREAT! HE BROUGHT US GOOD LUCK!
HM?
SPIN
YOU ALL RIGHT, SONNY?
YE-- YEAH.
EVERY-WHERE I GO, IT'S IDEA-THIS, IDEA-THAT...
GRRR
IDEA REALLY COULD DO ANYTHING. HMM...THEN WHY SHOULD HIS CLONE BE SO... USELESS...?
......
IT KIND OF MAKES ME VAGUELY FURIOUS.
HEY NOW, I'LL BE DARNED IF YOU DON'T LOOK A BIT LIKE IDEA YOURSELF.
OH?!
STARE
SHOCK
OH-- UMM-- REALLY?
NAW, I'M SURE I AIN'T HALF AS HANDSOME AS HE WAS...
OH MAN... I CAN'T LET THEM KNOW I'M IDEA'S CLONE...AND I'M RUNNING OUT OF TIME!!

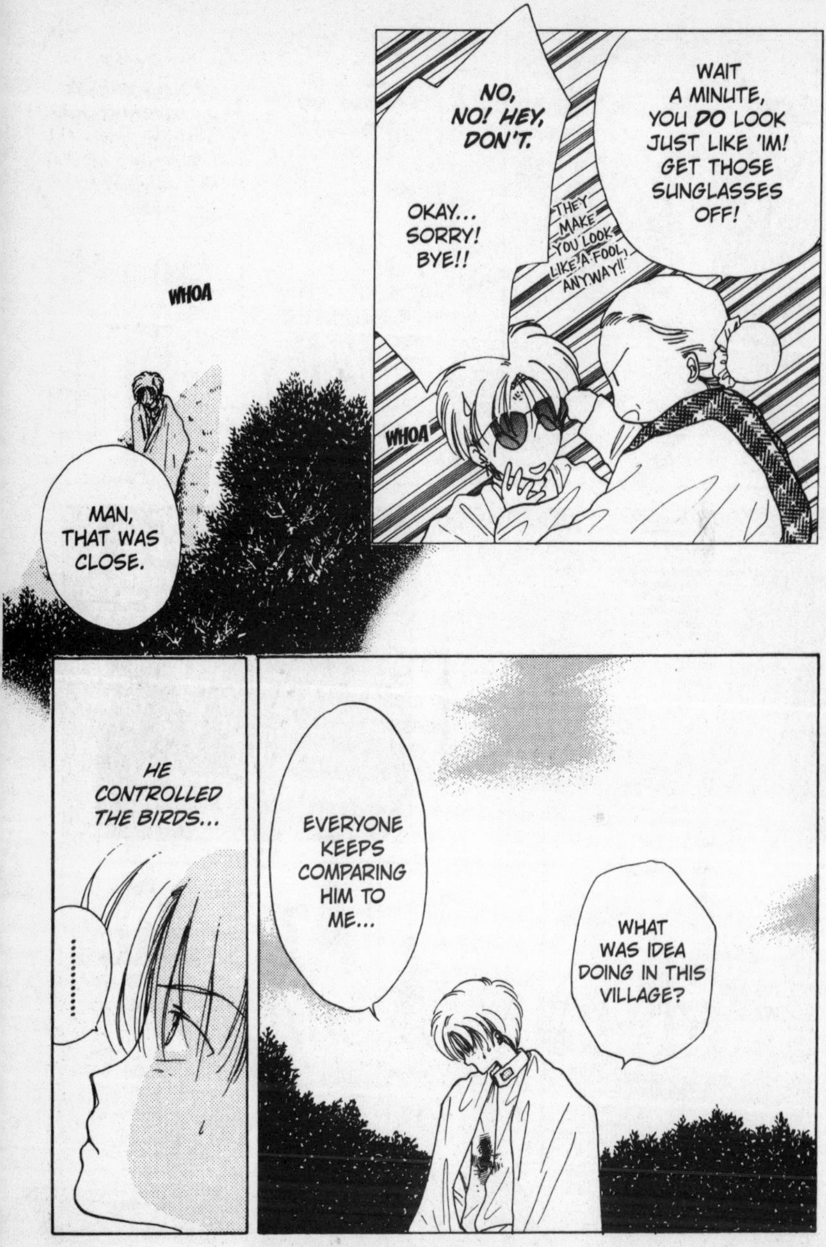
WAIT A MINUTE, YOU DO LOOK JUST LIKE 'IM! GET THOSE SUNGLASSES OFF!
NO, NO! HEY, DON'T.
THEY MAKE YOU LOOK LIKE A FOOL, ANYWAY!!
OKAY... SORRY! BYE!!
WHOA
WHOA
MAN, THAT WAS CLOSE.
EVERYONE KEEPS COMPARING HIM TO ME...
WHAT WAS IDEA DOING IN THIS VILLAGE?
HE CONTROLLED THE BIRDS...
....

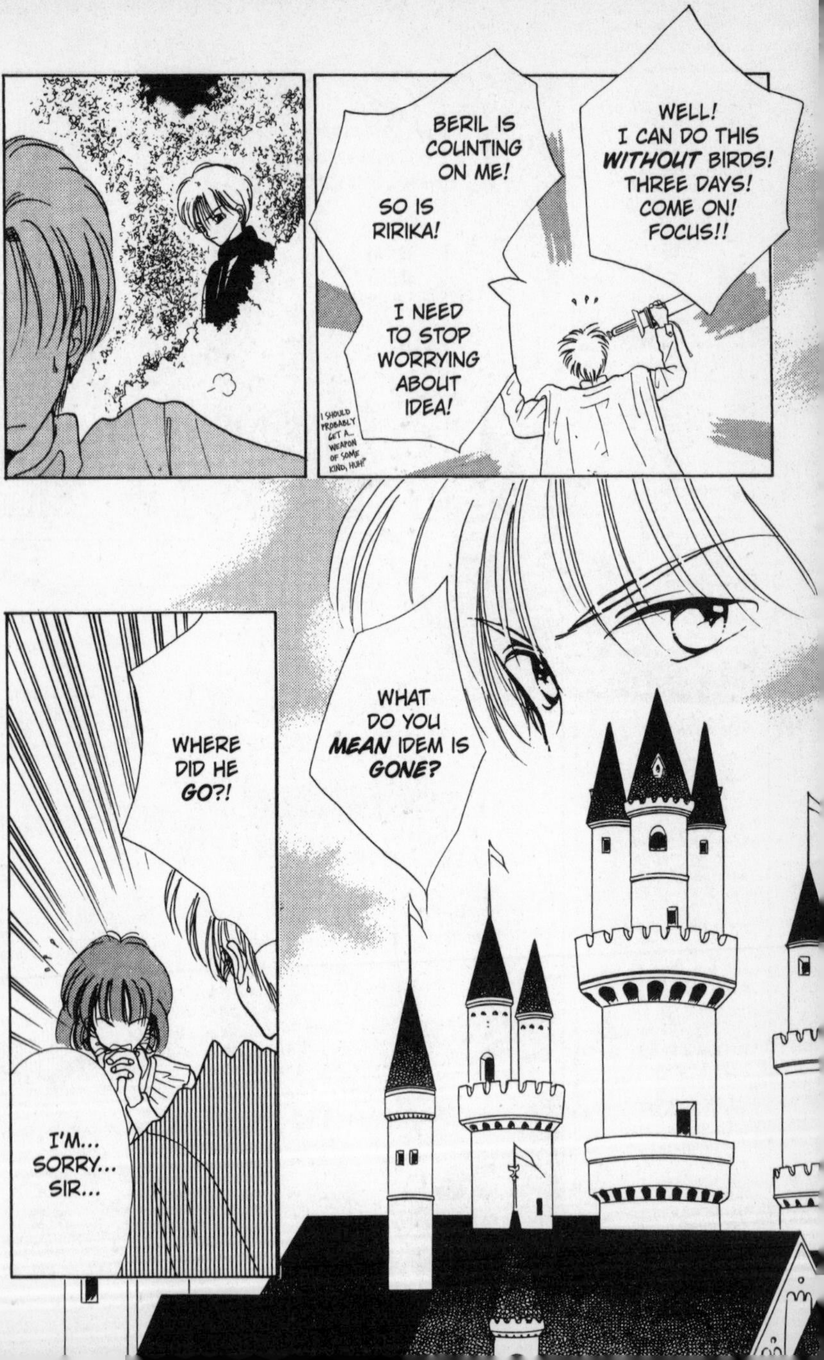
WELL! I CAN DO THIS WITHOUT BIRDS! THREE DAYS! COME ON! FOCUS!!
BERIL IS COUNTING ON ME!
SO IS RIRIKA!
I NEED TO STOP WORRYING ABOUT IDEA!
I SHOULD PROBABLY GET A... WEAPON OF SOME KIND, HUH?
WHAT DO YOU MEAN IDEM IS GONE?
WHERE DID HE GO?!
I'M... SORRY... SIR...

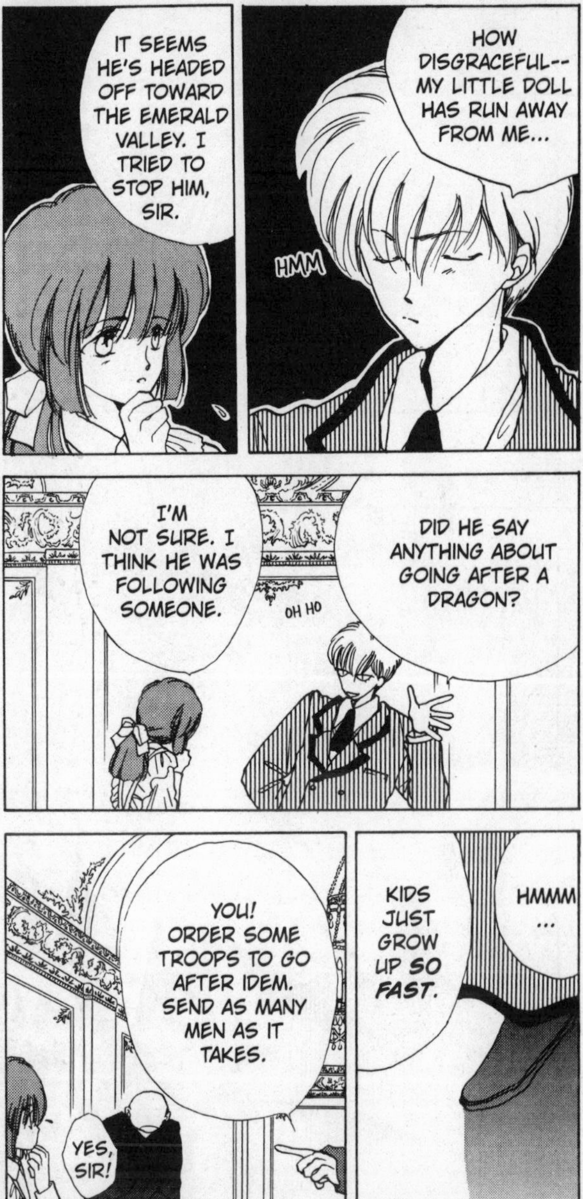
HOW DISGRACEFUL-- MY LITTLE DOLL HAS RUN AWAY FROM ME...
HMM
IT SEEMS HE'S HEADED OFF TOWARD THE EMERALD VALLEY. I TRIED TO STOP HIM, SIR.
DID HE SAY ANYTHING ABOUT GOING AFTER A DRAGON?
I'M NOT SURE. I THINK HE WAS FOLLOWING SOMEONE.
OH HO
HMMM ...
KIDS JUST GROW UP *SO FAST.*
YOU! ORDER SOME TROOPS TO GO AFTER IDEM. SEND AS MANY MEN AS IT TAKES.
YES, SIR!

OKAY, SO ACTUALLY, IT ***WAS*** BECAUSE OF THE TYPHOON. THE WEATHER WAS PERFECTLY CLEAR IN NAGOYA, AND TOTALLY STORMY IN TOKYO. SO THERE WE WERE, SITTING ON THE SHINKANSEN, LOOKING OUT THE WINDOW AT THE SKY, CLEAR AND BLUE, NOT A HINT OF TYPHOON. AND THE TRAIN WAS STOPPED BECAUSE OF A TYPHOON. IT WAS SO SURREAL. I THOUGHT ABOUT IT FOR A COUPLE OF MINUTES. UP WHERE THE TYPHOON WAS RAGING, TRAINS WERE STOPPED, SO THE TRAINS BEHIND THOSE TRAINS HAD TO STOP SO THEY WOULDN'T RUN INTO THE TRAINS IN FRONT OF THEM. SOMEHOW THIS CHAIN OF STOPPED TRAINS EXTENDED ALL THE WAY OUT INTO THE MIDDLE OF NOWHERE, FAR FROM THE STORM. AND SO I REALIZED: THIS WHOLE WORLD IS CONNECTED; EVEN PLACES WHERE IT'S RAINING ARE CONNECTED TO PLACES WHERE IT'S NOT RAINING.

I KEPT THINKING: THE TRAIN IS GOING TO MOVE AGAIN. I THOUGHT, LET'S JUST WAIT TEN MORE MINUTES. IT'LL BE MOVING IN TEN MORE MINUTES. TEN MINUTES PASSED. THE TRAIN STILL WASN'T MOVING. LET'S WAIT TEN MORE MINUTES, I THOUGHT.

THIS PROCESS REPEATED SEVENTEEN MORE TIMES.

IT TOOK THREE HOURS FOR THE TRAIN TO FINALLY BEGIN MOVING AGAIN.

THE TRAIN HAD RUN FOR FIFTY MINUTES BEFORE STOPPING FOR THREE HOURS, AND THEN RUNNING FOR TEN MORE MINUTES. AND THEN, WE WERE IN NAGOYA. AND THAT WAS WHEN...

(CONTINUED)

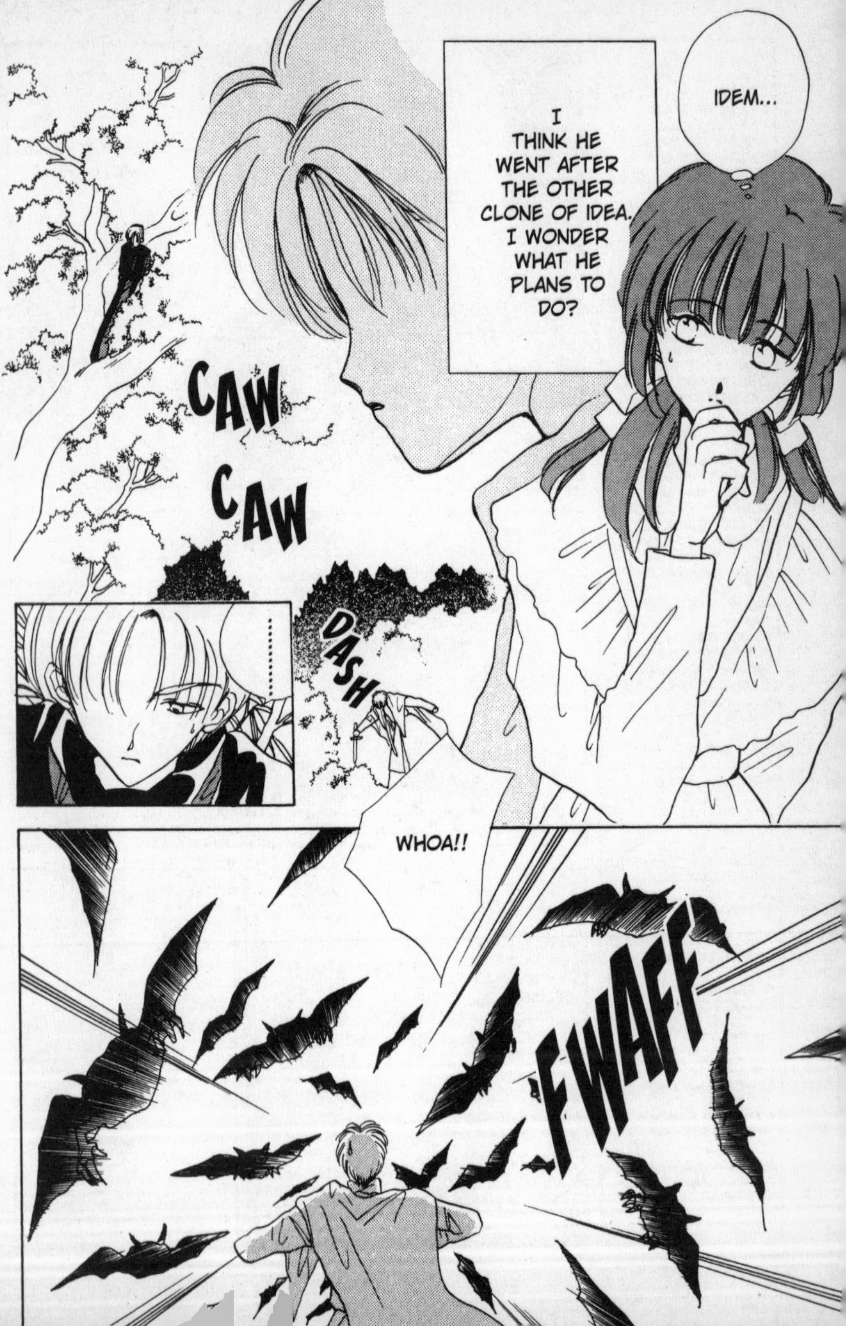
IDEM...
I THINK HE WENT AFTER THE OTHER CLONE OF IDEA. I WONDER WHAT HE PLANS TO DO?
CAW
CAW
......
DASH
WHOA!!
FWAFF

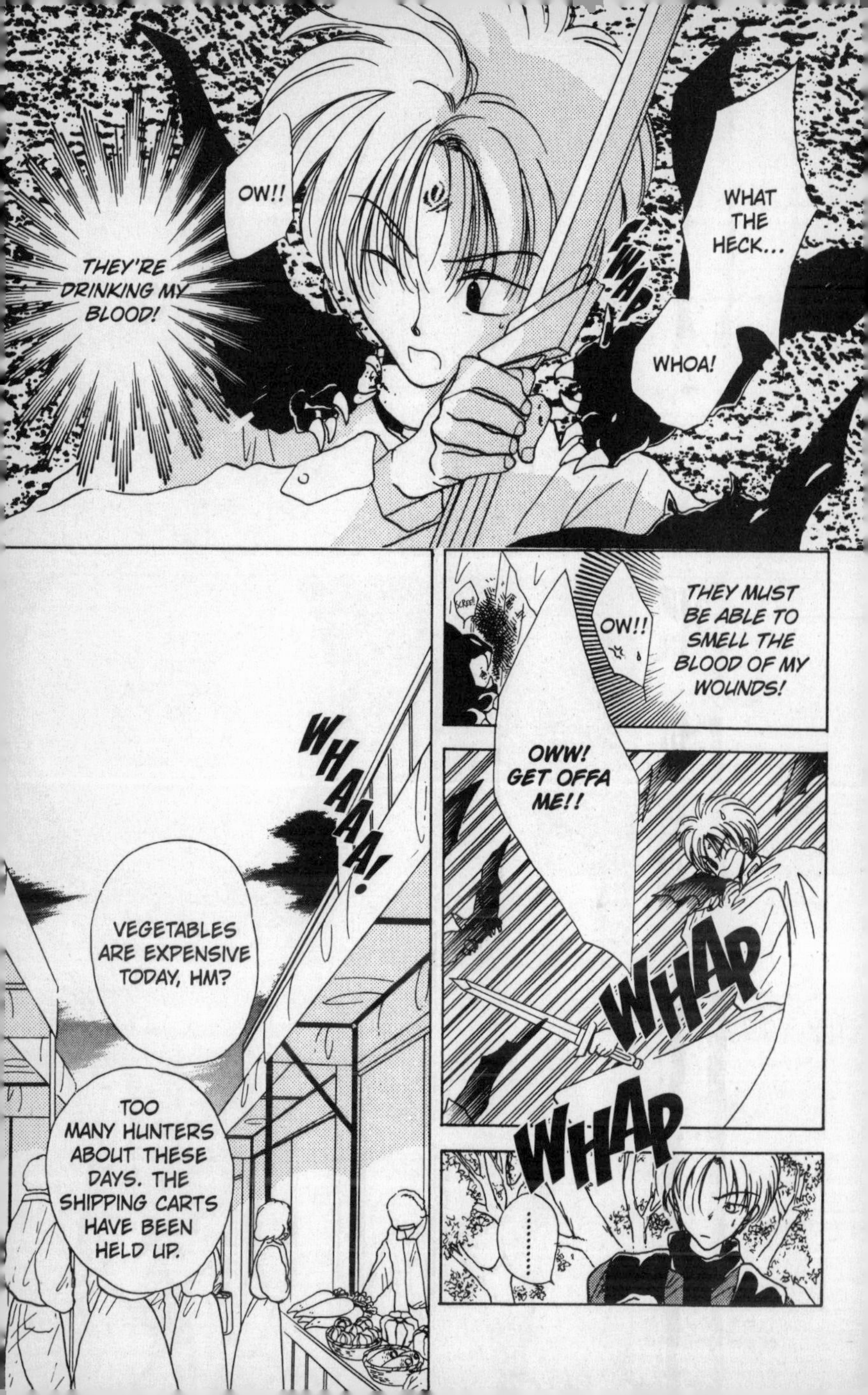
WHAT THE HECK...
WHOA!
FWAP
OW!!
THEY'RE DRINKING MY BLOOD!
THEY MUST BE ABLE TO SMELL THE BLOOD OF MY WOUNDS!
OW!!
OWW! GET OFFA ME!!
WHAP
WHAP
......
WHAAAA!
VEGETABLES ARE EXPENSIVE TODAY, HM?
TOO MANY HUNTERS ABOUT THESE DAYS. THE SHIPPING CARTS HAVE BEEN HELD UP.

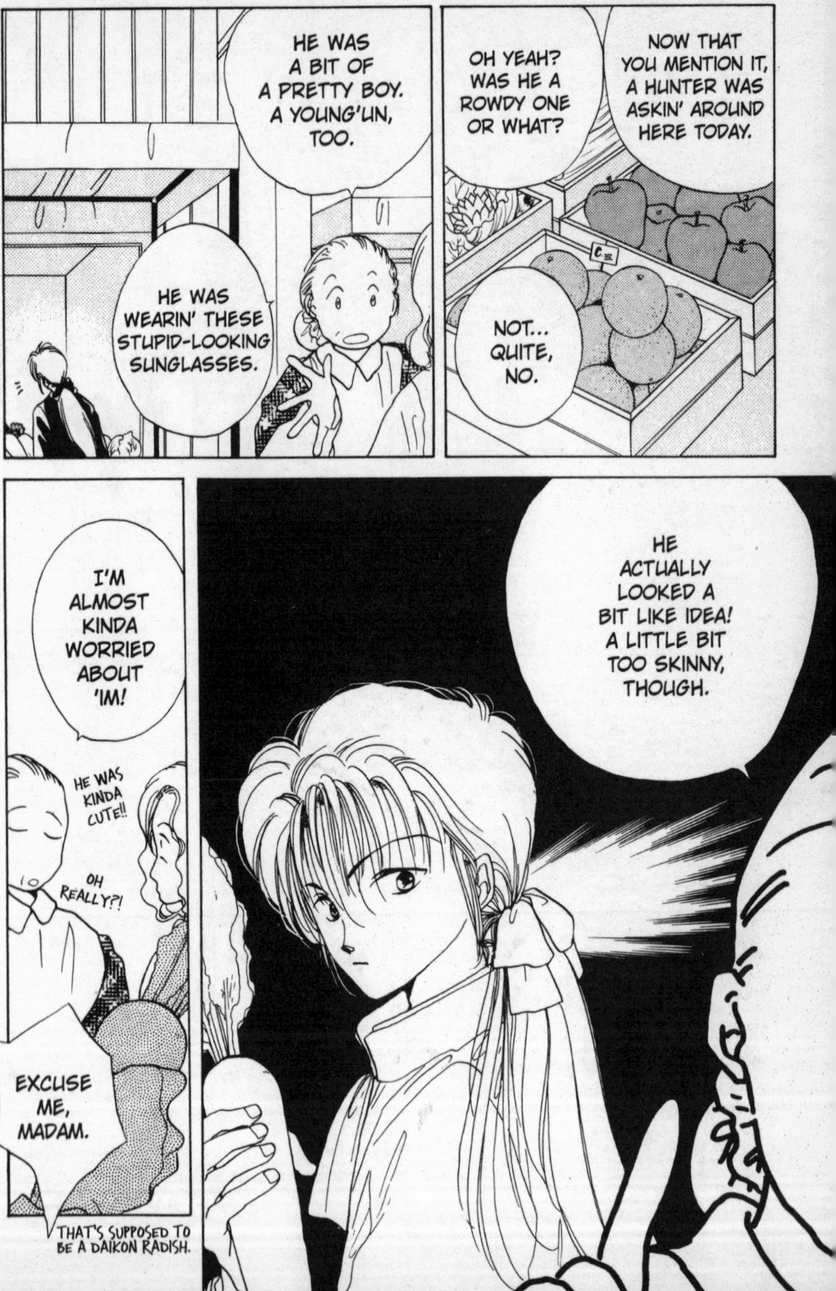
NOW THAT YOU MENTION IT, A HUNTER WAS ASKIN' AROUND HERE TODAY.
OH YEAH? WAS HE A ROWDY ONE OR WHAT?
NOT... QUITE, NO.
HE WAS A BIT OF A PRETTY BOY. A YOUNG'UN, TOO.
HE WAS WEARIN' THESE STUPID-LOOKING SUNGLASSES.
HE ACTUALLY LOOKED A BIT LIKE IDEA! A LITTLE BIT TOO SKINNY, THOUGH.
I'M ALMOST KINDA WORRIED ABOUT 'IM!
HE WAS KINDA CUTE!!
OH REALLY?!
EXCUSE ME, MADAM.
THAT'S SUPPOSED TO BE A DAIKON RADISH.

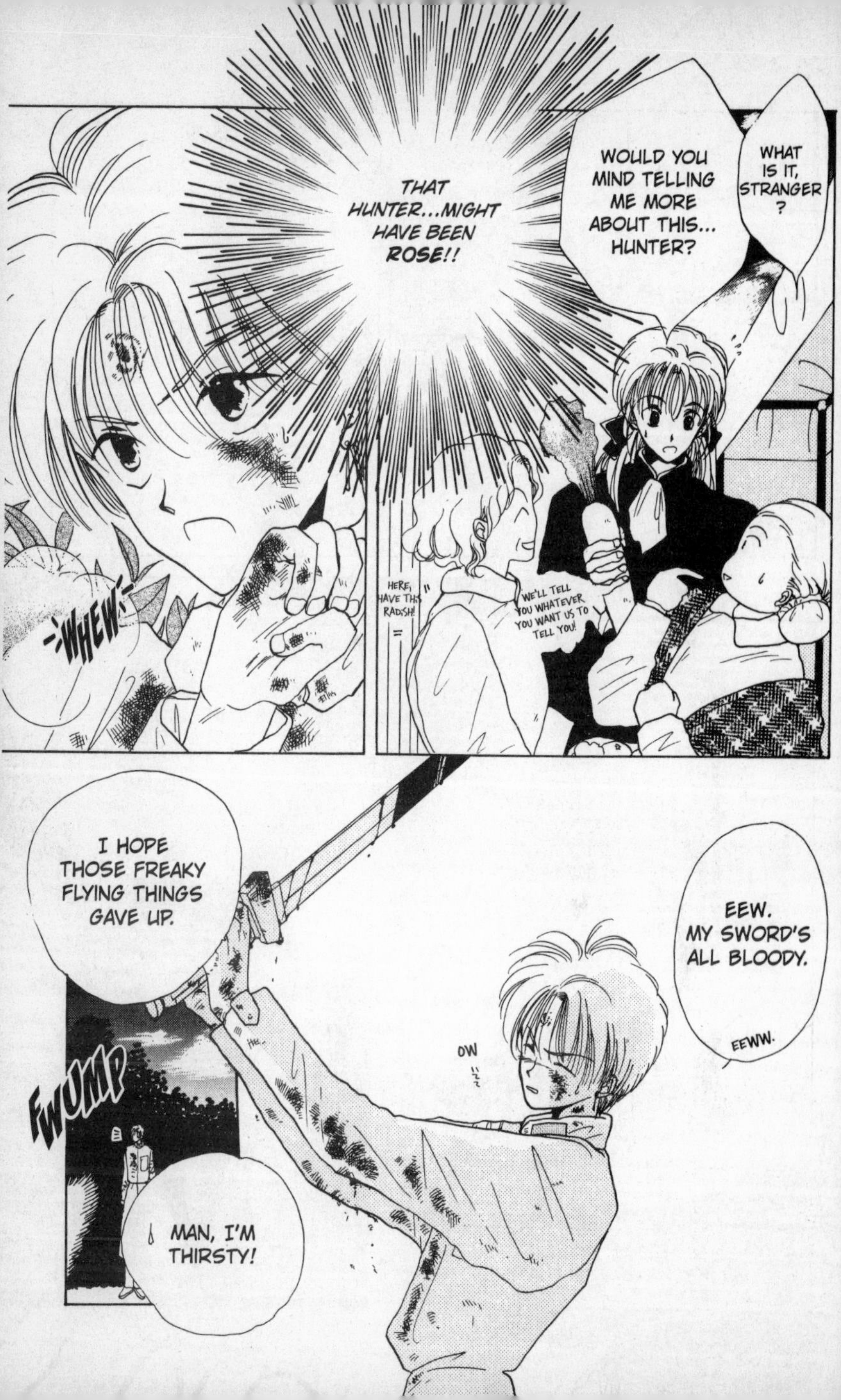
WHAT IS IT, STRANGER?
WOULD YOU MIND TELLING ME MORE ABOUT THIS... HUNTER?
HERE, HAVE THIS RADISH!
WE'LL TELL YOU WHATEVER YOU WANT US TO TELL YOU!
THAT HUNTER...MIGHT HAVE BEEN ROSE!!
WHEW
EEW. MY SWORD'S ALL BLOODY.
EEWW.
OW
I HOPE THOSE FREAKY FLYING THINGS GAVE UP.
FWUMP
MAN, I'M THIRSTY!

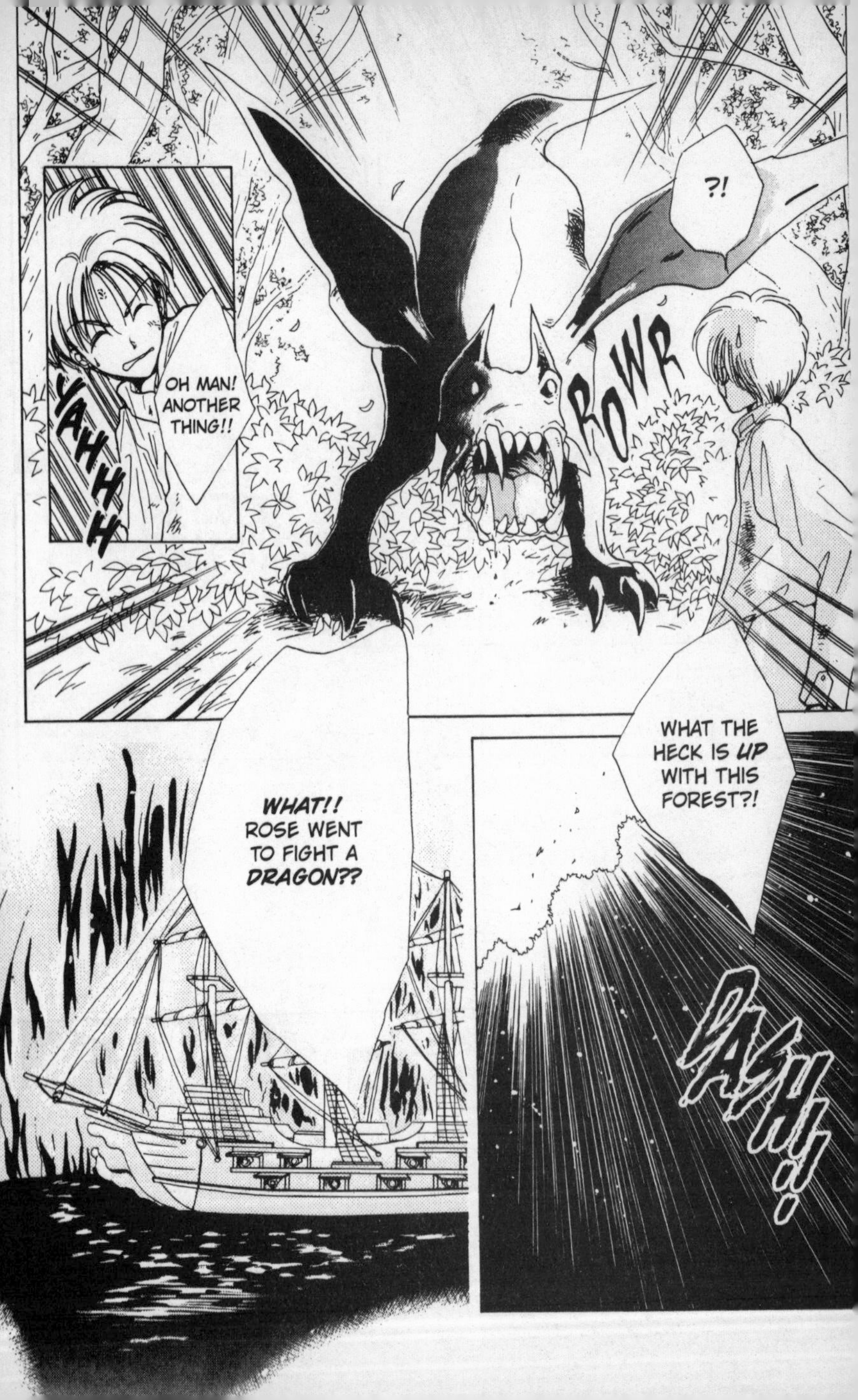
?!
ROWR
WHAT THE HECK IS *UP* WITH THIS FOREST?!
OH MAN! ANOTHER THING!!
YAHHHH
DASH!!
WHAT!! ROSE WENT TO FIGHT A ***DRAGON??***

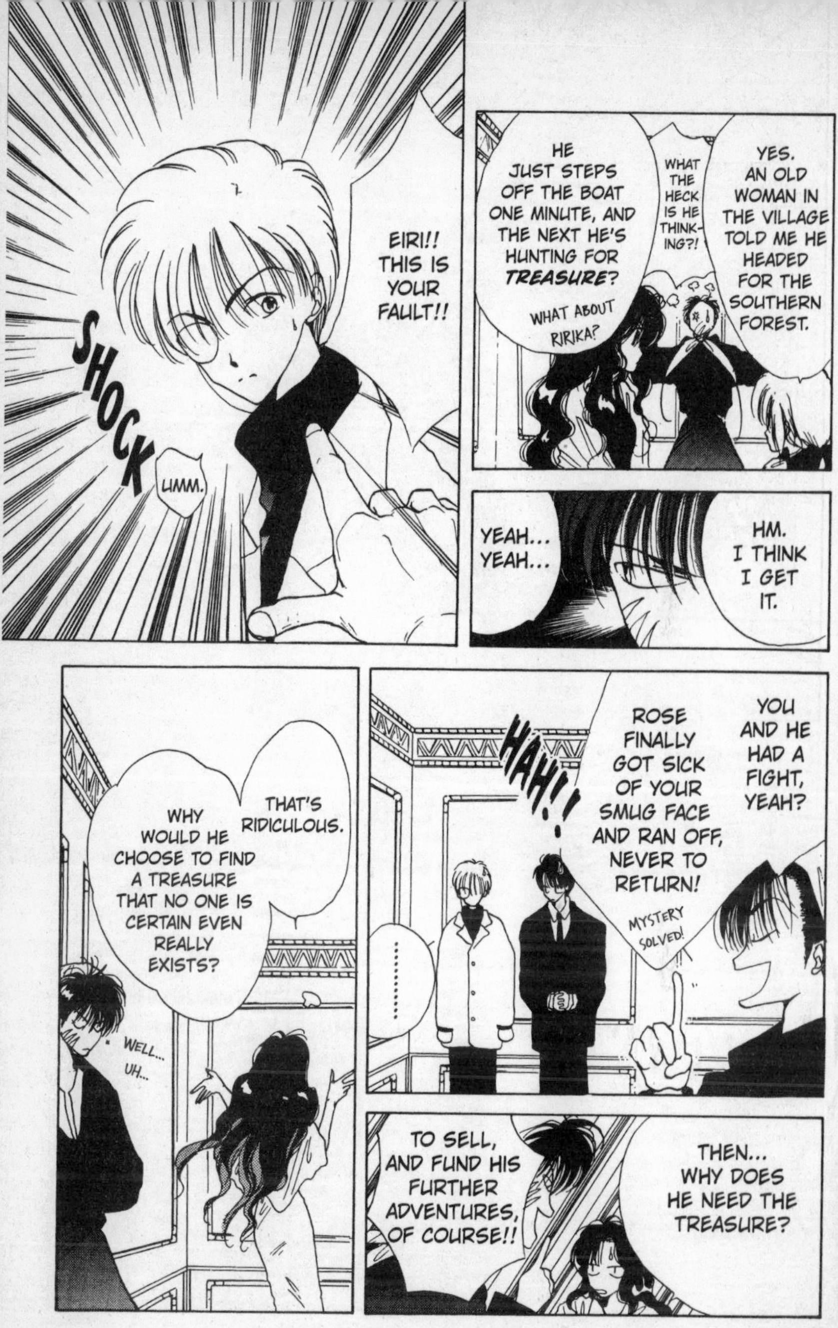
YES. AN OLD WOMAN IN THE VILLAGE TOLD ME HE HEADED FOR THE SOUTHERN FOREST.
WHAT THE HECK IS HE THINKING?!
HE JUST STEPS OFF THE BOAT ONE MINUTE, AND THE NEXT HE'S HUNTING FOR *TREASURE*?
WHAT ABOUT RIRIKA?
HM. I THINK I GET IT.
YEAH... YEAH...
EIRI!! THIS IS YOUR FAULT!!
SHOCK
UMM.
YOU AND HE HAD A FIGHT, YEAH?
ROSE FINALLY GOT SICK OF YOUR SMUG FACE AND RAN OFF, NEVER TO RETURN!
HAH!!
MYSTERY SOLVED!
......
THEN... WHY DOES HE NEED THE TREASURE?
TO SELL, AND FUND HIS FURTHER ADVENTURES, OF COURSE!!
THAT'S RIDICULOUS.
WHY WOULD HE CHOOSE TO FIND A TREASURE THAT NO ONE IS CERTAIN EVEN REALLY EXISTS?
WELL... UH...

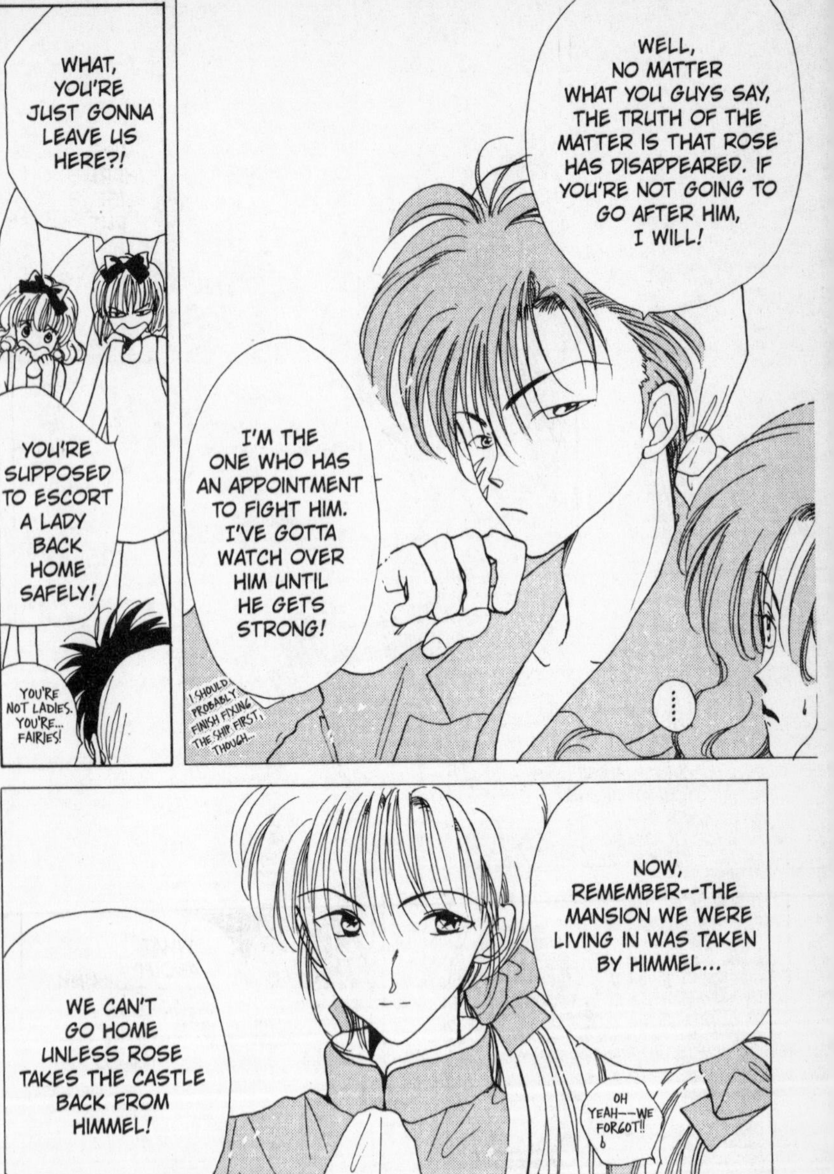
WELL, NO MATTER WHAT YOU GUYS SAY, THE TRUTH OF THE MATTER IS THAT ROSE HAS DISAPPEARED. IF YOU'RE NOT GOING TO GO AFTER HIM, I WILL!
I'M THE ONE WHO HAS AN APPOINTMENT TO FIGHT HIM. I'VE GOTTA WATCH OVER HIM UNTIL HE GETS STRONG!
I SHOULD PROBABLY FINISH FIXING THE SHIP FIRST, THOUGH...
......
WHAT, YOU'RE JUST GONNA LEAVE US HERE?!
YOU'RE SUPPOSED TO ESCORT A LADY BACK HOME SAFELY!
YOU'RE NOT LADIES. YOU'RE... FAIRIES!
NOW, REMEMBER--THE MANSION WE WERE LIVING IN WAS TAKEN BY HIMMEL...
OH YEAH--WE FORGOT!!
WE CAN'T GO HOME UNLESS ROSE TAKES THE CASTLE BACK FROM HIMMEL!

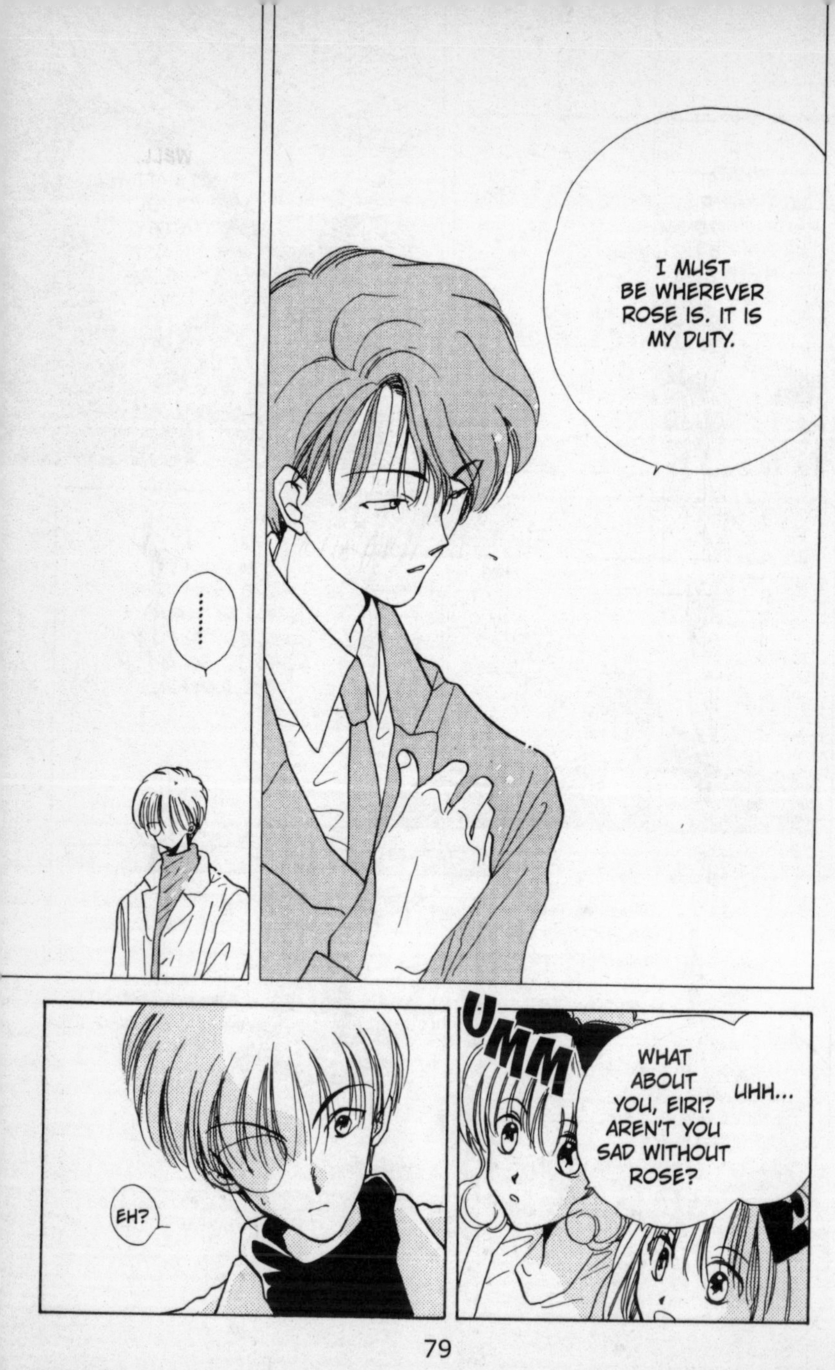

I MUST BE WHEREVER ROSE IS. IT IS MY DUTY.
......
UMM
WHAT ABOUT YOU, EIRI? AREN'T YOU SAD WITHOUT ROSE?
UHH...
EH?

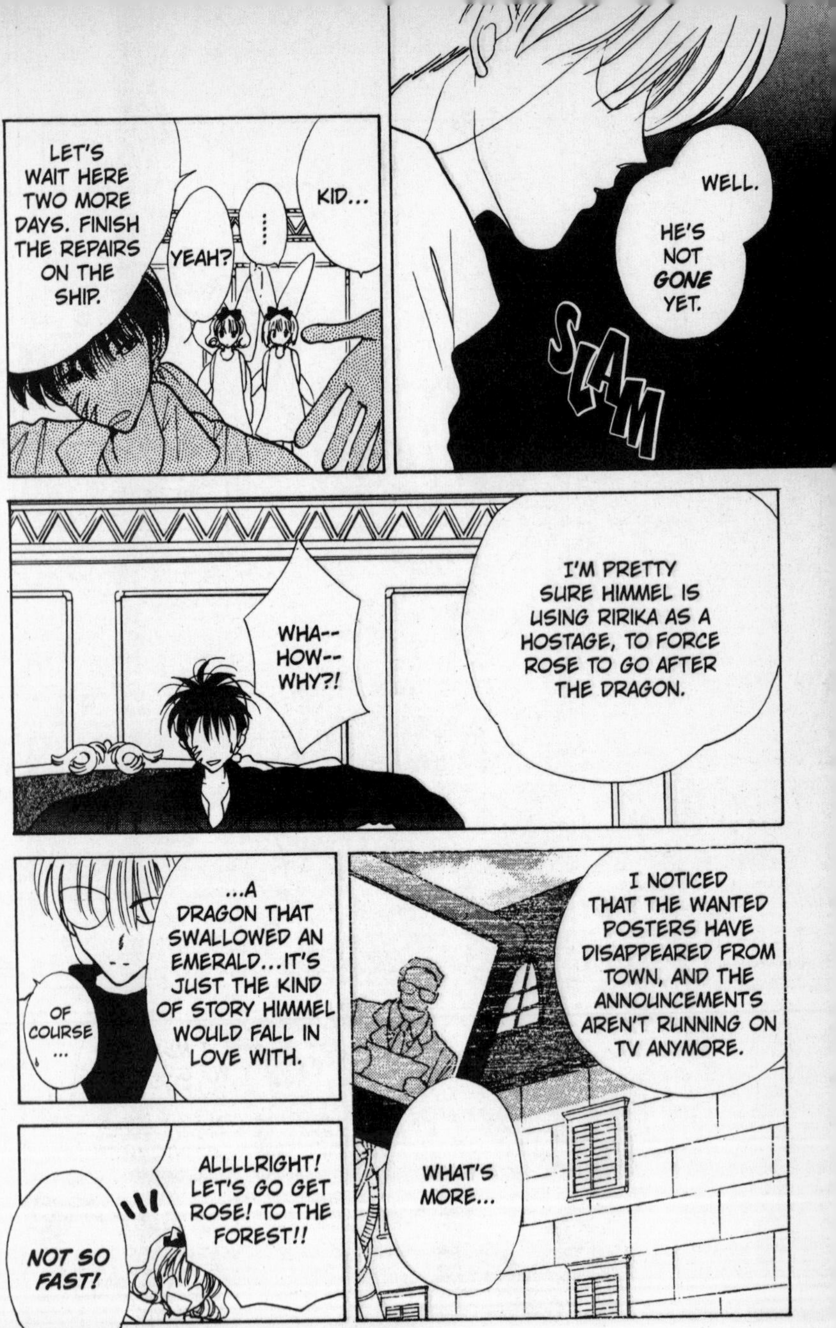
WELL.
HE'S NOT GONE YET.
SLAM
LET'S WAIT HERE TWO MORE DAYS. FINISH THE REPAIRS ON THE SHIP.
KID...
......
YEAH?
I'M PRETTY SURE HIMMEL IS USING RIRIKA AS A HOSTAGE, TO FORCE ROSE TO GO AFTER THE DRAGON.
WHA-- HOW-- WHY?!
I NOTICED THAT THE WANTED POSTERS HAVE DISAPPEARED FROM TOWN, AND THE ANNOUNCEMENTS AREN'T RUNNING ON TV ANYMORE.
WHAT'S MORE...
...A DRAGON THAT SWALLOWED AN EMERALD...IT'S JUST THE KIND OF STORY HIMMEL WOULD FALL IN LOVE WITH.
OF COURSE ...
ALLLLRIGHT! LET'S GO GET ROSE! TO THE FOREST!!
NOT SO FAST!

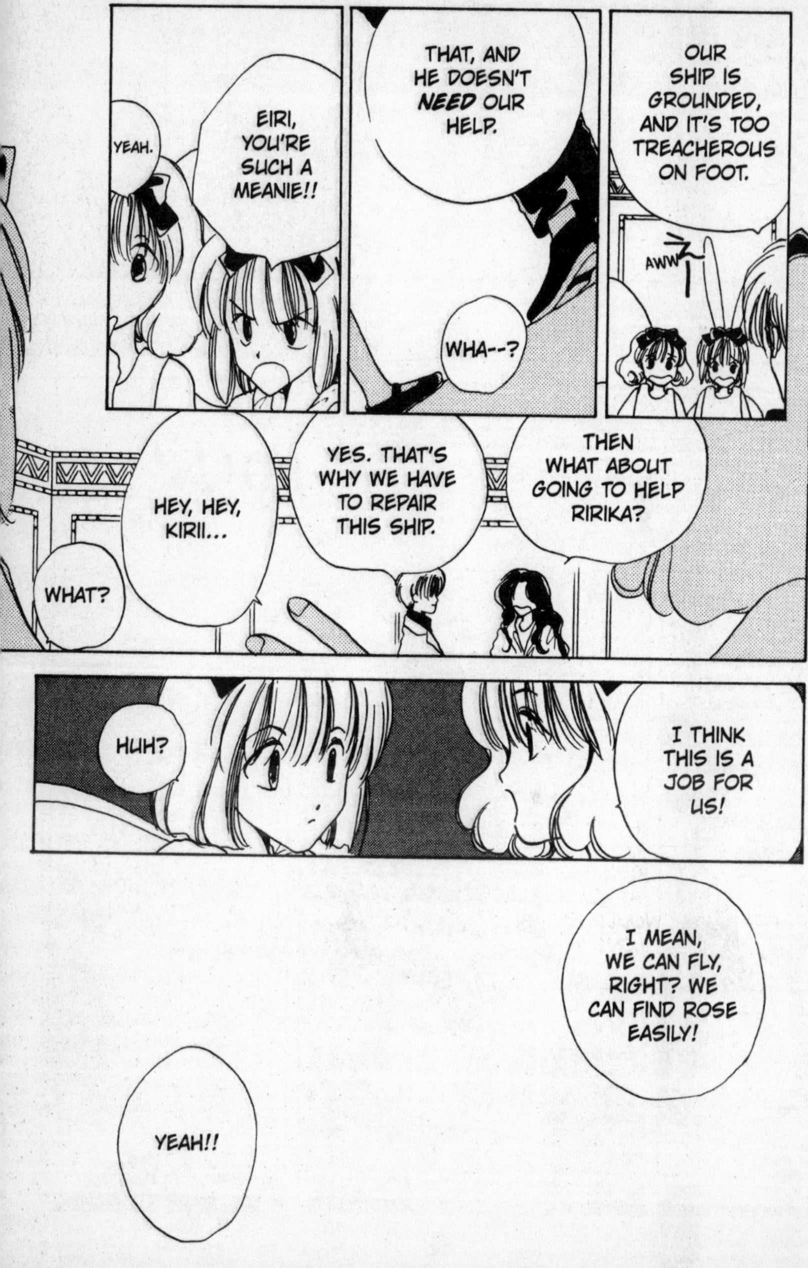
OUR SHIP IS GROUNDED, AND IT'S TOO TREACHEROUS ON FOOT.
AWW
THAT, AND HE DOESN'T *NEED* OUR HELP.
WHA--?
EIRI, YOU'RE SUCH A MEANIE!!
YEAH.
THEN WHAT ABOUT GOING TO HELP RIRIKA?
YES. THAT'S WHY WE HAVE TO REPAIR THIS SHIP.
HEY, HEY, KIRII...
WHAT?
I THINK THIS IS A JOB FOR US!
HUH?
I MEAN, WE CAN FLY, RIGHT? WE CAN FIND ROSE EASILY!
YEAH!!

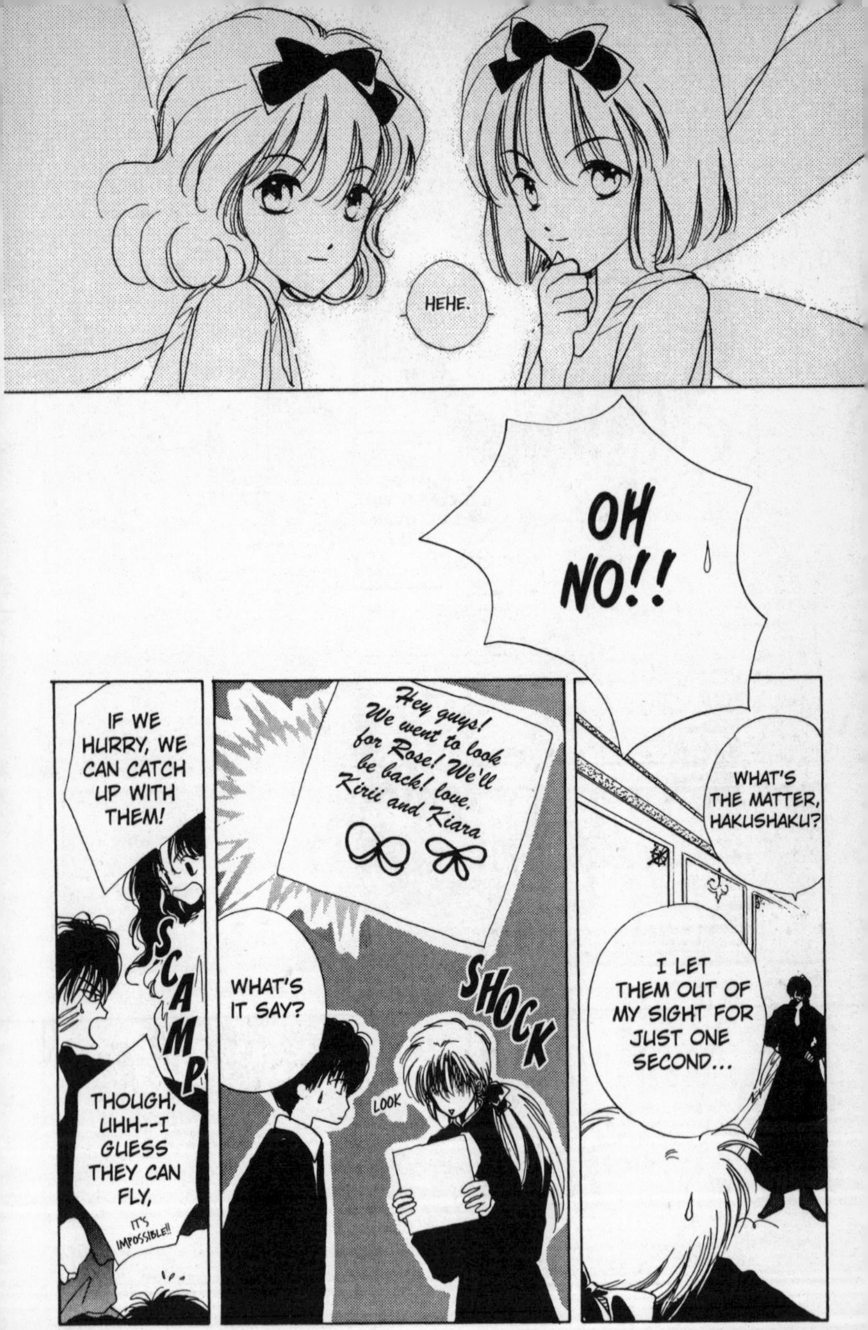
HEHE.
OH NO!!
WHAT'S THE MATTER, HAKUSHAKU?
I LET THEM OUT OF MY SIGHT FOR JUST ONE SECOND...
Hey guys! We went to look for Rose! We'll be back! love, Kirii and Kiara
SHOCK
WHAT'S IT SAY?
LOOK
IF WE HURRY, WE CAN CATCH UP WITH THEM!
SCAMP
THOUGH, UHH--I GUESS THEY CAN FLY,
IT'S IMPOSSIBLE!!

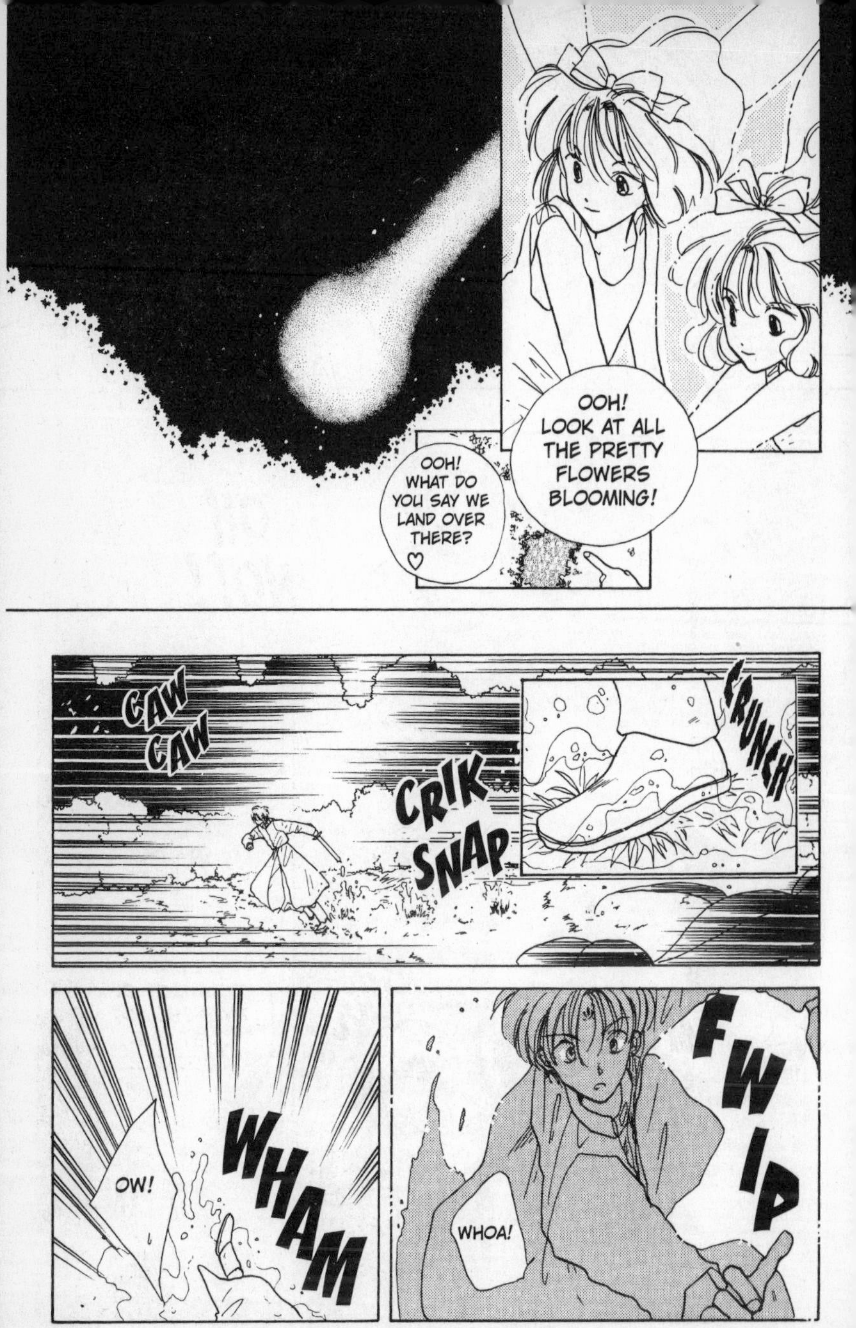
OOH! LOOK AT ALL THE PRETTY FLOWERS BLOOMING!
OOH! WHAT DO YOU SAY WE LAND OVER THERE? ♡
CRUNCH
CAW CAW
CRIK SNAP
FWIP
WHOA!
WHAM
OW!

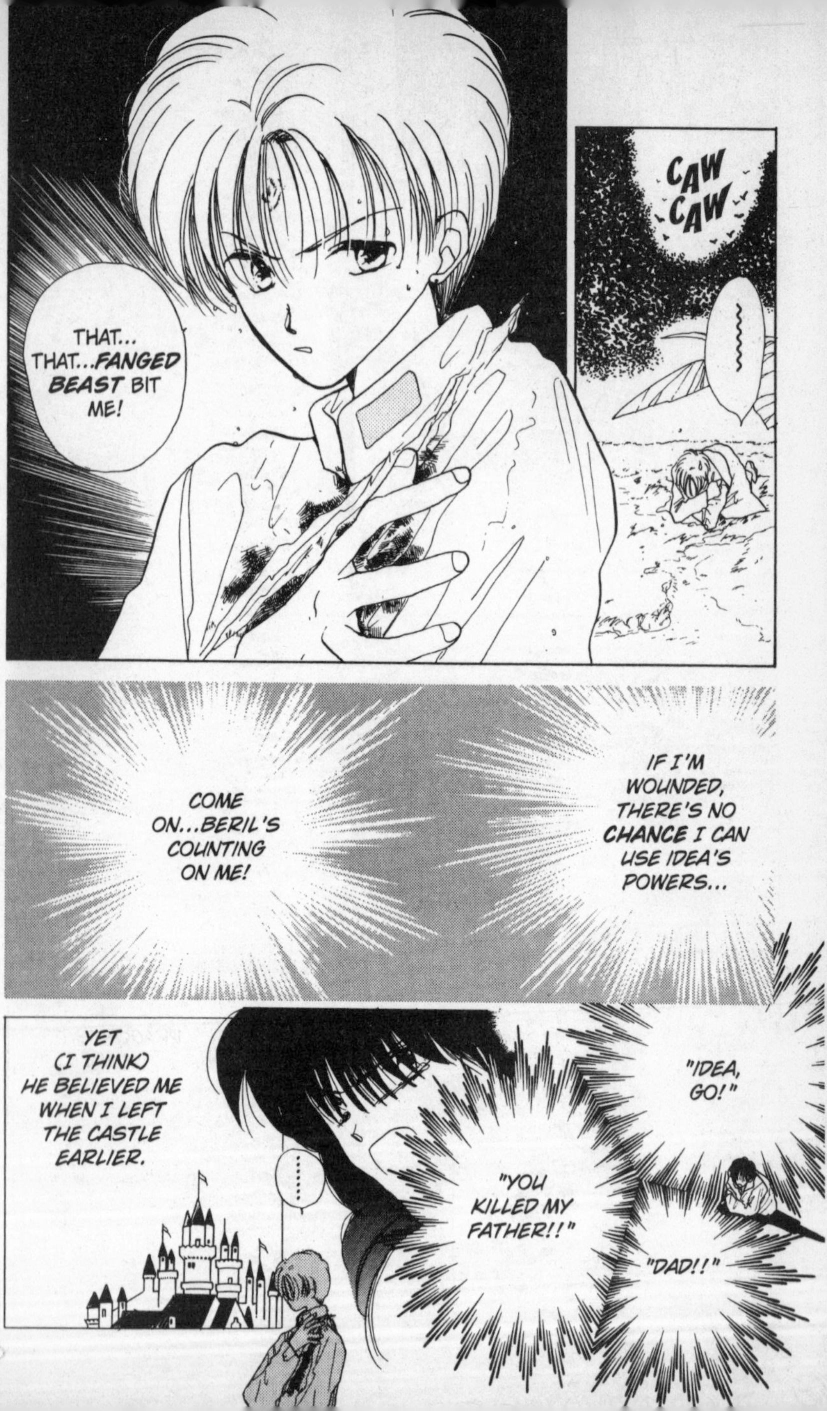
CAW CAW
THAT... THAT...FANGED BEAST BIT ME!
IF I'M WOUNDED, THERE'S NO CHANCE I CAN USE IDEA'S POWERS...
COME ON...BERIL'S COUNTING ON ME!
"IDEA, GO!"
"YOU KILLED MY FATHER!!"
"DAD!!"
YET (I THINK) HE BELIEVED ME WHEN I LEFT THE CASTLE EARLIER.
......

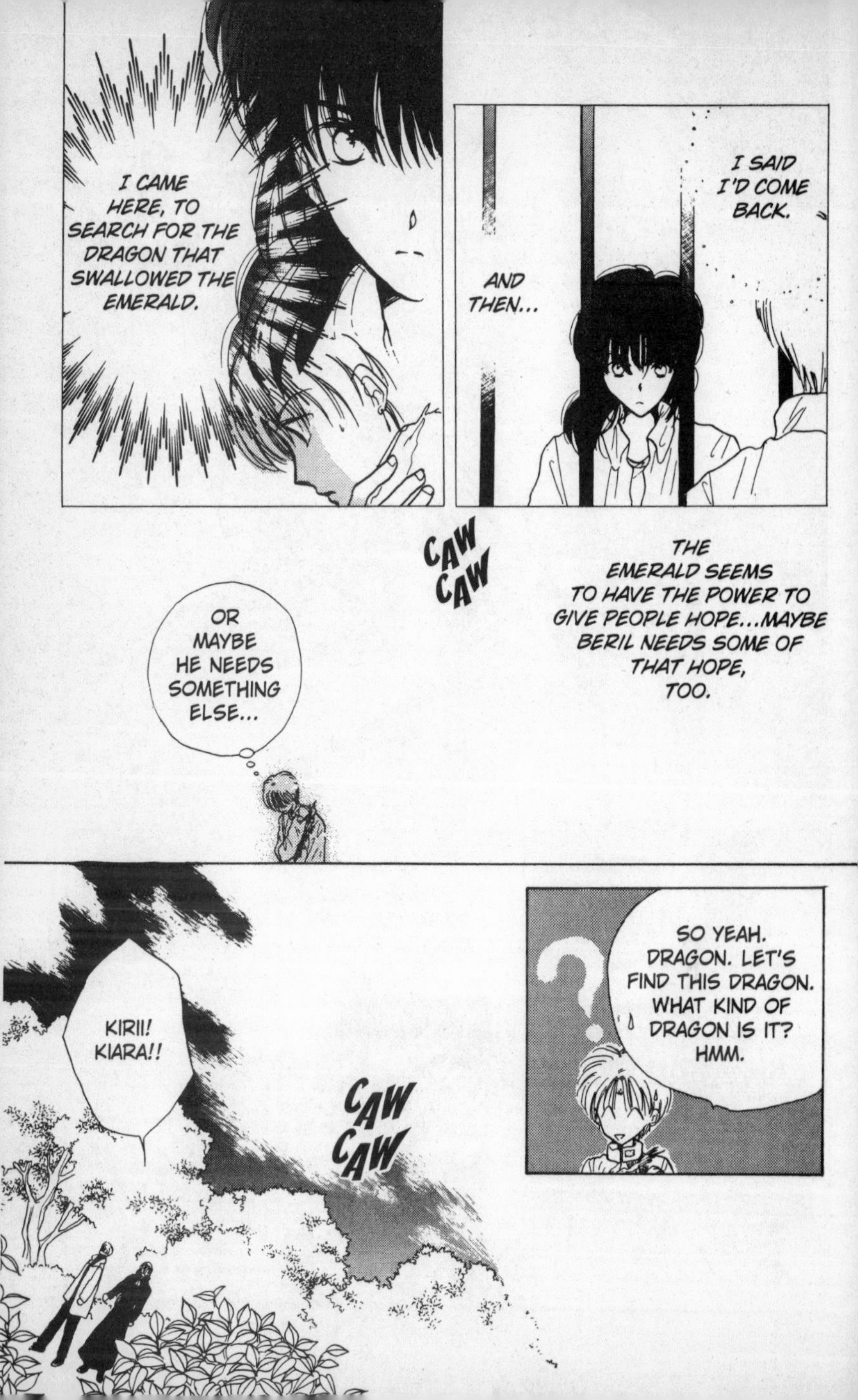
I SAID I'D COME BACK.
AND THEN...
I CAME HERE, TO SEARCH FOR THE DRAGON THAT SWALLOWED THE EMERALD.
THE EMERALD SEEMS TO HAVE THE POWER TO GIVE PEOPLE HOPE...MAYBE BERIL NEEDS SOME OF THAT HOPE, TOO.
CAW CAW
OR MAYBE HE NEEDS SOMETHING ELSE...
SO YEAH. DRAGON. LET'S FIND THIS DRAGON. WHAT KIND OF DRAGON IS IT? HMM.
CAW CAW
KIRII! KIARA!!

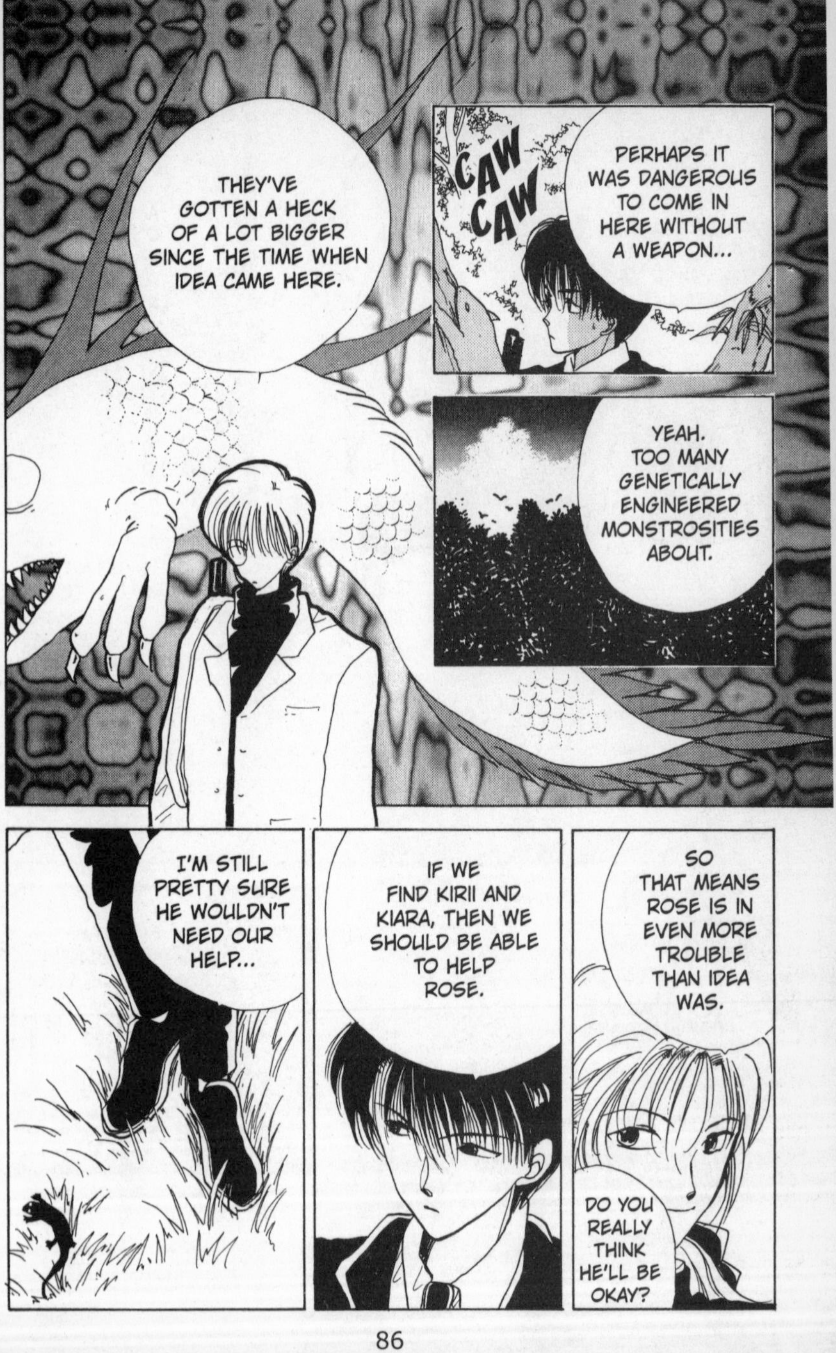
CAW CAW
PERHAPS IT WAS DANGEROUS TO COME IN HERE WITHOUT A WEAPON...
YEAH. TOO MANY GENETICALLY ENGINEERED MONSTROSITIES ABOUT.
THEY'VE GOTTEN A HECK OF A LOT BIGGER SINCE THE TIME WHEN IDEA CAME HERE.
SO THAT MEANS ROSE IS IN EVEN MORE TROUBLE THAN IDEA WAS.
DO YOU REALLY THINK HE'LL BE OKAY?
IF WE FIND KIRII AND KIARA, THEN WE SHOULD BE ABLE TO HELP ROSE.
I'M STILL PRETTY SURE HE WOULDN'T NEED OUR HELP...

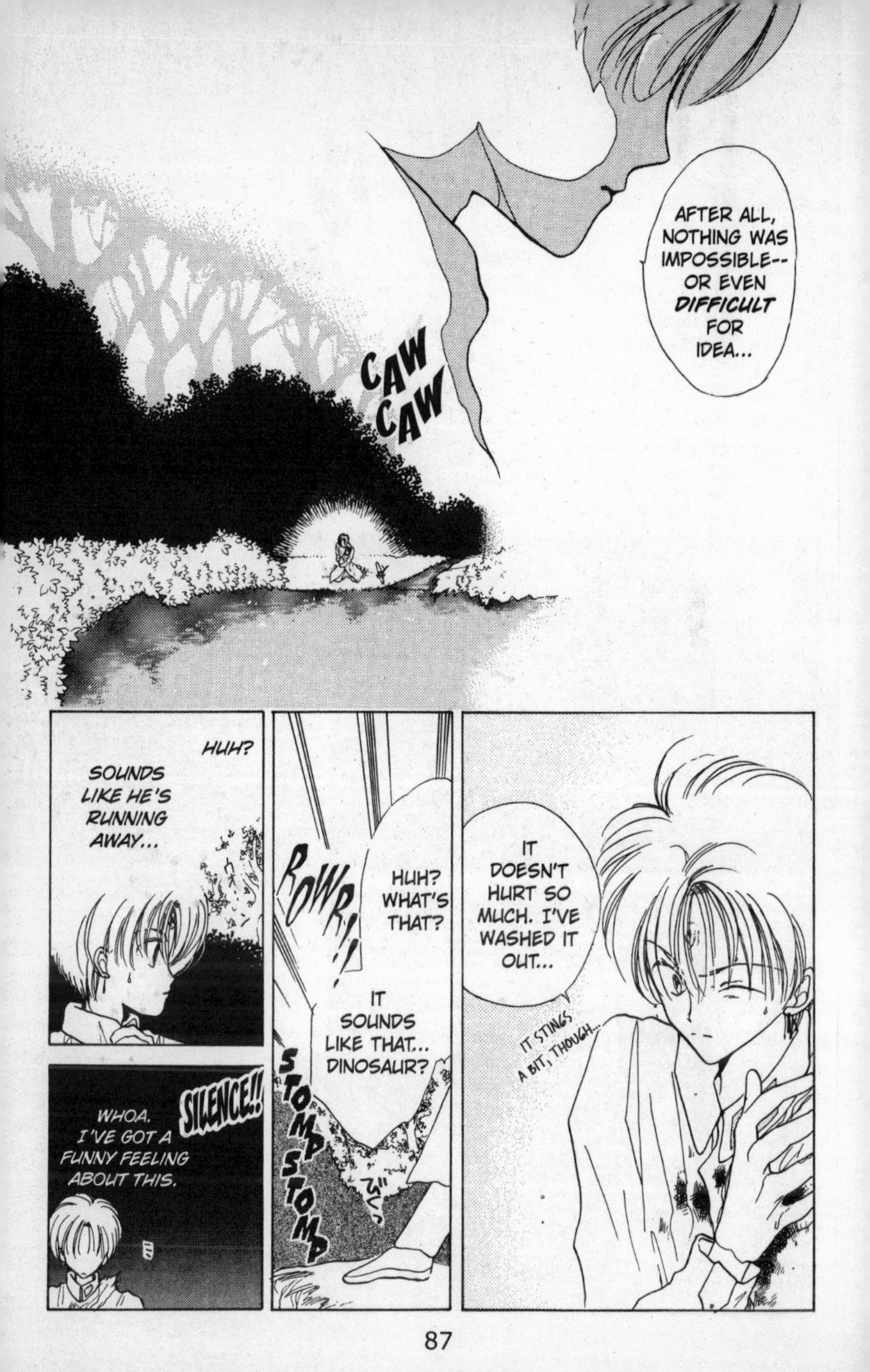

AFTER ALL, NOTHING WAS IMPOSSIBLE-- OR EVEN *DIFFICULT* FOR IDEA...
CAW CAW
IT DOESN'T HURT SO MUCH. I'VE WASHED IT OUT...
IT STINGS A BIT, THOUGH...
ROWR!!
HUH? WHAT'S THAT?
IT SOUNDS LIKE THAT... DINOSAUR?
STOMP STOMP
HUH?
SOUNDS LIKE HE'S RUNNING AWAY...
SILENCE!!
WHOA. I'VE GOT A FUNNY FEELING ABOUT THIS.

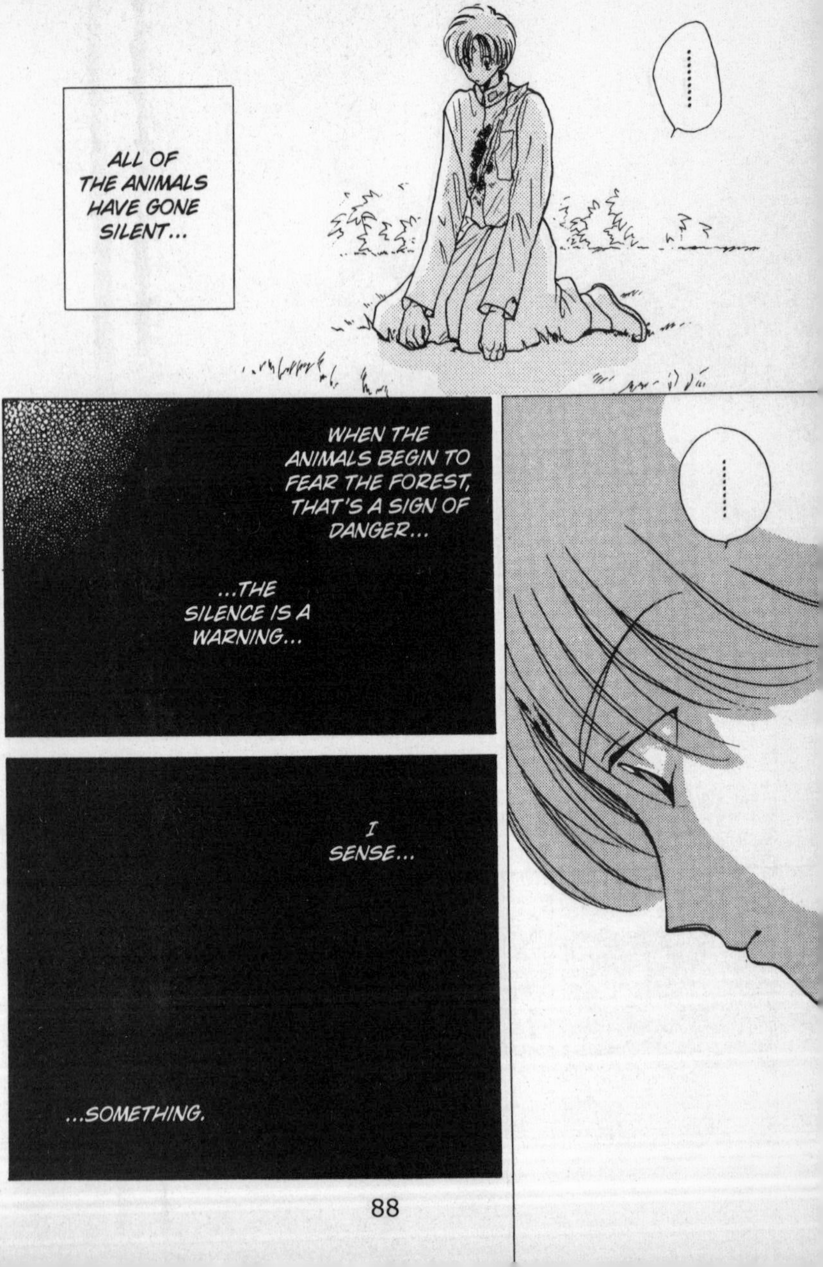
ALL OF THE ANIMALS HAVE GONE SILENT...
......
......
WHEN THE ANIMALS BEGIN TO FEAR THE FOREST, THAT'S A SIGN OF DANGER...
...THE SILENCE IS A WARNING...
I SENSE...
...SOMETHING.

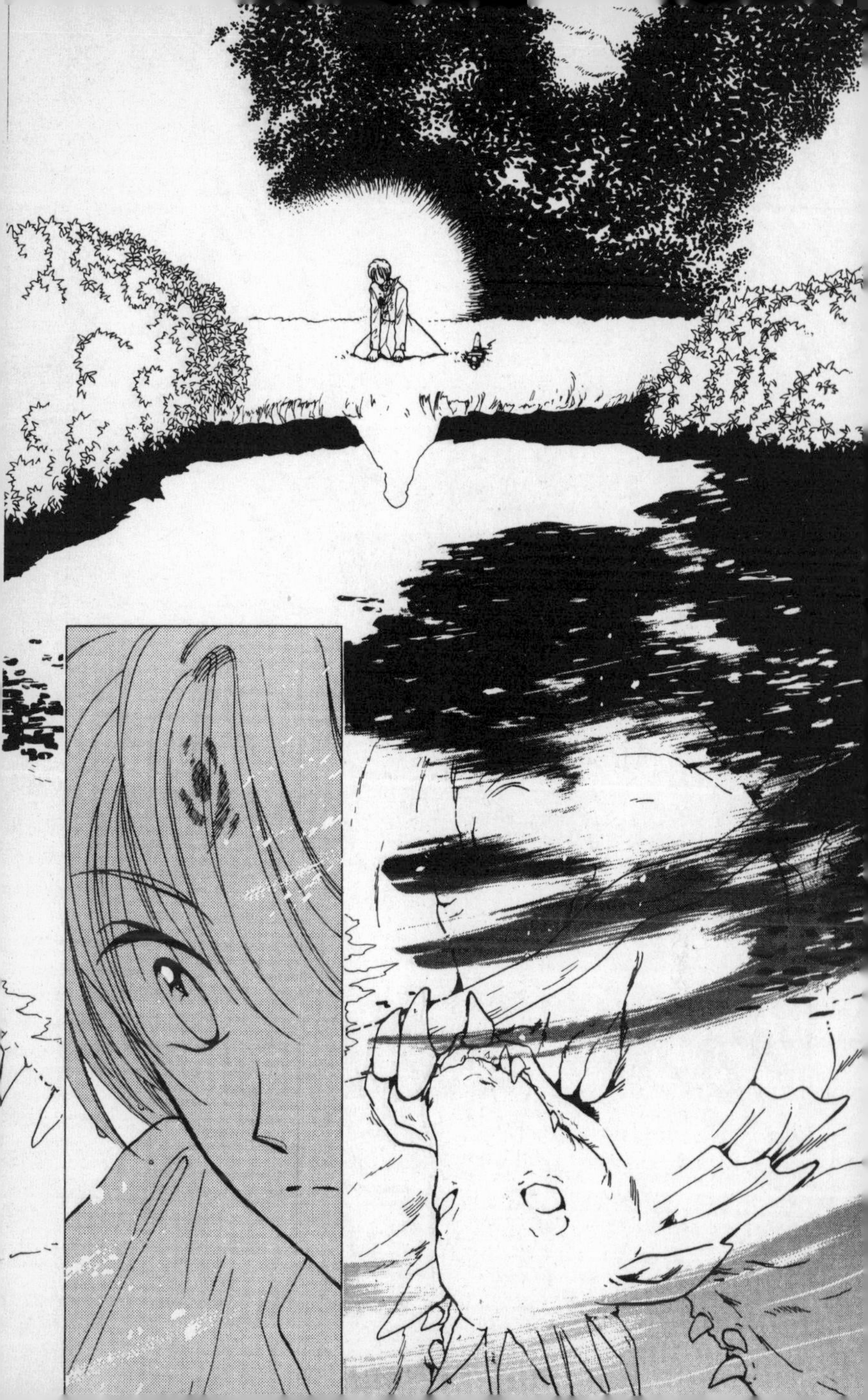

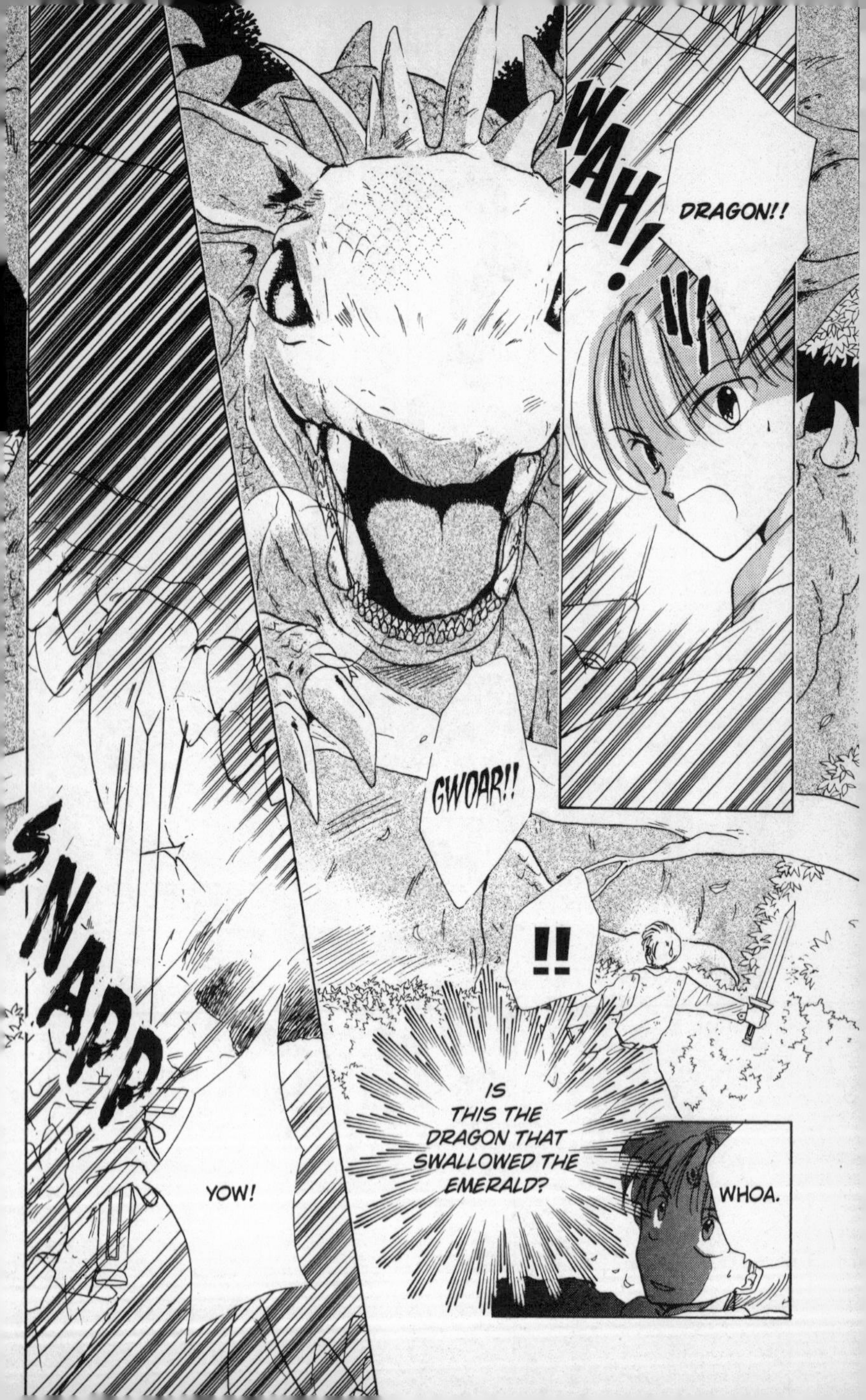
WAH!
DRAGON!!
!!
GWOAR!!
!!
IS THIS THE DRAGON THAT SWALLOWED THE EMERALD?
WHOA.
SNAPP
YOW!

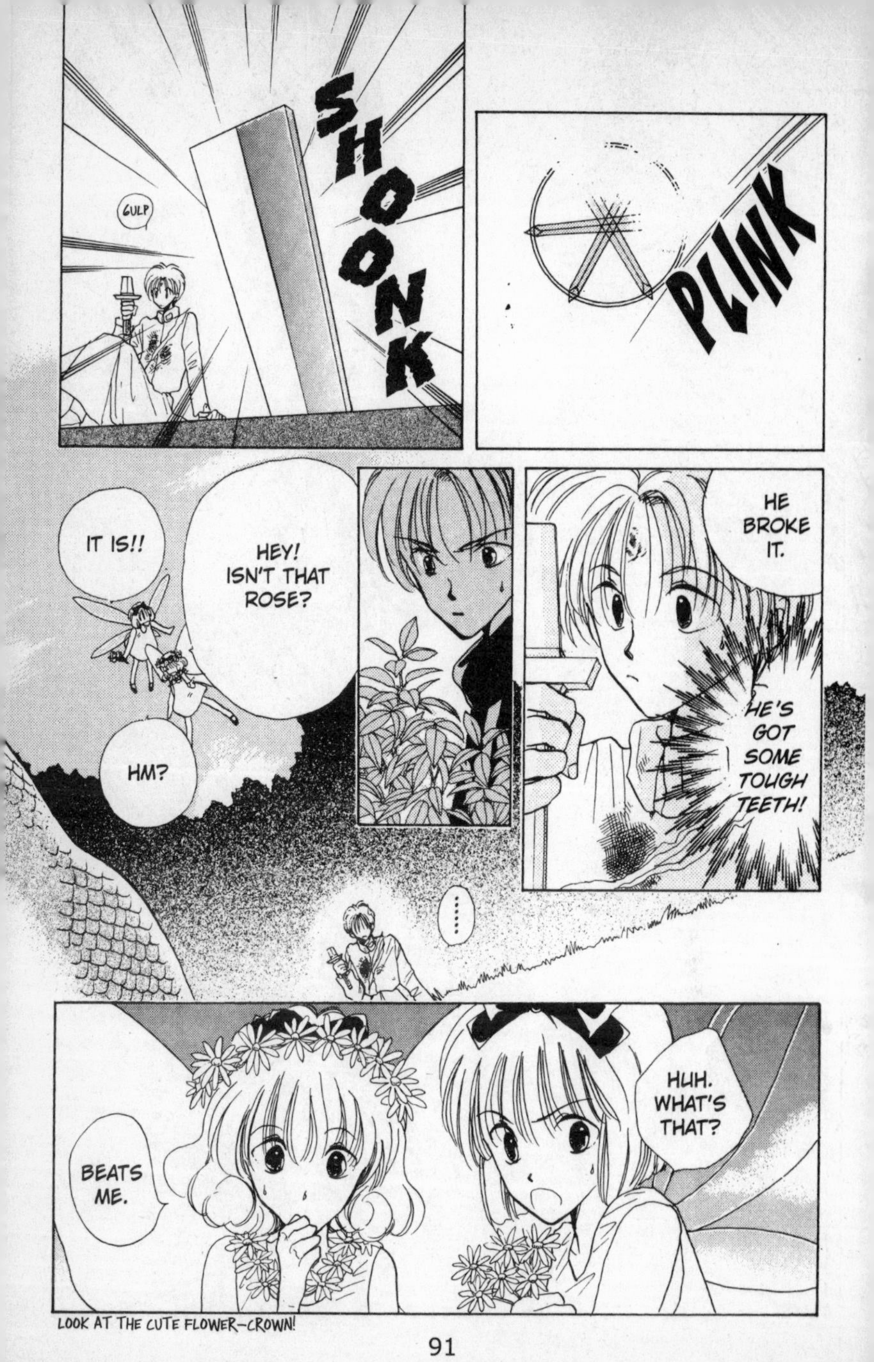
PLINK
SHOONK
GULP
HE BROKE IT.
HE'S GOT SOME TOUGH TEETH!
HEY! ISN'T THAT ROSE?
IT IS!!
HM?
......
HUH. WHAT'S THAT?
BEATS ME.
LOOK AT THE CUTE FLOWER-CROWN!

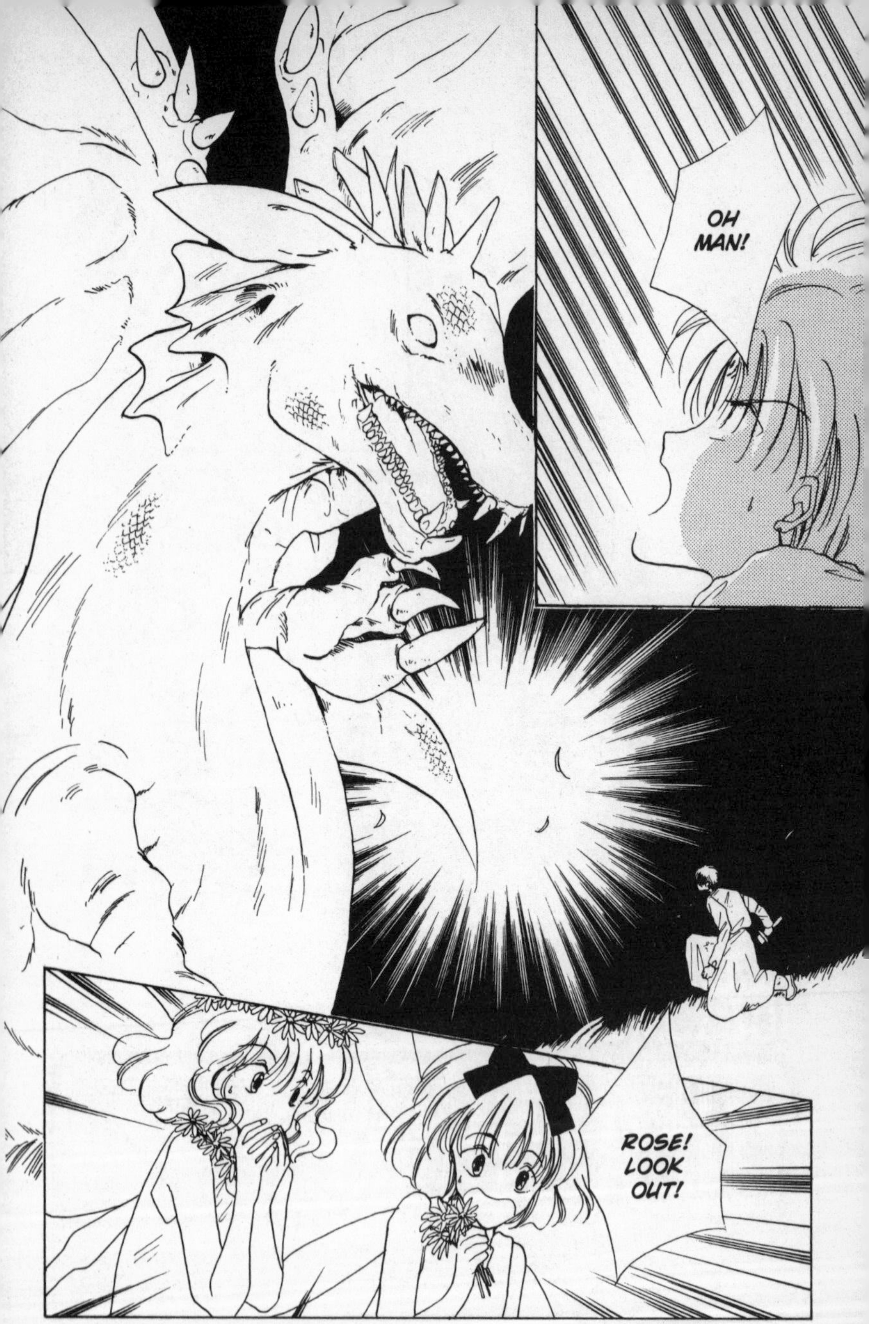
OH MAN!
ROSE! LOOK OUT!

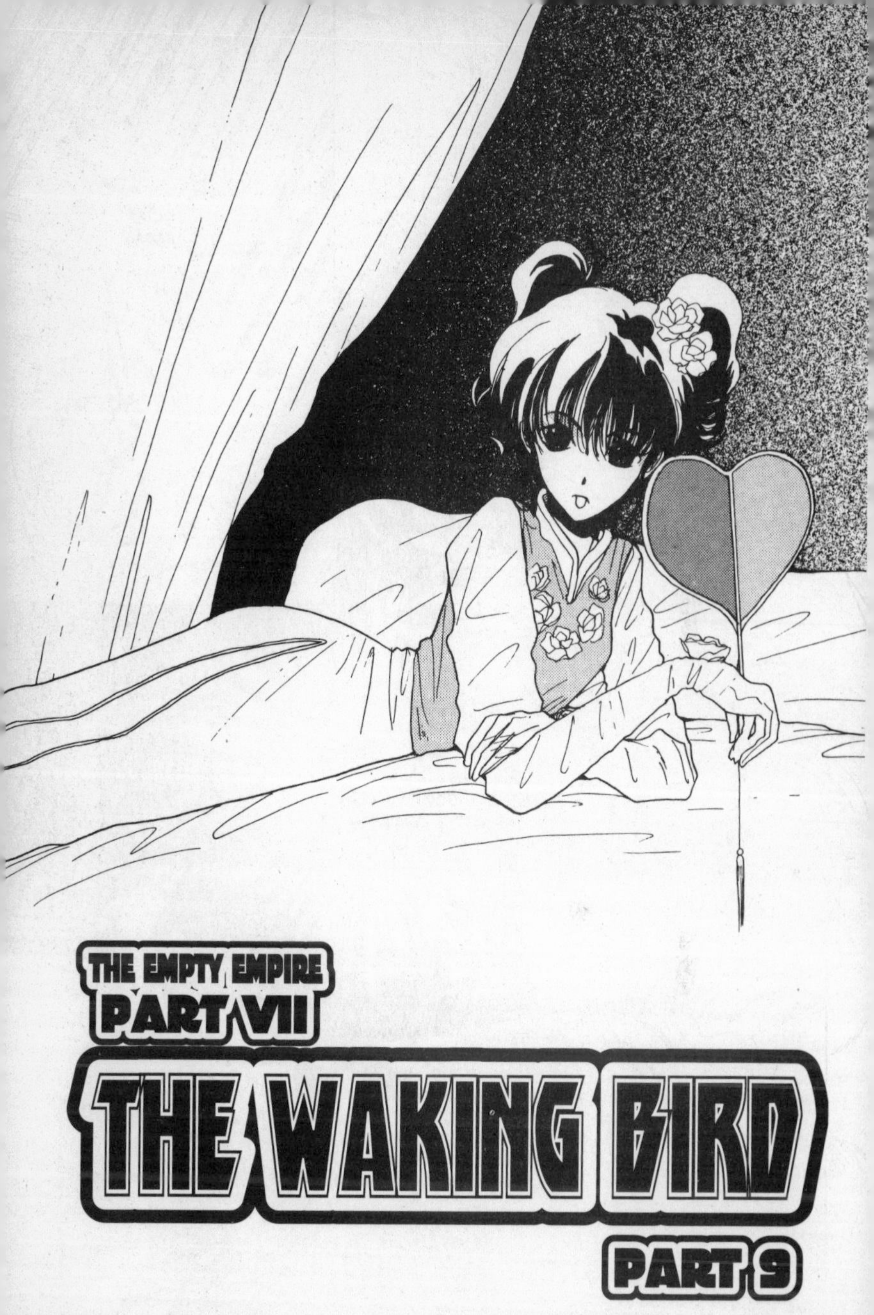

THE EMPTY EMPIRE
PART VII

THE WAKING BIRD

PART 9

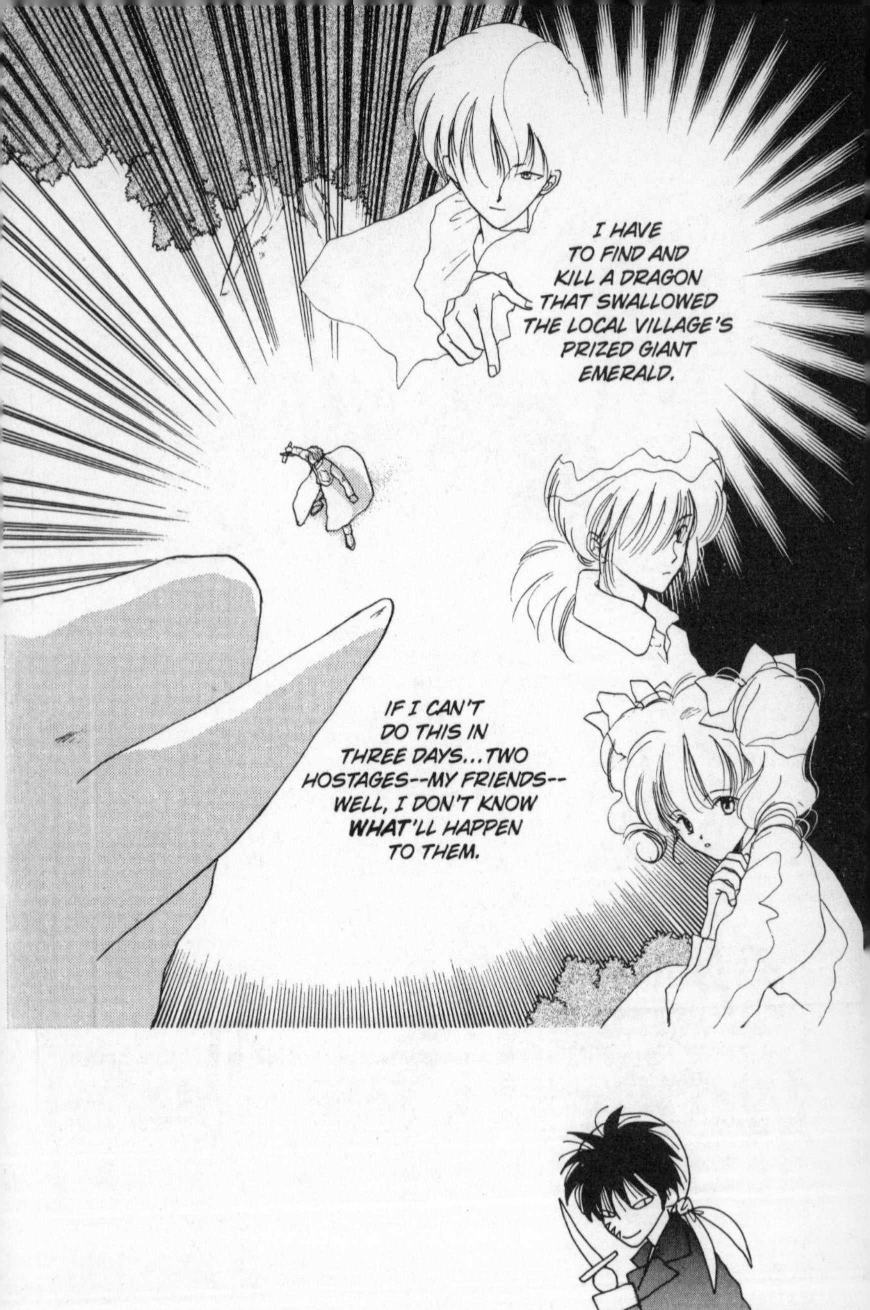
I HAVE TO FIND AND KILL A DRAGON THAT SWALLOWED THE LOCAL VILLAGE'S PRIZED GIANT EMERALD.
IF I CAN'T DO THIS IN THREE DAYS...TWO HOSTAGES--MY FRIENDS--WELL, I DON'T KNOW **WHAT**'LL HAPPEN TO THEM.

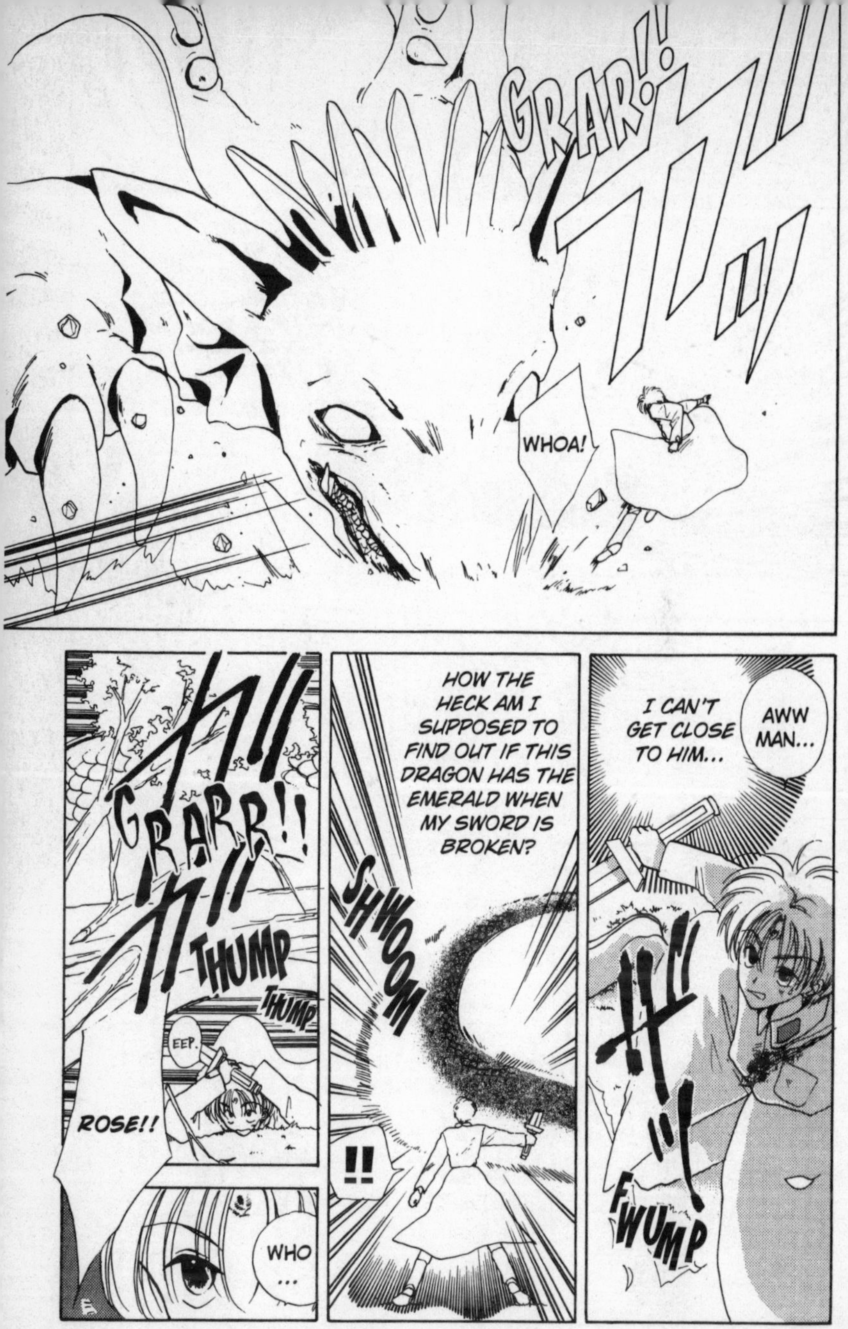
GRAR!!
WHOA!
AWW MAN...
I CAN'T GET CLOSE TO HIM...
FWUMP
HOW THE HECK AM I SUPPOSED TO FIND OUT IF THIS DRAGON HAS THE EMERALD WHEN MY SWORD IS BROKEN?
SHWOOOM
!!
GRARR!!
THUMP
THUMP
EEP.
ROSE!!
WHO ...

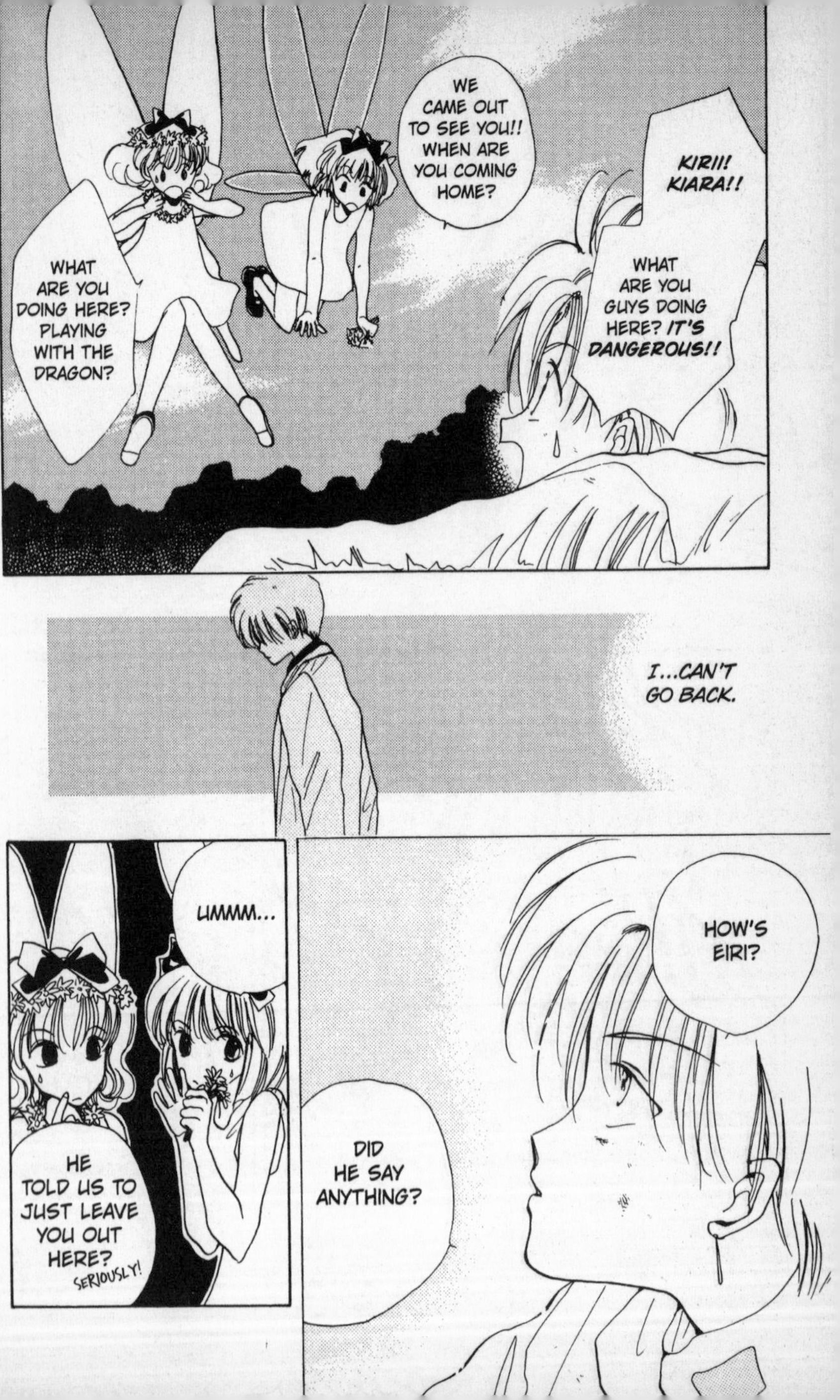
KIRI!! KIARA!!
WHAT ARE YOU GUYS DOING HERE? IT'S DANGEROUS!!
WE CAME OUT TO SEE YOU!! WHEN ARE YOU COMING HOME?
WHAT ARE YOU DOING HERE? PLAYING WITH THE DRAGON?
I...CAN'T GO BACK.
HOW'S EIRI?
DID HE SAY ANYTHING?
UMMM...
HE TOLD US TO JUST LEAVE YOU OUT HERE?
SERIOUSLY!

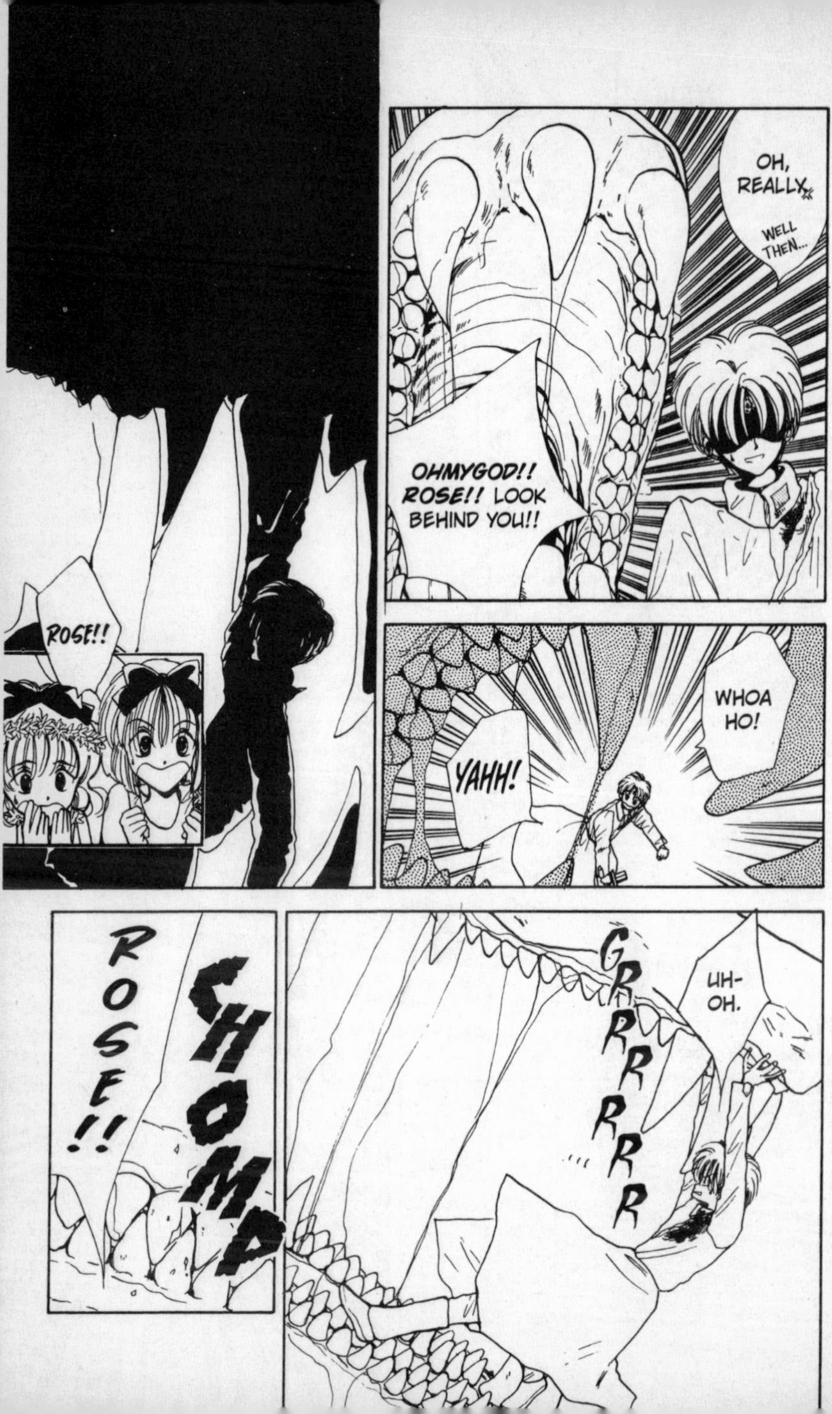
OH, REALLY
WELL THEN...
OHMYGOD!! ROSE!! LOOK BEHIND YOU!!
WHOA HO!
YAHH!
ROSE!!
UH-OH.
GRRRRRRR
...
ROSE!!
CHOMP

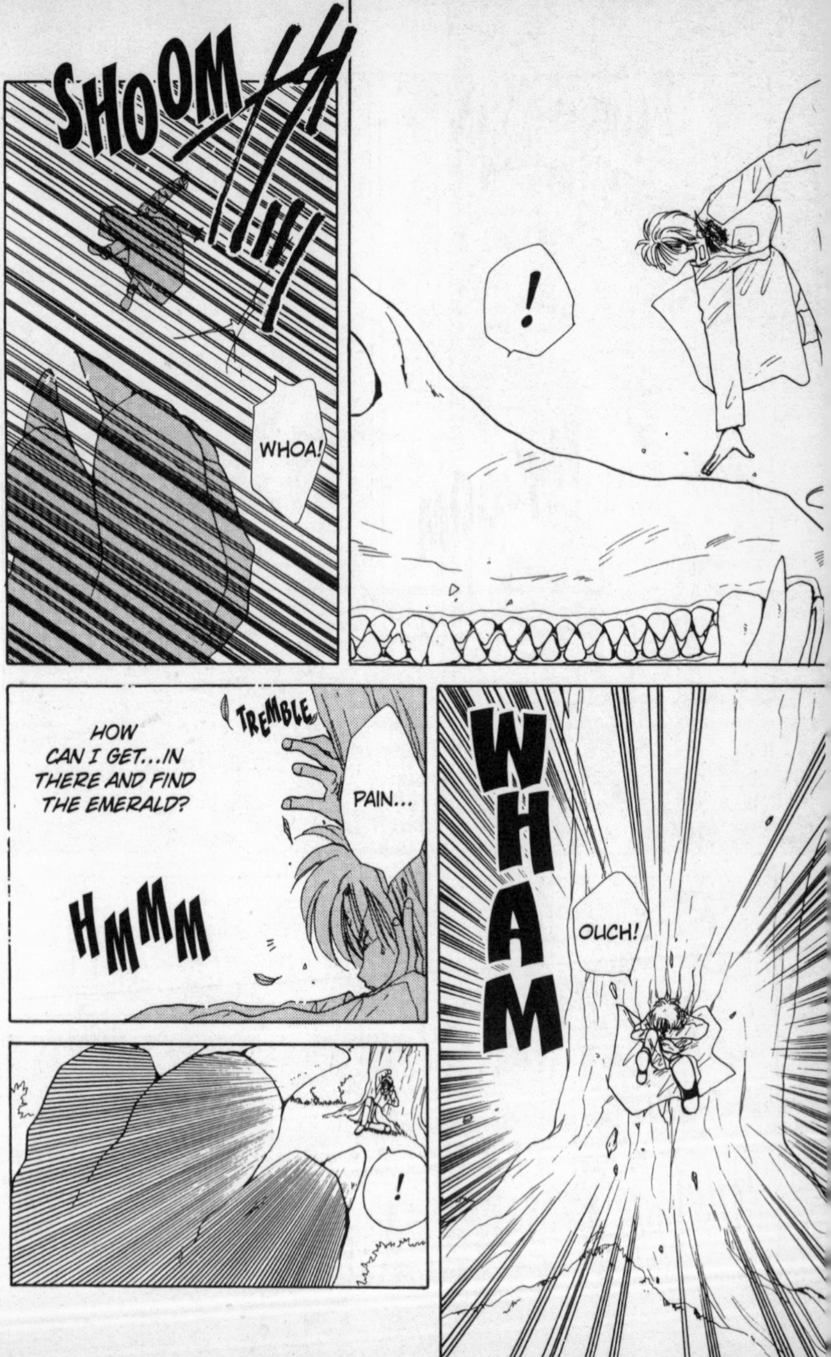
!
SHOOM
WHOA!
WHAM
OUCH!
TREMBLE
PAIN...
HOW CAN I GET...IN THERE AND FIND THE EMERALD?
HMMM
!

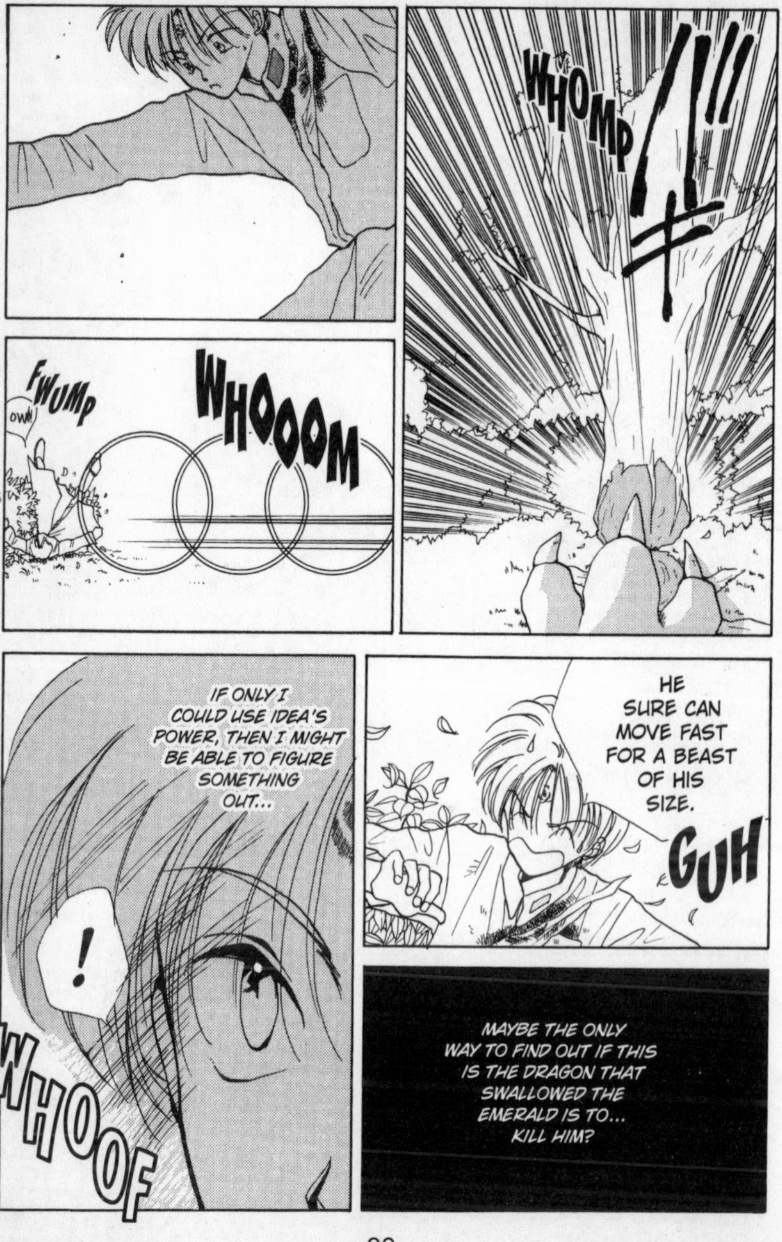
WHOMP
FWUMP
OW!!
WHOOOM
HE SURE CAN MOVE FAST FOR A BEAST OF HIS SIZE.
GUH
MAYBE THE ONLY WAY TO FIND OUT IF THIS IS THE DRAGON THAT SWALLOWED THE EMERALD IS TO... KILL HIM?
IF ONLY I COULD USE IDEA'S POWER, THEN I MIGHT BE ABLE TO FIGURE SOMETHING OUT...
!
WHOOF

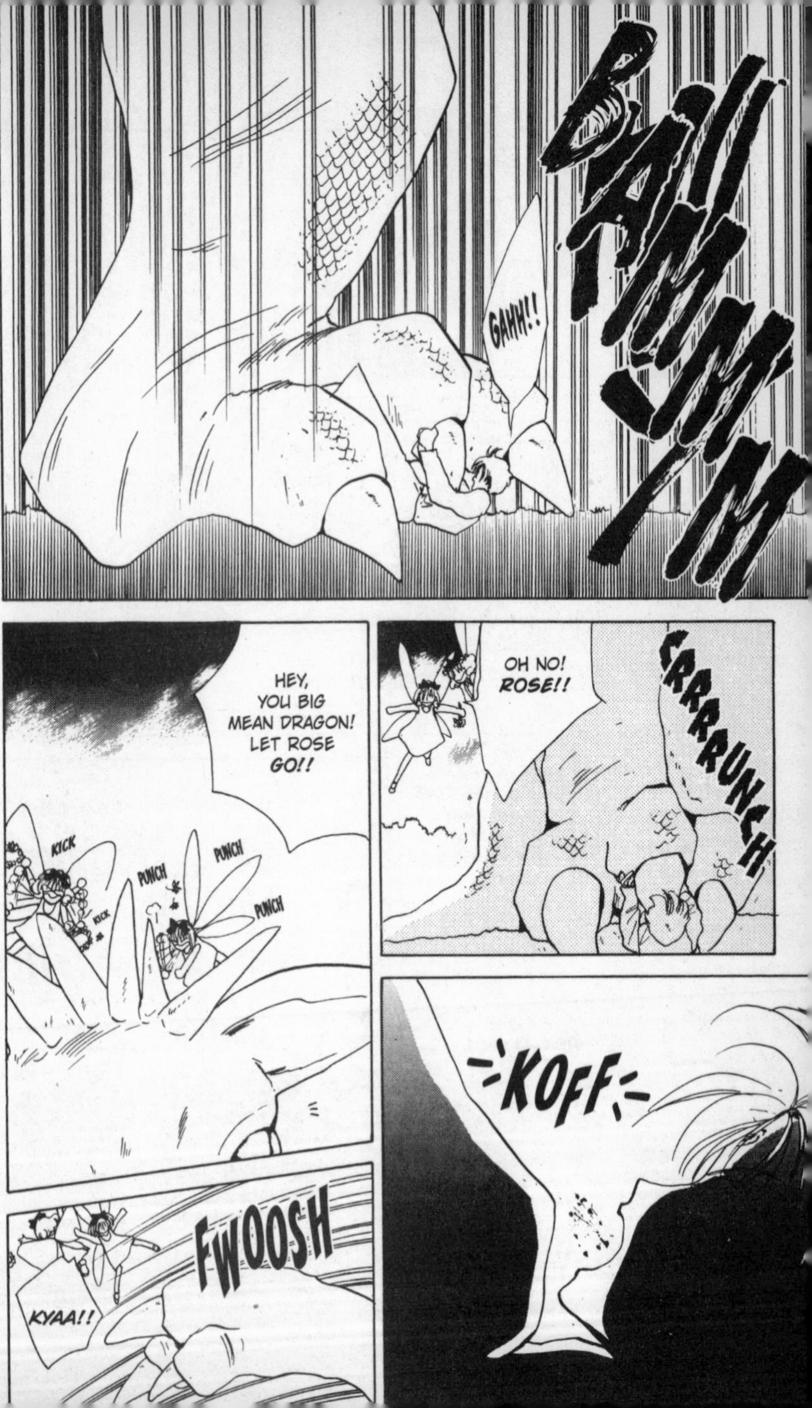
BAMMMM
GAHH!!
OH NO! ROSE!!
CRRRRUNCH
HEY, YOU BIG MEAN DRAGON! LET ROSE GO!!
KICK
KICK
PUNCH
PUNCH
PUNCH
-KOFF-
FWOOSH
KYAA!!

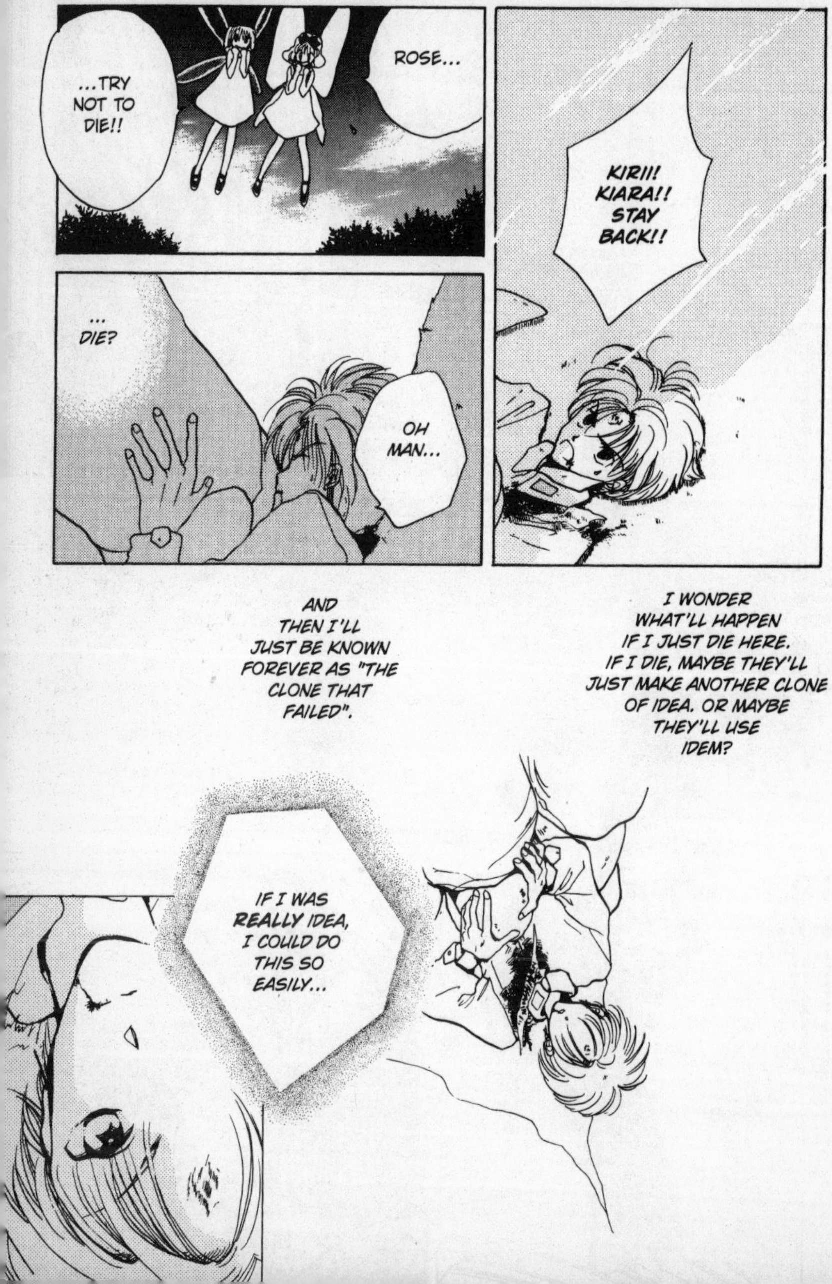
KIRII! KIARA!! STAY BACK!!
ROSE...
...TRY NOT TO DIE!!
... DIE?
OH MAN...
I WONDER WHAT'LL HAPPEN IF I JUST DIE HERE. IF I DIE, MAYBE THEY'LL JUST MAKE ANOTHER CLONE OF IDEA. OR MAYBE THEY'LL USE IDEM?
AND THEN I'LL JUST BE KNOWN FOREVER AS "THE CLONE THAT FAILED".
IF I WAS REALLY IDEA, I COULD DO THIS SO EASILY...

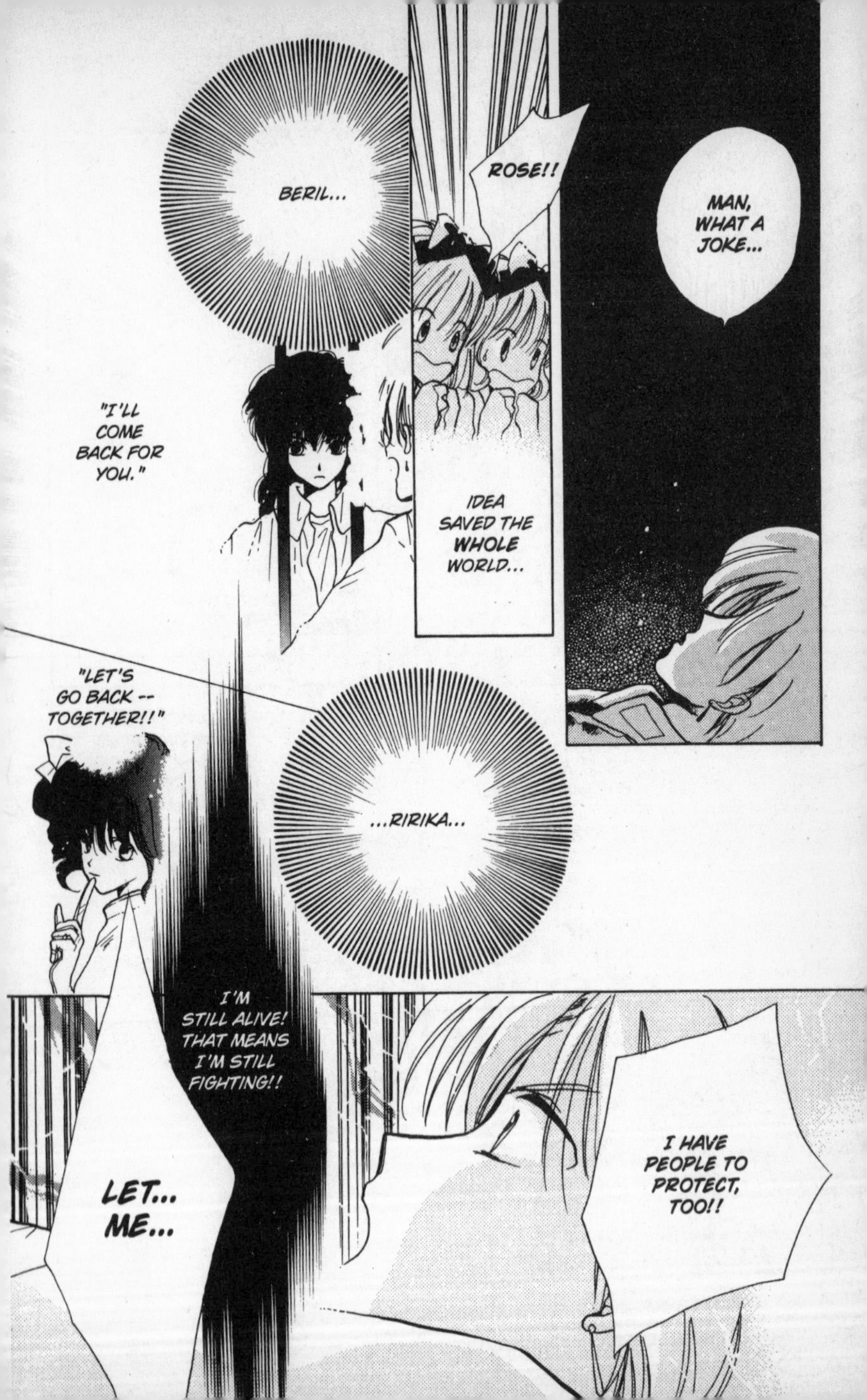
MAN, WHAT A JOKE...
ROSE!!
IDEA SAVED THE WHOLE WORLD...
BERIL...
"I'LL COME BACK FOR YOU."
...RIRIKA...
"LET'S GO BACK -- TOGETHER!!"
I HAVE PEOPLE TO PROTECT, TOO!!
I'M STILL ALIVE! THAT MEANS I'M STILL FIGHTING!!
LET... ME...

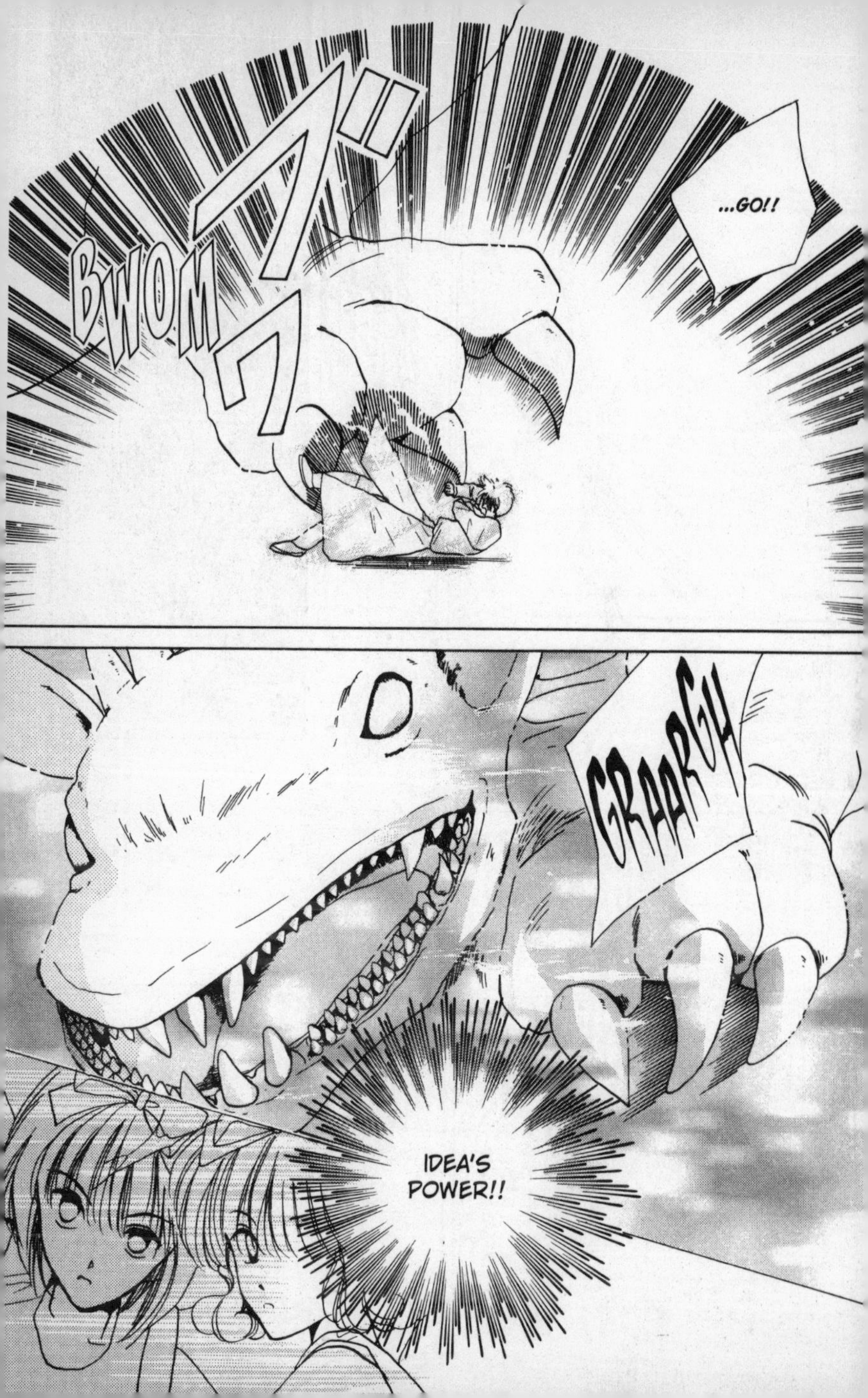
...GO!!
BWOM
GRAARGH
IDEA'S POWER!!

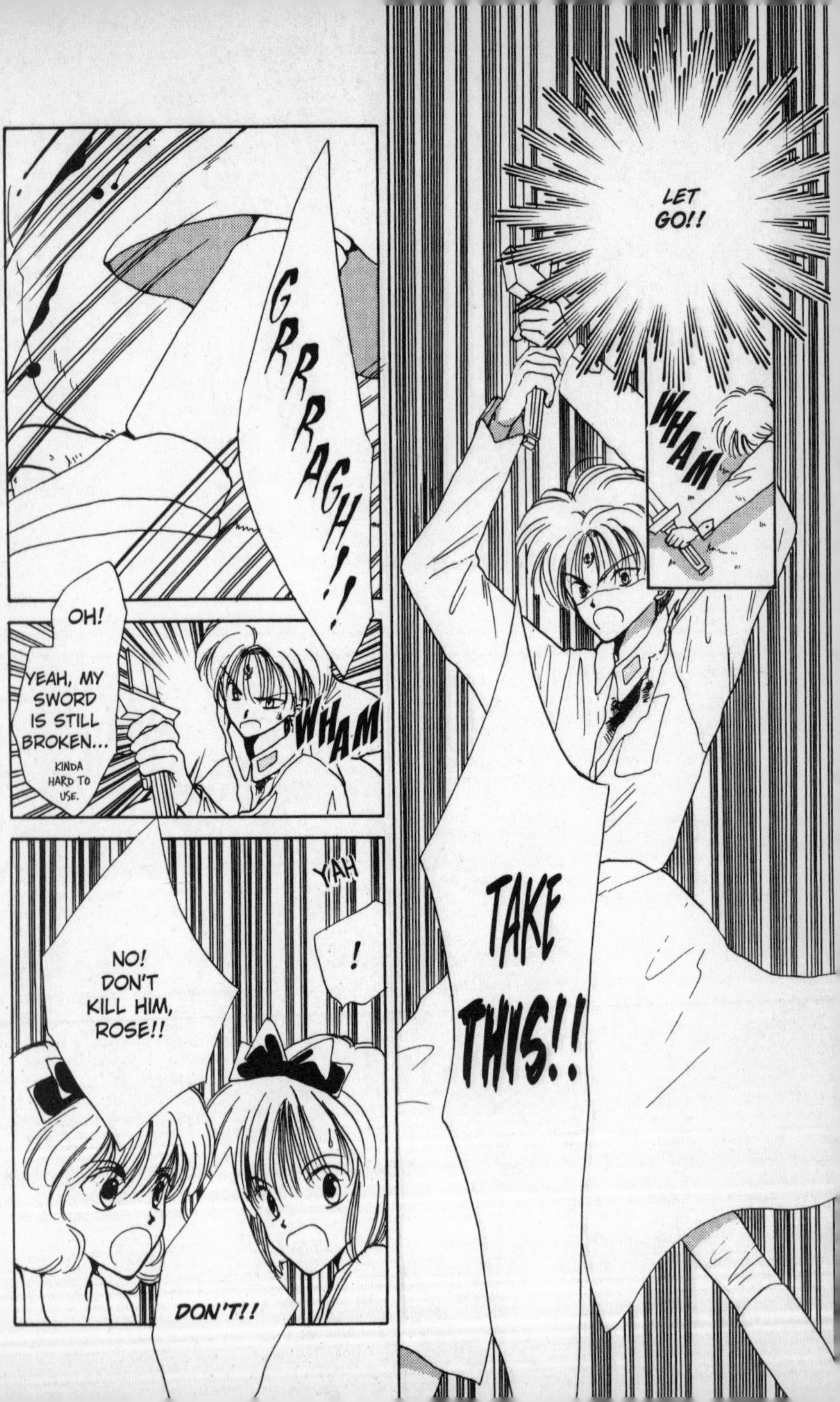
LET GO!!
WHAM
TAKE THIS!!
GRRRAGH!!
OH!
YEAH, MY SWORD IS STILL BROKEN...
KINDA HARD TO USE.
WHAM
YAH
!
NO! DON'T KILL HIM, ROSE!!
DON'T!!

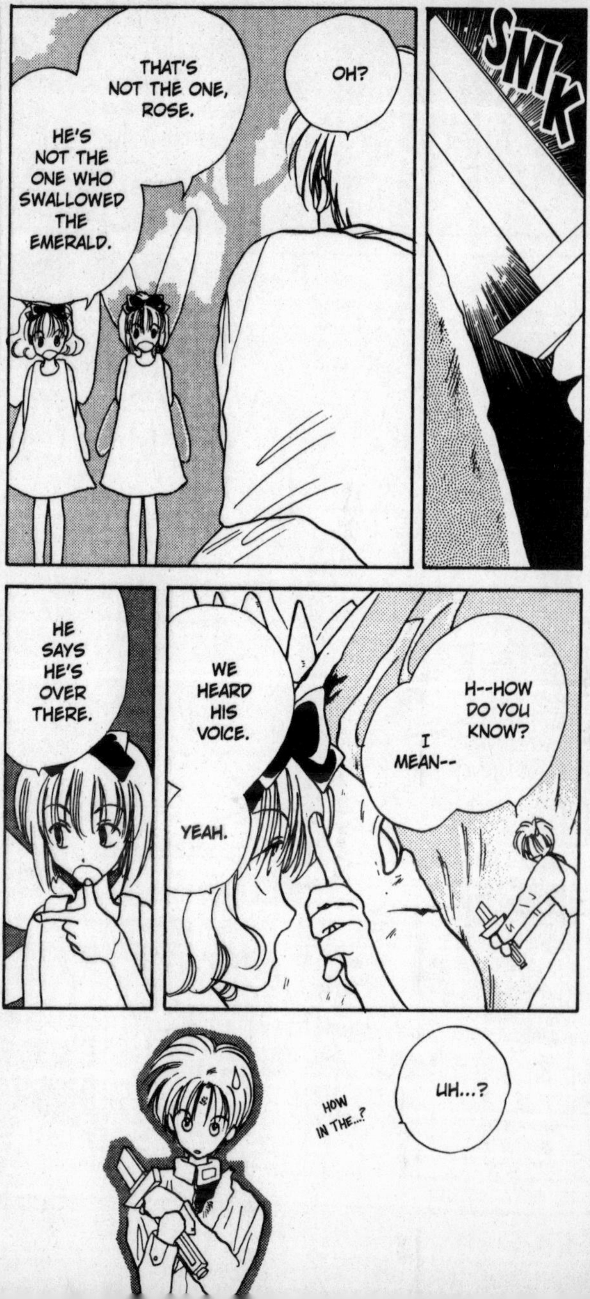

SNIK
OH?
THAT'S NOT THE ONE, ROSE.
HE'S NOT THE ONE WHO SWALLOWED THE EMERALD.
H--HOW DO YOU KNOW?
I MEAN--
WE HEARD HIS VOICE.
YEAH.
HE SAYS HE'S OVER THERE.
UH...?
HOW IN THE...?

WHEN WE GOT TO NAGOYA, WE COULDN'T EVEN GET OFF THE TRAIN FOR A FEW MINUTES-- THERE WERE SO MANY PEOPLE WAITING ON THE PLATFORM BECAUSE THE TRAINS HAD BEEN STOPPED. AND WHEN WE FINALLY ***DID*** GET OFF THE TRAIN, ALL OF THE VENDING MACHINES WERE SOLD OUT OF ***EVERY*** DRINK, EVEN THE ONES WE DIDN'T ***WANT***. HERE WE WERE, ON A BEAUTIFUL DAY, FAR FROM ANY KIND OF STORM, AND HERE WERE THESE VENDING MACHINES, WHICH WOULD HAVE BEEN FULL ON ANY OTHER DAY, EMPTY BECAUSE OF A TYPHOON THAT NO ONE HERE COULD SEE.
WE'D JUST SPENT FOUR HOURS ON A TRAIN, TO MAKE A ONE-HOUR TRIP. EVENTUALLY, WE FOUND THE EXPERIENCE KIND OF FUNNY. WE WEREN'T EVEN BORED WHILE WE WERE WAITING, ACTUALLY. WE JUST TALKED AND TALKED AND TALKED THE WHOLE TIME. IT WAS ONE OF THOSE CLASSIC, LEGENDARY, SUPER-LONG "GIRL TALK" SESSIONS, IF YOU KNOW WHAT I MEAN.
THE NEXT STEP WAS TO TAKE A LOCAL TRAIN TO THE PARTICULAR STATION IN NAGOYA WHERE WE WERE HEADED. AND -- HAH! -- ***THAT'S*** WHERE WE GOT HOPELESSLY LOST FOR ***ANOTHER*** TWO HOURS.

(CONTINUED)

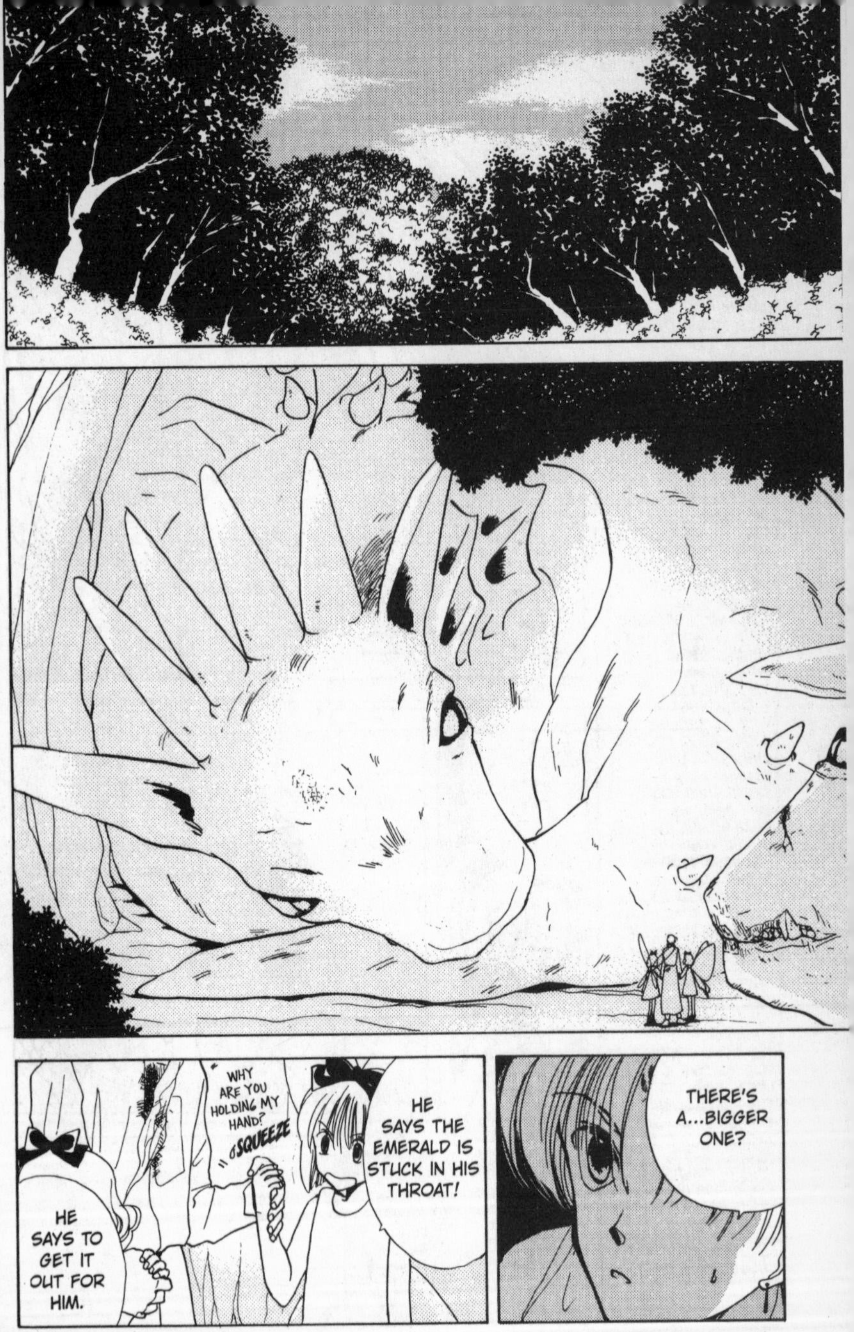
THERE'S A...BIGGER ONE?
HE SAYS THE EMERALD IS STUCK IN HIS THROAT!
WHY ARE YOU HOLDING MY HAND?
SQUEEZE
HE SAYS TO GET IT OUT FOR HIM.

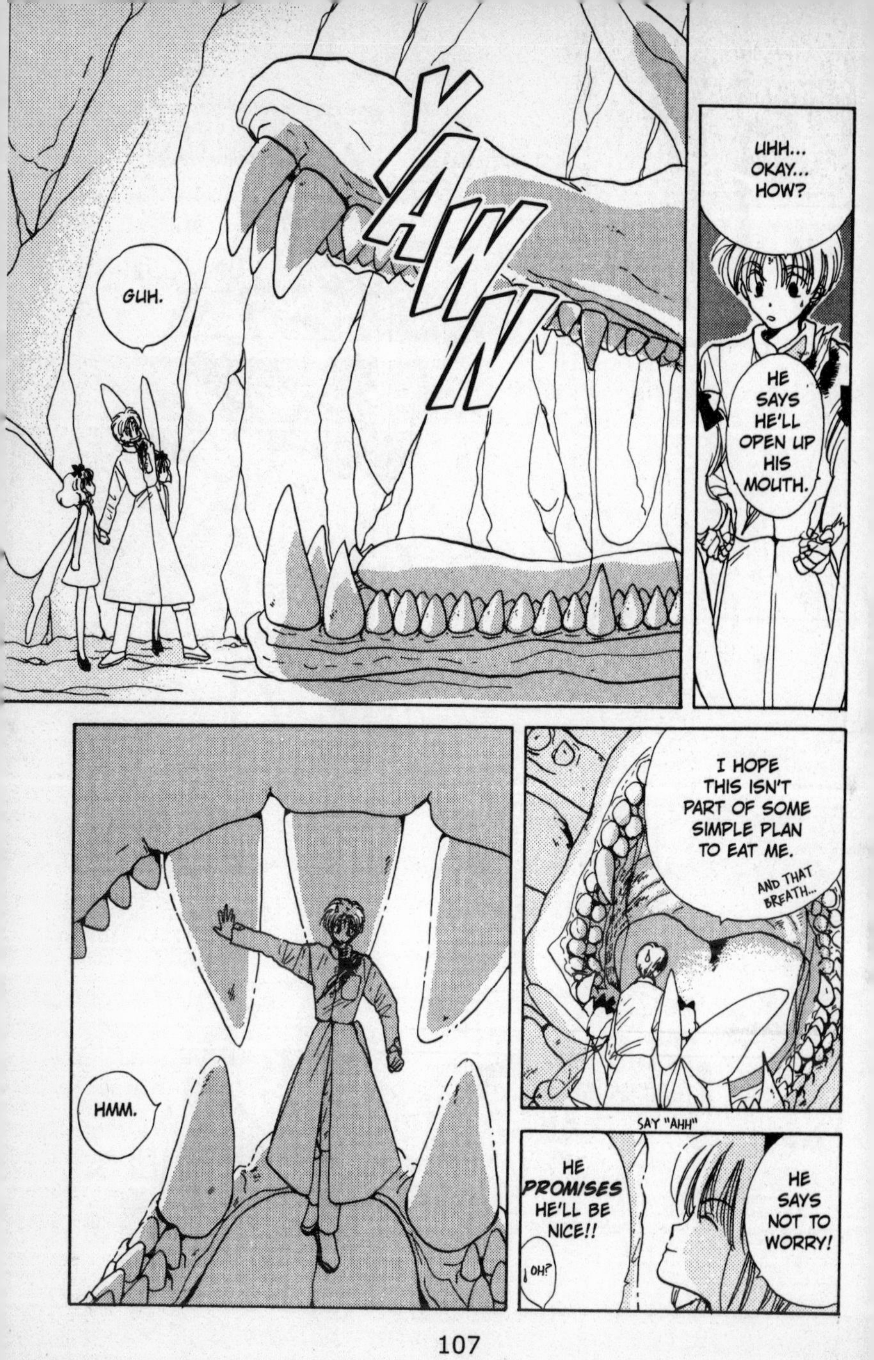
UHH... OKAY... HOW?
HE SAYS HE'LL OPEN UP HIS MOUTH.
YAWN
GUH.
I HOPE THIS ISN'T PART OF SOME SIMPLE PLAN TO EAT ME.
AND THAT BREATH...
SAY "AHH"
HE SAYS NOT TO WORRY!
HE **PROMISES** HE'LL BE NICE!!
OH?
HMM.

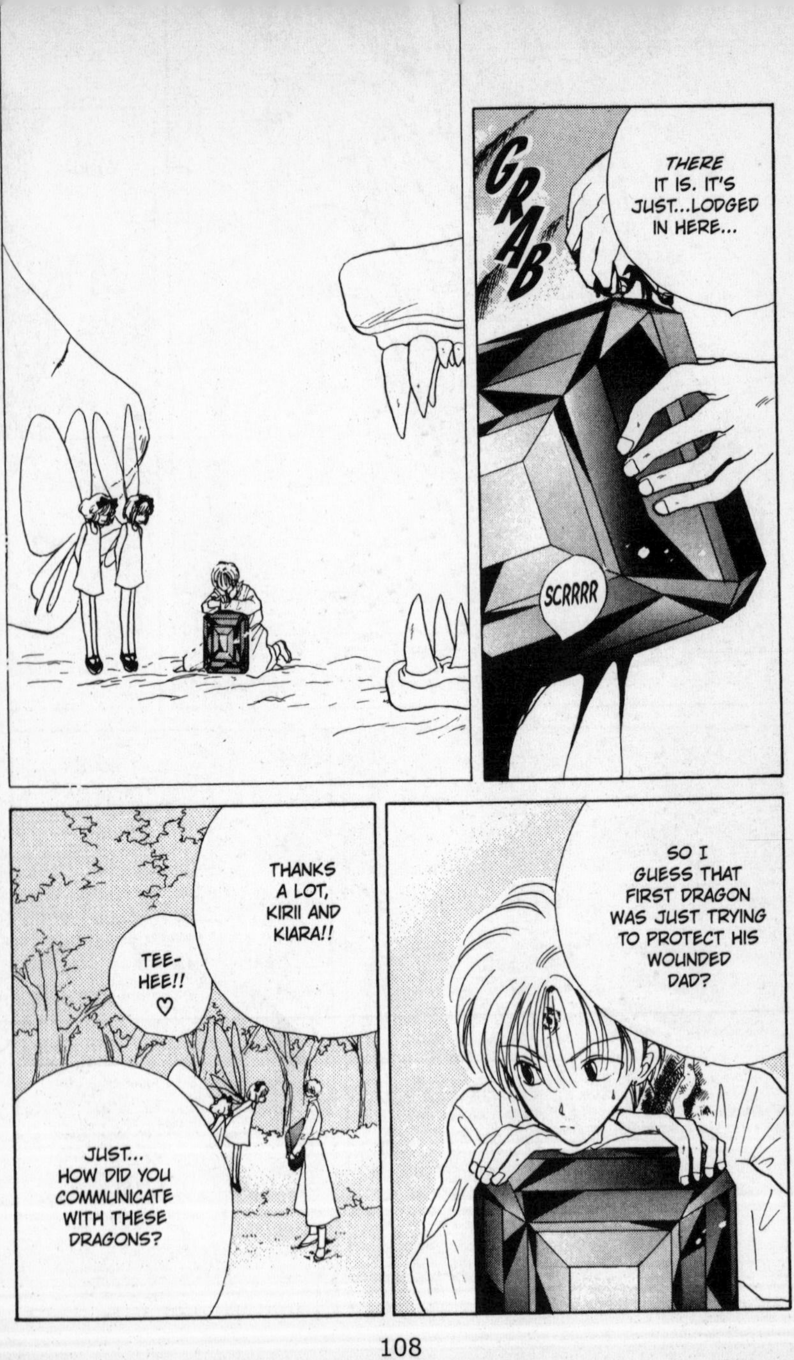
GRAB
THERE IT IS. IT'S JUST...LODGED IN HERE...
SCRRRR
SO I GUESS THAT FIRST DRAGON WAS JUST TRYING TO PROTECT HIS WOUNDED DAD?
THANKS A LOT, KIRII AND KIARA!!
TEE-HEE!! ♡
JUST... HOW DID YOU COMMUNICATE WITH THESE DRAGONS?

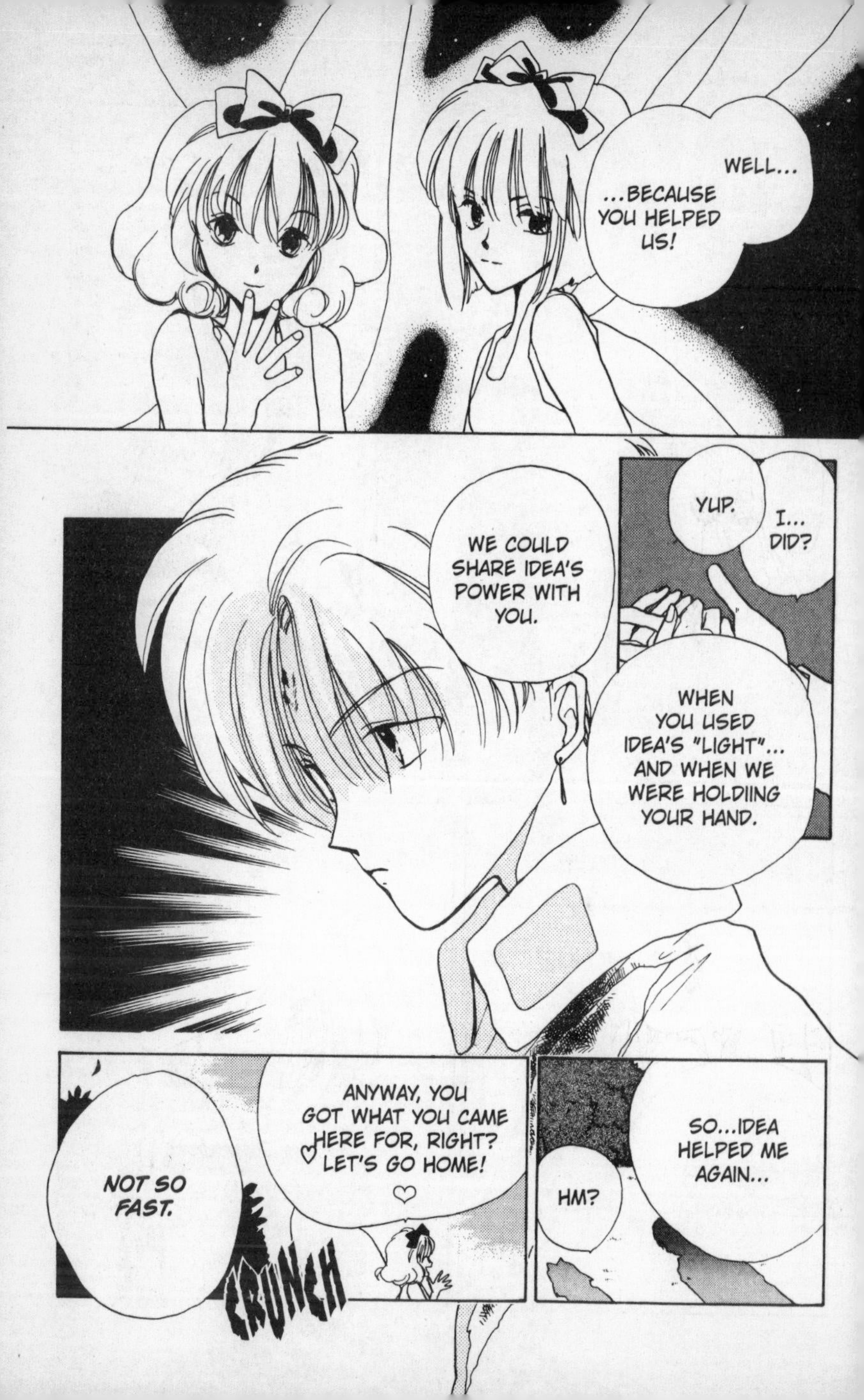
WELL...
...BECAUSE YOU HELPED US!
I... DID?
YUP.
WE COULD SHARE IDEA'S POWER WITH YOU.
WHEN YOU USED IDEA'S "LIGHT"... AND WHEN WE WERE HOLDIING YOUR HAND.
SO...IDEA HELPED ME AGAIN...
HM?
ANYWAY, YOU GOT WHAT YOU CAME HERE FOR, RIGHT? LET'S GO HOME! ♡
CRUNCH
NOT SO FAST.

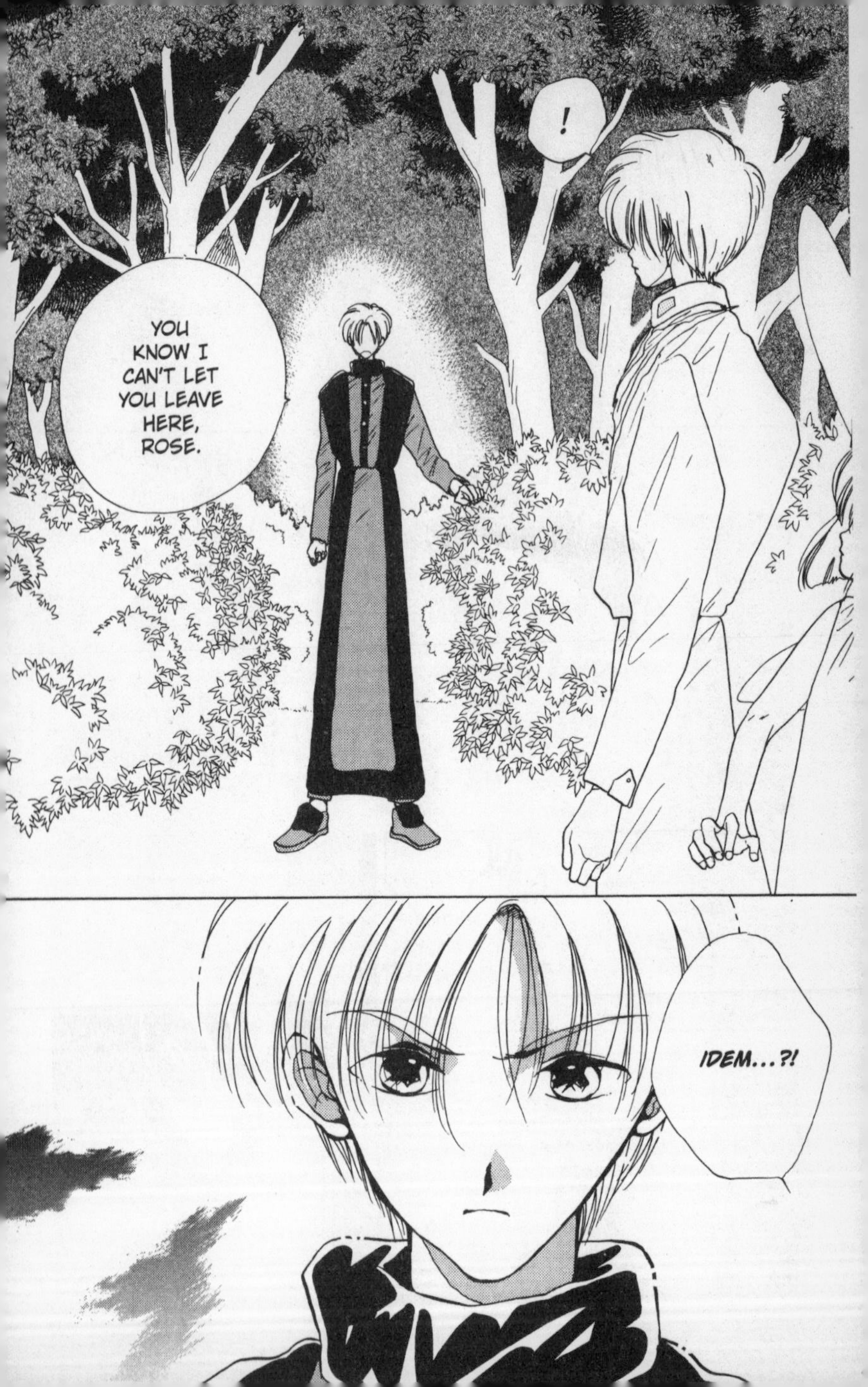
!
YOU KNOW I CAN'T LET YOU LEAVE HERE, ROSE.
IDEM...?!

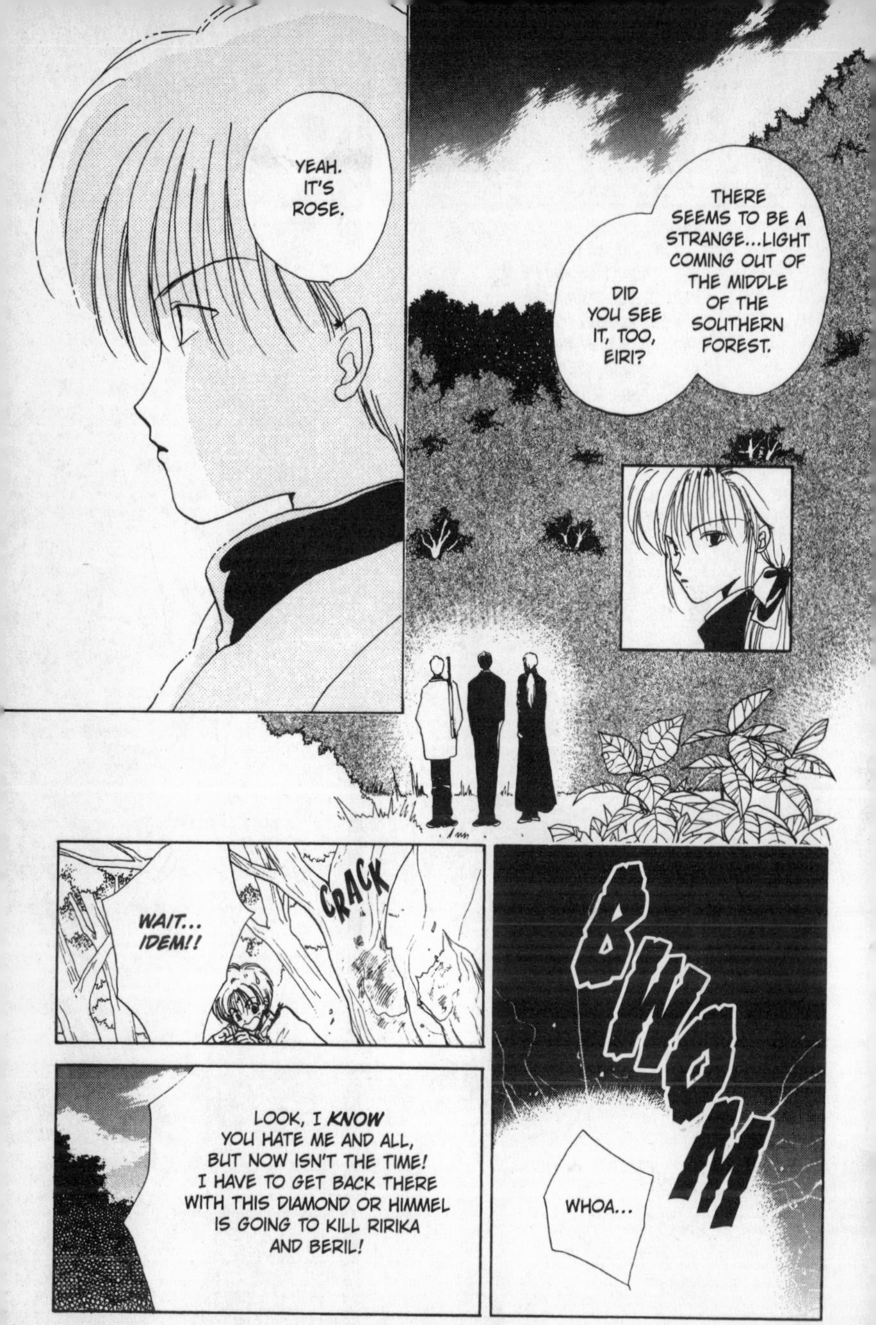
THERE SEEMS TO BE A STRANGE...LIGHT COMING OUT OF THE MIDDLE OF THE SOUTHERN FOREST.
DID YOU SEE IT, TOO, EIRI?
YEAH. IT'S ROSE.
BWOM
WHOA...
CRACK
WAIT... IDEM!!
LOOK, I KNOW YOU HATE ME AND ALL, BUT NOW ISN'T THE TIME! I HAVE TO GET BACK THERE WITH THIS DIAMOND OR HIMMEL IS GOING TO KILL RIRIKA AND BERIL!

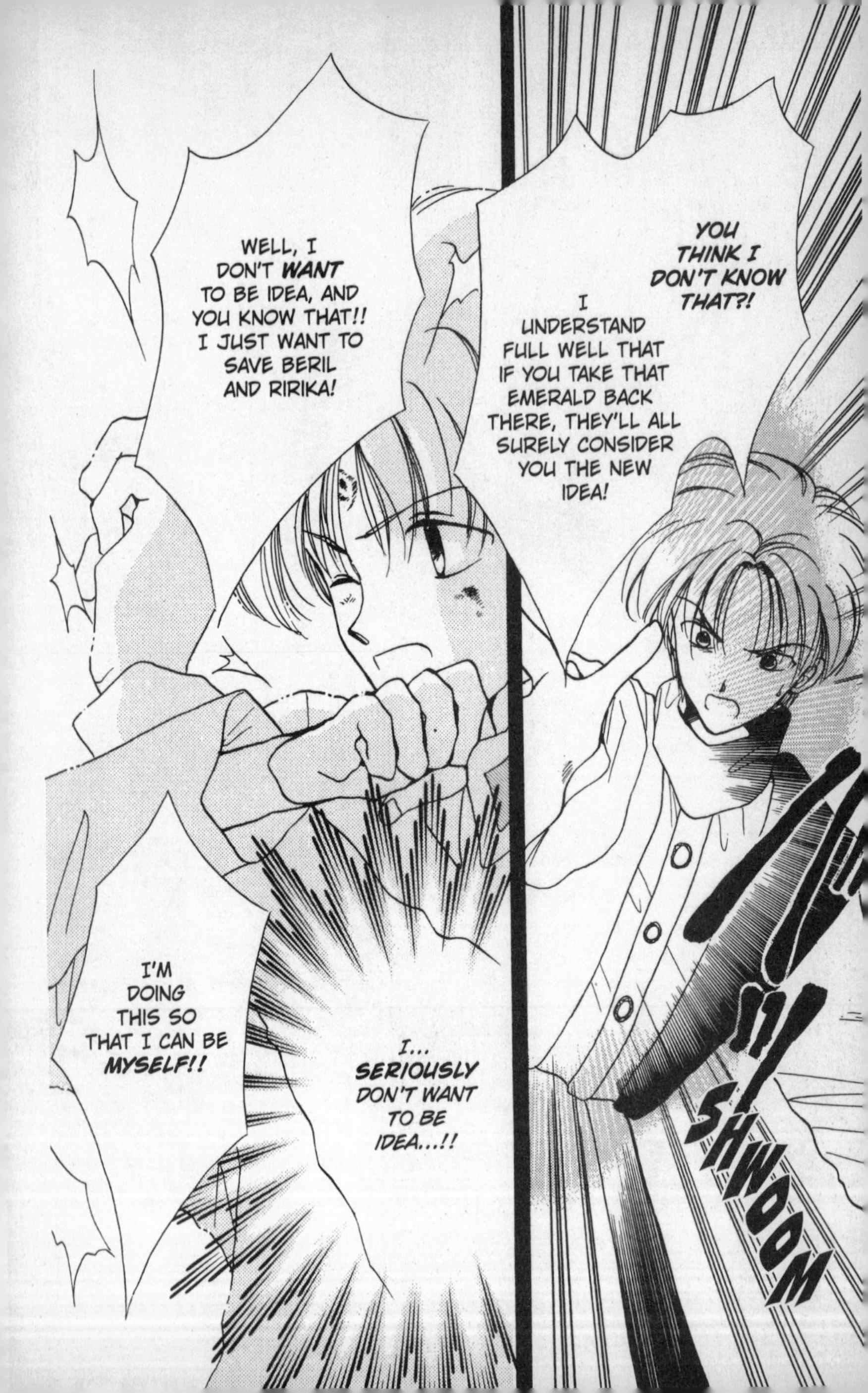
YOU THINK I DON'T KNOW THAT?!
I UNDERSTAND FULL WELL THAT IF YOU TAKE THAT EMERALD BACK THERE, THEY'LL ALL SURELY CONSIDER YOU THE NEW IDEA!
SHWOOM
WELL, I DON'T WANT TO BE IDEA, AND YOU KNOW THAT!! I JUST WANT TO SAVE BERIL AND RIRIKA!
I'M DOING THIS SO THAT I CAN BE MYSELF!!
I... SERIOUSLY DON'T WANT TO BE IDEA...!!

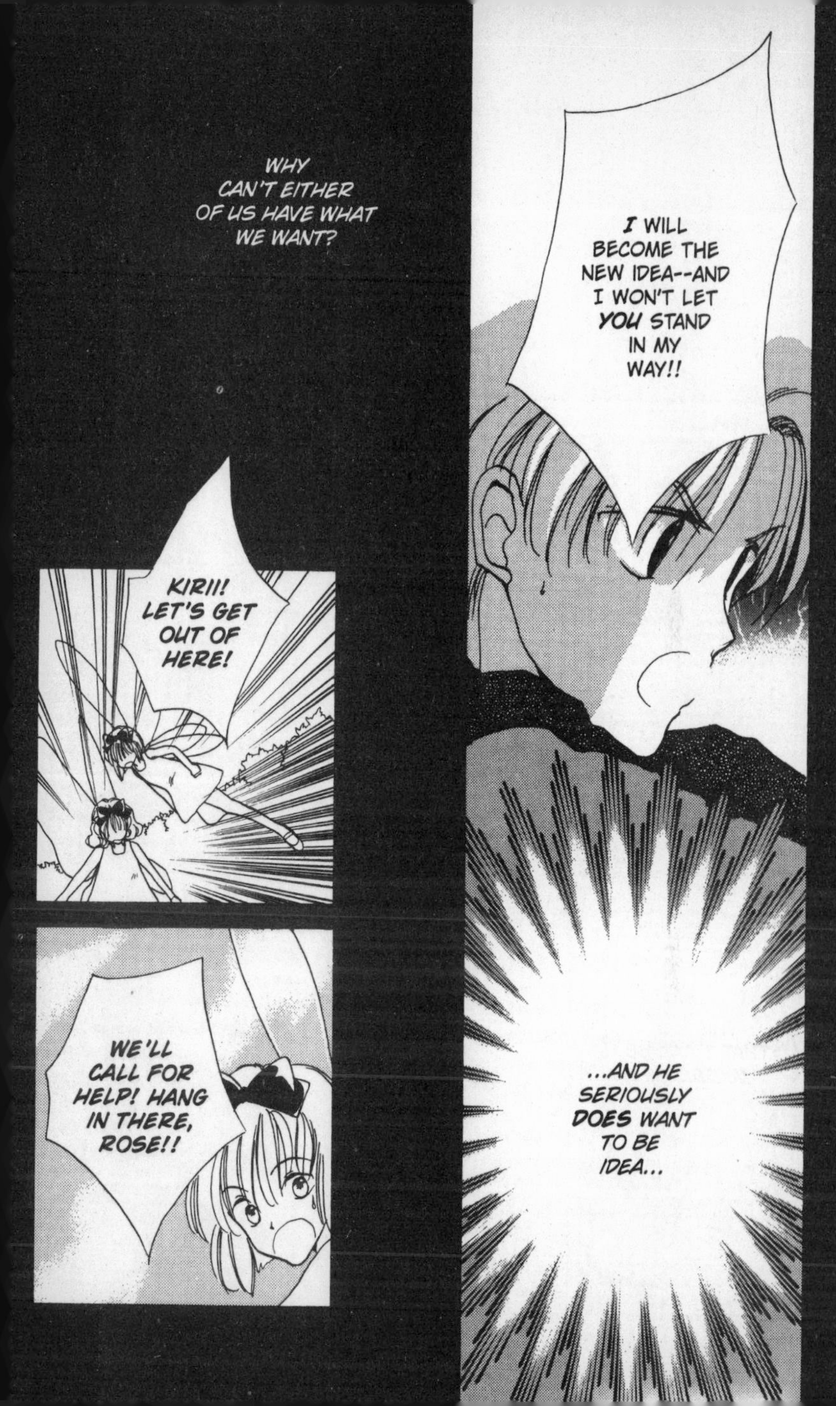
I WILL BECOME THE NEW IDEA--AND I WON'T LET YOU STAND IN MY WAY!!
...AND HE SERIOUSLY DOES WANT TO BE IDEA...
WHY CAN'T EITHER OF US HAVE WHAT WE WANT?
KIRII! LET'S GET OUT OF HERE!
WE'LL CALL FOR HELP! HANG IN THERE, ROSE!!

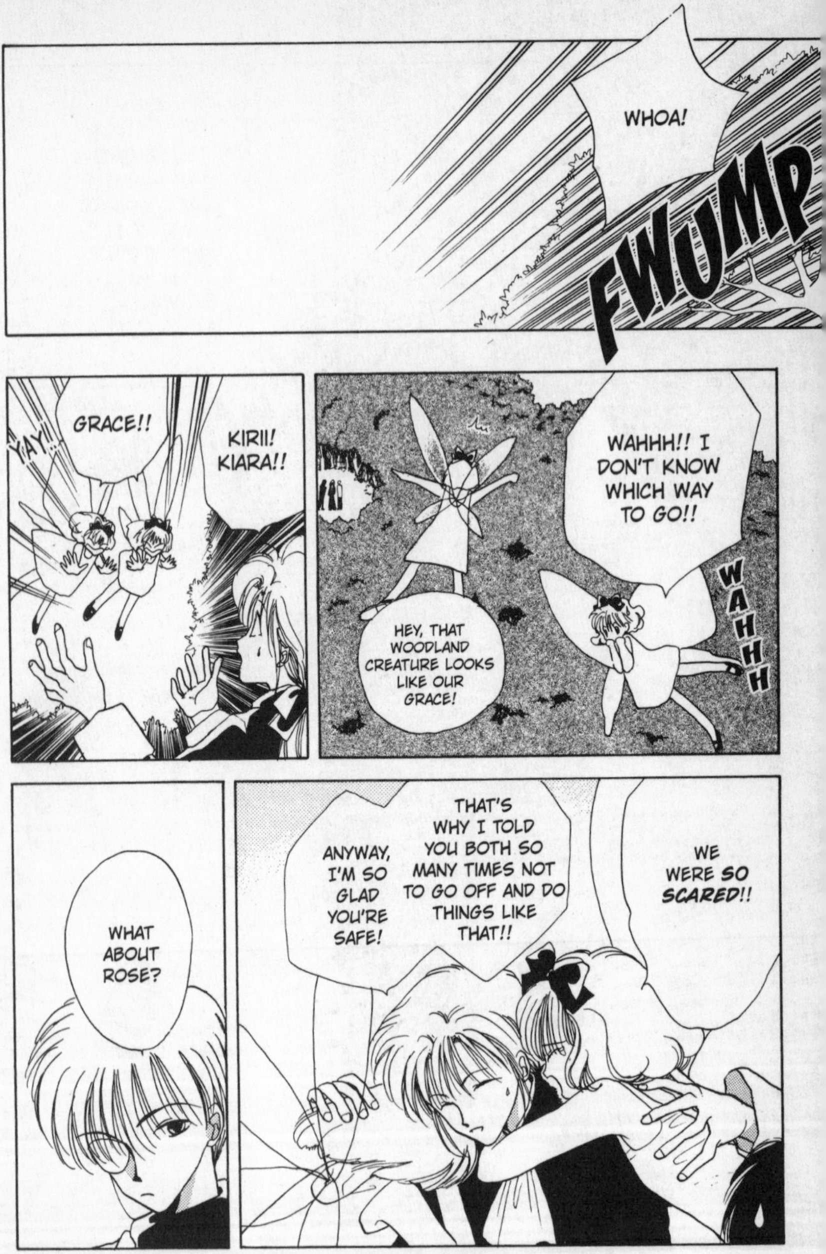
WHOA!
FWUMP
WAHHH!! I DON'T KNOW WHICH WAY TO GO!!
WAHHH
HEY, THAT WOODLAND CREATURE LOOKS LIKE OUR GRACE!
KIRII! KIARA!!
GRACE!!
YAY!!
WE WERE SO ***SCARED***!!
THAT'S WHY I TOLD YOU BOTH SO MANY TIMES NOT TO GO OFF AND DO THINGS LIKE THAT!!
ANYWAY, I'M SO GLAD YOU'RE SAFE!
WHAT ABOUT ROSE?

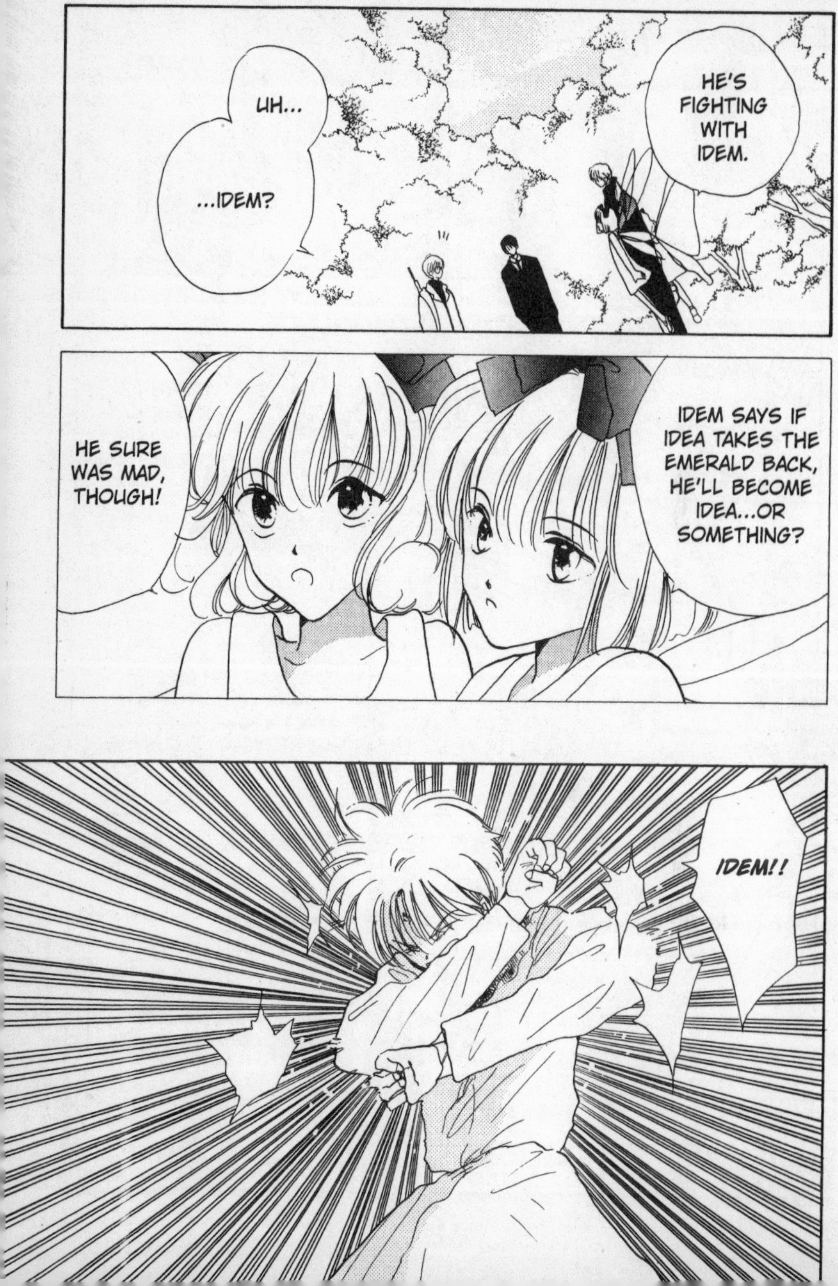
HE'S FIGHTING WITH IDEM.
UH...
...IDEM?
IDEM SAYS IF IDEA TAKES THE EMERALD BACK, HE'LL BECOME IDEA...OR SOMETHING?
HE SURE WAS MAD, THOUGH!
IDEM!!

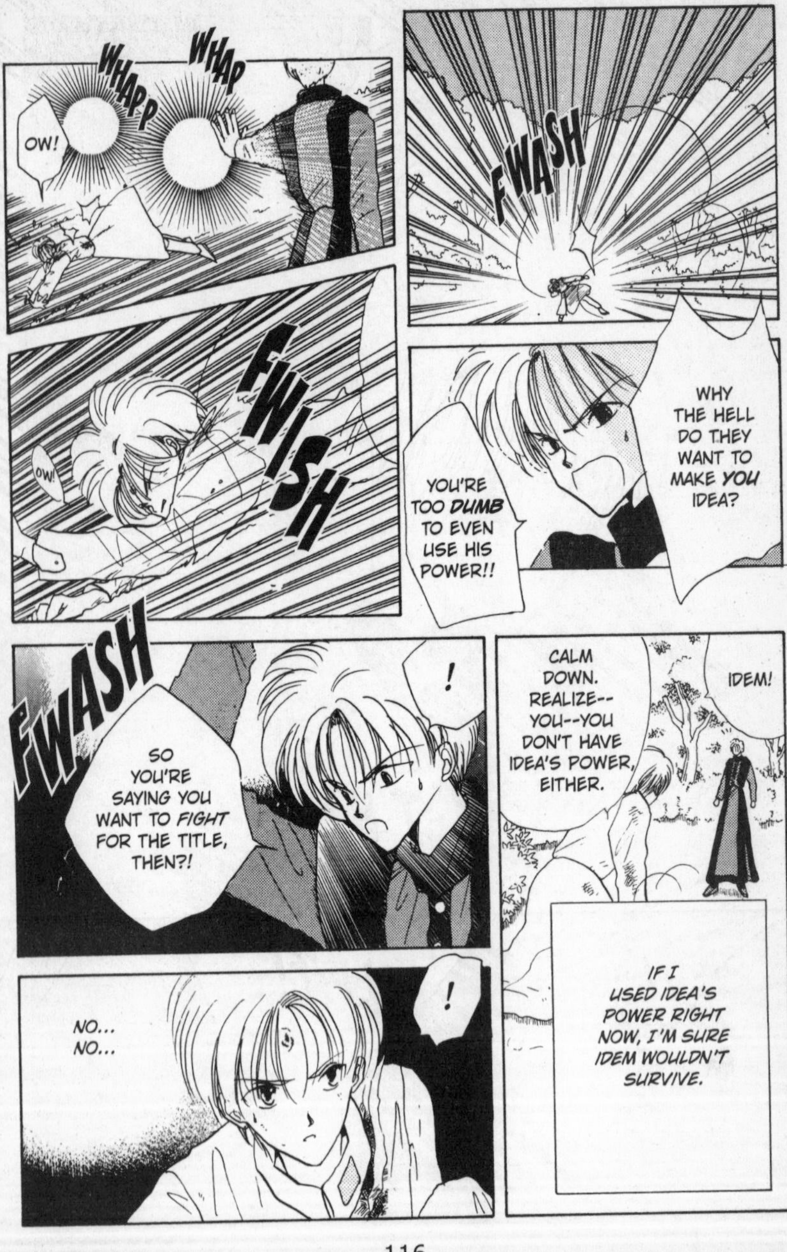

FWASH
WHAP
WHAPP
OW!
WHY THE HELL DO THEY WANT TO MAKE *YOU* IDEA?
YOU'RE TOO **DUMB** TO EVEN USE HIS POWER!!
FWISH
OW!
IDEM!
CALM DOWN. REALIZE-- YOU--YOU DON'T HAVE IDEA'S POWER, EITHER.
IF I USED IDEA'S POWER RIGHT NOW, I'M SURE IDEM WOULDN'T SURVIVE.
!
FWASH
SO YOU'RE SAYING YOU WANT TO *FIGHT* FOR THE TITLE, THEN?!
!
NO... NO...

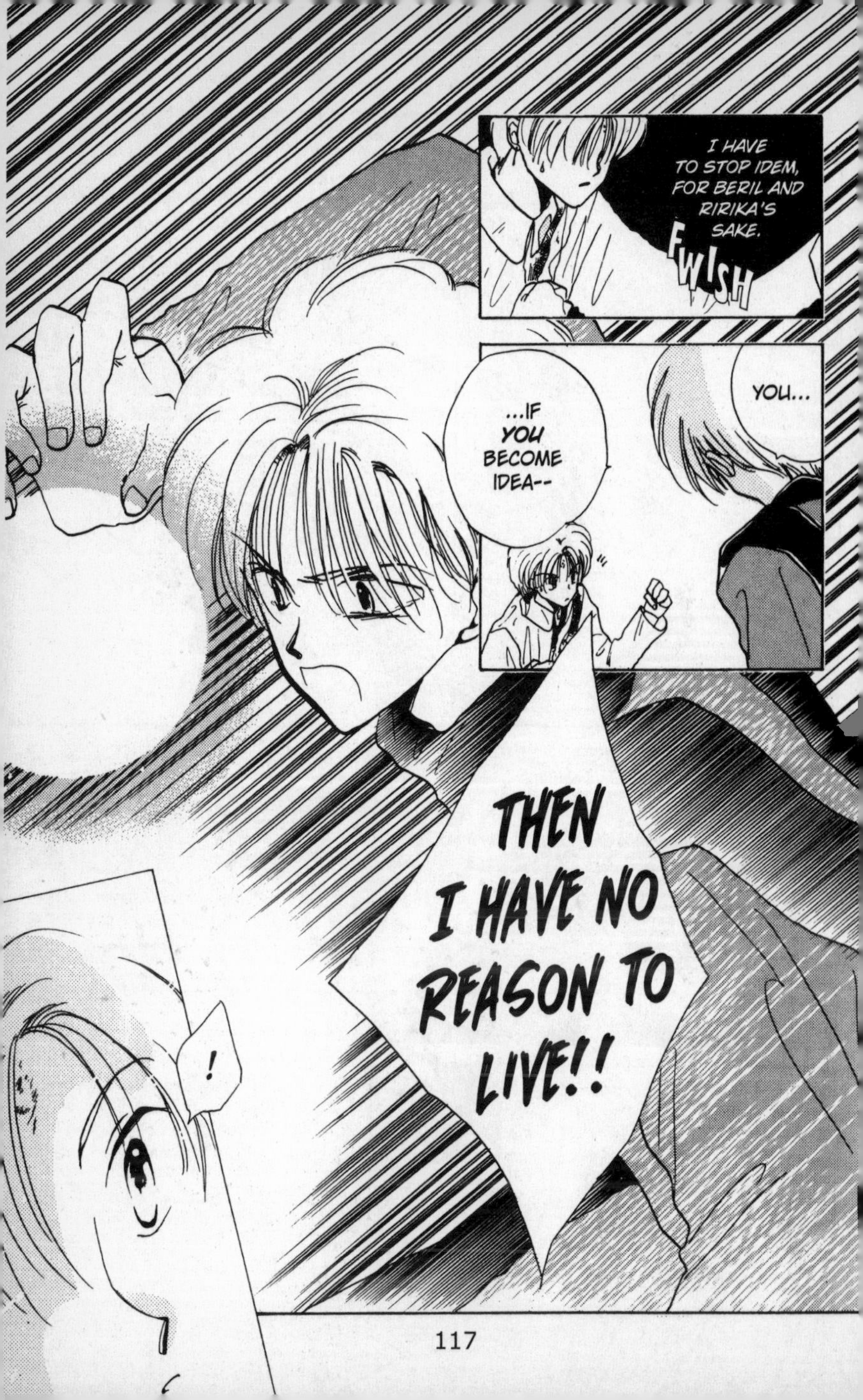
I HAVE TO STOP IDEM, FOR BERIL AND RIRIKA'S SAKE.
FWISH
YOU...
...IF YOU BECOME IDEA--
THEN I HAVE NO REASON TO LIVE!!
!

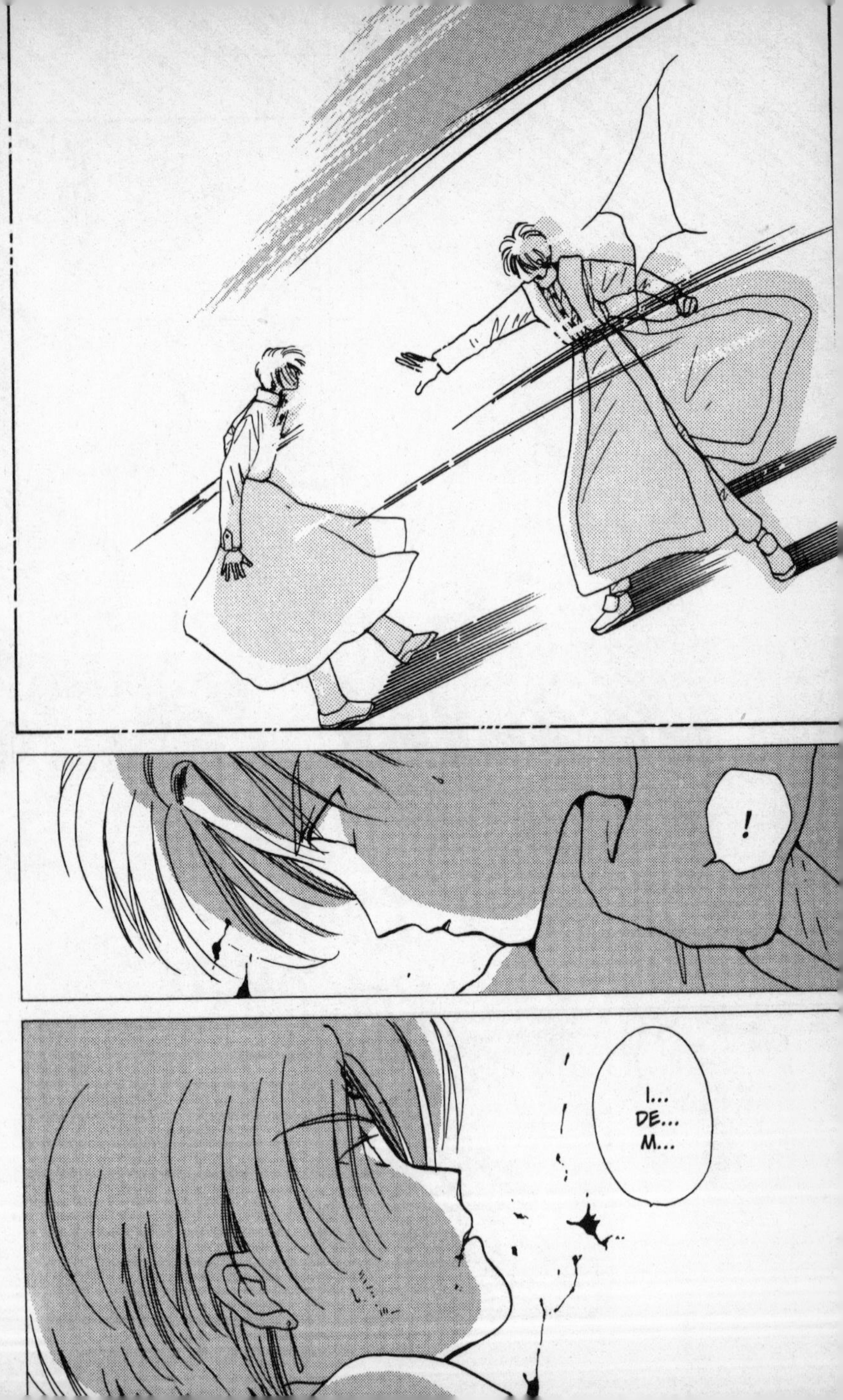
!
I... DE... M...

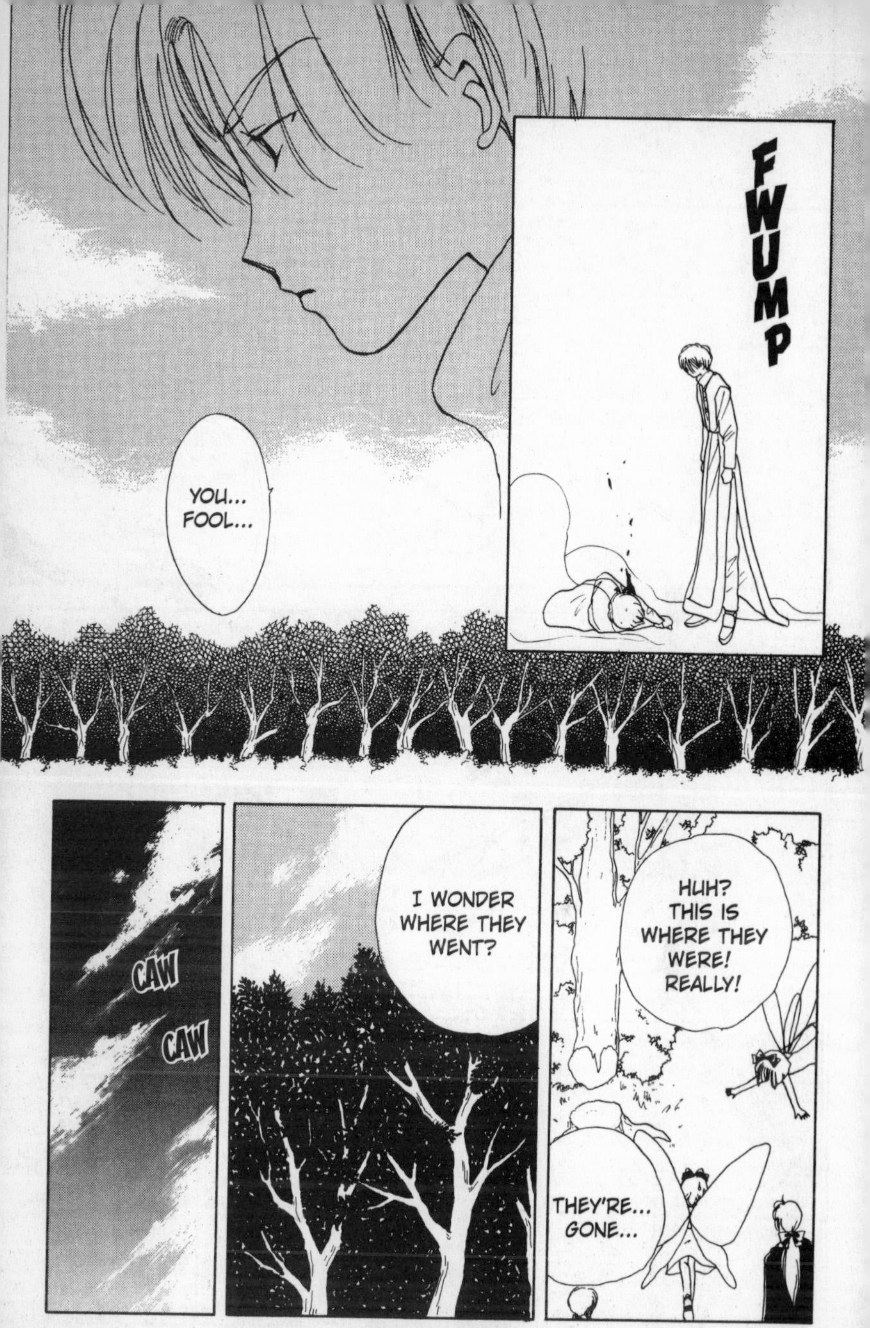
FWUMP
YOU... FOOL...
HUH? THIS IS WHERE THEY WERE! REALLY!
THEY'RE... GONE...
I WONDER WHERE THEY WENT?
CAW
CAW

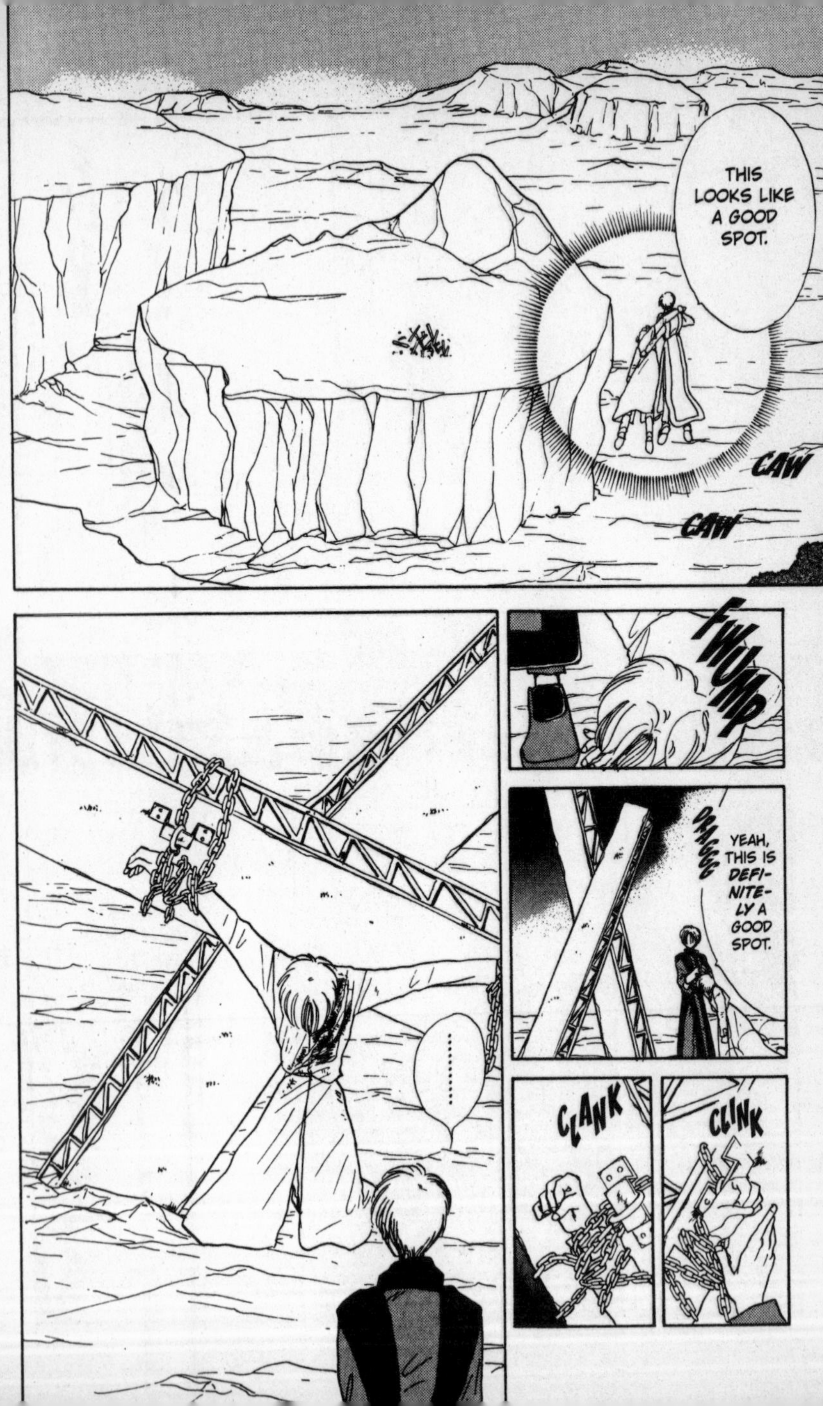
THIS LOOKS LIKE A GOOD SPOT.
CAW
CAW
FWUMP
DRAGGG
YEAH, THIS IS *DEFINITELY* A GOOD SPOT.
CLINK
CLANK
......

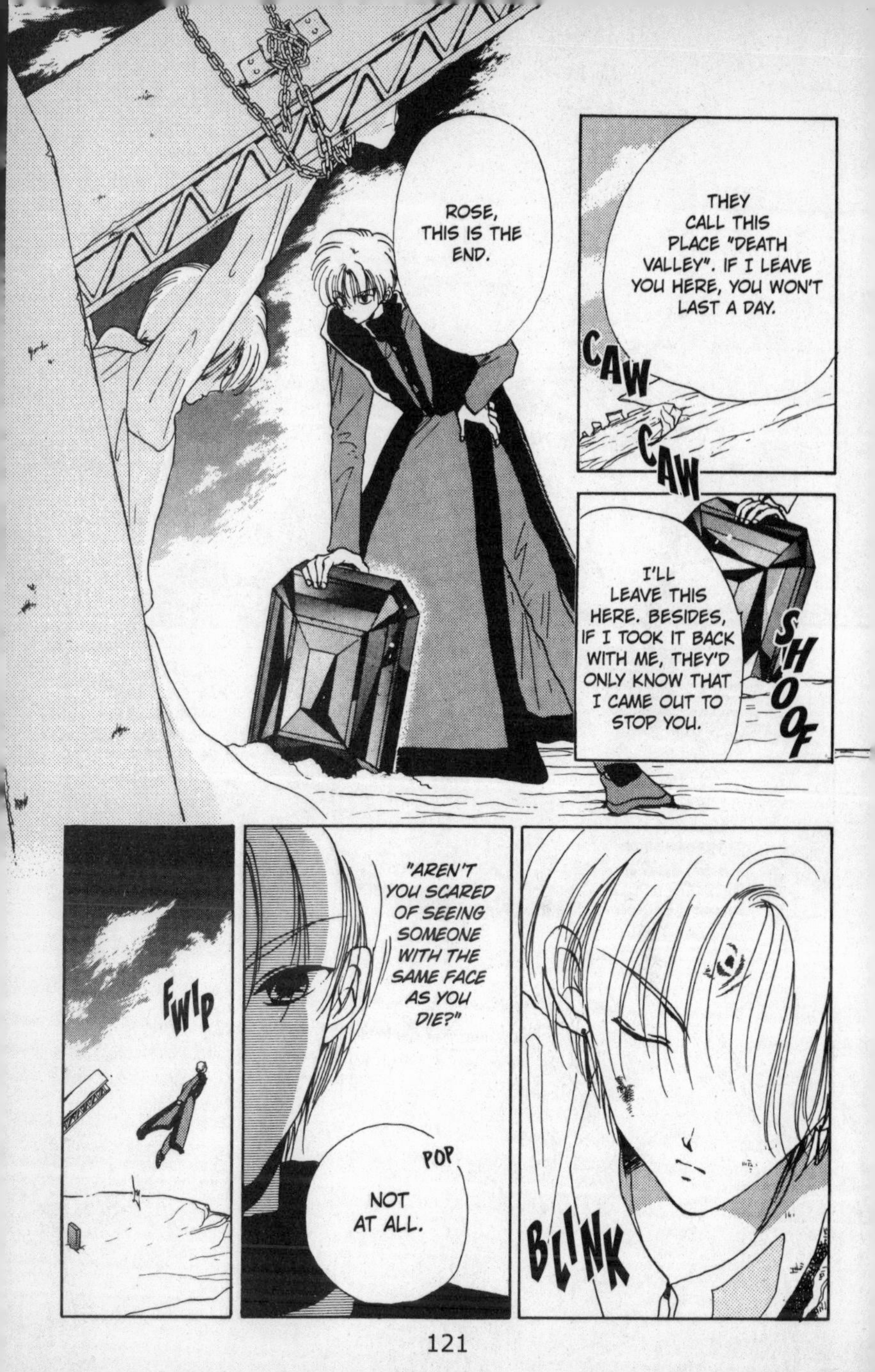
THEY CALL THIS PLACE "DEATH VALLEY". IF I LEAVE YOU HERE, YOU WON'T LAST A DAY.
CAW
CAW
I'LL LEAVE THIS HERE. BESIDES, IF I TOOK IT BACK WITH ME, THEY'D ONLY KNOW THAT I CAME OUT TO STOP YOU.
SHOOF
ROSE, THIS IS THE END.
BLINK
"AREN'T YOU SCARED OF SEEING SOMEONE WITH THE SAME FACE AS YOU DIE?"
POP
NOT AT ALL.
FWIP

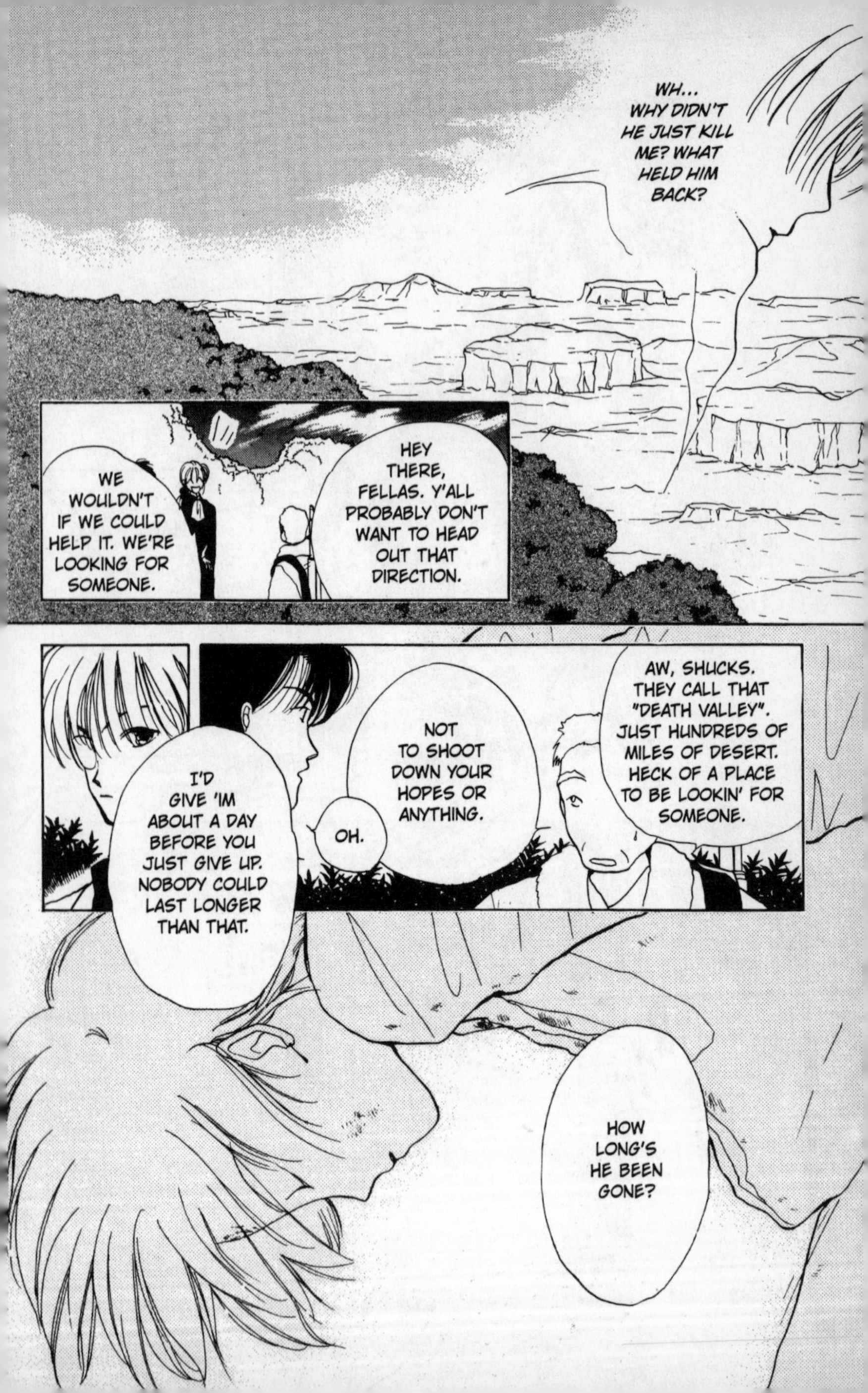
WH... WHY DIDN'T HE JUST KILL ME? WHAT HELD HIM BACK?
HEY THERE, FELLAS. Y'ALL PROBABLY DON'T WANT TO HEAD OUT THAT DIRECTION.
WE WOULDN'T IF WE COULD HELP IT. WE'RE LOOKING FOR SOMEONE.
AW, SHUCKS. THEY CALL THAT "DEATH VALLEY". JUST HUNDREDS OF MILES OF DESERT. HECK OF A PLACE TO BE LOOKIN' FOR SOMEONE.
NOT TO SHOOT DOWN YOUR HOPES OR ANYTHING.
OH.
I'D GIVE 'IM ABOUT A DAY BEFORE YOU JUST GIVE UP. NOBODY COULD LAST LONGER THAN THAT.
HOW LONG'S HE BEEN GONE?

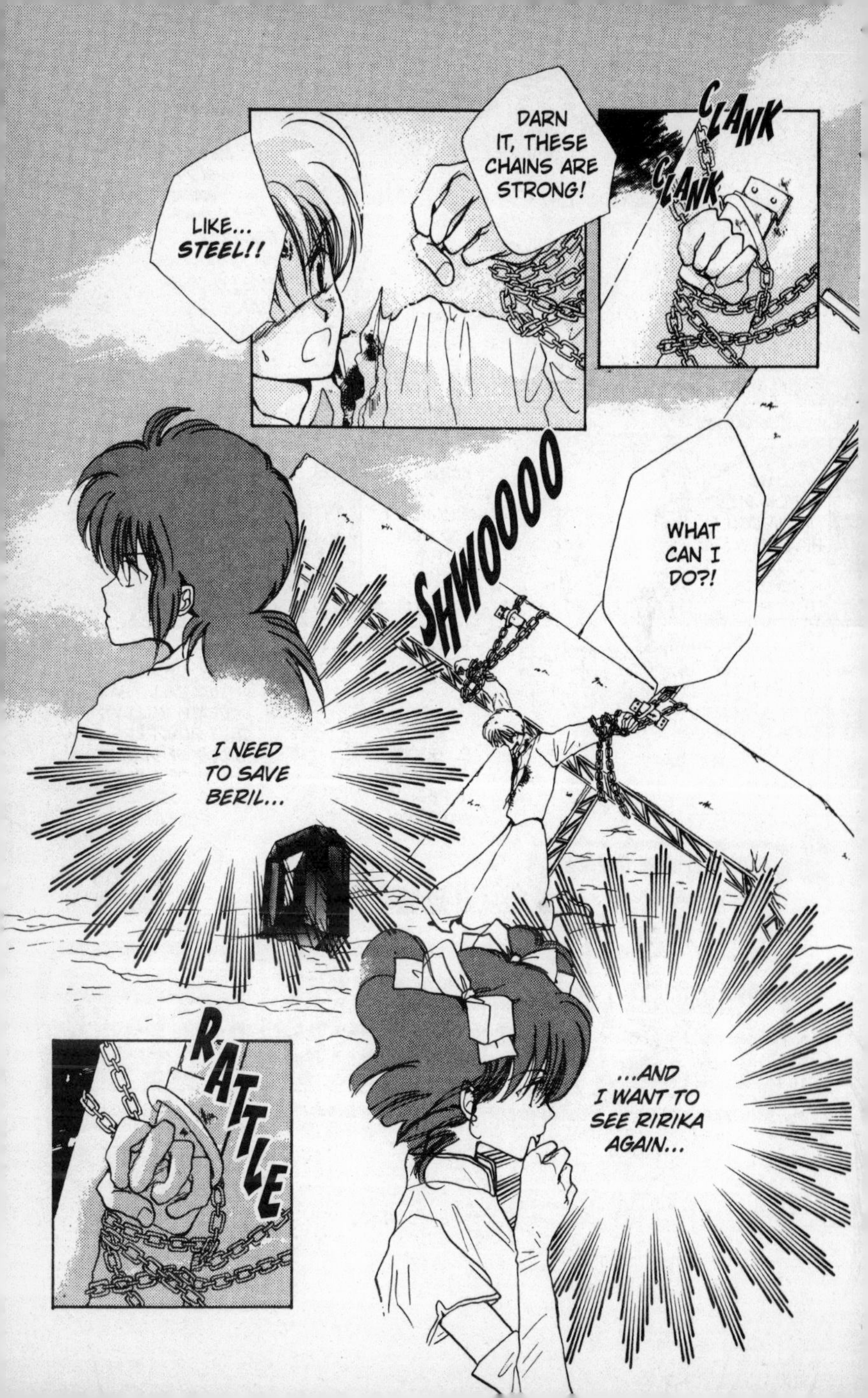
CLANK
CLANK
DARN IT, THESE CHAINS ARE STRONG!
LIKE... STEEL!!
WHAT CAN I DO?!
SHWOOOO
I NEED TO SAVE BERIL...
...AND I WANT TO SEE RIRIKA AGAIN...
RATTLE

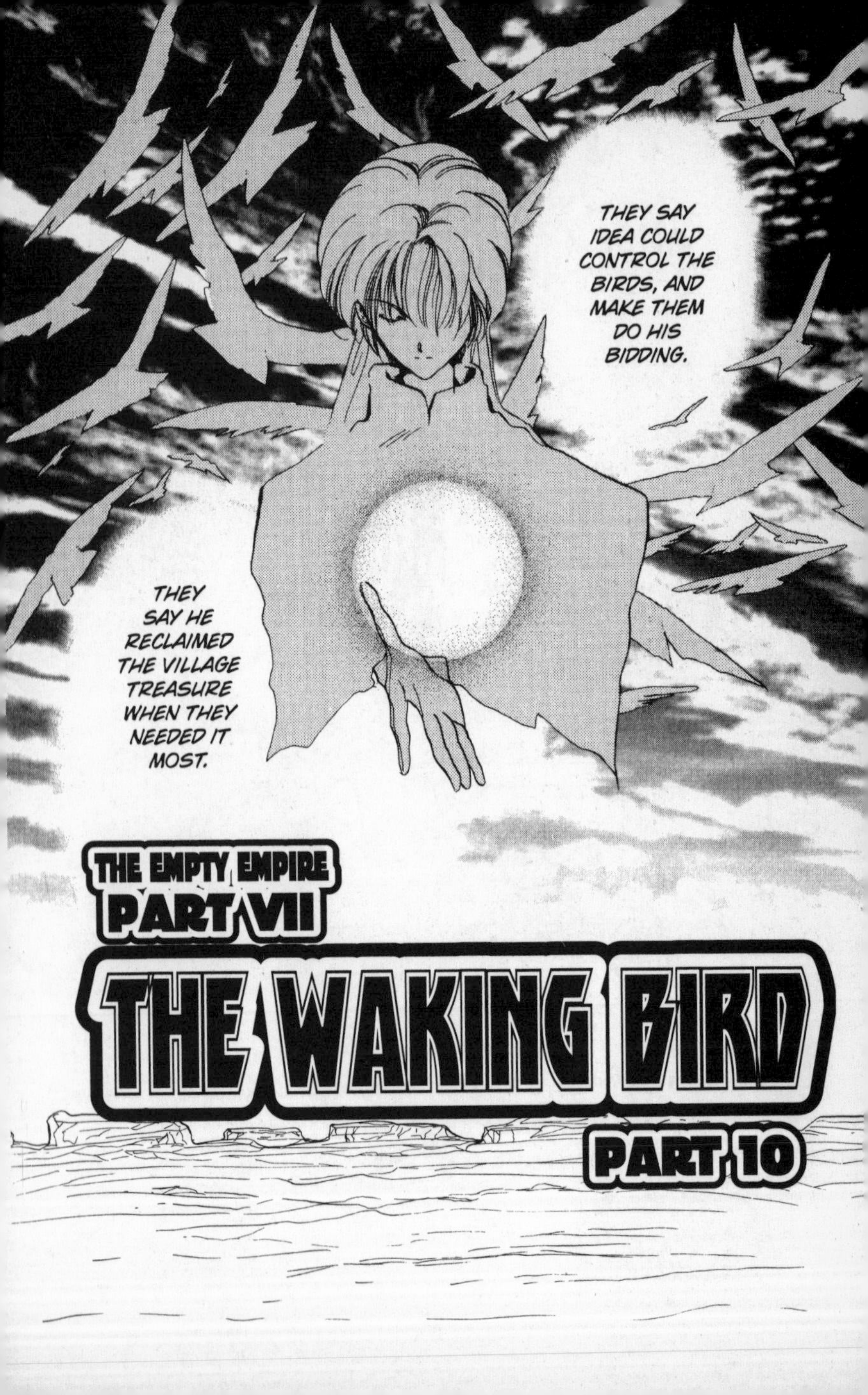

THEY SAY IDEA COULD CONTROL THE BIRDS, AND MAKE THEM DO HIS BIDDING.
THEY SAY HE RECLAIMED THE VILLAGE TREASURE WHEN THEY NEEDED IT MOST.
THE EMPTY EMPIRE PART VII
THE WAKING BIRD
PART 10

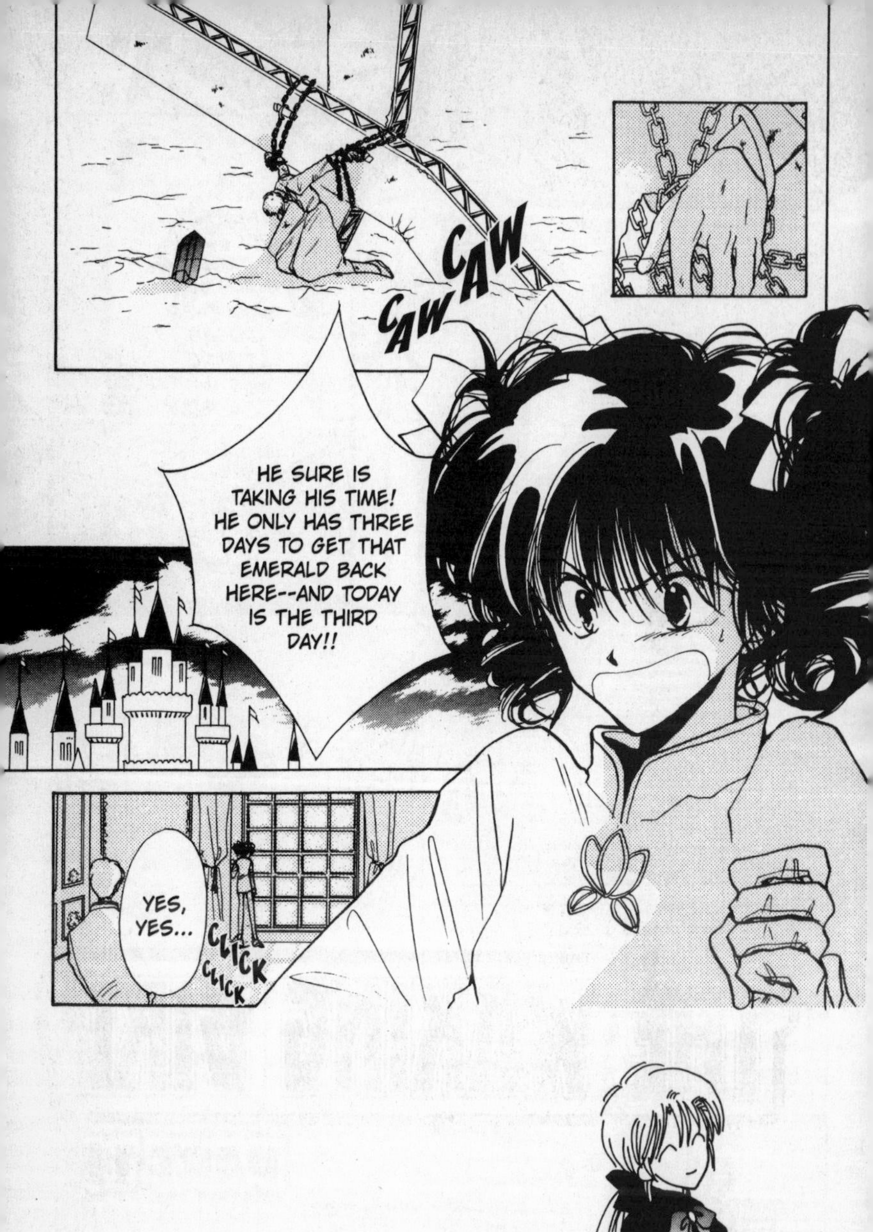
CAW CAW
CAW
HE SURE IS TAKING HIS TIME! HE ONLY HAS THREE DAYS TO GET THAT EMERALD BACK HERE--AND TODAY IS THE THIRD DAY!!
YES, YES...
CLICK CLICK

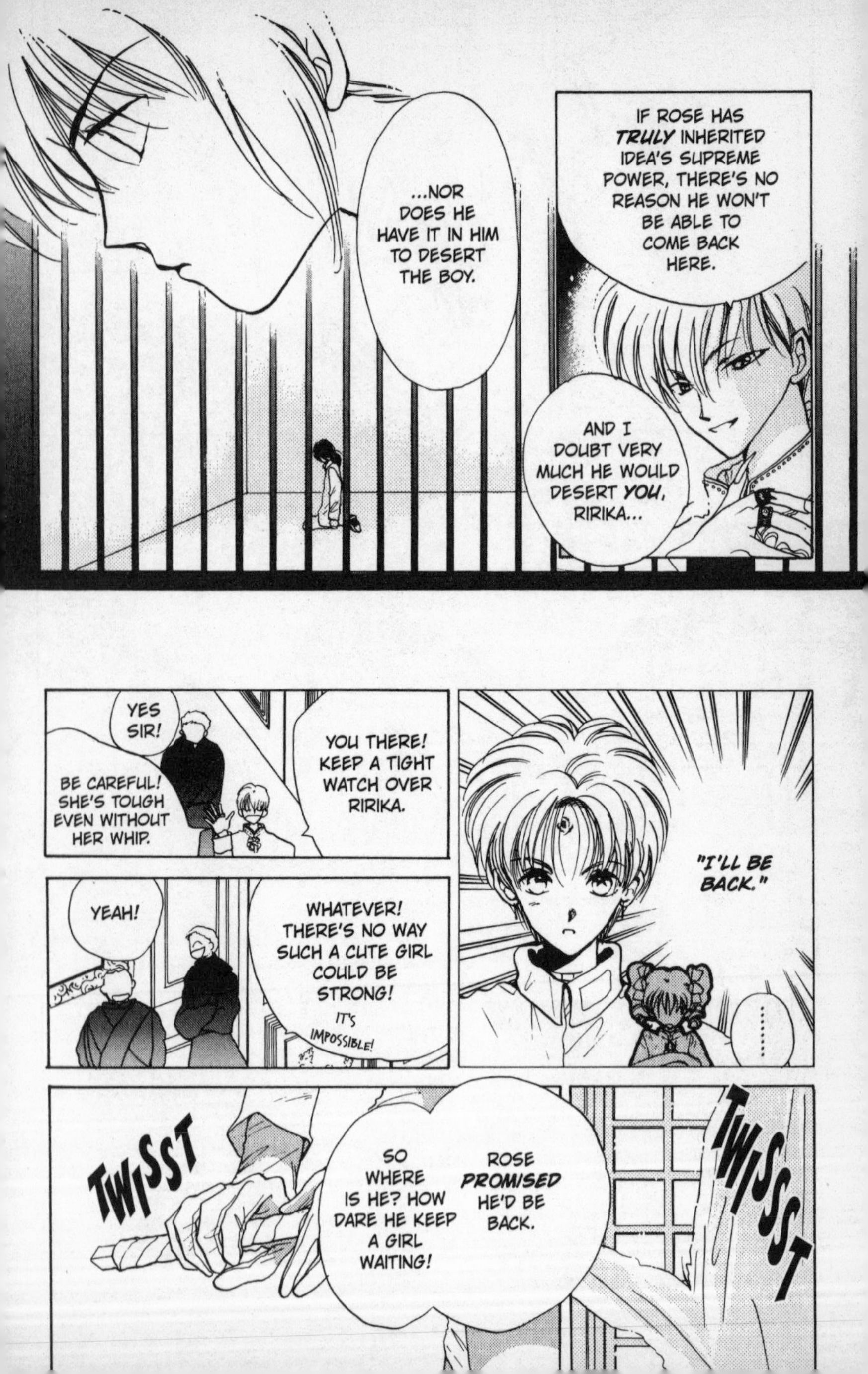
...NOR DOES HE HAVE IT IN HIM TO DESERT THE BOY.
IF ROSE HAS TRULY INHERITED IDEA'S SUPREME POWER, THERE'S NO REASON HE WON'T BE ABLE TO COME BACK HERE.
AND I DOUBT VERY MUCH HE WOULD DESERT YOU, RIRIKA...
"I'LL BE BACK."
......
YOU THERE! KEEP A TIGHT WATCH OVER RIRIKA.
YES SIR!
BE CAREFUL! SHE'S TOUGH EVEN WITHOUT HER WHIP.
WHATEVER! THERE'S NO WAY SUCH A CUTE GIRL COULD BE STRONG!
IT'S IMPOSSIBLE!
YEAH!
TWISSST
ROSE PROMISED HE'D BE BACK.
SO WHERE IS HE? HOW DARE HE KEEP A GIRL WAITING!
TWISST

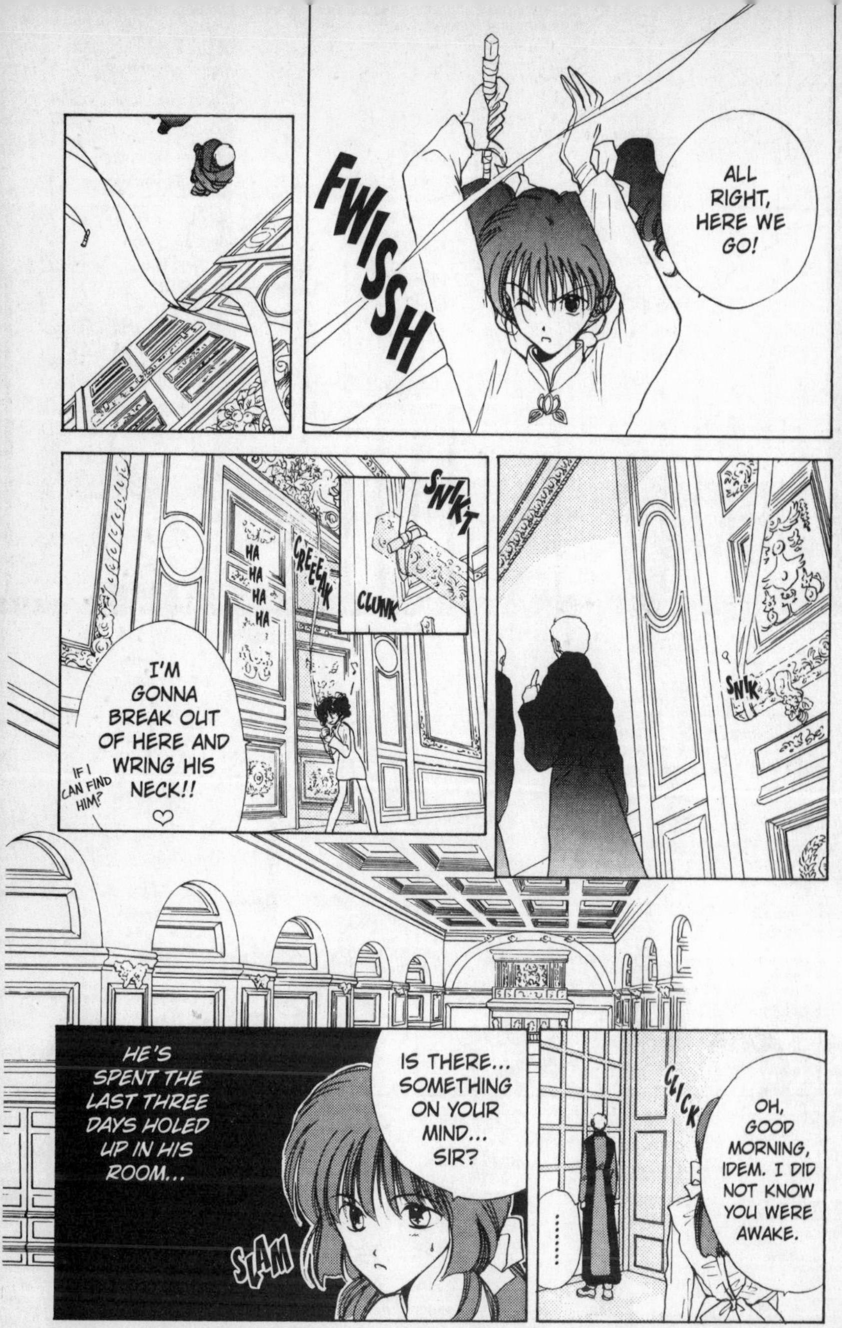
ALL RIGHT, HERE WE GO!
FWISSH
SNIK
SNIKT
CLUNK
CREEEAK
HA HA HA HA
I'M GONNA BREAK OUT OF HERE AND WRING HIS NECK!! ♡
IF I CAN FIND HIM?
CLICK
OH, GOOD MORNING, IDEM. I DID NOT KNOW YOU WERE AWAKE.
......
IS THERE... SOMETHING ON YOUR MIND... SIR?
HE'S SPENT THE LAST THREE DAYS HOLED UP IN HIS ROOM...
SLAM

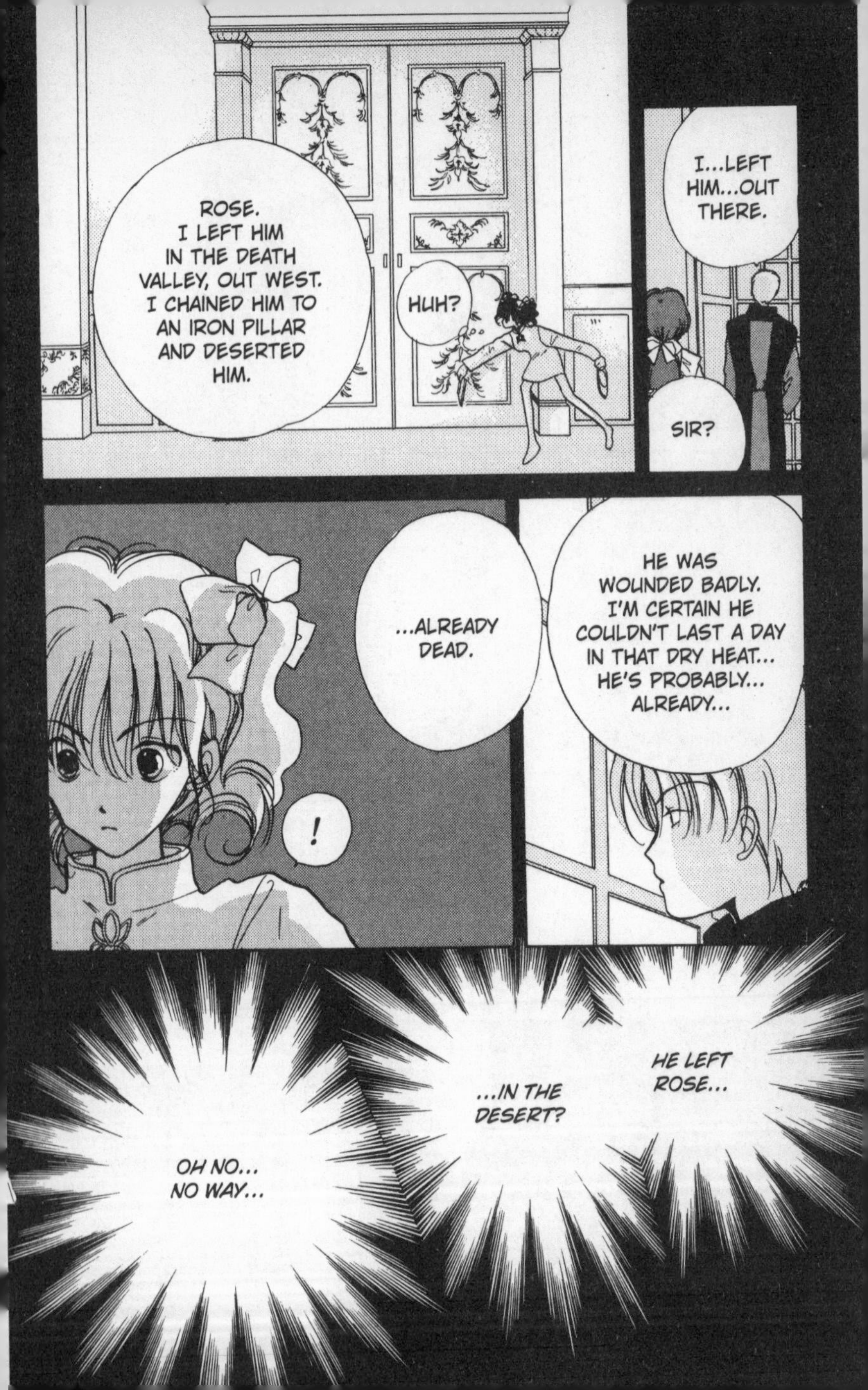
I...LEFT HIM...OUT THERE.
SIR?
ROSE. I LEFT HIM IN THE DEATH VALLEY, OUT WEST. I CHAINED HIM TO AN IRON PILLAR AND DESERTED HIM.
HUH?
HE WAS WOUNDED BADLY. I'M CERTAIN HE COULDN'T LAST A DAY IN THAT DRY HEAT... HE'S PROBABLY... ALREADY...
...ALREADY DEAD.
!
HE LEFT ROSE...
...IN THE DESERT?
OH NO... NO WAY...

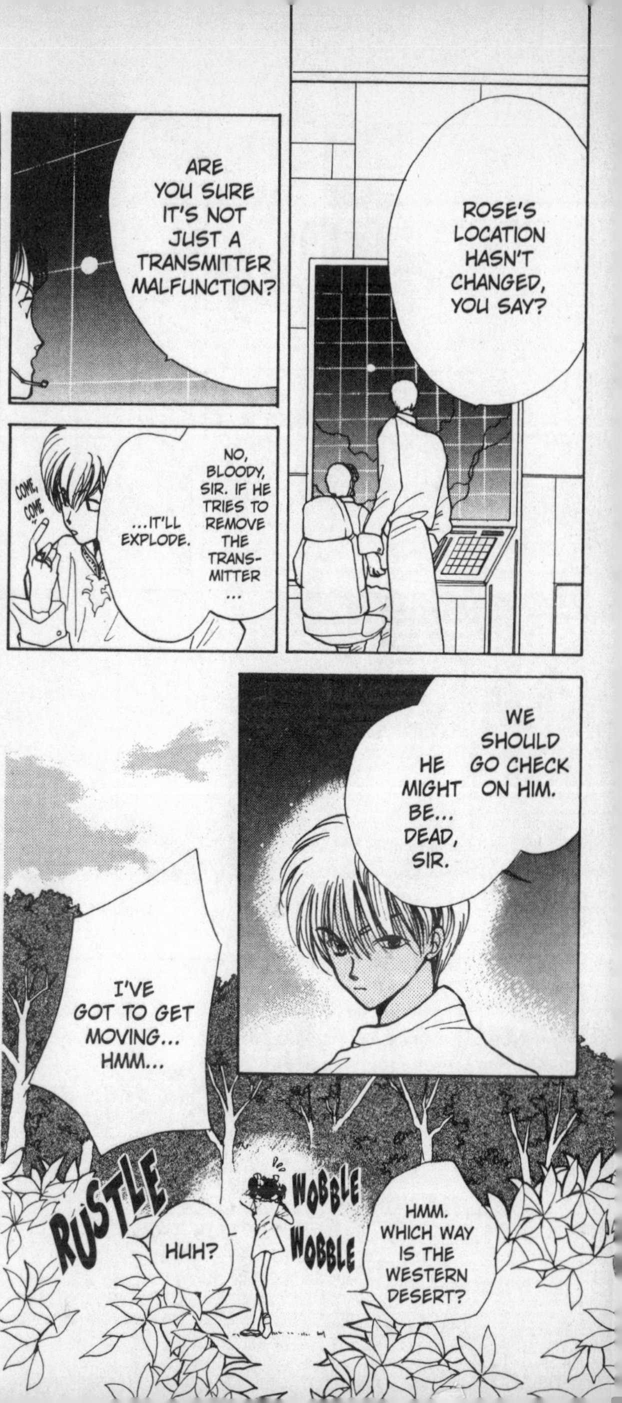
ROSE'S LOCATION HASN'T CHANGED, YOU SAY?
ARE YOU SURE IT'S NOT JUST A TRANSMITTER MALFUNCTION?
NO, BLOODY, SIR. IF HE TRIES TO REMOVE THE TRANSMITTER...
...IT'LL EXPLODE.
COME, COME
WE SHOULD GO CHECK ON HIM.
HE MIGHT BE... DEAD, SIR.
I'VE GOT TO GET MOVING... HMM...
HMM. WHICH WAY IS THE WESTERN DESERT?
WOBBLE WOBBLE
HUH?
RUSTLE

IT TOOK US A TOTAL OF SIX HOURS TO GET TO NAGOYA STATION. SO I SAID TO MY FRIEND "WAIT... WE'RE STILL IN JAPAN?" IT FELT LIKE WE'D TAKEN A LONG TRIP TO SOME EXOTIC LAND, SO IT WAS KIND OF A WEIRD LITTLE DISAPPOINTMENT THAT WE WERE STILL IN JAPAN.

WELL, WE HAD PLENTY OF FUN IN NAGOYA, ONCE WE GOT OUR BEARINGS STRAIGHT. IT'S KIND OF STRANGE; WHEN WE'RE WORKING, IT FEELS SO BAD TO WASTE TIME. THOUGH BECAUSE IT WAS A VACATION, WE WERE ABLE TO ACTUALLY ENJOY BEING DELAYED ON THE TRAIN.

I LOVE THE HANDBAG I BOUGHT IN NAGOYA. IT'S ONE OF THESE PIERO GUIDI BAGS!

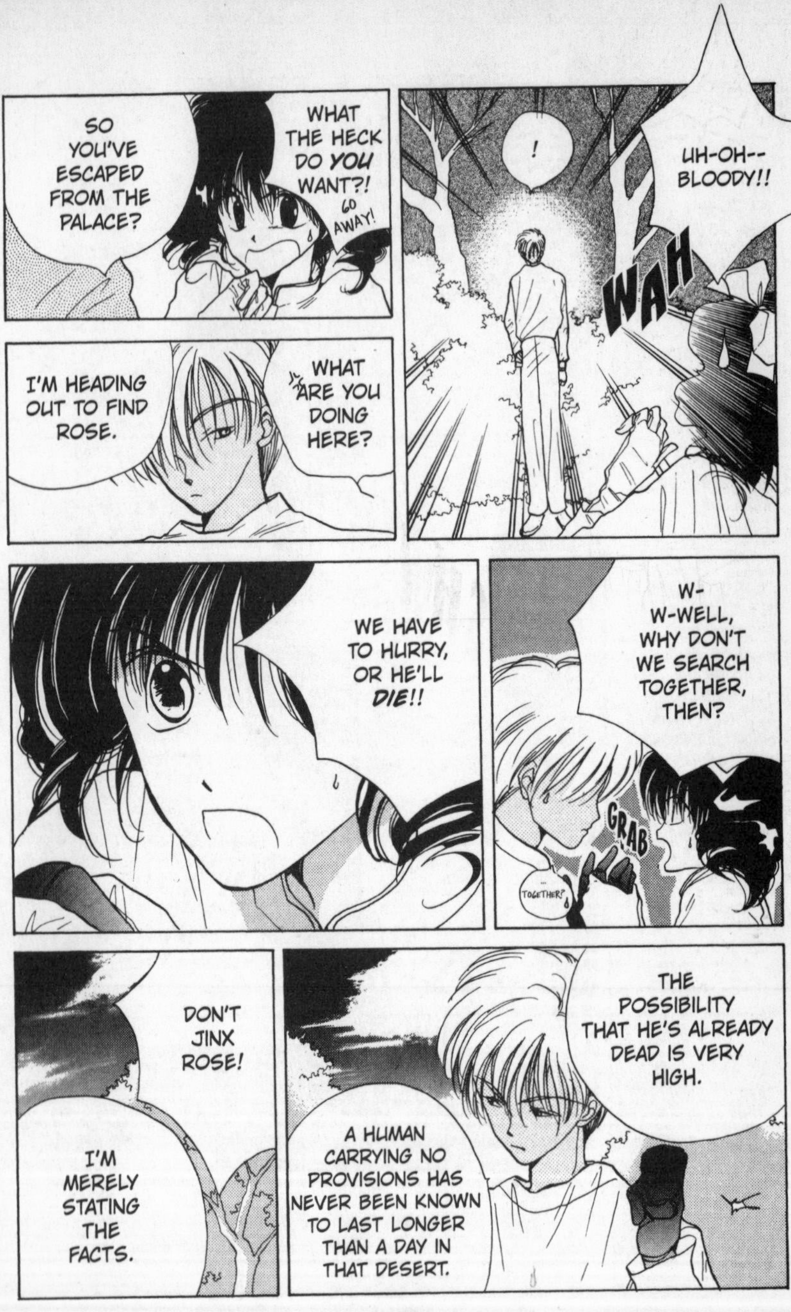
!
UH-OH-- BLOODY!!
WAH
WHAT THE HECK DO *YOU* WANT?!
GO AWAY!
SO YOU'VE ESCAPED FROM THE PALACE?
WHAT ARE YOU DOING HERE?
I'M HEADING OUT TO FIND ROSE.
W- W-WELL, WHY DON'T WE SEARCH TOGETHER, THEN?
GRAB
...TOGETHER?
WE HAVE TO HURRY, OR HE'LL *DIE*!!
THE POSSIBILITY THAT HE'S ALREADY DEAD IS VERY HIGH.
A HUMAN CARRYING NO PROVISIONS HAS NEVER BEEN KNOWN TO LAST LONGER THAN A DAY IN THAT DESERT.
DON'T JINX ROSE!
I'M MERELY STATING THE FACTS.

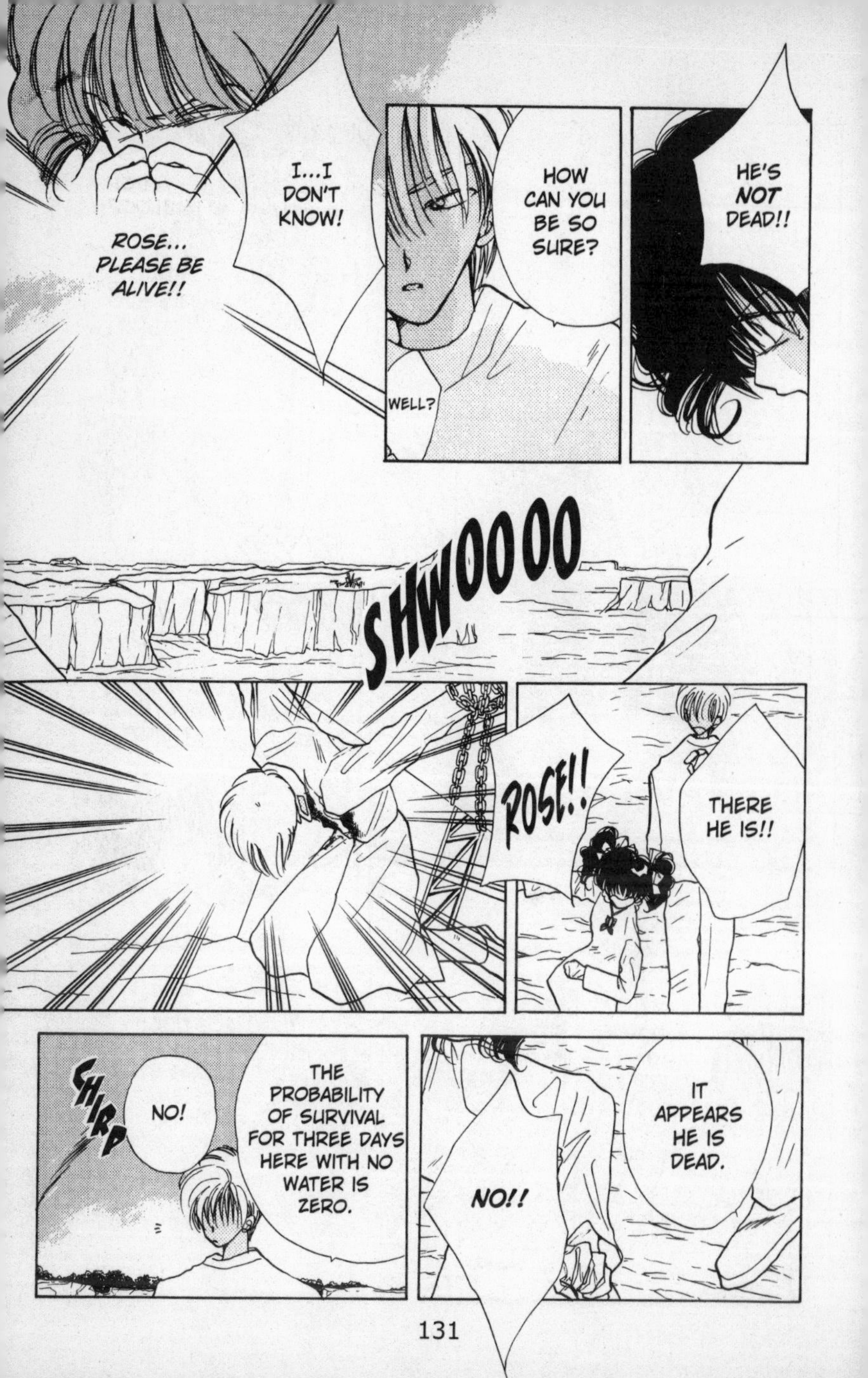
HE'S NOT DEAD!!
HOW CAN YOU BE SO SURE?
WELL?
I...I DON'T KNOW!
ROSE... PLEASE BE ALIVE!!
SHWOOOO
THERE HE IS!!
ROSE!!
IT APPEARS HE IS DEAD.
NO!!
THE PROBABILITY OF SURVIVAL FOR THREE DAYS HERE WITH NO WATER IS ZERO.
NO!
CHIRP

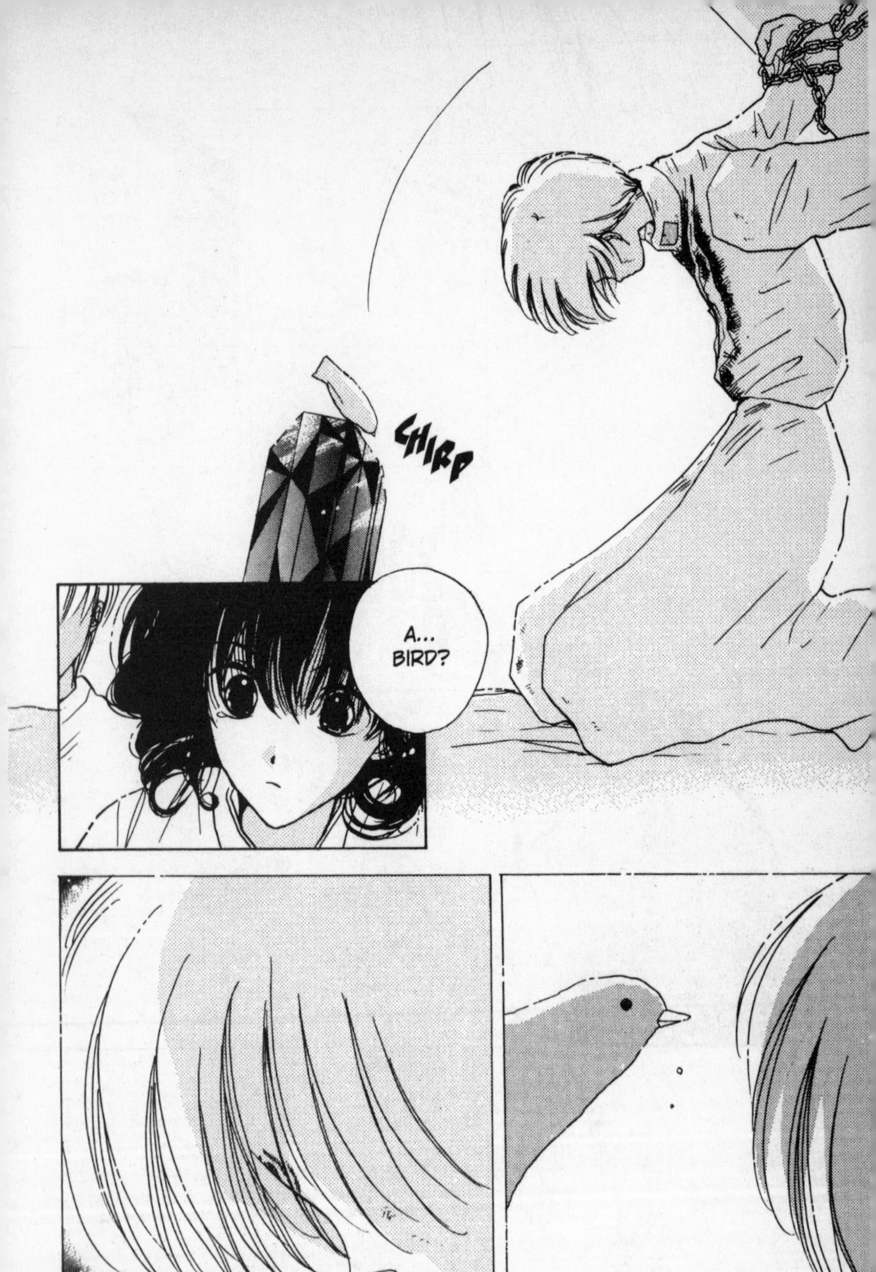
CHIRP
A... BIRD?

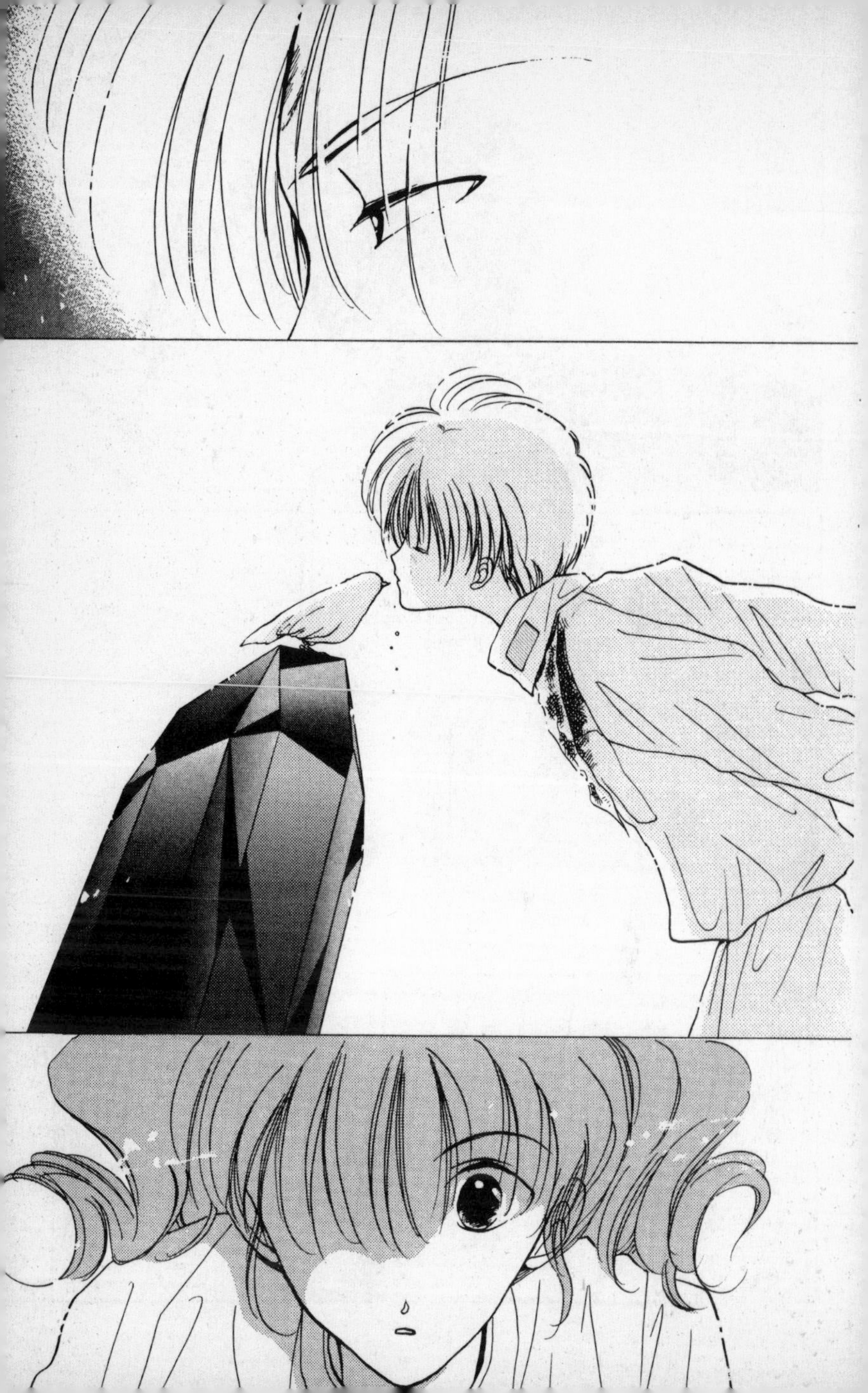

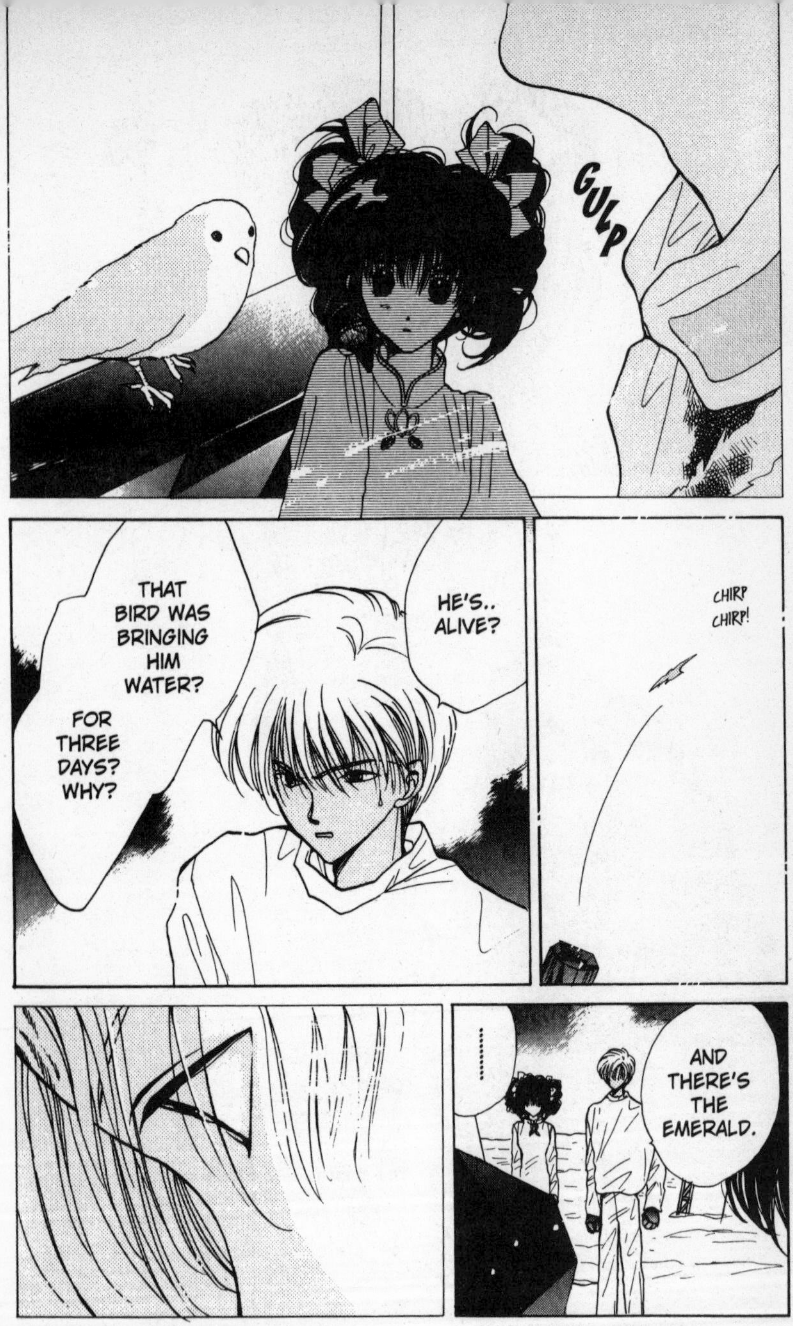
GULP
CHIRP CHIRP!
HE'S.. ALIVE?
THAT BIRD WAS BRINGING HIM WATER?
FOR THREE DAYS? WHY?
AND THERE'S THE EMERALD.
......

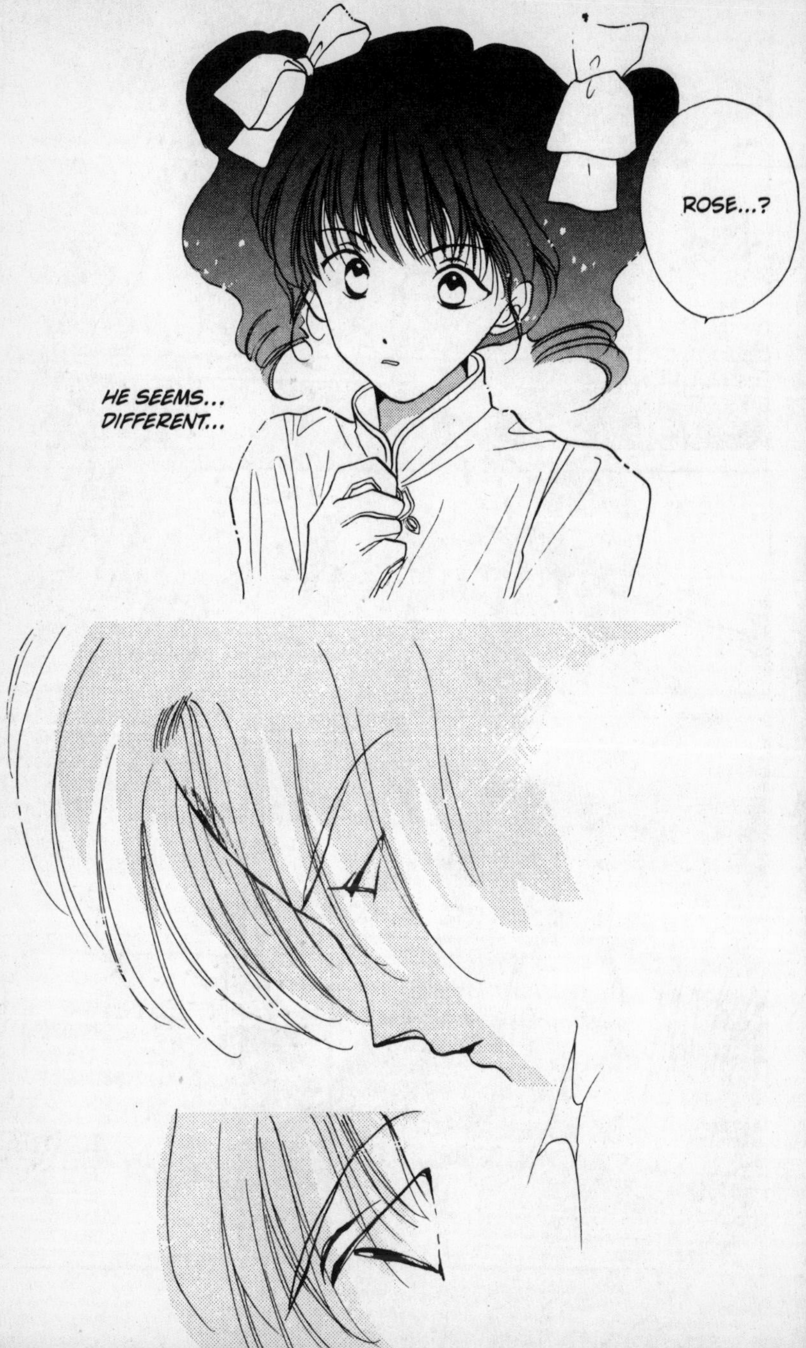
ROSE...?
HE SEEMS... DIFFERENT...

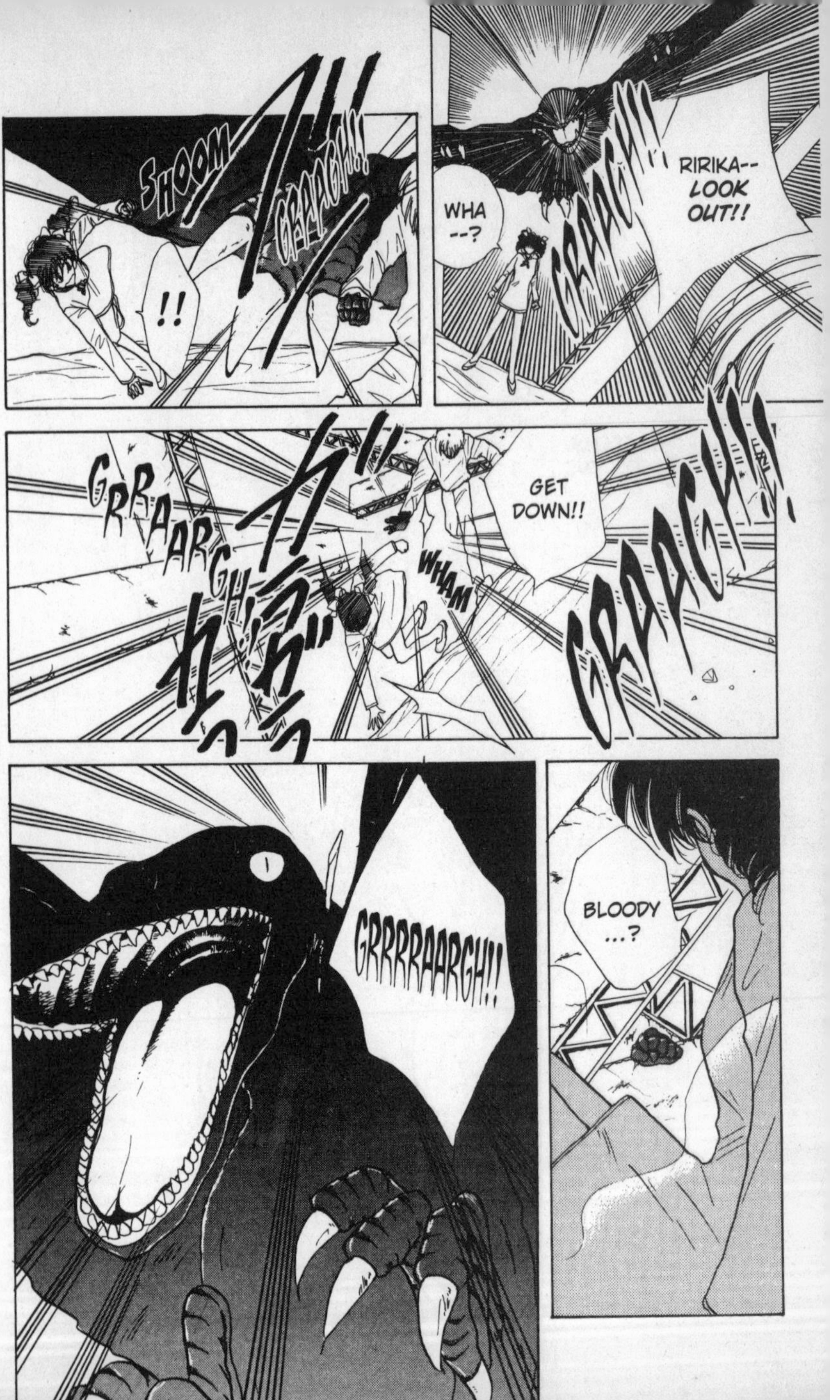
RIRIKA-- LOOK OUT!!
WHA --?
GRAAGH!!
SHOOM
GRAAGH!!
!!
GET DOWN!!
GRAAGH!!
WHAM
GRRAARGH!!
BLOODY ...?
GRRRRAARGH!!

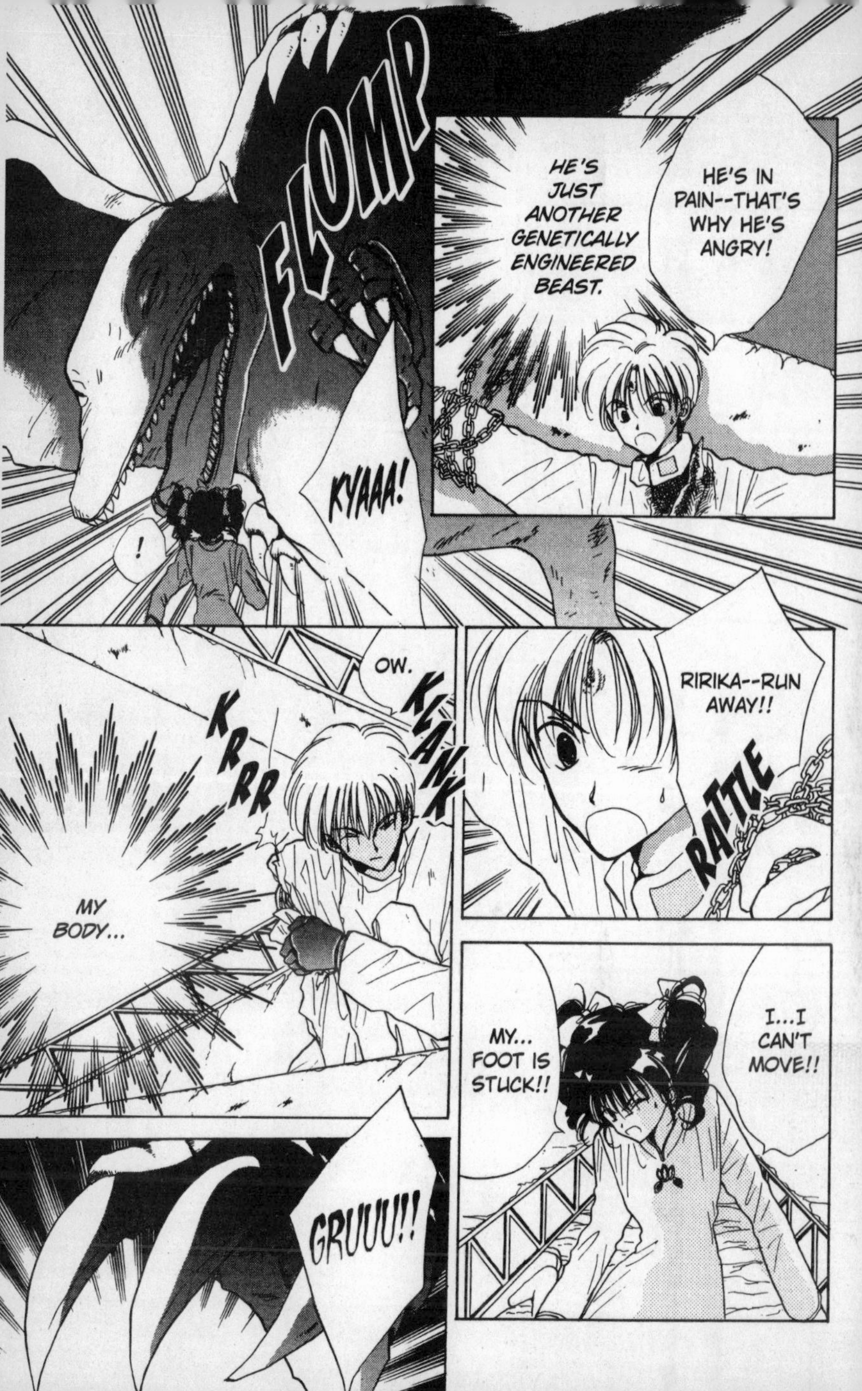
HE'S IN PAIN--THAT'S WHY HE'S ANGRY!
HE'S JUST ANOTHER GENETICALLY ENGINEERED BEAST.
FLOMP
KYAAA!
!
RIRIKA--RUN AWAY!!
RATTLE
OW.
KLANK
KRRR
MY BODY...
I...I CAN'T MOVE!!
MY... FOOT IS STUCK!!
GRUUU!!

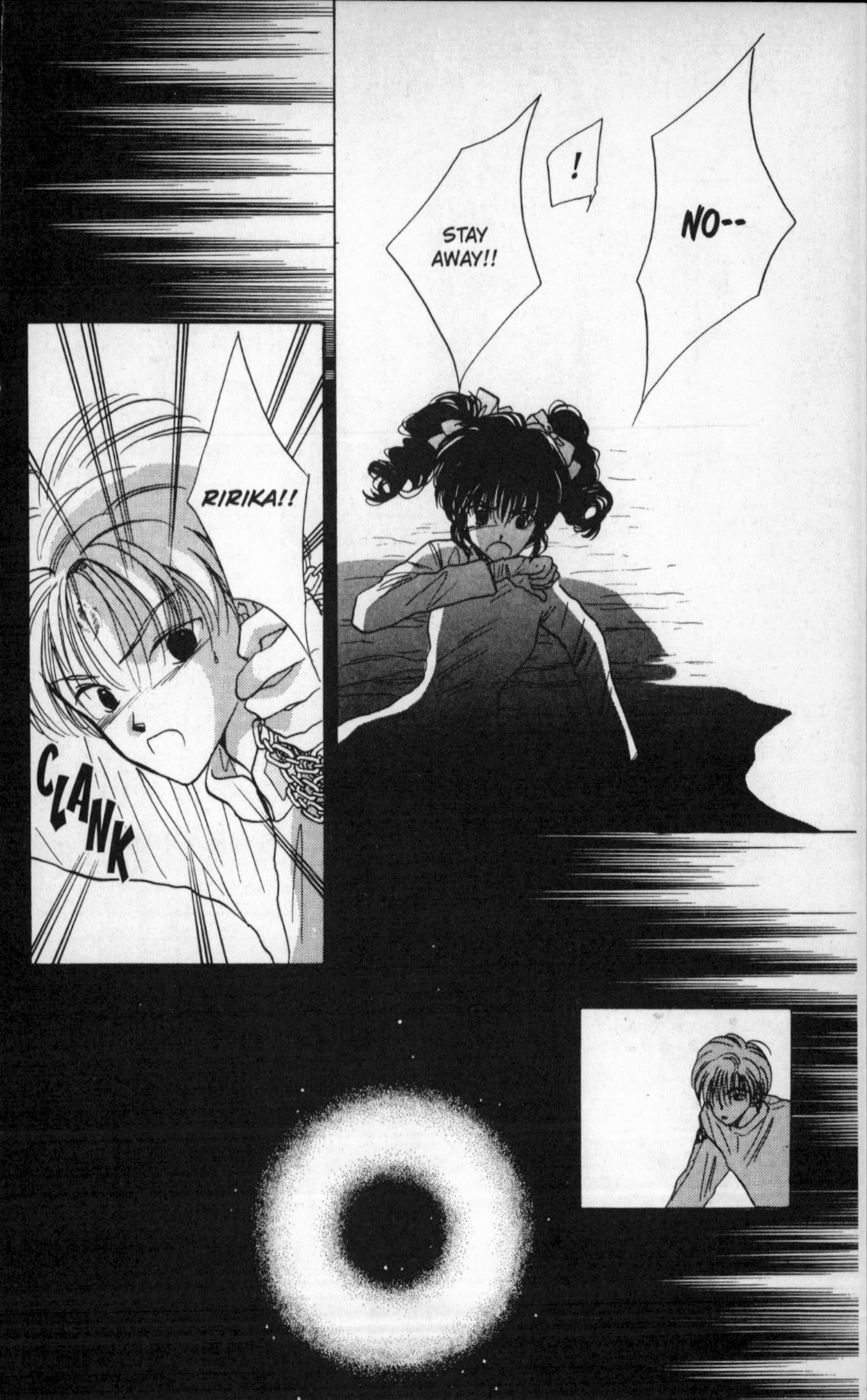
NO--
!
STAY AWAY!!
RIRIKA!!
CLANK

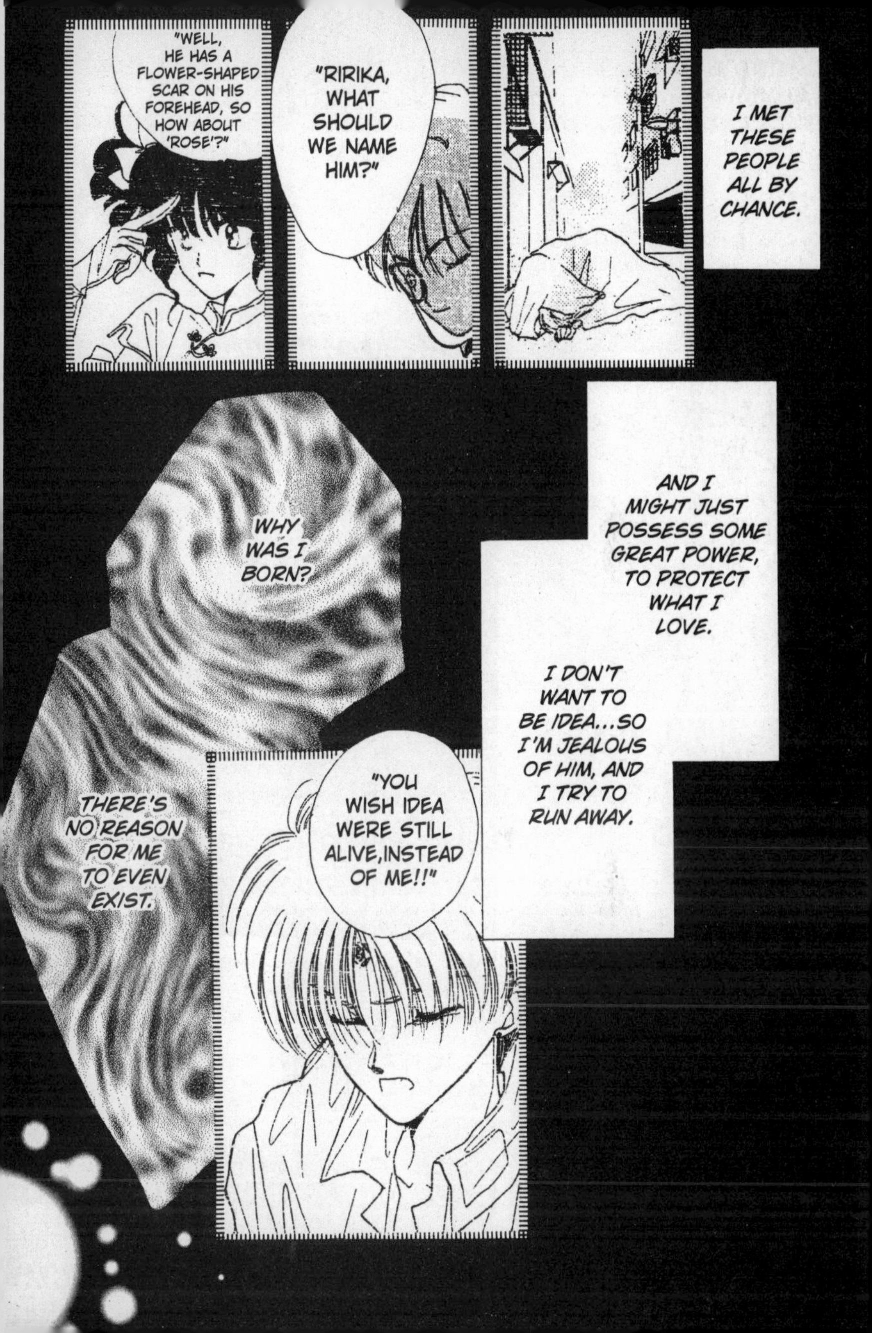
I MET THESE PEOPLE ALL BY CHANCE.
"RIRIKA, WHAT SHOULD WE NAME HIM?"
"WELL, HE HAS A FLOWER-SHAPED SCAR ON HIS FOREHEAD, SO HOW ABOUT 'ROSE'?"
AND I MIGHT JUST POSSESS SOME GREAT POWER, TO PROTECT WHAT I LOVE.
I DON'T WANT TO BE IDEA...SO I'M JEALOUS OF HIM, AND I TRY TO RUN AWAY.
WHY WAS I BORN?
"YOU WISH IDEA WERE STILL ALIVE,INSTEAD OF ME!!"
THERE'S NO REASON FOR ME TO EVEN EXIST.

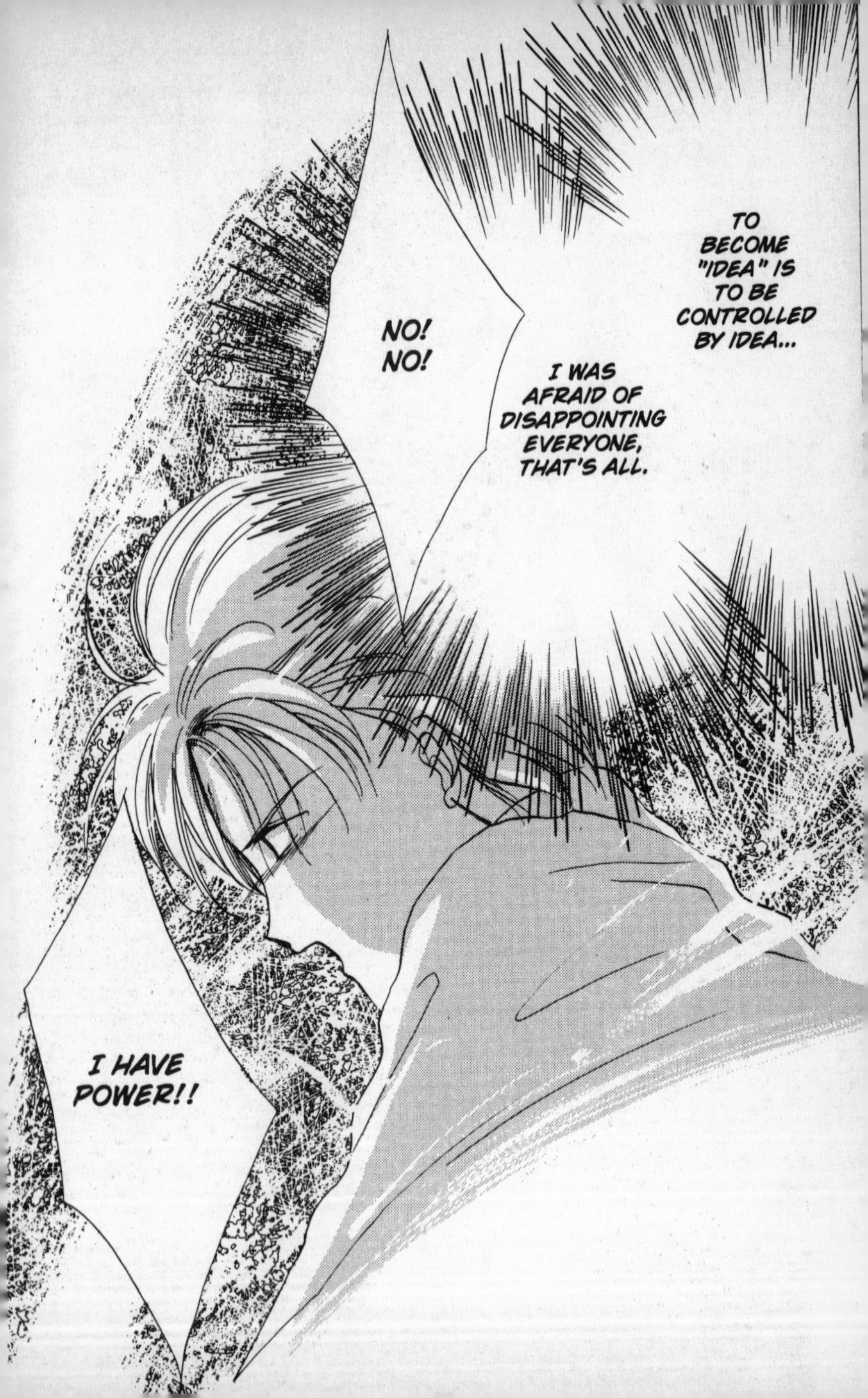
TO BECOME "IDEA" IS TO BE CONTROLLED BY IDEA...
I WAS AFRAID OF DISAPPOINTING EVERYONE, THAT'S ALL.
NO! NO!
I HAVE POWER!!

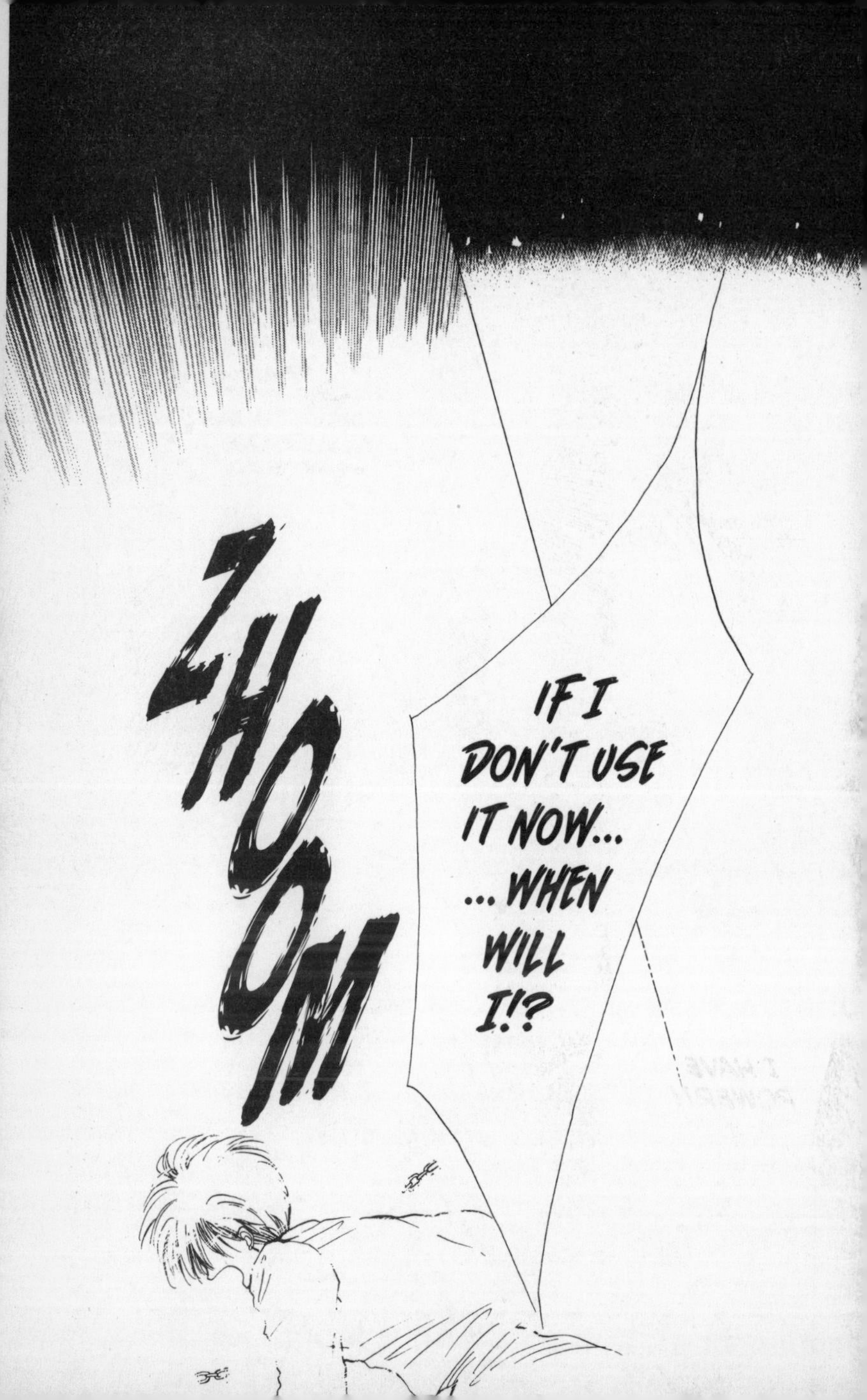
ZHOOM
IF I DON'T USE IT NOW... ...WHEN WILL I!?

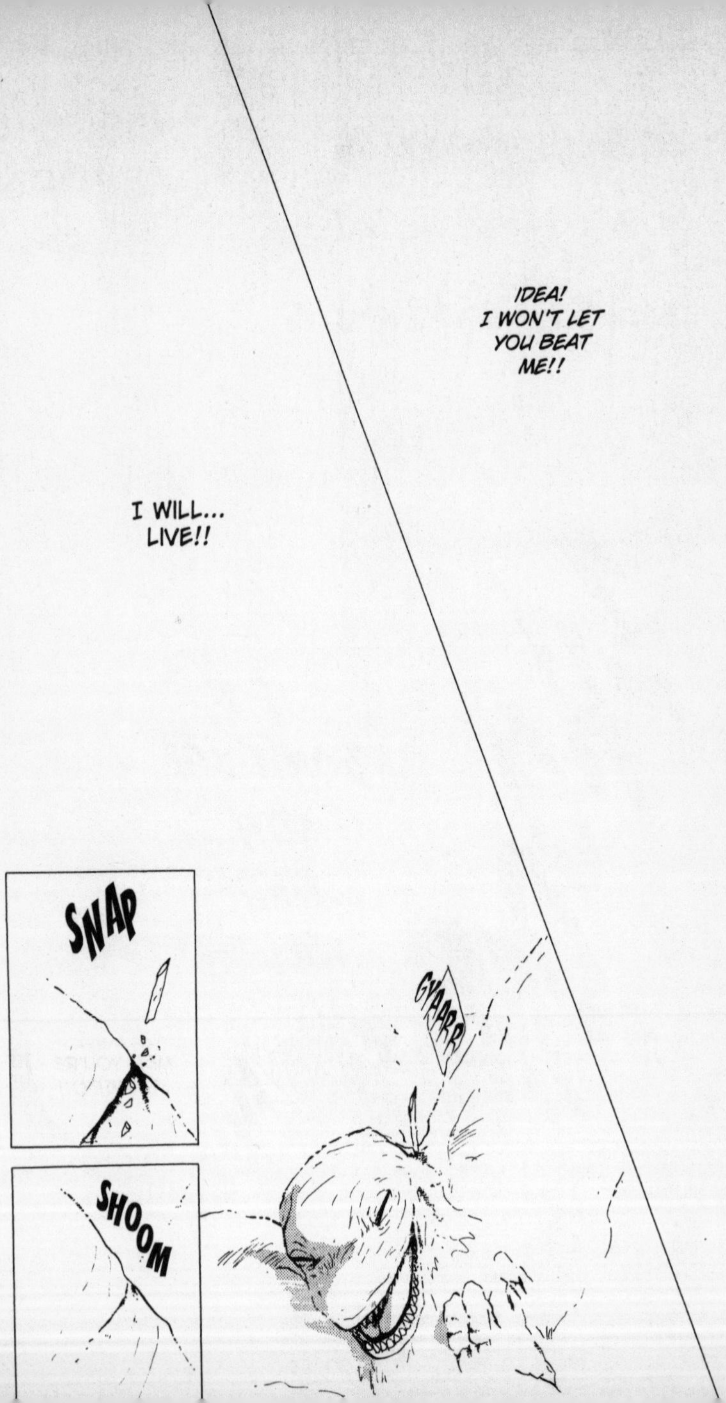
IDEA! I WON'T LET YOU BEAT ME!!
GYAARR
I WILL... LIVE!!
SNAP
SHOOM

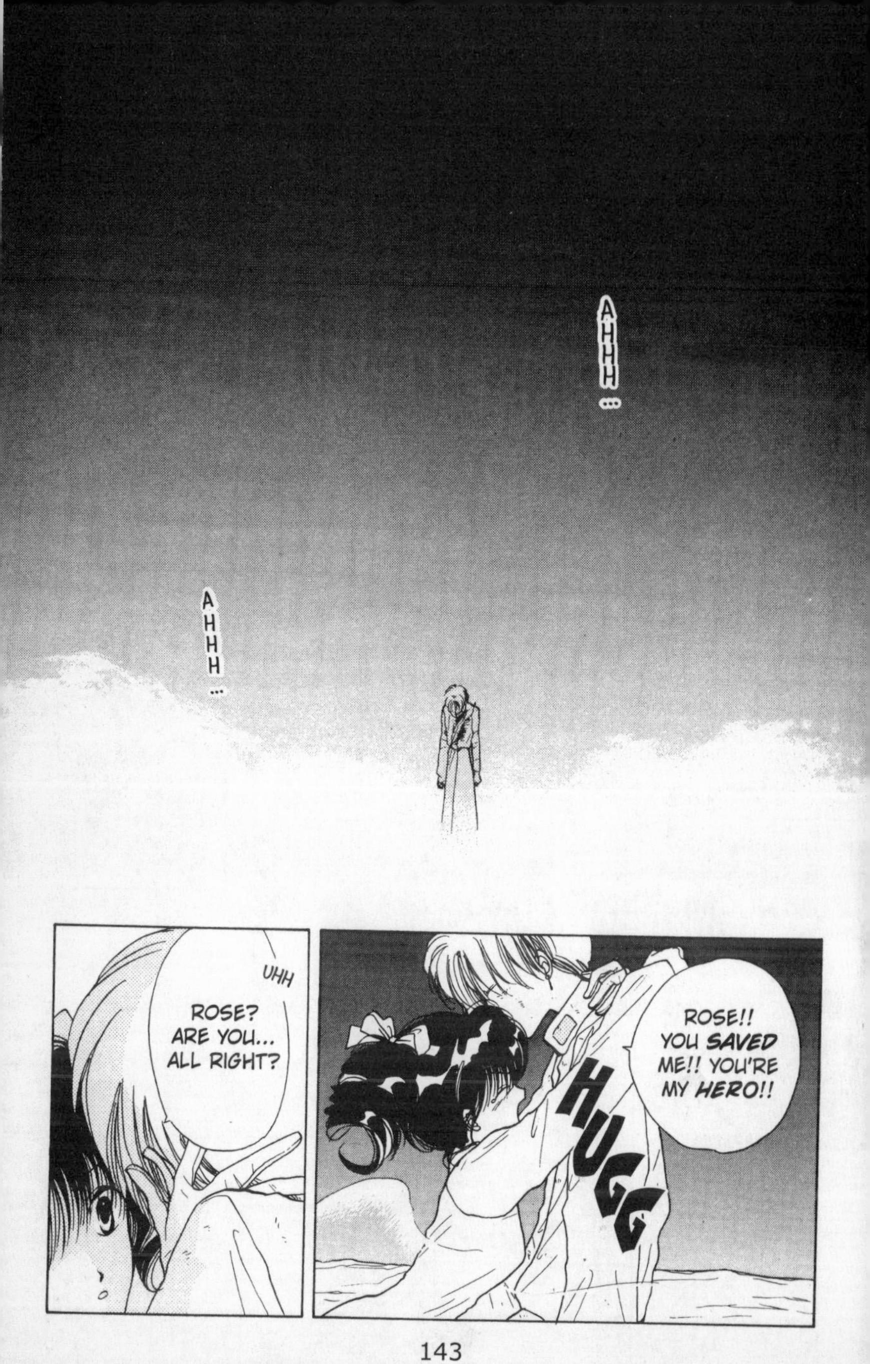
AHHHH...
AHHH...
HUGG
ROSE!! YOU *SAVED* ME!! YOU'RE MY *HERO*!!
UHH
ROSE? ARE YOU... ALL RIGHT?

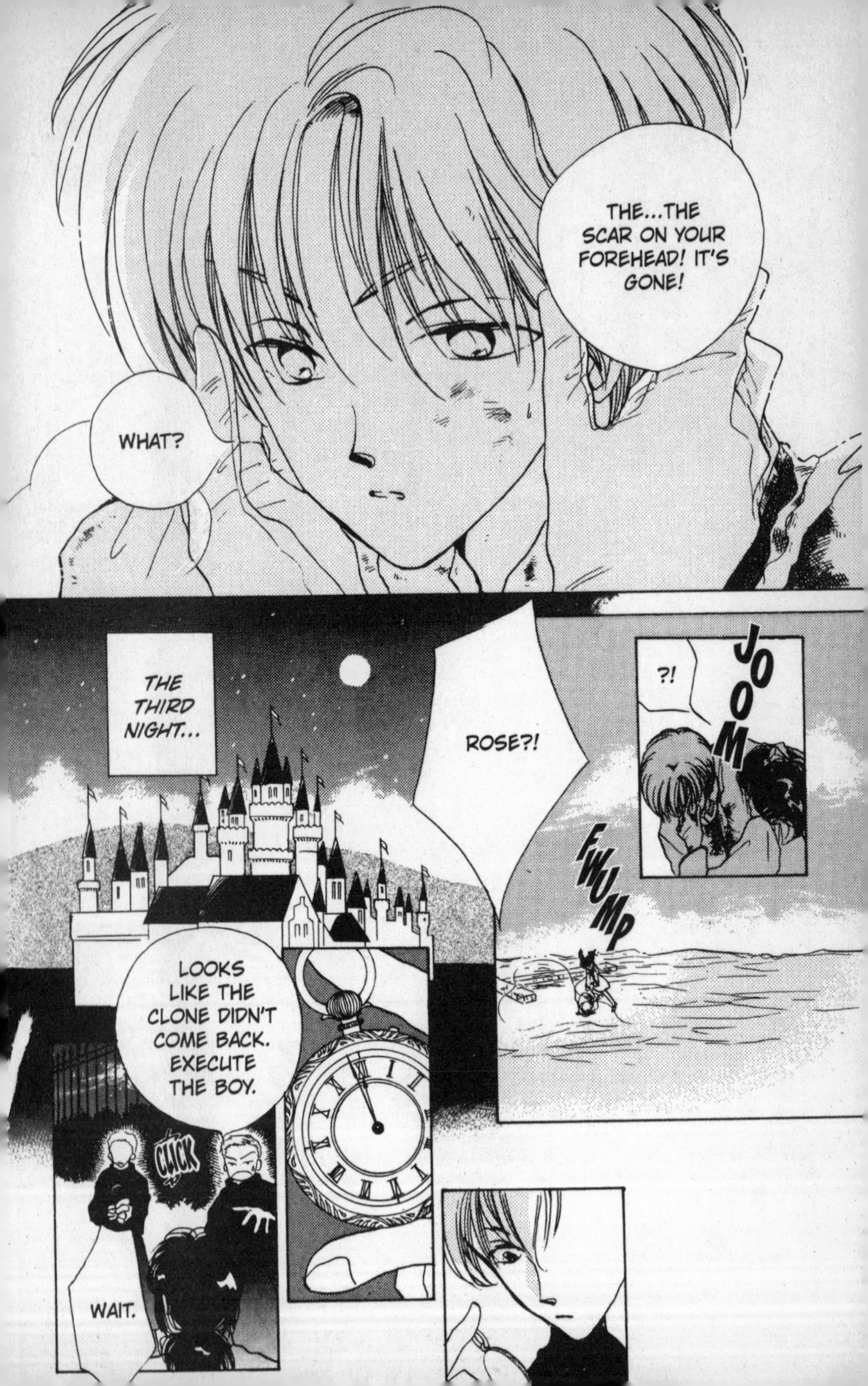
THE...THE SCAR ON YOUR FOREHEAD! IT'S GONE!
WHAT?
?!
JOOOM
ROSE?!
FWUMP
THE THIRD NIGHT...
LOOKS LIKE THE CLONE DIDN'T COME BACK. EXECUTE THE BOY.
CLICK
WAIT.

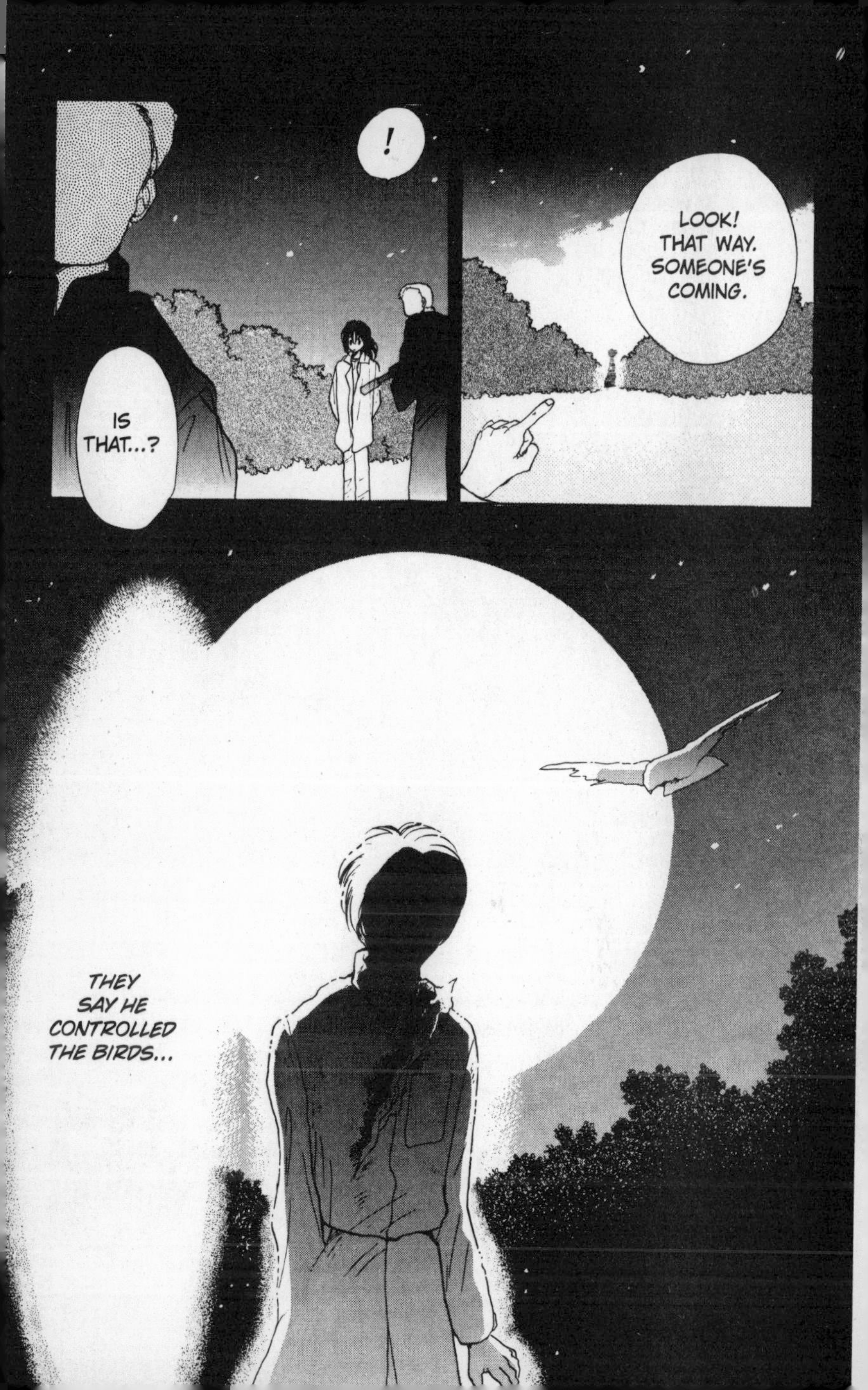
LOOK! THAT WAY. SOMEONE'S COMING.
!
IS THAT...?
THEY SAY HE CONTROLLED THE BIRDS...

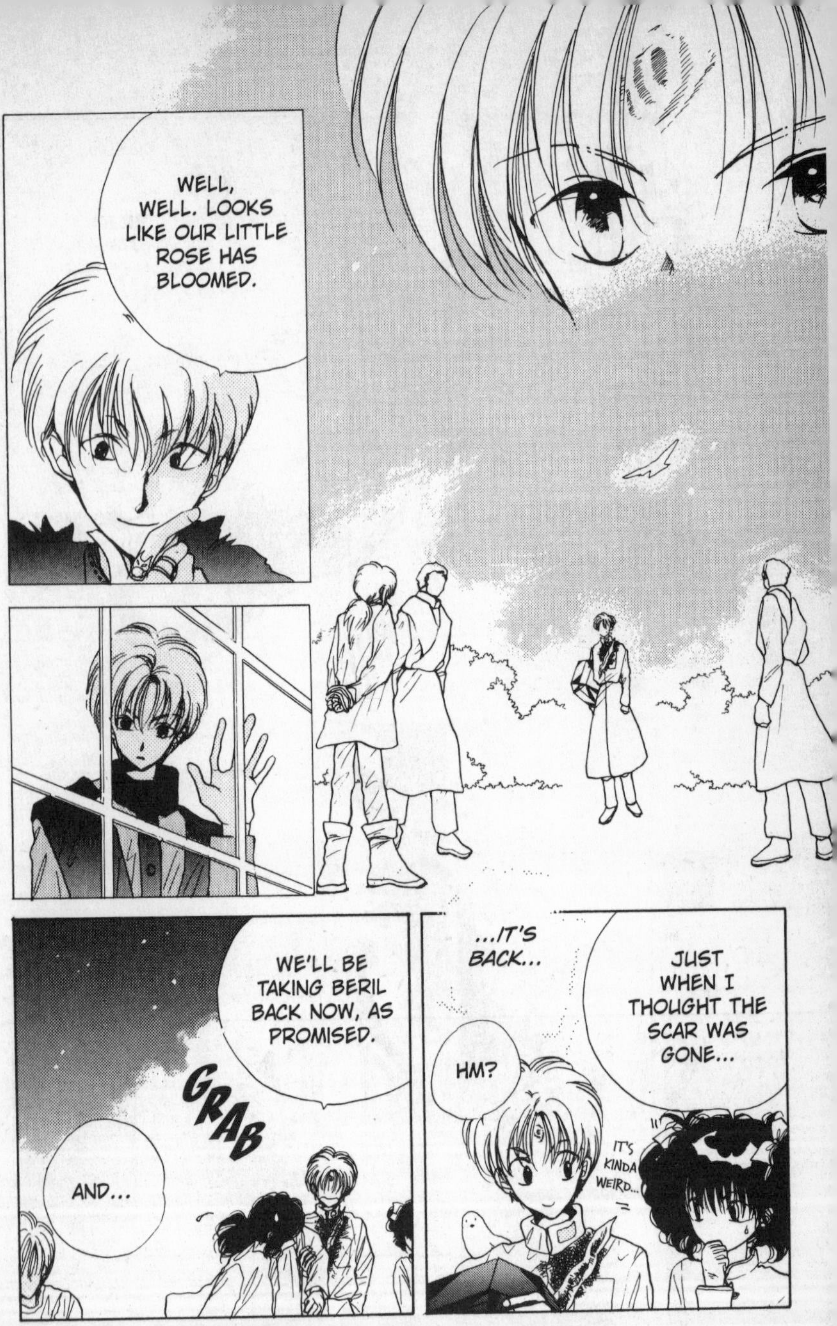
WELL, WELL. LOOKS LIKE OUR LITTLE ROSE HAS BLOOMED.
JUST WHEN I THOUGHT THE SCAR WAS GONE...
...IT'S BACK...
IT'S KINDA WEIRD...
HM?
WE'LL BE TAKING BERIL BACK NOW, AS PROMISED.
GRAB
AND...

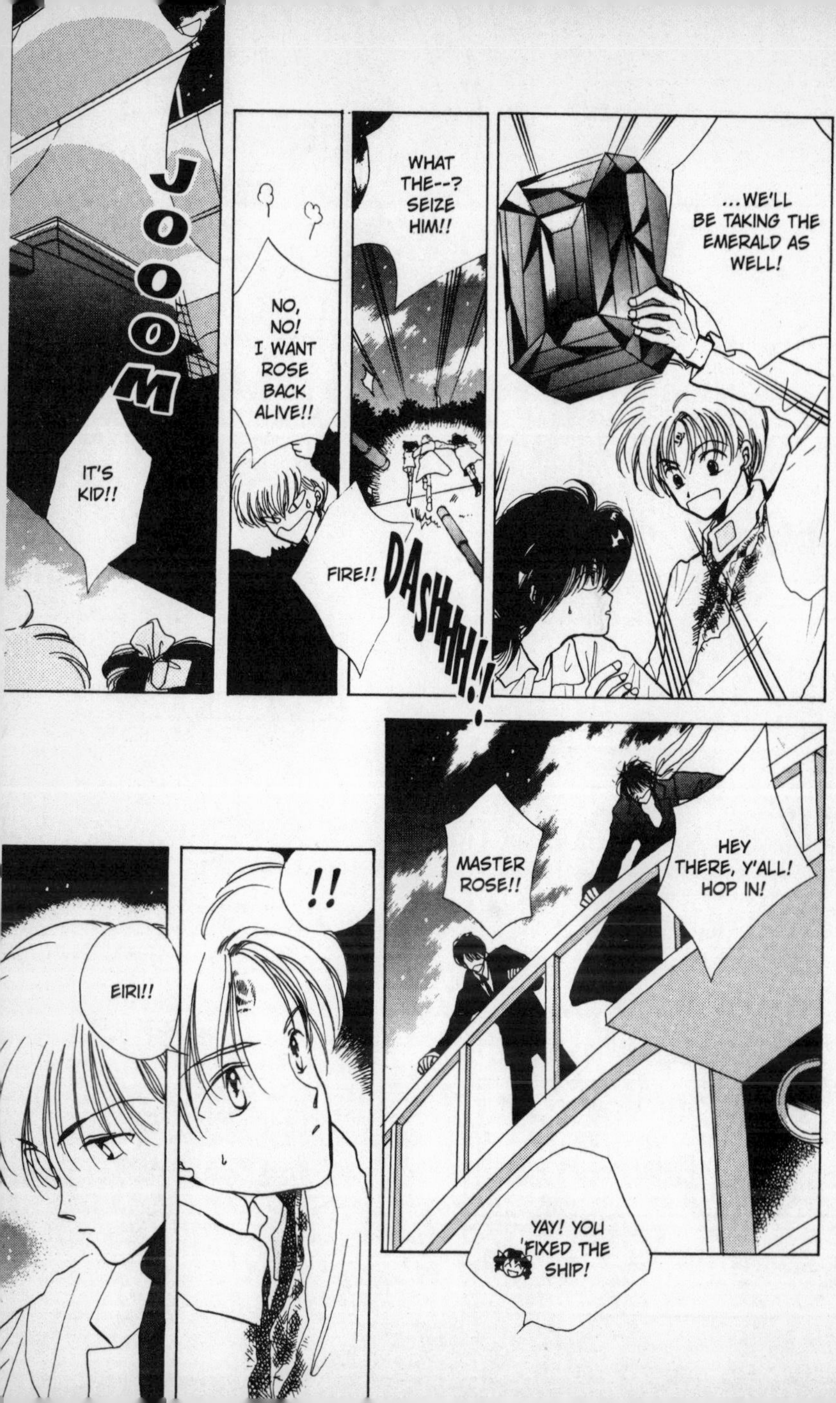
...WE'LL BE TAKING THE EMERALD AS WELL!
WHAT THE--? SEIZE HIM!!
DASHHH!!
NO, NO! I WANT ROSE BACK ALIVE!!
FIRE!!
JOOOOM
IT'S KID!!
HEY THERE, Y'ALL! HOP IN!
MASTER ROSE!!
YAY! YOU FIXED THE SHIP!
!!
EIRI!!

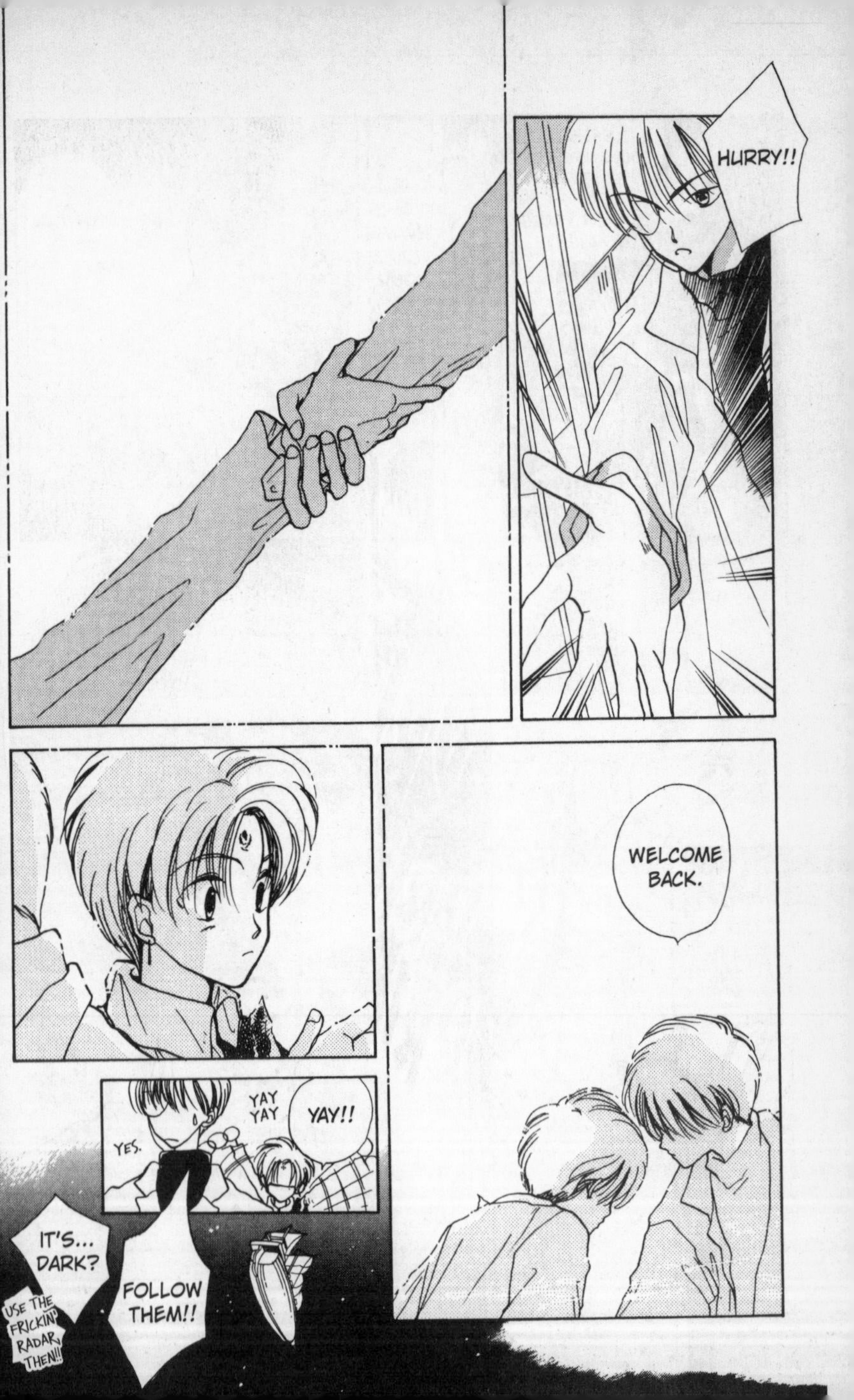
HURRY!!
WELCOME BACK.
YAY!!
YAY YAY
YES.
FOLLOW THEM!!
IT'S... DARK?
USE THE FRICKIN' RADAR, THEN!!

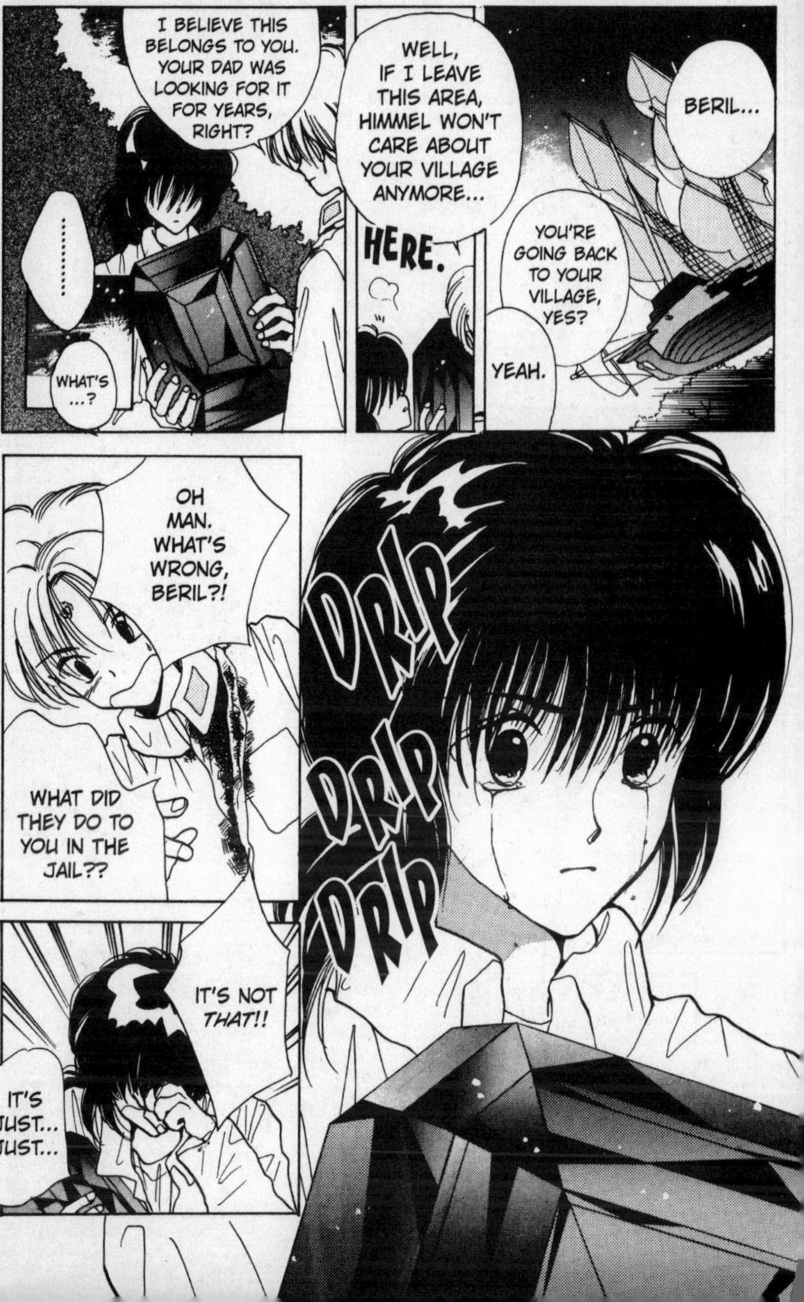
BERIL...
YOU'RE GOING BACK TO YOUR VILLAGE, YES?
YEAH.
WELL, IF I LEAVE THIS AREA, HIMMEL WON'T CARE ABOUT YOUR VILLAGE ANYMORE...
HERE.
I BELIEVE THIS BELONGS TO YOU. YOUR DAD WAS LOOKING FOR IT FOR YEARS, RIGHT?
....
WHAT'S ...?
DRIP
DRIP
DRIP
OH MAN. WHAT'S WRONG, BERIL?!
WHAT DID THEY DO TO YOU IN THE JAIL??
IT'S NOT *THAT*!!
IT'S JUST... JUST...

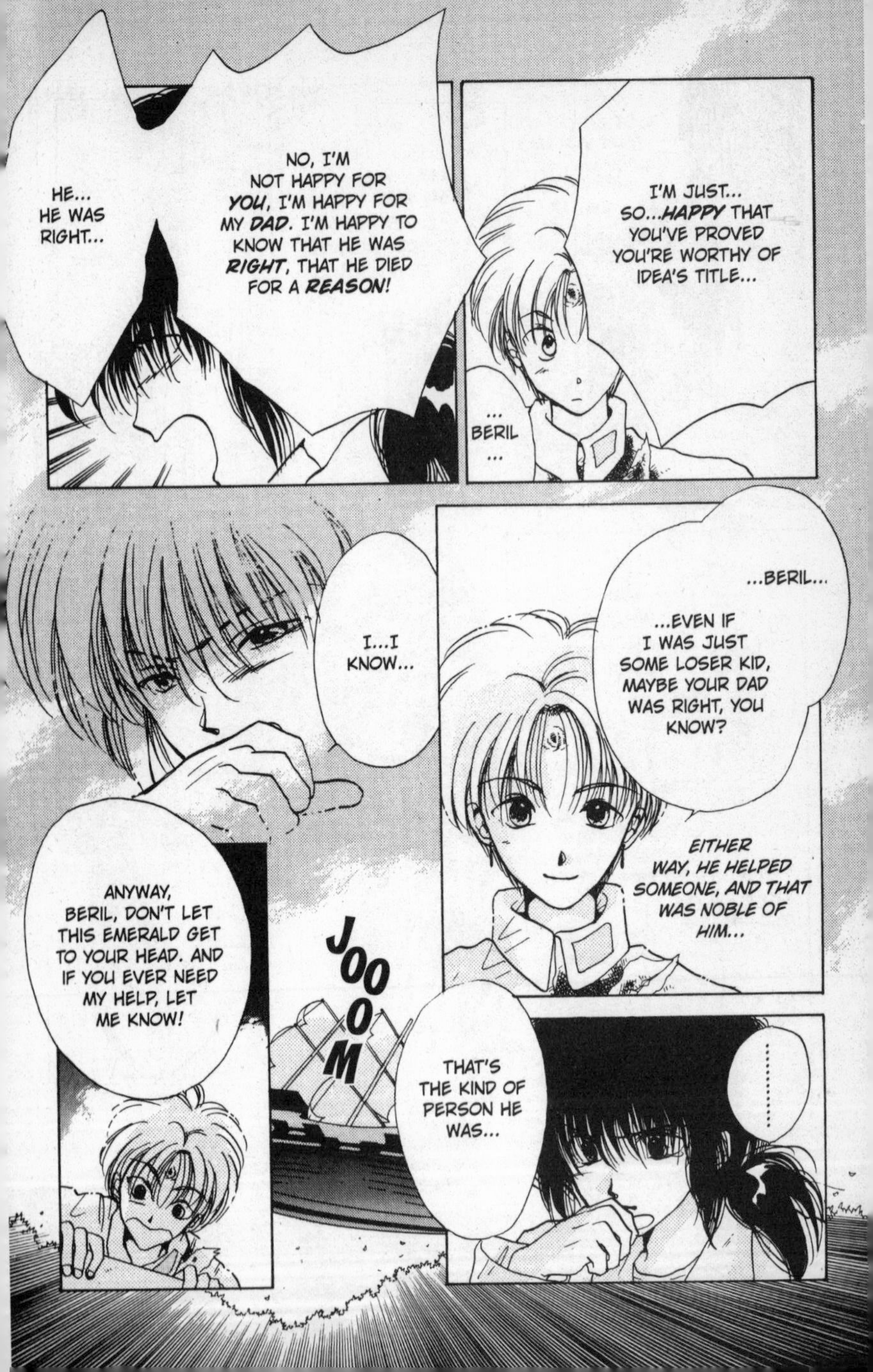

I'M JUST... SO...HAPPY THAT YOU'VE PROVED YOU'RE WORTHY OF IDEA'S TITLE...
... BERIL ...
NO, I'M NOT HAPPY FOR YOU, I'M HAPPY FOR MY DAD. I'M HAPPY TO KNOW THAT HE WAS RIGHT, THAT HE DIED FOR A REASON!
HE... HE WAS RIGHT...
...BERIL...
...EVEN IF I WAS JUST SOME LOSER KID, MAYBE YOUR DAD WAS RIGHT, YOU KNOW?
EITHER WAY, HE HELPED SOMEONE, AND THAT WAS NOBLE OF HIM...
I...I KNOW...
......
THAT'S THE KIND OF PERSON HE WAS...
JOOOOM
ANYWAY, BERIL, DON'T LET THIS EMERALD GET TO YOUR HEAD. AND IF YOU EVER NEED MY HELP, LET ME KNOW!

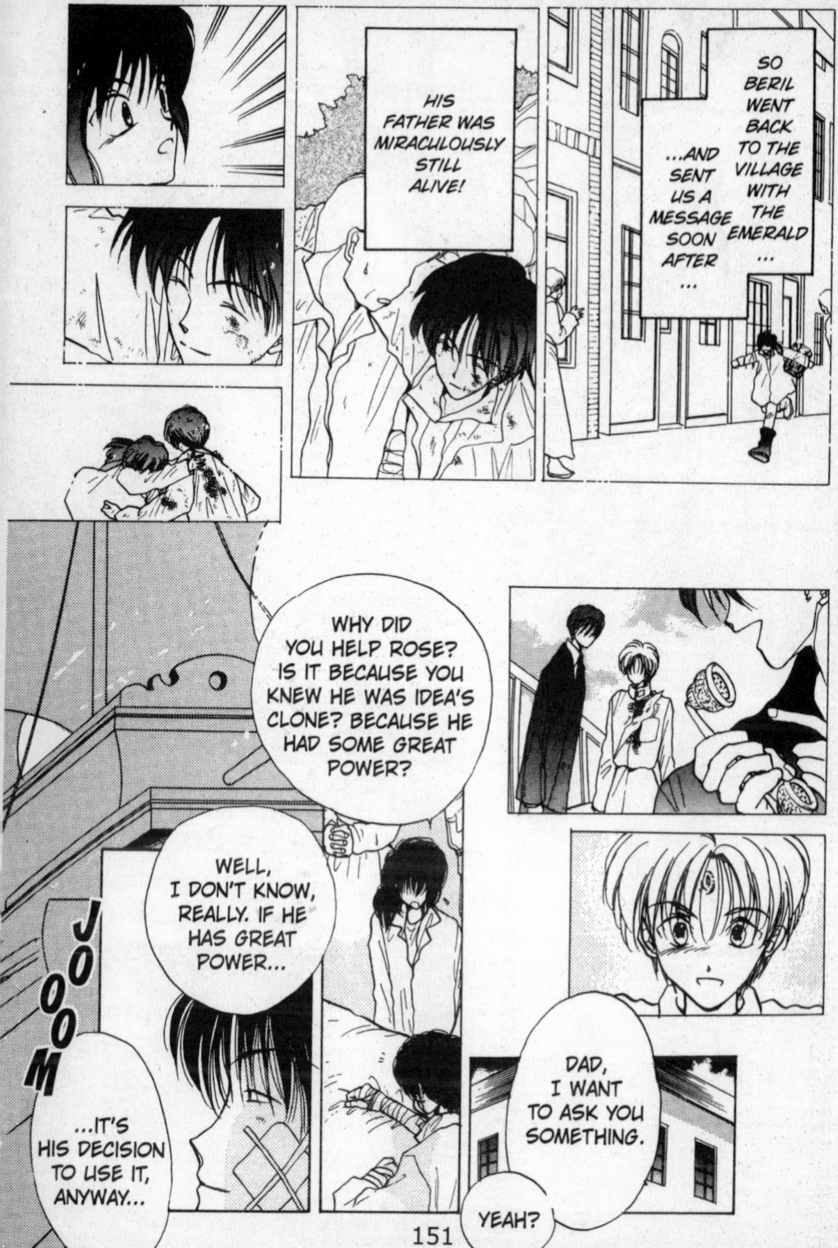
SO BERIL WENT BACK TO THE VILLAGE WITH THE EMERALD...
...AND SENT US A MESSAGE SOON AFTER...
HIS FATHER WAS MIRACULOUSLY STILL ALIVE!
DAD, I WANT TO ASK YOU SOMETHING.
YEAH?
WHY DID YOU HELP ROSE? IS IT BECAUSE YOU KNEW HE WAS IDEA'S CLONE? BECAUSE HE HAD SOME GREAT POWER?
WELL, I DON'T KNOW, REALLY. IF HE HAS GREAT POWER...
...IT'S HIS DECISION TO USE IT, ANYWAY...
JOOOOM

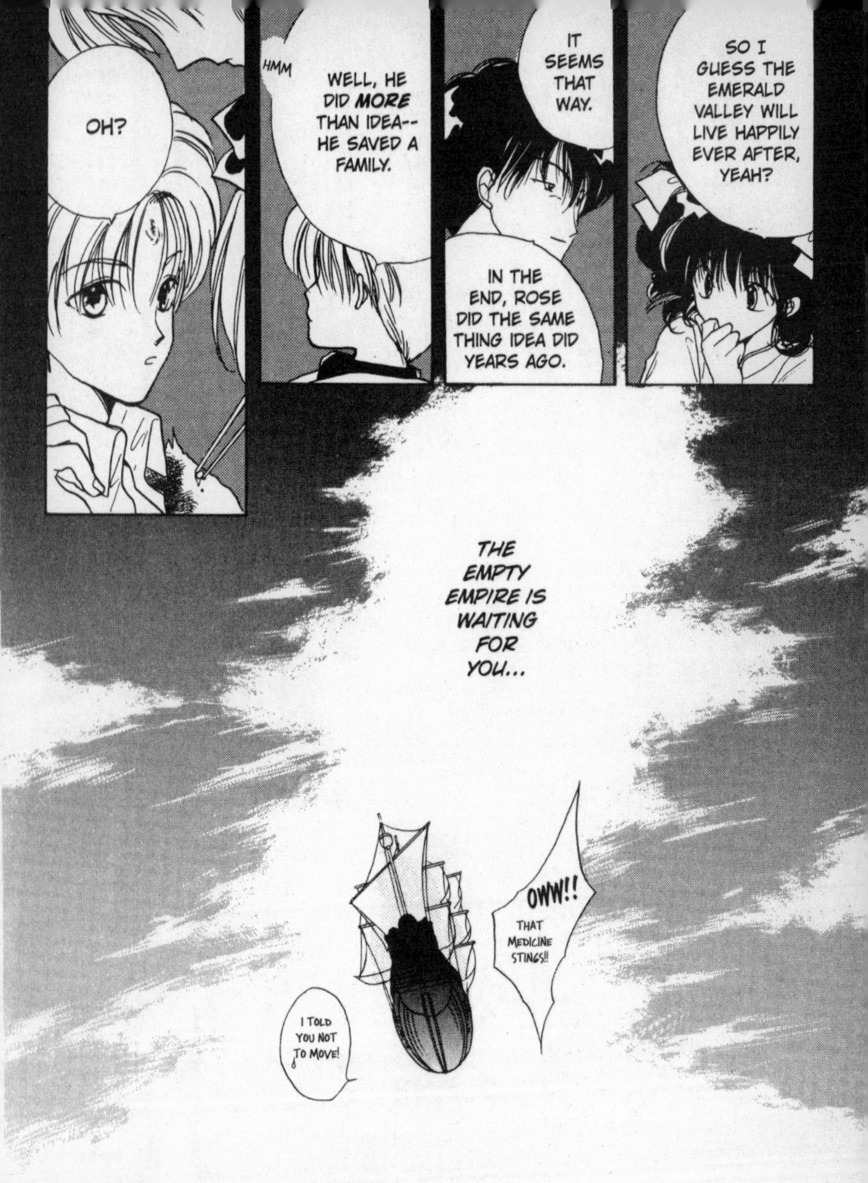
SO I GUESS THE EMERALD VALLEY WILL LIVE HAPPILY EVER AFTER, YEAH?
IT SEEMS THAT WAY.
IN THE END, ROSE DID THE SAME THING IDEA DID YEARS AGO.
HMM
WELL, HE DID MORE THAN IDEA-- HE SAVED A FAMILY.
OH?
THE EMPTY EMPIRE IS WAITING FOR YOU...
OWW!! THAT MEDICINE STINGS!!
I TOLD YOU NOT TO MOVE!

"THE WAKING BIRD" / END.

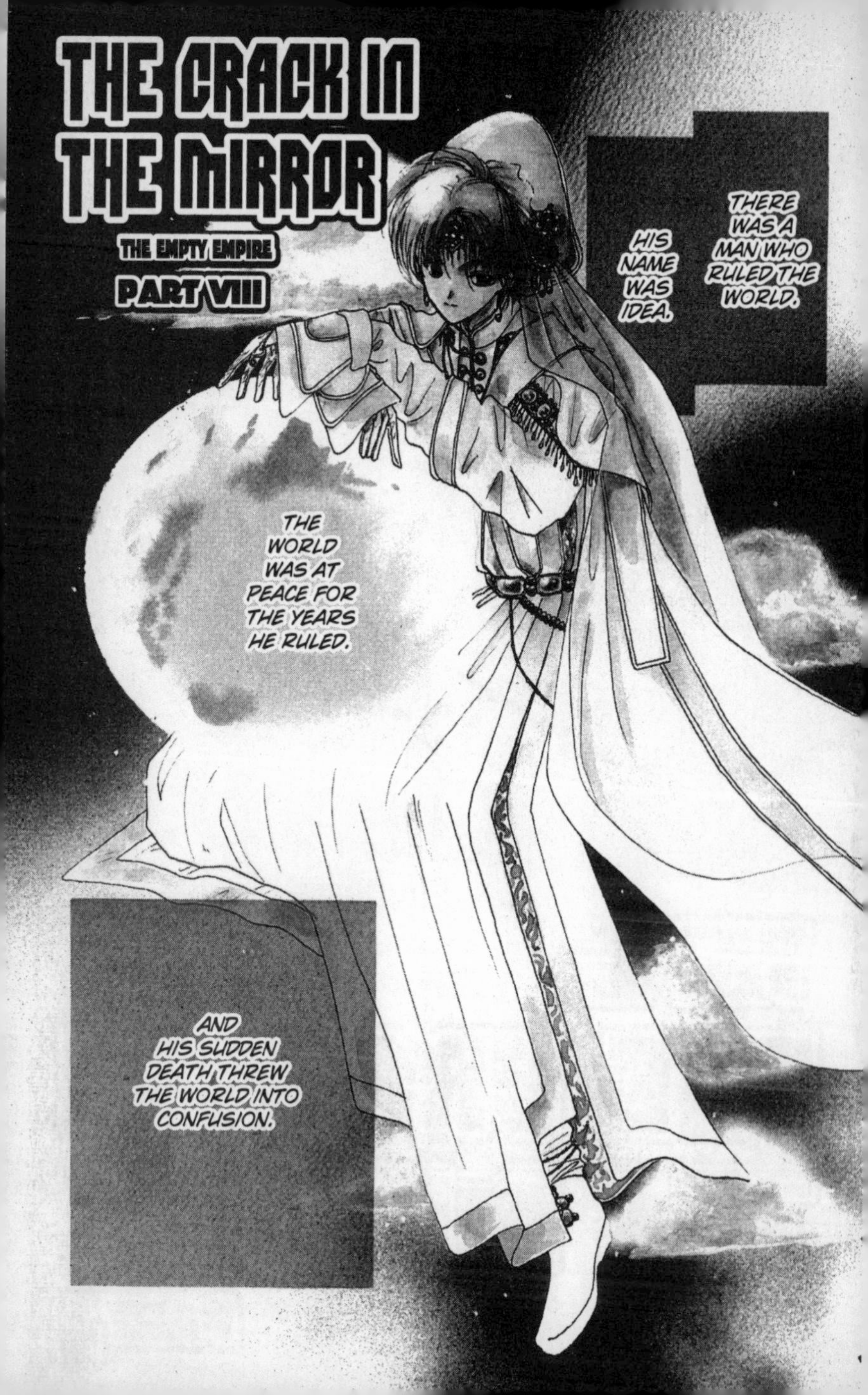
THE CRACK IN THE MIRROR
THE EMPTY EMPIRE
PART VIII
THERE WAS A MAN WHO RULED THE WORLD.
HIS NAME WAS IDEA.
THE WORLD WAS AT PEACE FOR THE YEARS HE RULED.
AND HIS SUDDEN DEATH THREW THE WORLD INTO CONFUSION.

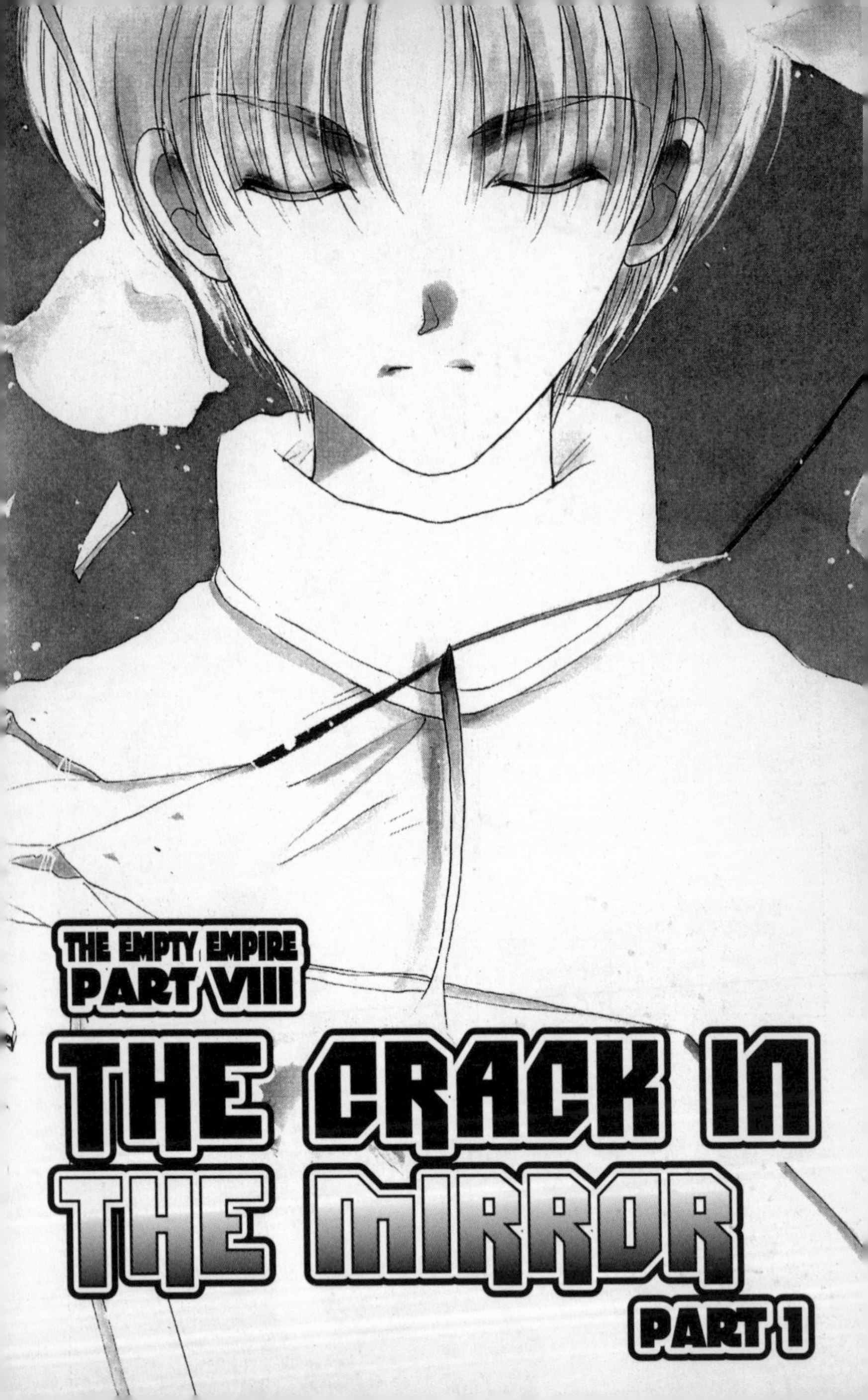
THE EMPTY EMPIRE
PART VIII
THE CRACK IN
THE MIRROR
PART 1

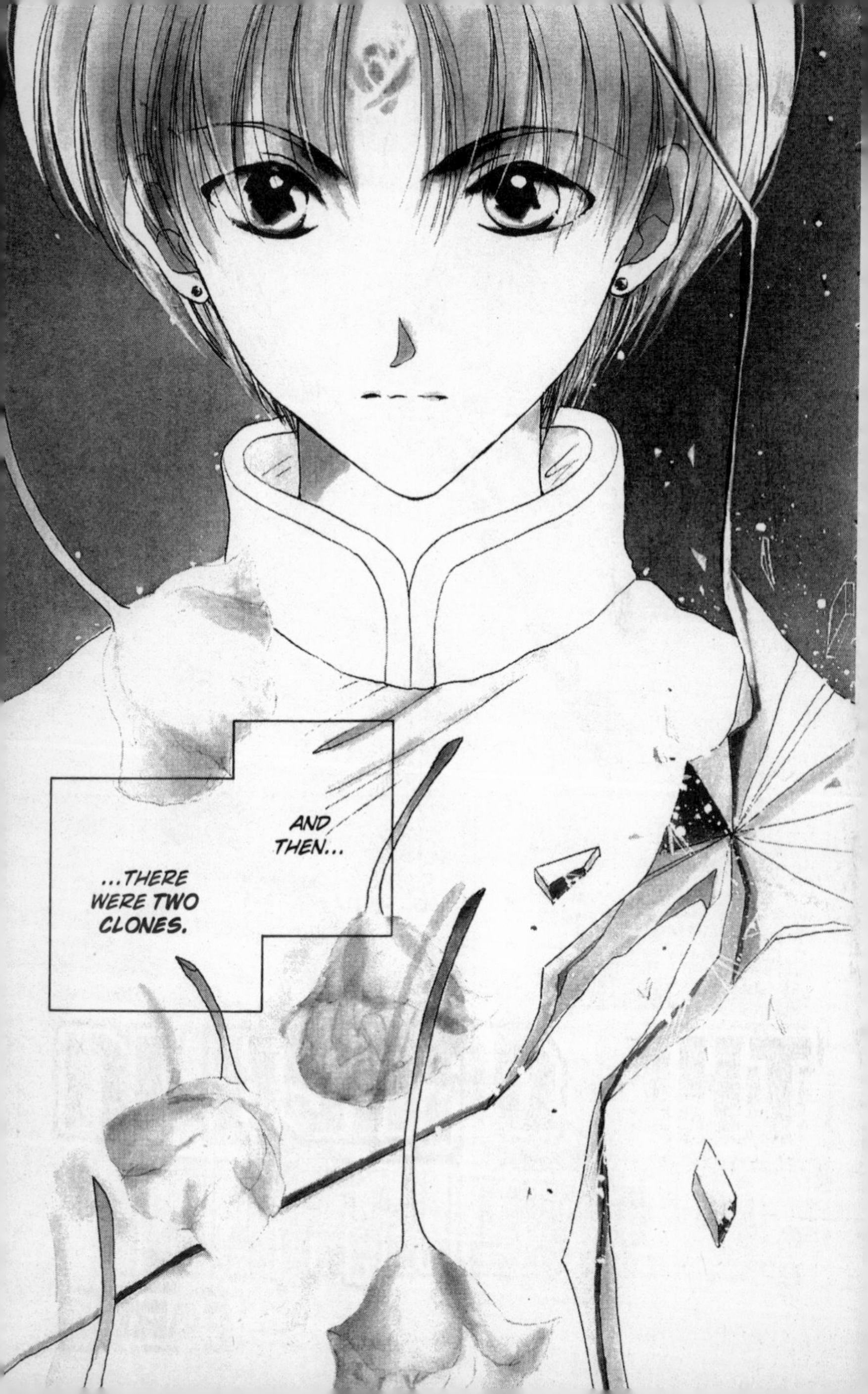
AND THEN...
...THERE WERE TWO CLONES.

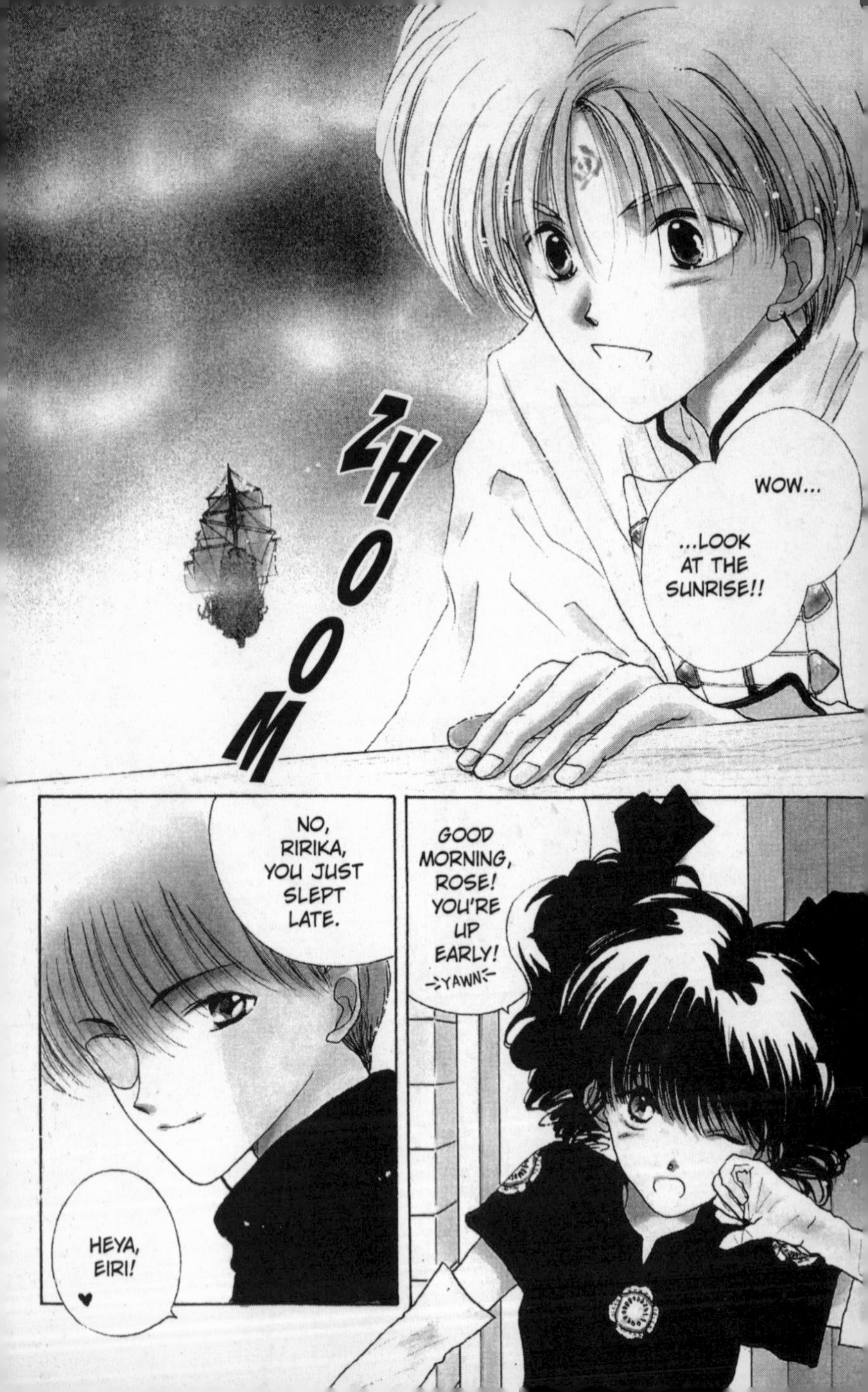
WOW...
...LOOK AT THE SUNRISE!!
ZHOOM
GOOD MORNING, ROSE! YOU'RE UP EARLY!
YAWN
NO, RIRIKA, YOU JUST SLEPT LATE.
HEYA, EIRI! ♥

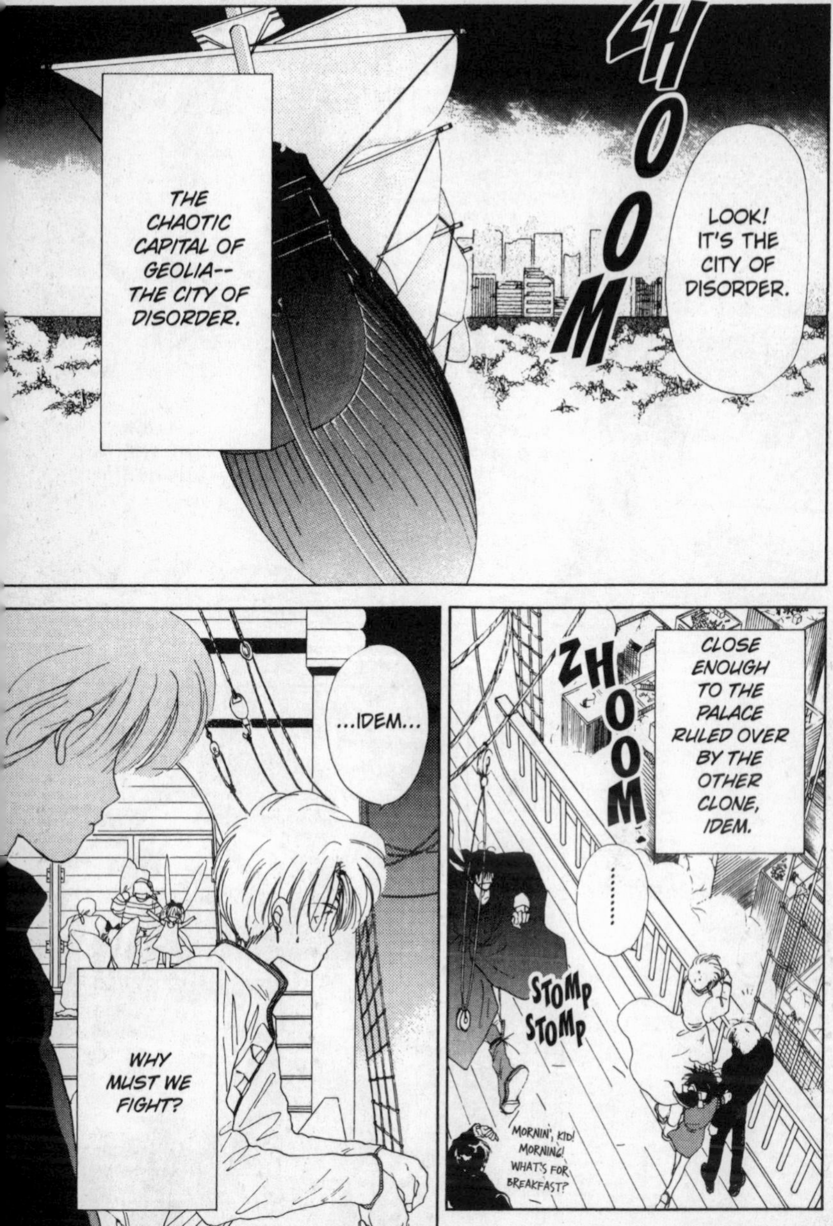
ZHOOOM
LOOK! IT'S THE CITY OF DISORDER.
THE CHAOTIC CAPITAL OF GEOLIA-- THE CITY OF DISORDER.
ZHOOOM
CLOSE ENOUGH TO THE PALACE RULED OVER BY THE OTHER CLONE, IDEM.
......
STOMP STOMP
MORNIN', KID!
MORNING!
WHAT'S FOR BREAKFAST?
...IDEM...
WHY MUST WE FIGHT?

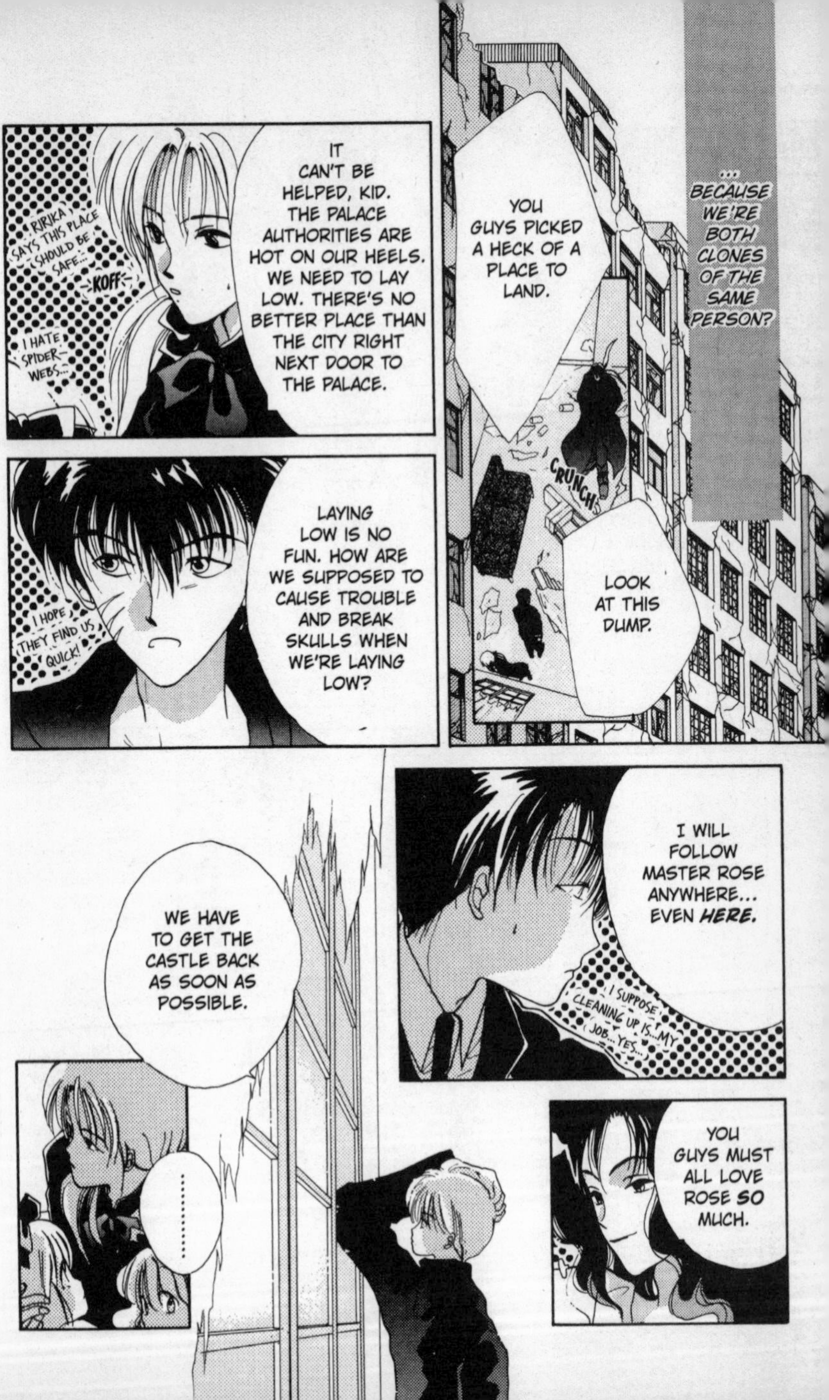
...BECAUSE WE'RE BOTH CLONES OF THE SAME PERSON?
YOU GUYS PICKED A HECK OF A PLACE TO LAND.
CRUNCH
LOOK AT THIS DUMP.
IT CAN'T BE HELPED, KID. THE PALACE AUTHORITIES ARE HOT ON OUR HEELS. WE NEED TO LAY LOW. THERE'S NO BETTER PLACE THAN THE CITY RIGHT NEXT DOOR TO THE PALACE.
RIRIKA SAYS THIS PLACE SHOULD BE SAFE...
-KOFF-
I HATE SPIDER-WEBS...
LAYING LOW IS NO FUN. HOW ARE WE SUPPOSED TO CAUSE TROUBLE AND BREAK SKULLS WHEN WE'RE LAYING LOW?
I HOPE THEY FIND US QUICK!
I WILL FOLLOW MASTER ROSE ANYWHERE... EVEN *HERE.*
I SUPPOSE CLEANING UP IS... MY JOB... YES...
WE HAVE TO GET THE CASTLE BACK AS SOON AS POSSIBLE.
YOU GUYS MUST ALL LOVE ROSE SO MUCH.
......

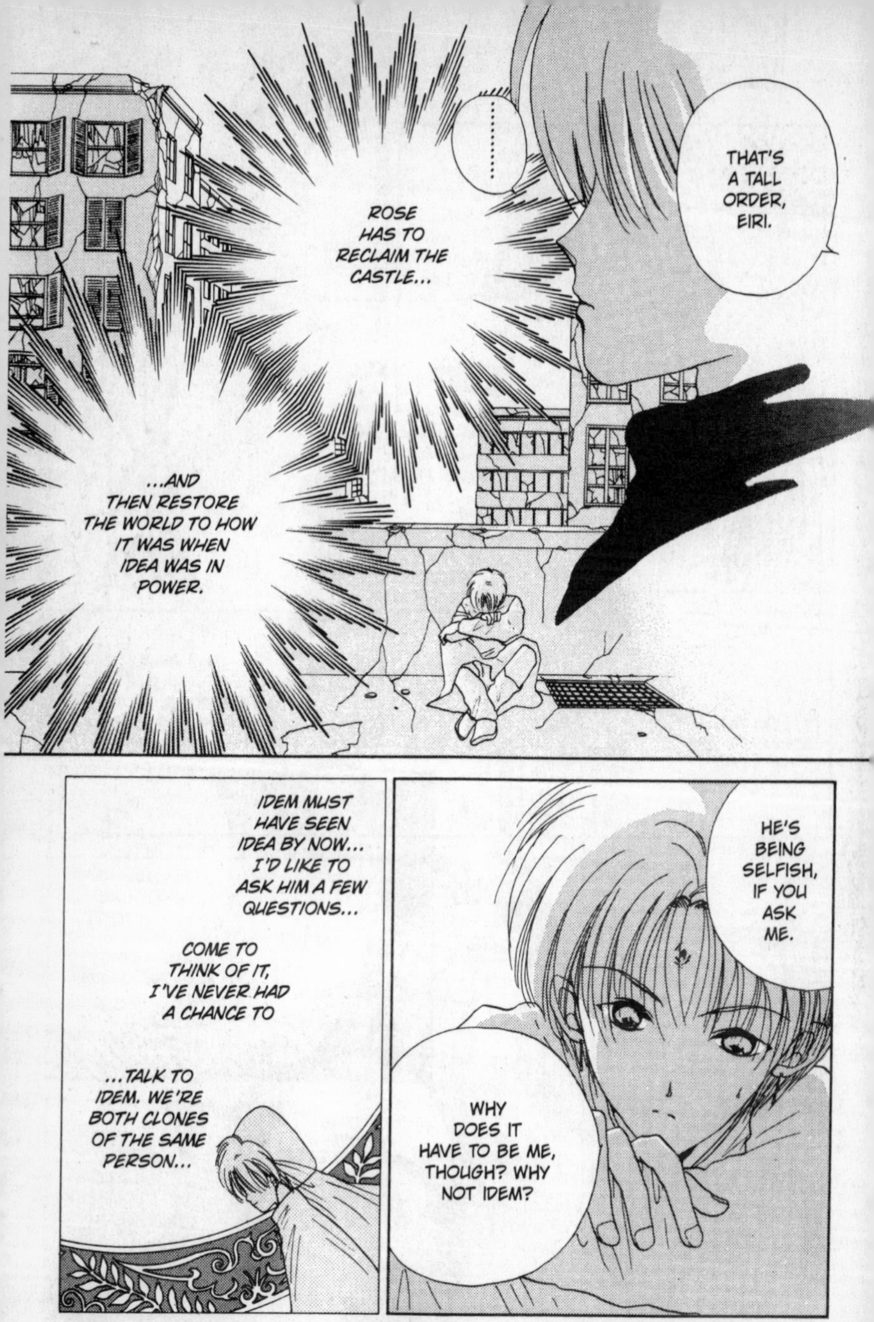
……
THAT'S A TALL ORDER, EIRI.
ROSE HAS TO RECLAIM THE CASTLE…
…AND THEN RESTORE THE WORLD TO HOW IT WAS WHEN IDEA WAS IN POWER.
HE'S BEING SELFISH, IF YOU ASK ME.
WHY DOES IT HAVE TO BE ME, THOUGH? WHY NOT IDEM?
IDEM MUST HAVE SEEN IDEA BY NOW… I'D LIKE TO ASK HIM A FEW QUESTIONS…
COME TO THINK OF IT, I'VE NEVER HAD A CHANCE TO
…TALK TO IDEM. WE'RE BOTH CLONES OF THE SAME PERSON…

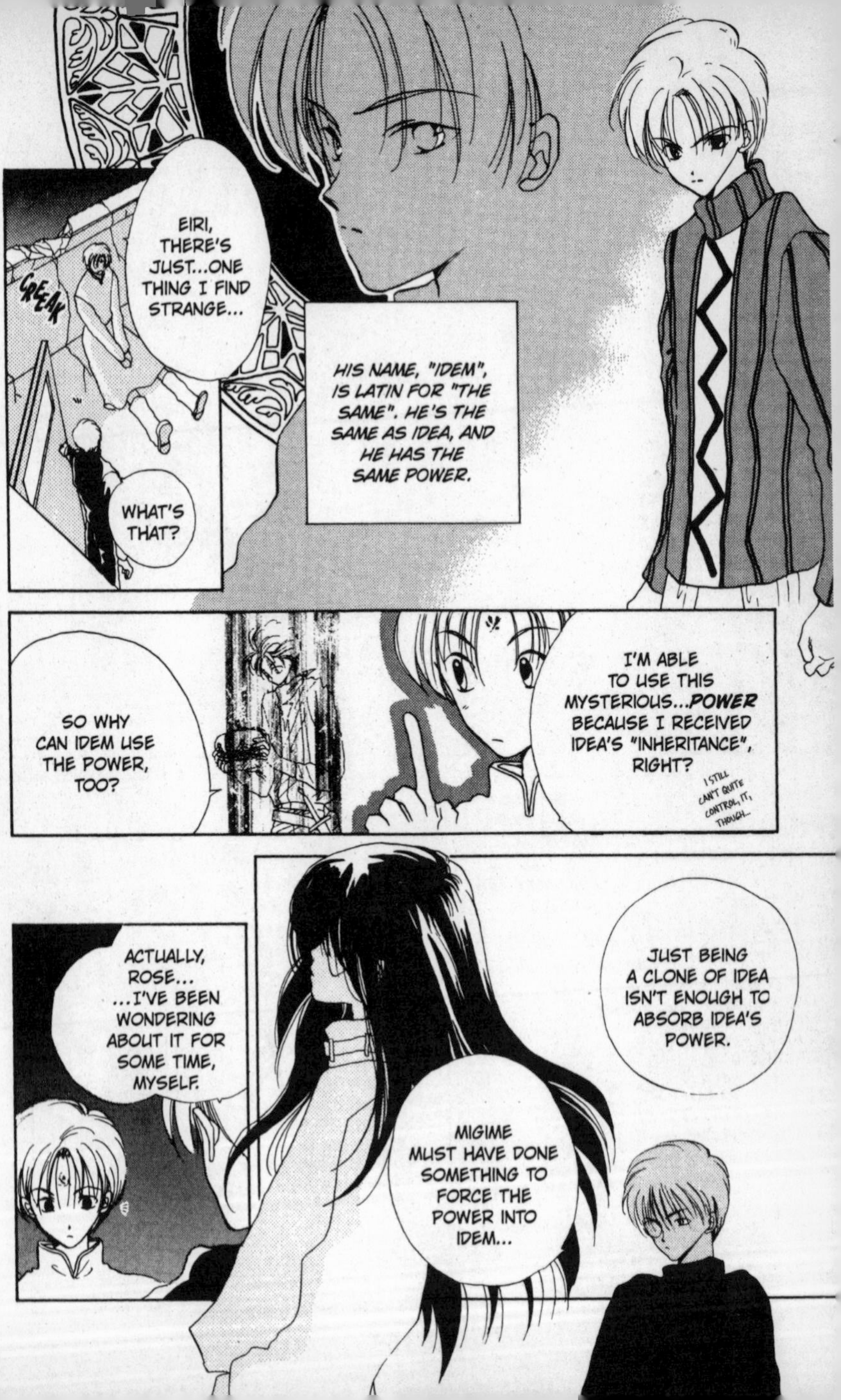
EIRI, THERE'S JUST...ONE THING I FIND STRANGE...
CREEAK
WHAT'S THAT?
HIS NAME, "IDEM", IS LATIN FOR "THE SAME". HE'S THE SAME AS IDEA, AND HE HAS THE SAME POWER.
I'M ABLE TO USE THIS MYSTERIOUS...POWER BECAUSE I RECEIVED IDEA'S "INHERITANCE", RIGHT?
I STILL CAN'T QUITE CONTROL, IT, THOUGH...
SO WHY CAN IDEM USE THE POWER, TOO?
JUST BEING A CLONE OF IDEA ISN'T ENOUGH TO ABSORB IDEA'S POWER.
MIGIME MUST HAVE DONE SOMETHING TO FORCE THE POWER INTO IDEM...
ACTUALLY, ROSE... ...I'VE BEEN WONDERING ABOUT IT FOR SOME TIME, MYSELF.

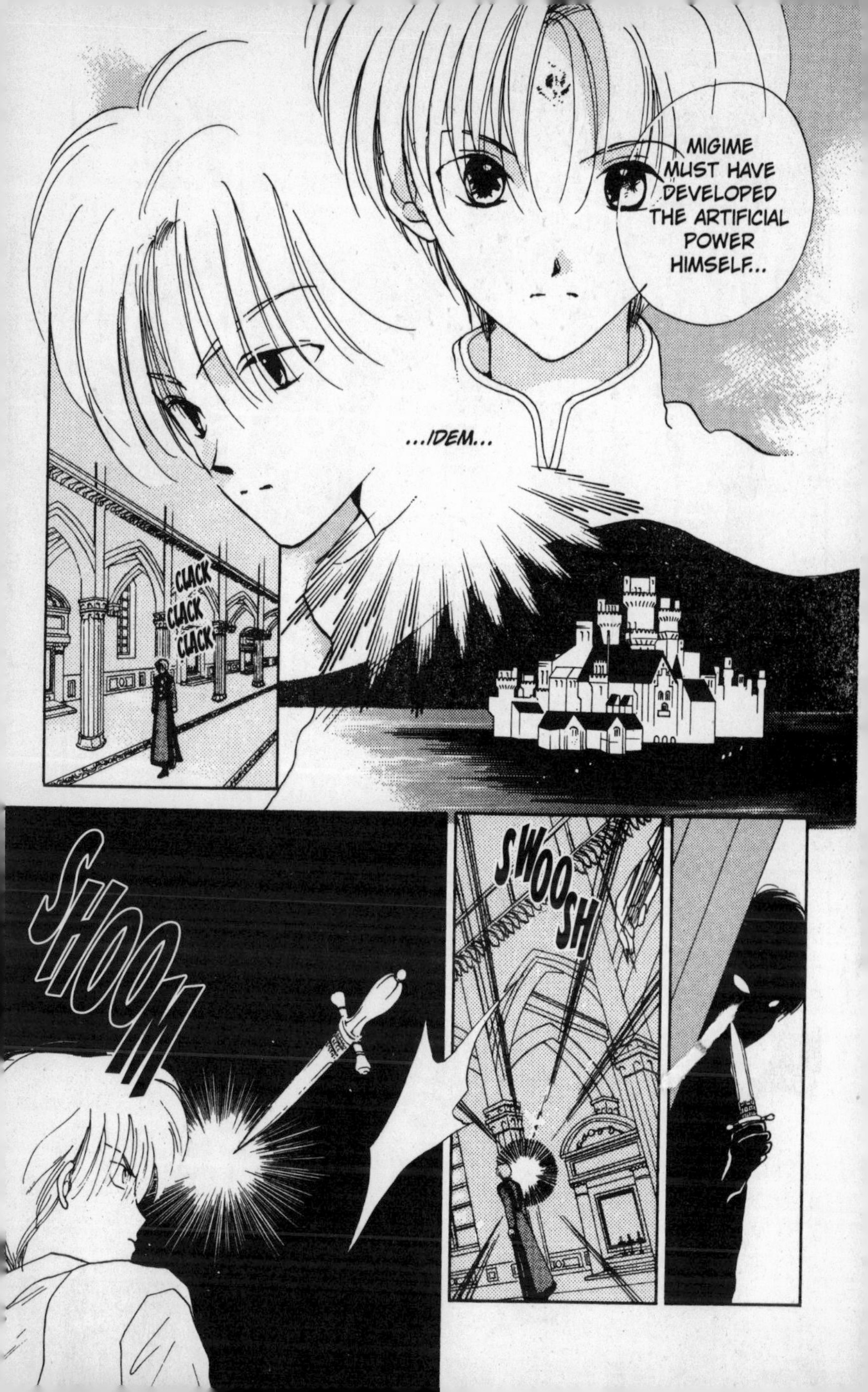
MIGIME MUST HAVE DEVELOPED THE ARTIFICIAL POWER HIMSELF...
...IDEM...
CLACK
CLACK
CLACK
SWOOSH
SHOOM

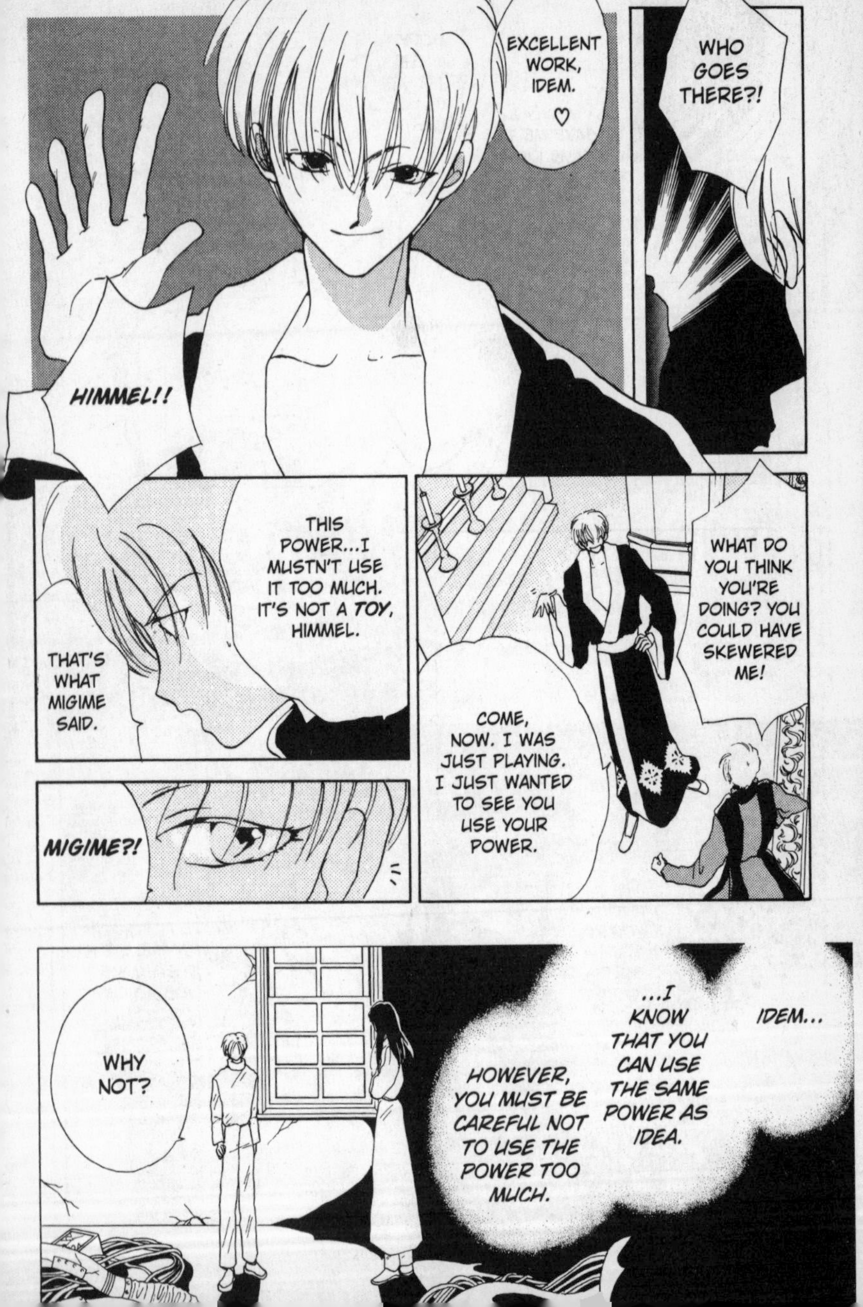

WHO GOES THERE?!
EXCELLENT WORK, IDEM. ♡
HIMMEL!!
WHAT DO YOU THINK YOU'RE DOING? YOU COULD HAVE SKEWERED ME!
COME, NOW. I WAS JUST PLAYING. I JUST WANTED TO SEE YOU USE YOUR POWER.
THIS POWER...I MUSTN'T USE IT TOO MUCH. IT'S NOT A *TOY*, HIMMEL.
THAT'S WHAT MIGIME SAID.
MIGIME?!
IDEM...
...I KNOW THAT YOU CAN USE THE SAME POWER AS IDEA.
HOWEVER, YOU MUST BE CAREFUL NOT TO USE THE POWER TOO MUCH.
WHY NOT?

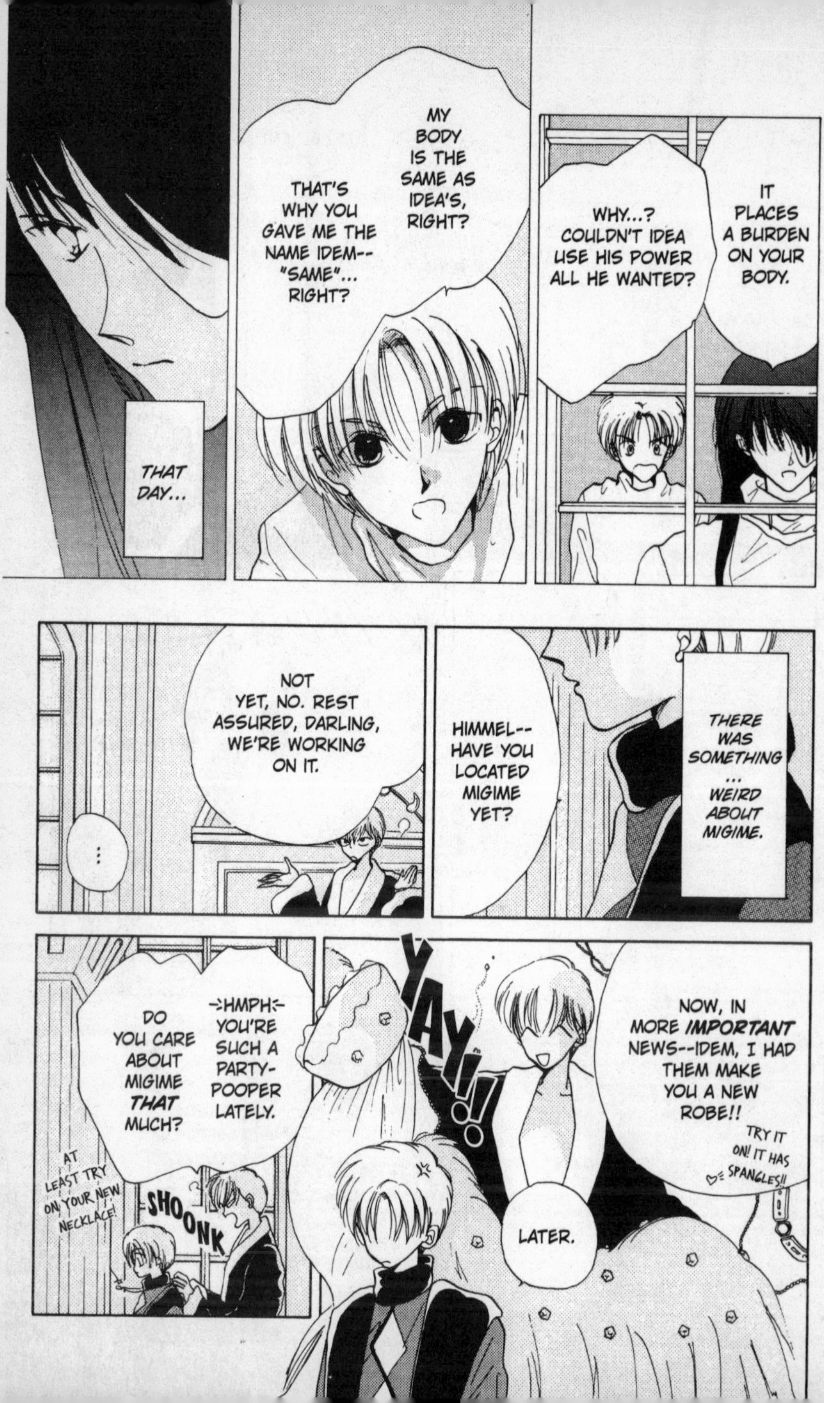
IT PLACES A BURDEN ON YOUR BODY.
WHY...? COULDN'T IDEA USE HIS POWER ALL HE WANTED?
MY BODY IS THE SAME AS IDEA'S, RIGHT?
THAT'S WHY YOU GAVE ME THE NAME IDEM-- "SAME"... RIGHT?
THAT DAY...
THERE WAS SOMETHING ... WEIRD ABOUT MIGIME.
HIMMEL-- HAVE YOU LOCATED MIGIME YET?
NOT YET, NO. REST ASSURED, DARLING, WE'RE WORKING ON IT.
...
NOW, IN MORE IMPORTANT NEWS--IDEM, I HAD THEM MAKE YOU A NEW ROBE!!
TRY IT ON! IT HAS SPANGLES!!
YAY!!
LATER.
HMPH YOU'RE SUCH A PARTY-POOPER LATELY.
DO YOU CARE ABOUT MIGIME THAT MUCH?
AT LEAST TRY ON YOUR NEW NECKLACE!
SHOONK

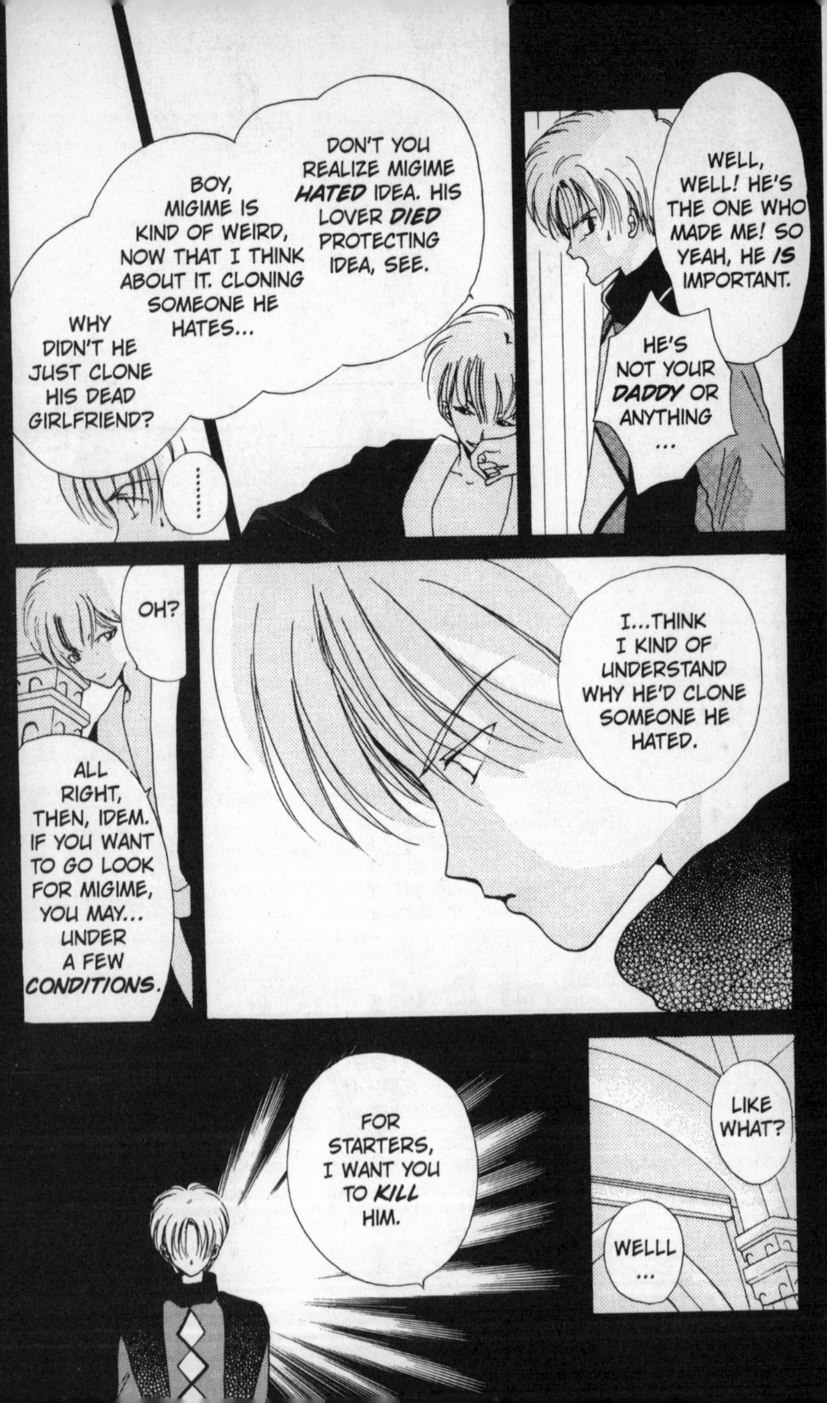
WELL, WELL! HE'S THE ONE WHO MADE ME! SO YEAH, HE IS IMPORTANT.
HE'S NOT YOUR DADDY OR ANYTHING ...
BOY, MIGIME IS KIND OF WEIRD, NOW THAT I THINK ABOUT IT. CLONING SOMEONE HE HATES...
WHY DIDN'T HE JUST CLONE HIS DEAD GIRLFRIEND?
DON'T YOU REALIZE MIGIME HATED IDEA. HIS LOVER DIED PROTECTING IDEA, SEE.
......
I...THINK I KIND OF UNDERSTAND WHY HE'D CLONE SOMEONE HE HATED.
OH?
ALL RIGHT, THEN, IDEM. IF YOU WANT TO GO LOOK FOR MIGIME, YOU MAY... UNDER A FEW CONDITIONS.
LIKE WHAT?
WELLL ...
FOR STARTERS, I WANT YOU TO KILL HIM.

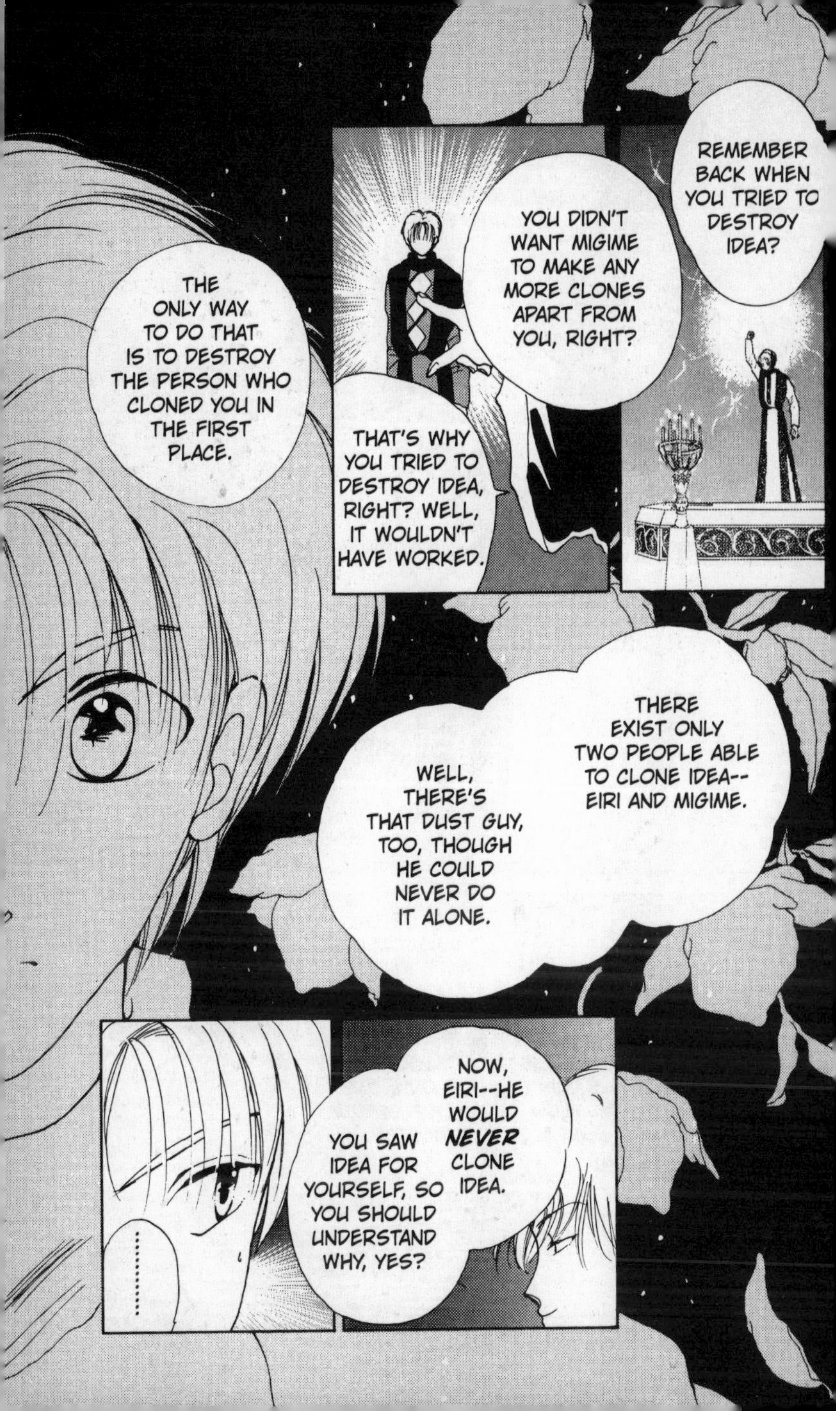
REMEMBER BACK WHEN YOU TRIED TO DESTROY IDEA?
YOU DIDN'T WANT MIGIME TO MAKE ANY MORE CLONES APART FROM YOU, RIGHT?
THAT'S WHY YOU TRIED TO DESTROY IDEA, RIGHT? WELL, IT WOULDN'T HAVE WORKED.
THE ONLY WAY TO DO THAT IS TO DESTROY THE PERSON WHO CLONED YOU IN THE FIRST PLACE.
THERE EXIST ONLY TWO PEOPLE ABLE TO CLONE IDEA-- EIRI AND MIGIME.
WELL, THERE'S THAT DUST GUY, TOO, THOUGH HE COULD NEVER DO IT ALONE.
NOW, EIRI--HE WOULD ***NEVER*** CLONE IDEA.
YOU SAW IDEA FOR YOURSELF, SO YOU SHOULD UNDERSTAND WHY, YES?
......

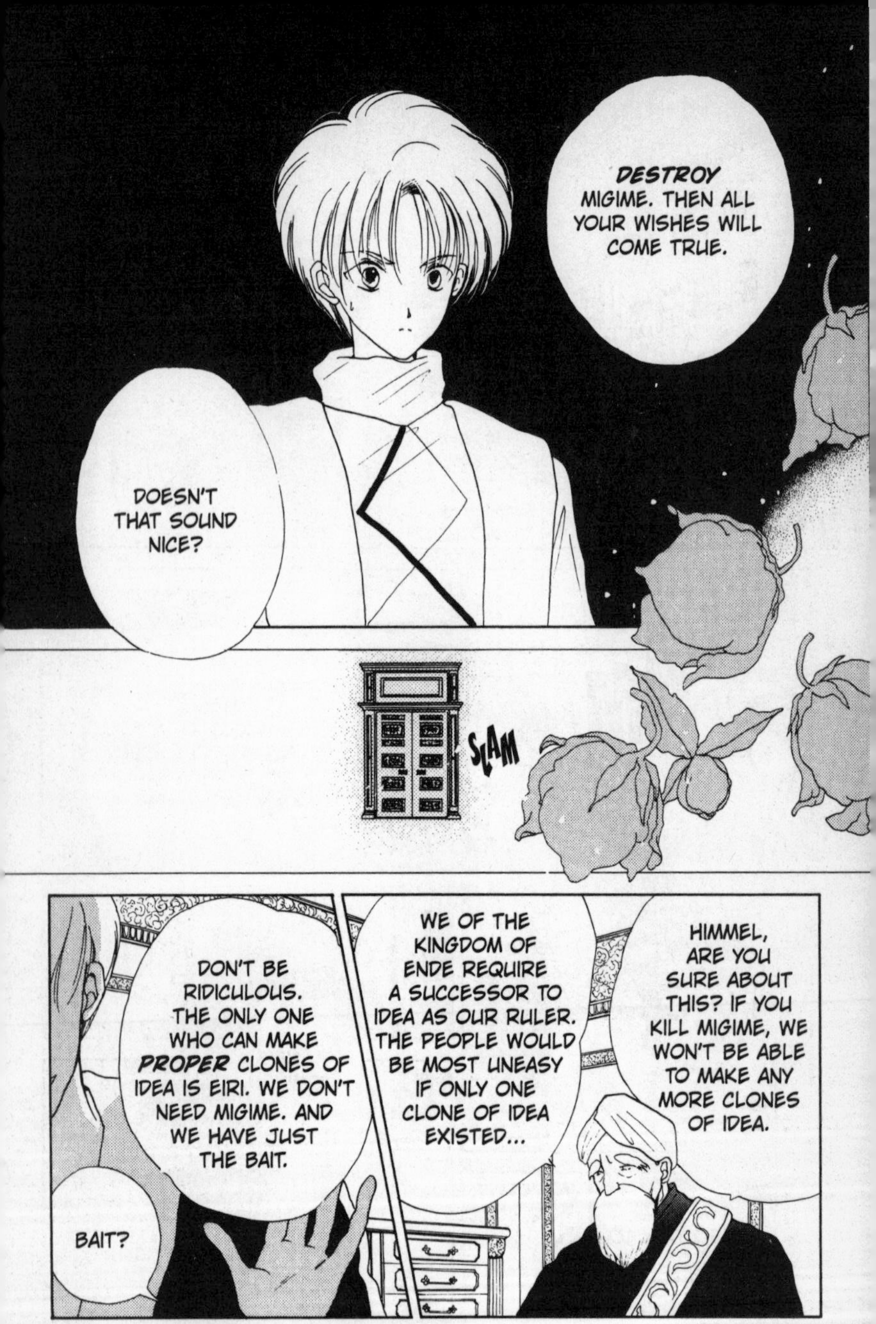
DESTROY MIGIME. THEN ALL YOUR WISHES WILL COME TRUE.
DOESN'T THAT SOUND NICE?
SLAM
HIMMEL, ARE YOU SURE ABOUT THIS? IF YOU KILL MIGIME, WE WON'T BE ABLE TO MAKE ANY MORE CLONES OF IDEA.
WE OF THE KINGDOM OF ENDE REQUIRE A SUCCESSOR TO IDEA AS OUR RULER. THE PEOPLE WOULD BE MOST UNEASY IF ONLY ONE CLONE OF IDEA EXISTED...
DON'T BE RIDICULOUS. THE ONLY ONE WHO CAN MAKE PROPER CLONES OF IDEA IS EIRI. WE DON'T NEED MIGIME. AND WE HAVE JUST THE BAIT.
BAIT?

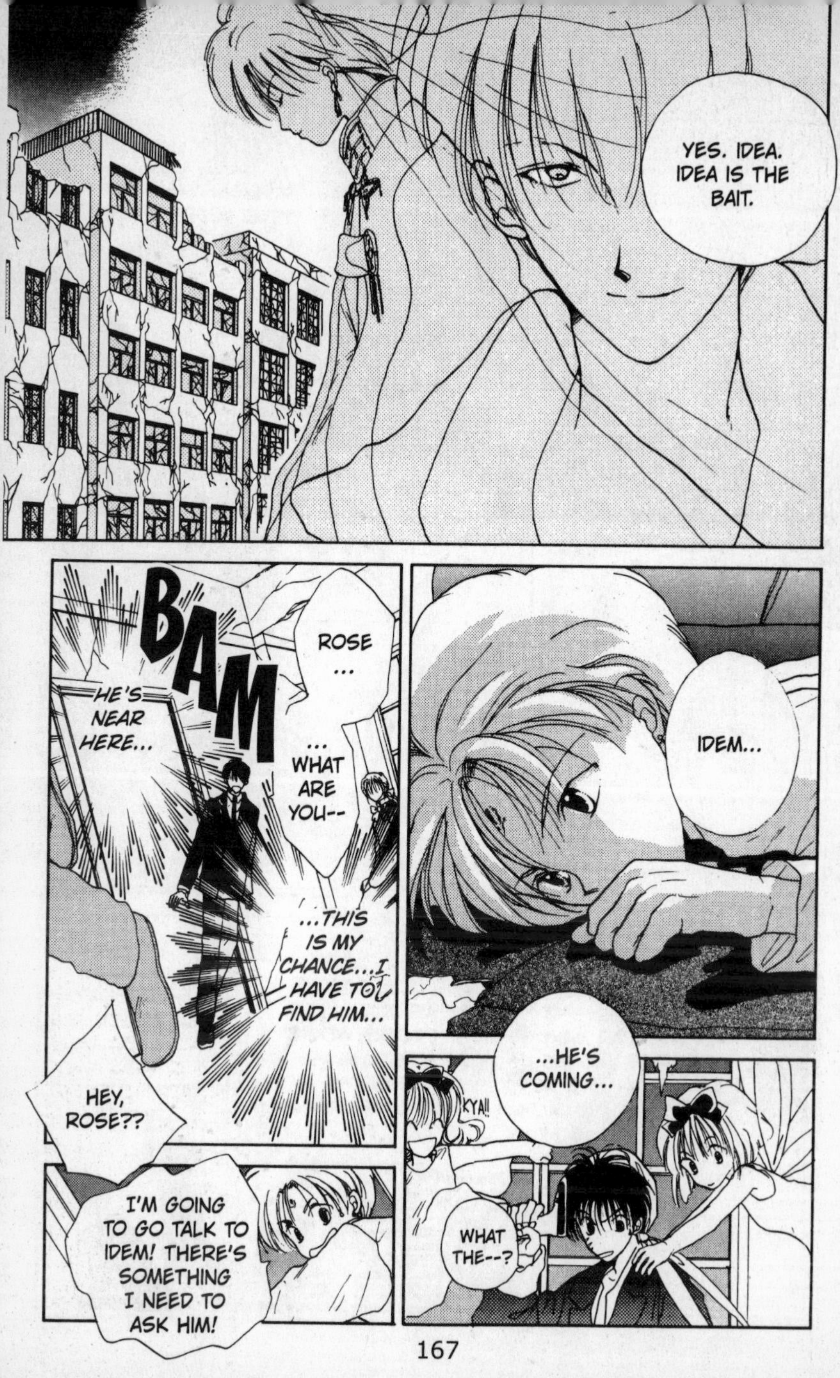
YES. IDEA. IDEA IS THE BAIT.
IDEM...
ROSE ...
BAM
... WHAT ARE YOU--
HE'S NEAR HERE...
...THIS IS MY CHANCE...I HAVE TO FIND HIM...
HEY, ROSE??
...HE'S COMING...
KYA!!
WHAT THE--?
I'M GOING TO GO TALK TO IDEM! THERE'S SOMETHING I NEED TO ASK HIM!

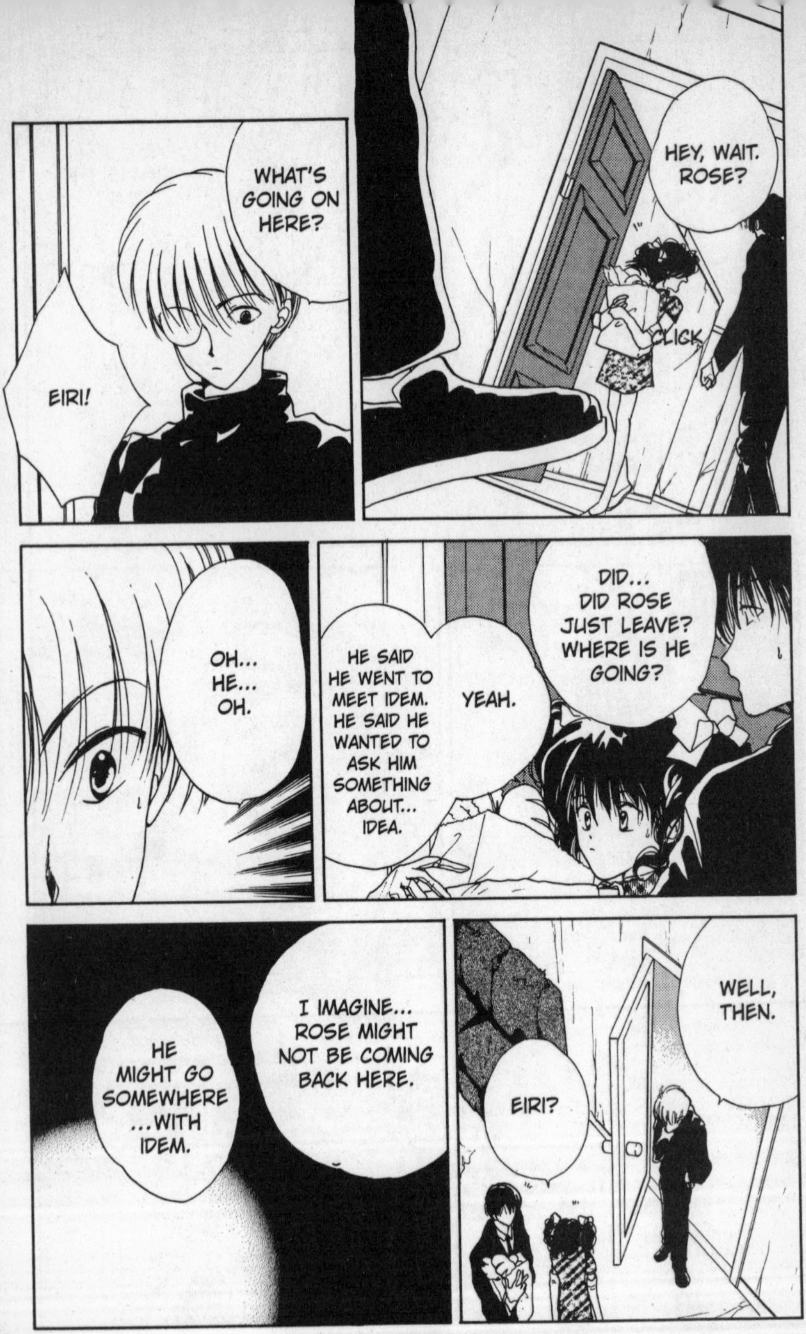
HEY, WAIT. ROSE?
CLICK
WHAT'S GOING ON HERE?
EIRI!
DID... DID ROSE JUST LEAVE? WHERE IS HE GOING?
YEAH.
HE SAID HE WENT TO MEET IDEM. HE SAID HE WANTED TO ASK HIM SOMETHING ABOUT... IDEA.
OH... HE... OH.
WELL, THEN.
EIRI?
I IMAGINE... ROSE MIGHT NOT BE COMING BACK HERE.
HE MIGHT GO SOMEWHERE ...WITH IDEM.

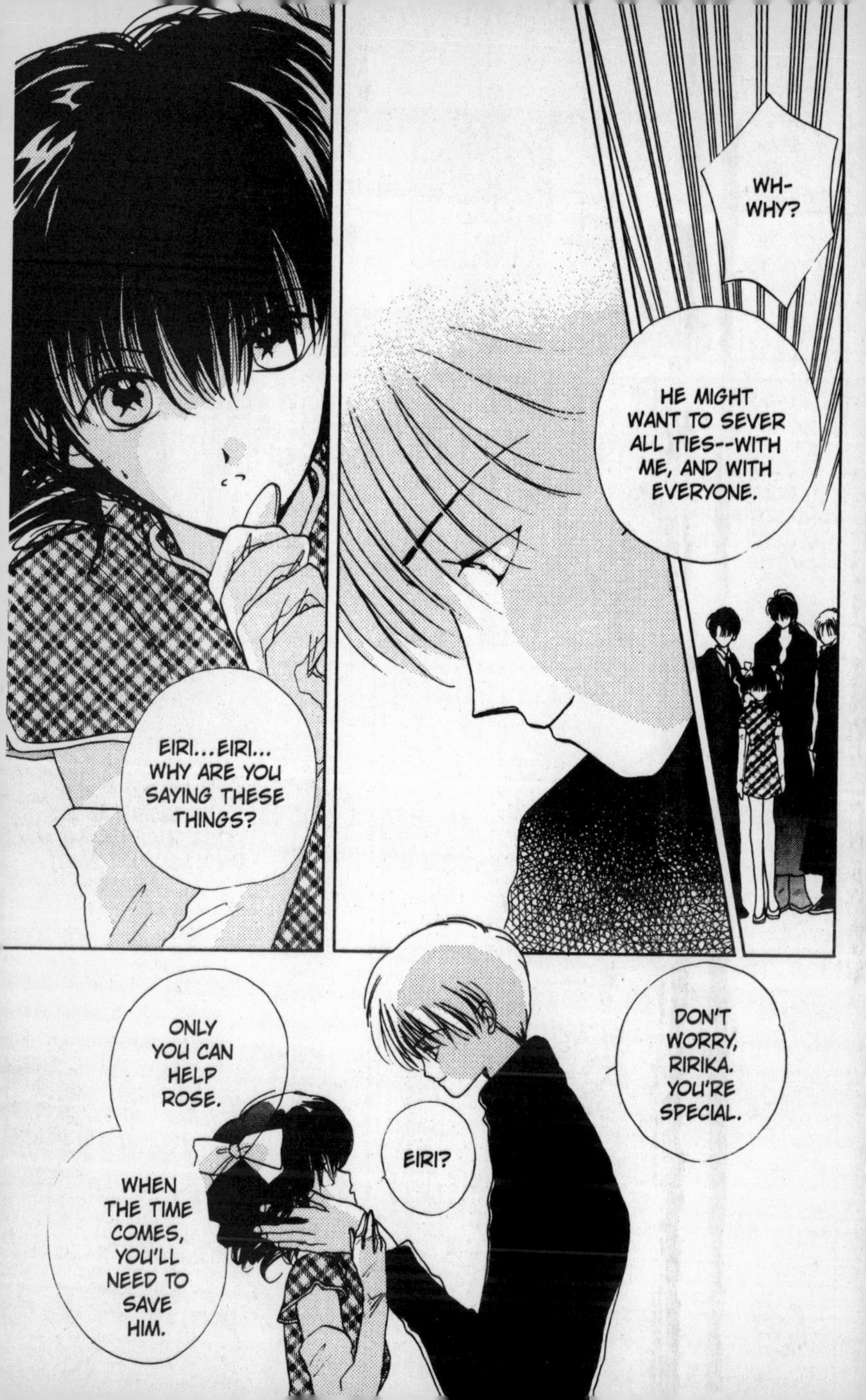
WH-
WHY?
HE MIGHT WANT TO SEVER ALL TIES--WITH ME, AND WITH EVERYONE.
EIRI...EIRI... WHY ARE YOU SAYING THESE THINGS?
DON'T WORRY, RIRIKA. YOU'RE SPECIAL.
EIRI?
ONLY YOU CAN HELP ROSE.
WHEN THE TIME COMES, YOU'LL NEED TO SAVE HIM.

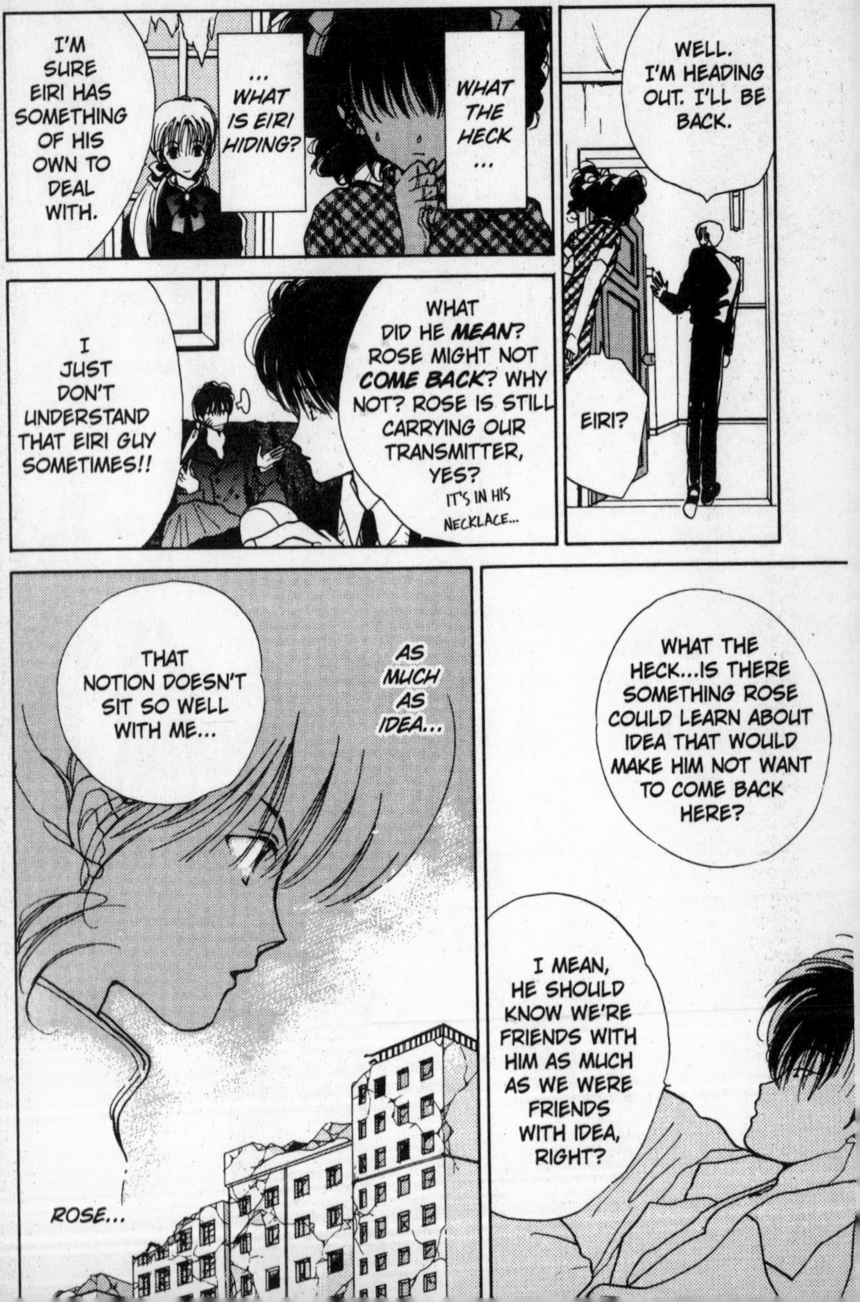
WELL. I'M HEADING OUT. I'LL BE BACK.
EIRI?
WHAT THE HECK ...
... WHAT IS EIRI HIDING?
I'M SURE EIRI HAS SOMETHING OF HIS OWN TO DEAL WITH.
WHAT DID HE *MEAN*? ROSE MIGHT NOT *COME BACK*? WHY NOT? ROSE IS STILL CARRYING OUR TRANSMITTER, YES?
IT'S IN HIS NECKLACE...
I JUST DON'T UNDERSTAND THAT EIRI GUY SOMETIMES!!
WHAT THE HECK...IS THERE SOMETHING ROSE COULD LEARN ABOUT IDEA THAT WOULD MAKE HIM NOT WANT TO COME BACK HERE?
I MEAN, HE SHOULD KNOW WE'RE FRIENDS WITH HIM AS MUCH AS WE WERE FRIENDS WITH IDEA, RIGHT?
AS MUCH AS IDEA...
THAT NOTION DOESN'T SIT SO WELL WITH ME...
ROSE...

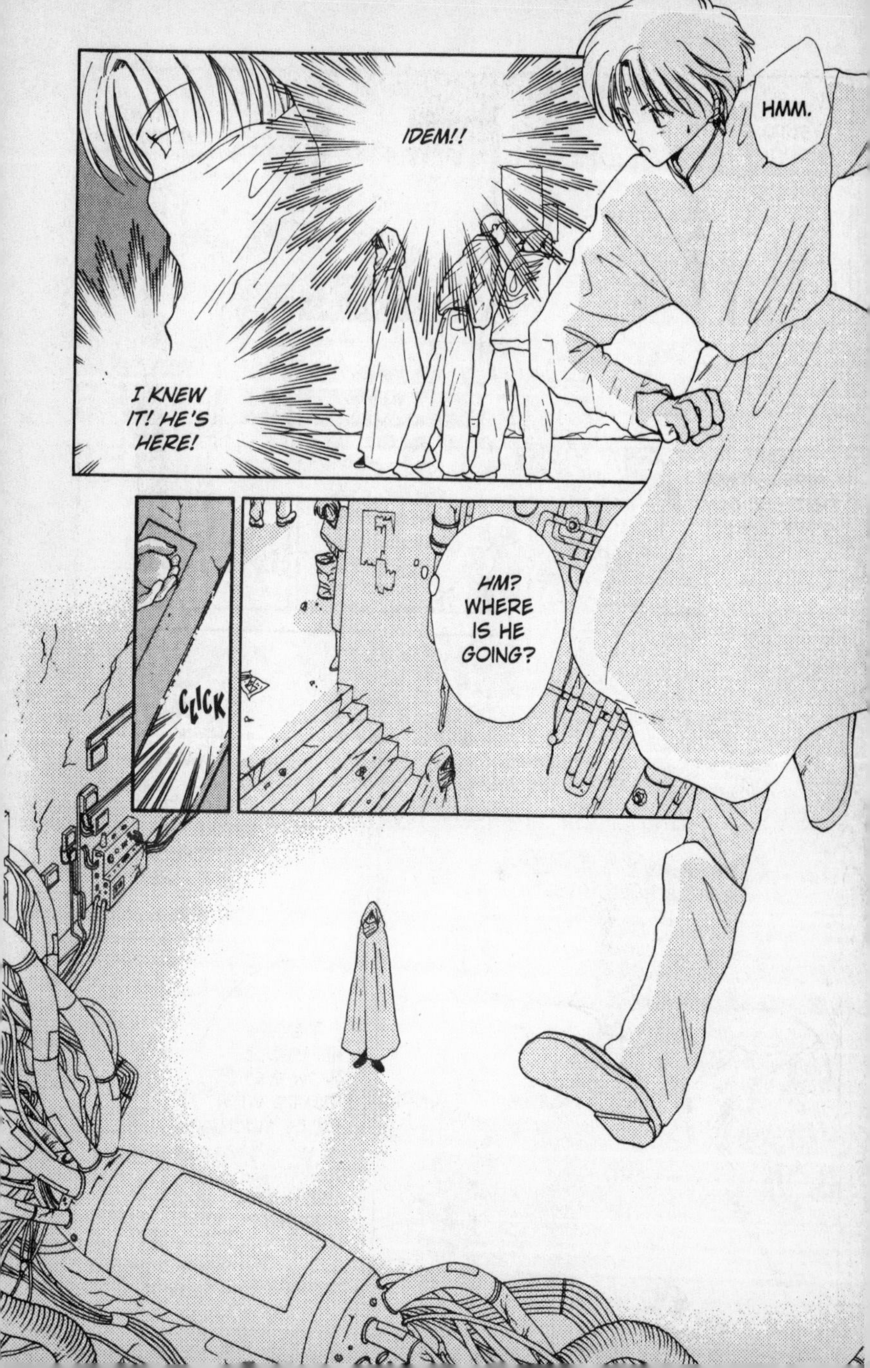
HMM.
IDEM!!
I KNEW IT! HE'S HERE!
HM? WHERE IS HE GOING?
CLICK

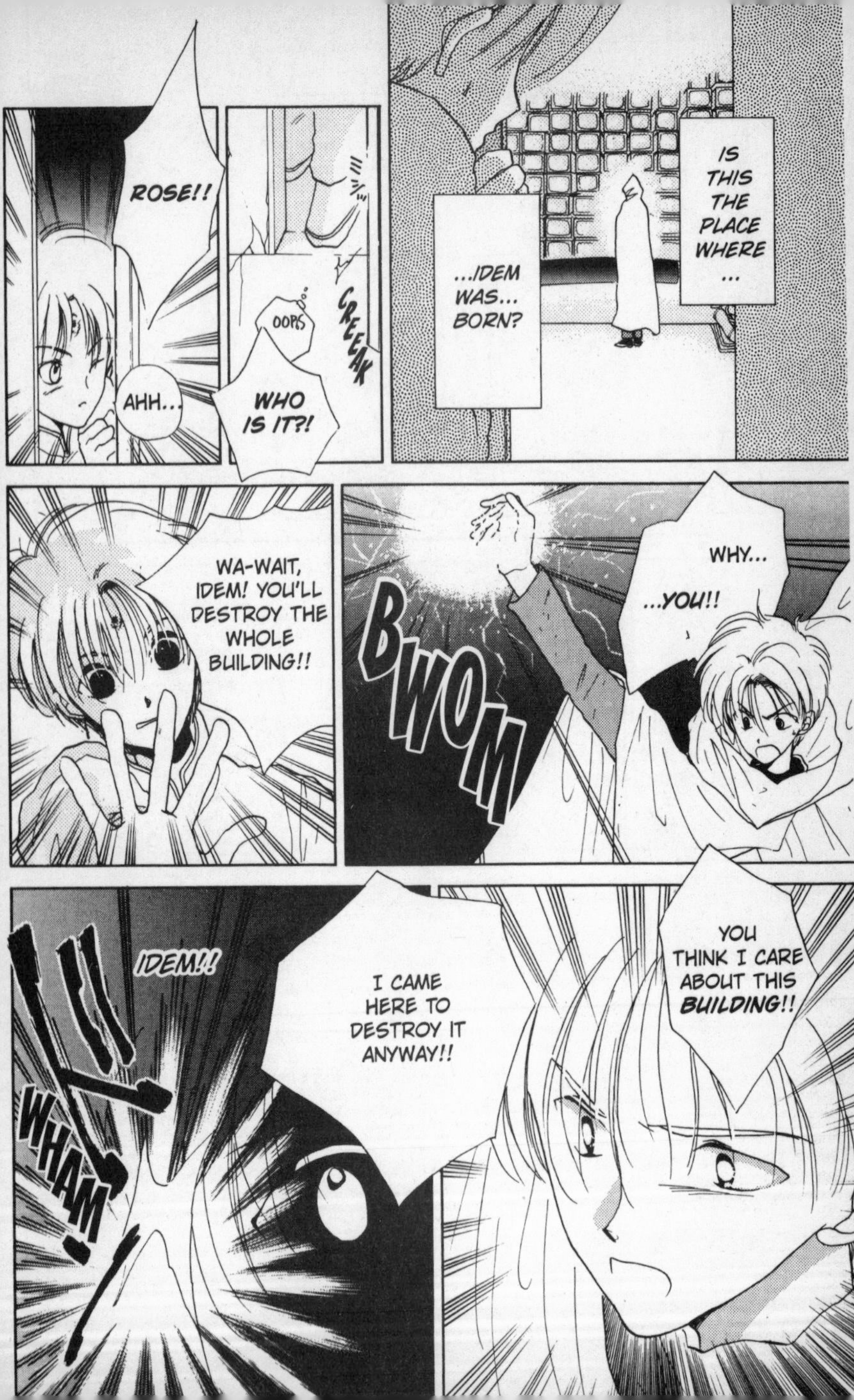
IS THIS THE PLACE WHERE...
...IDEM WAS... BORN?
CREEAK
OOPS
WHO IS IT?!
ROSE!!
AHH...
WHY...
...YOU!!
BWOM
WA-WAIT, IDEM! YOU'LL DESTROY THE WHOLE BUILDING!!
YOU THINK I CARE ABOUT THIS BUILDING!!
I CAME HERE TO DESTROY IT ANYWAY!!
IDEM!!
WHAM

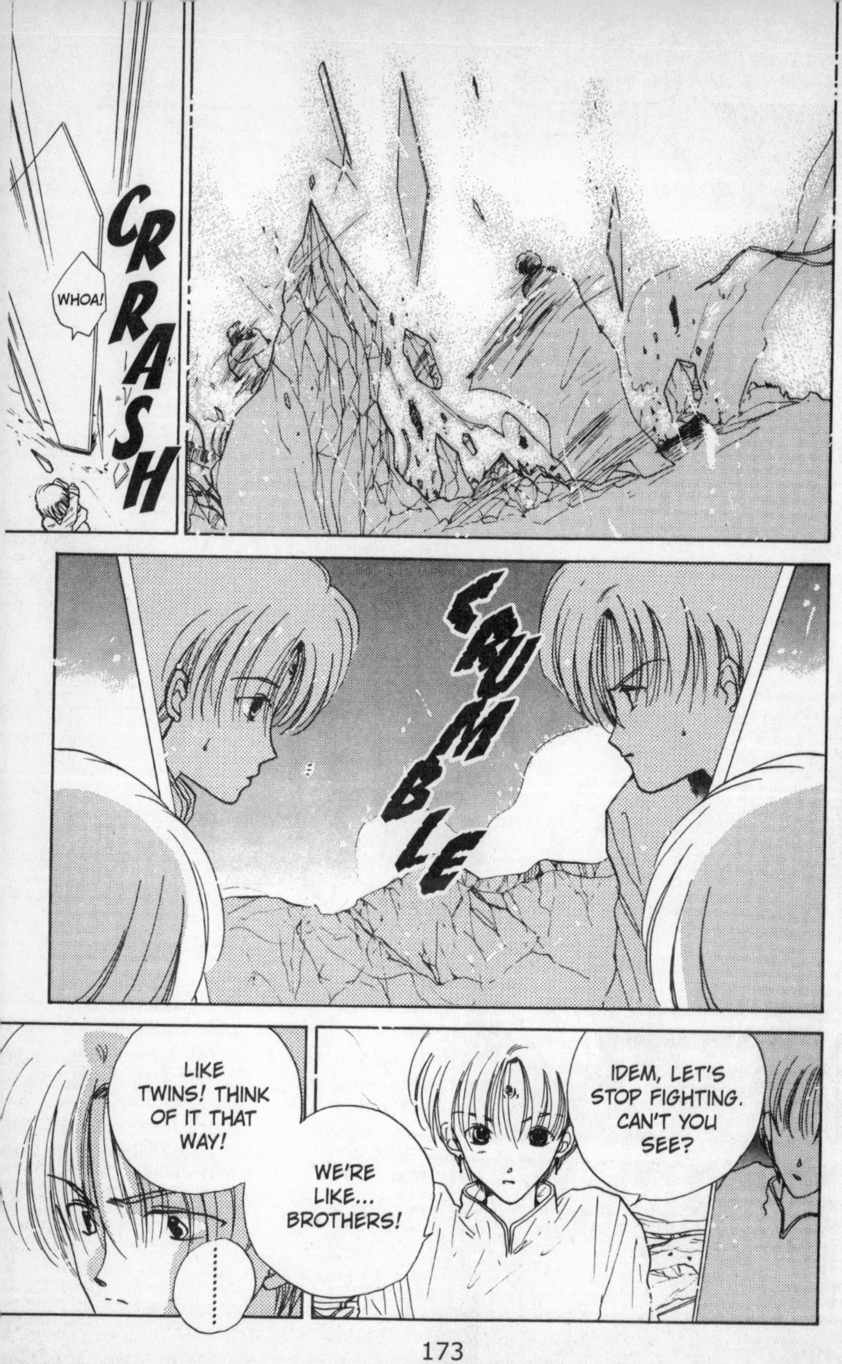
WHOA!
CRRASH
CRUMBLE
IDEM, LET'S STOP FIGHTING. CAN'T YOU SEE?
WE'RE LIKE... BROTHERS!
LIKE TWINS! THINK OF IT THAT WAY!
......

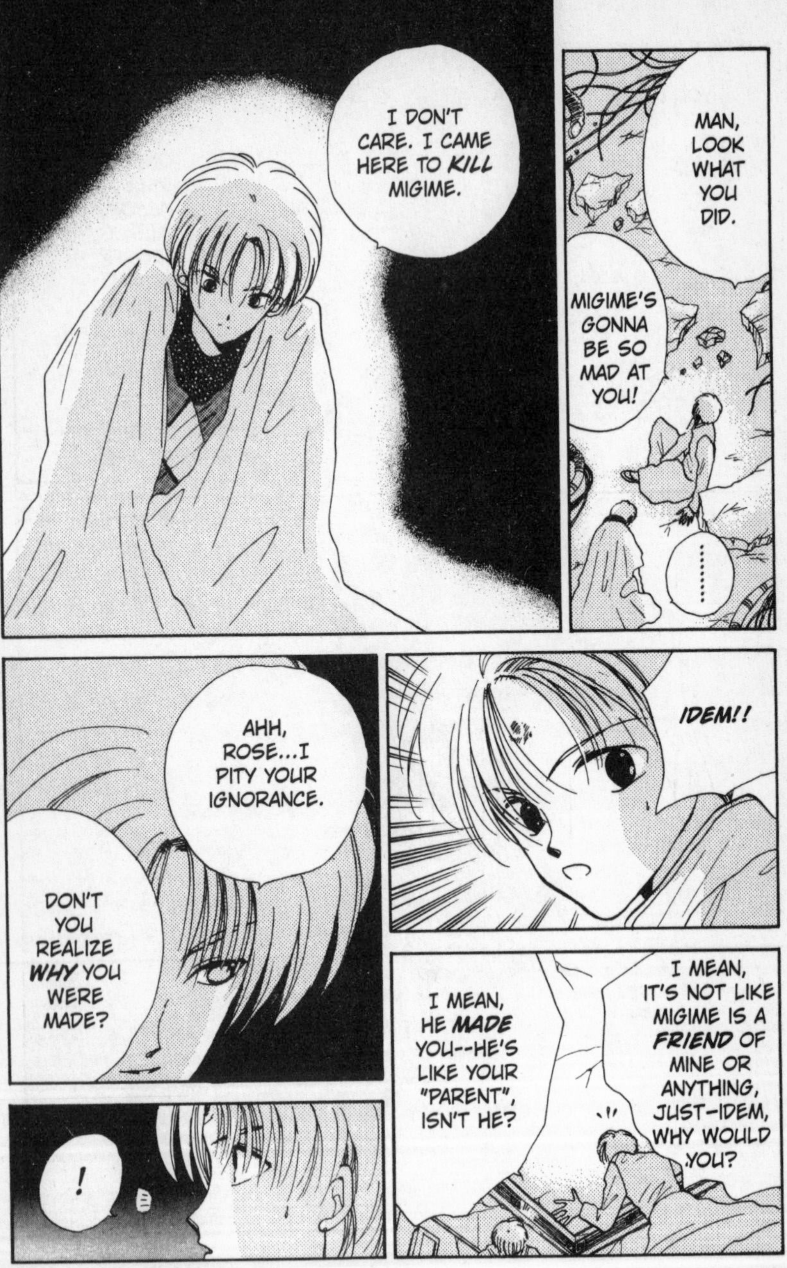
MAN, LOOK WHAT YOU DID.
MIGIME'S GONNA BE SO MAD AT YOU!
......
I DON'T CARE. I CAME HERE TO KILL MIGIME.
IDEM!!
I MEAN, IT'S NOT LIKE MIGIME IS A FRIEND OF MINE OR ANYTHING, JUST-IDEM, WHY WOULD YOU?
I MEAN, HE MADE YOU--HE'S LIKE YOUR "PARENT", ISN'T HE?
AHH, ROSE...I PITY YOUR IGNORANCE.
DON'T YOU REALIZE WHY YOU WERE MADE?
!

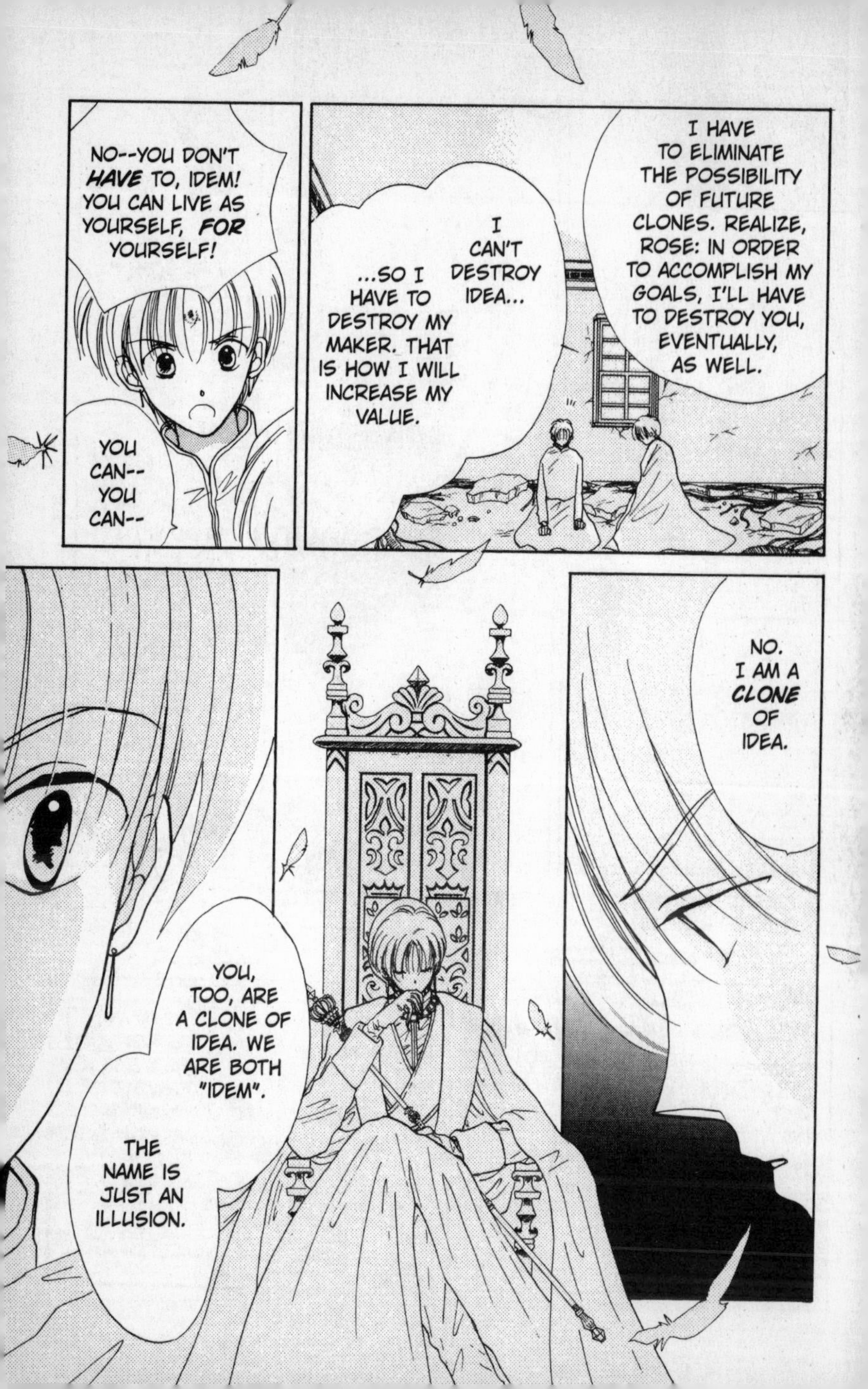
I HAVE TO ELIMINATE THE POSSIBILITY OF FUTURE CLONES. REALIZE, ROSE: IN ORDER TO ACCOMPLISH MY GOALS, I'LL HAVE TO DESTROY YOU, EVENTUALLY, AS WELL.
I CAN'T DESTROY IDEA...
...SO I HAVE TO DESTROY MY MAKER. THAT IS HOW I WILL INCREASE MY VALUE.
NO--YOU DON'T *HAVE* TO, IDEM! YOU CAN LIVE AS YOURSELF, *FOR* YOURSELF!
YOU CAN--YOU CAN--
NO. I AM A *CLONE* OF IDEA.
YOU, TOO, ARE A CLONE OF IDEA. WE ARE BOTH "IDEM".
THE NAME IS JUST AN ILLUSION.

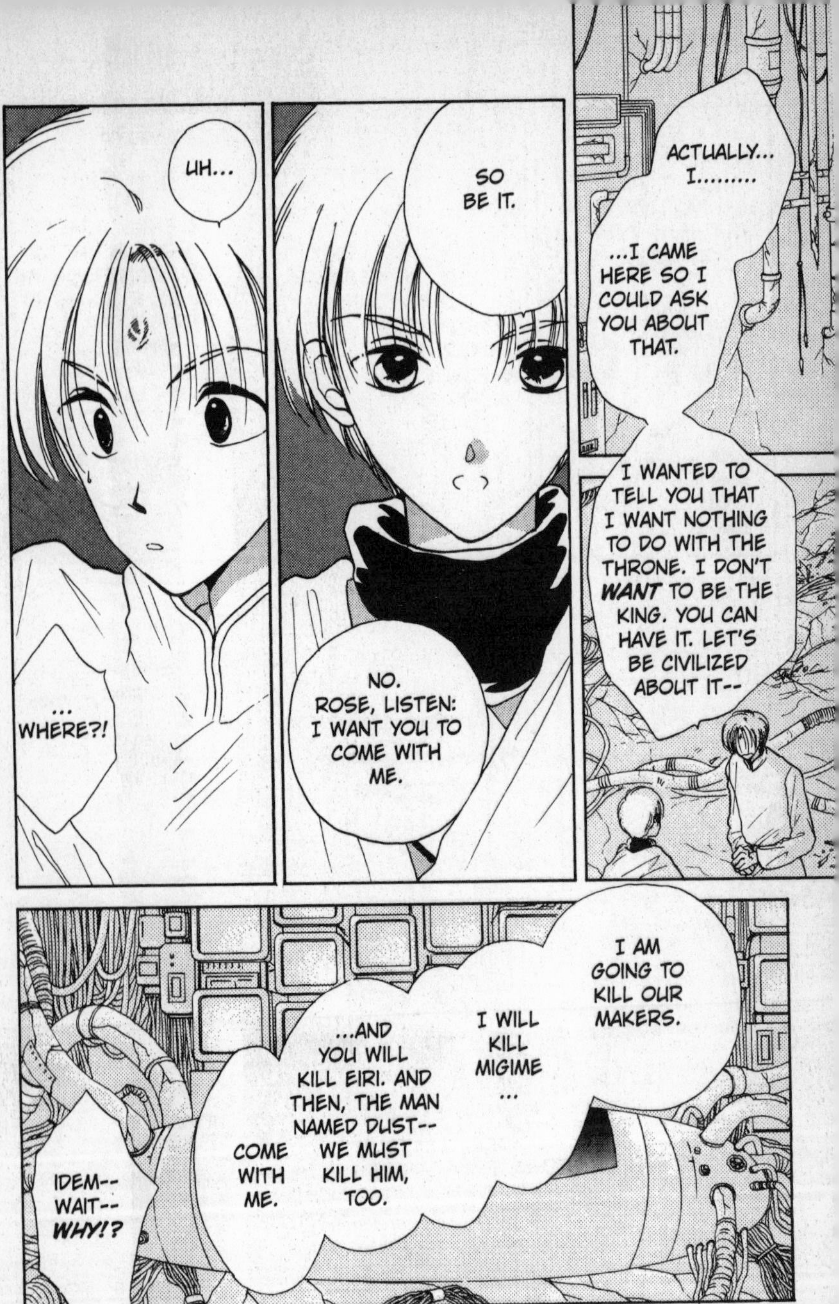
ACTUALLY... I.........
...I CAME HERE SO I COULD ASK YOU ABOUT THAT.
I WANTED TO TELL YOU THAT I WANT NOTHING TO DO WITH THE THRONE. I DON'T **WANT** TO BE THE KING. YOU CAN HAVE IT. LET'S BE CIVILIZED ABOUT IT--
SO BE IT.
NO. ROSE, LISTEN: I WANT YOU TO COME WITH ME.
UH...
... WHERE?!
I AM GOING TO KILL OUR MAKERS.
I WILL KILL MIGIME ...
...AND YOU WILL KILL EIRI. AND THEN, THE MAN NAMED DUST-- WE MUST KILL HIM, TOO.
COME WITH ME.
IDEM-- WAIT-- **WHY!?**

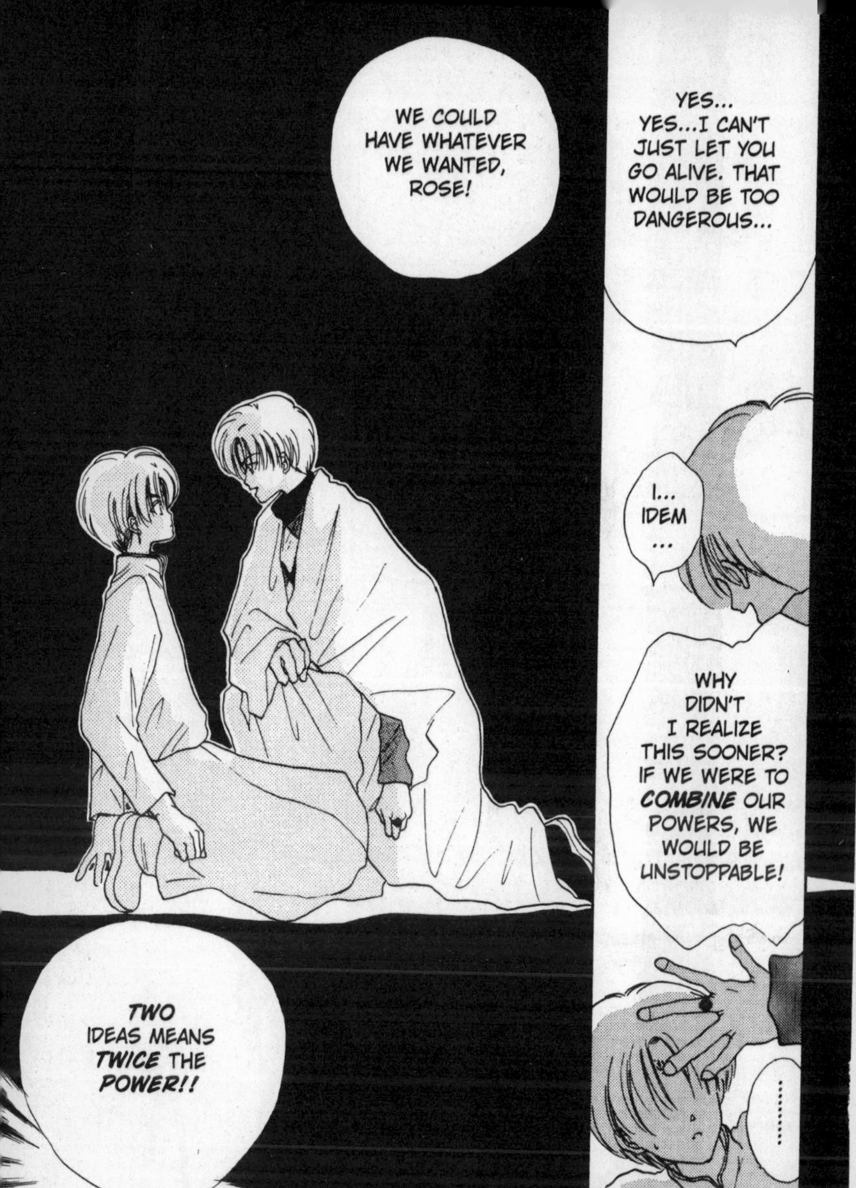
YES...
YES...I CAN'T JUST LET YOU GO ALIVE. THAT WOULD BE TOO DANGEROUS...
I... IDEM ...
WHY DIDN'T I REALIZE THIS SOONER? IF WE WERE TO *COMBINE* OUR POWERS, WE WOULD BE UNSTOPPABLE!
....
WE COULD HAVE WHATEVER WE WANTED, ROSE!
TWO IDEAS MEANS *TWICE* THE *POWER!!*

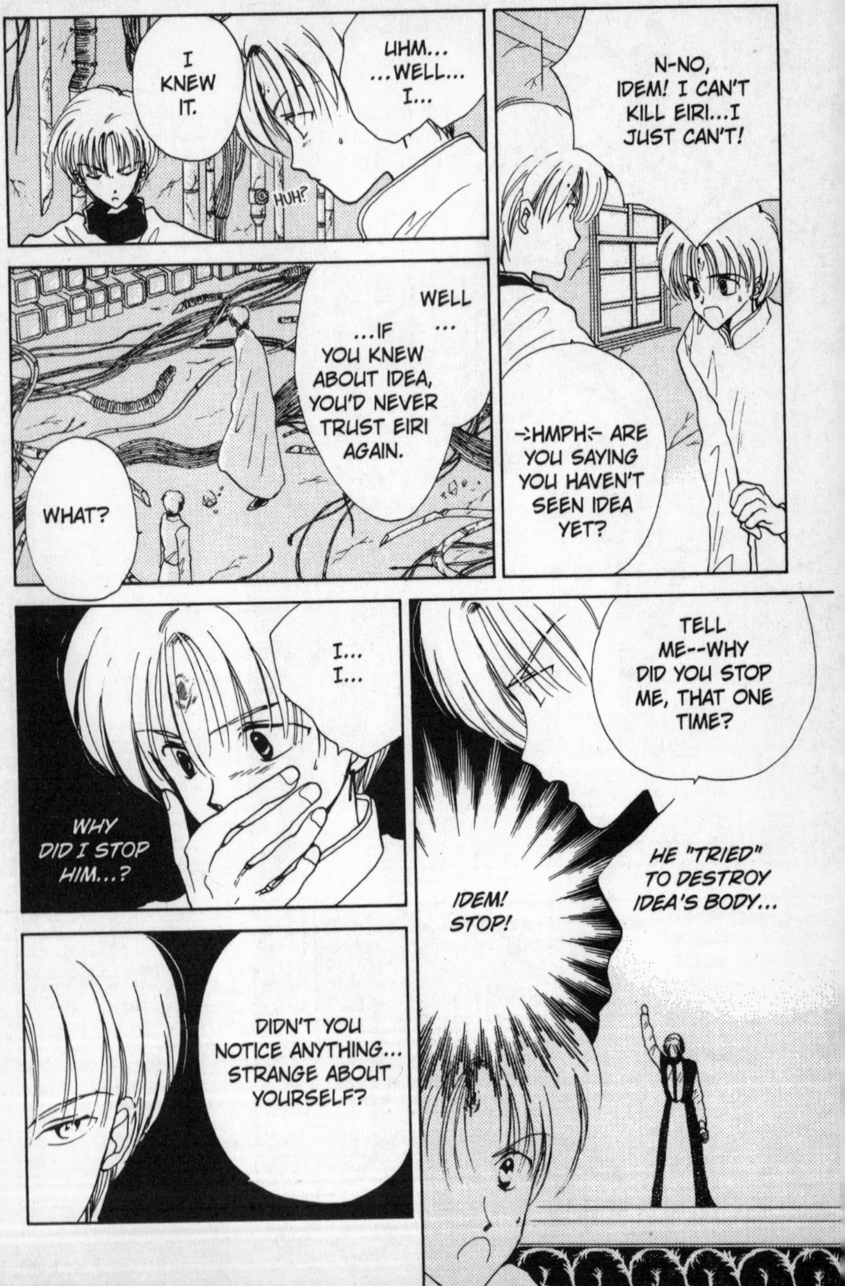
N-NO, IDEM! I CAN'T KILL EIRI...I JUST CAN'T!
≯HMPH≮ ARE YOU SAYING YOU HAVEN'T SEEN IDEA YET?
UHM... ...WELL... I...
I KNEW IT.
HUH?
WELL ... ...IF YOU KNEW ABOUT IDEA, YOU'D NEVER TRUST EIRI AGAIN.
WHAT?
TELL ME--WHY DID YOU STOP ME, THAT ONE TIME?
HE "TRIED" TO DESTROY IDEA'S BODY...
IDEM! STOP!
I... I...
WHY DID I STOP HIM...?
DIDN'T YOU NOTICE ANYTHING... STRANGE ABOUT YOURSELF?

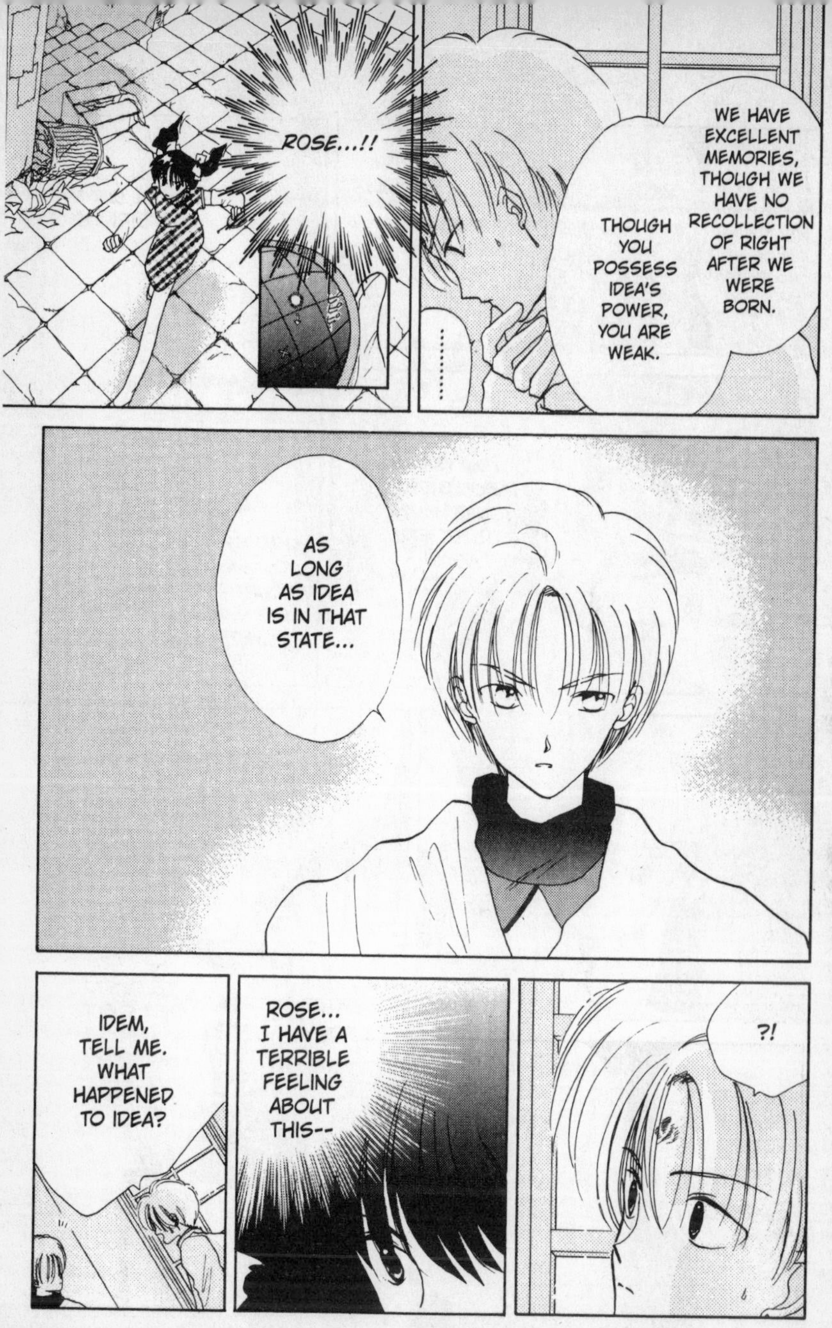
WE HAVE EXCELLENT MEMORIES, THOUGH WE HAVE NO RECOLLECTION OF RIGHT AFTER WE WERE BORN.
THOUGH YOU POSSESS IDEA'S POWER, YOU ARE WEAK.
......
ROSE...!!
AS LONG AS IDEA IS IN THAT STATE...
?!
ROSE... I HAVE A TERRIBLE FEELING ABOUT THIS--
IDEM, TELL ME. WHAT HAPPENED TO IDEA?

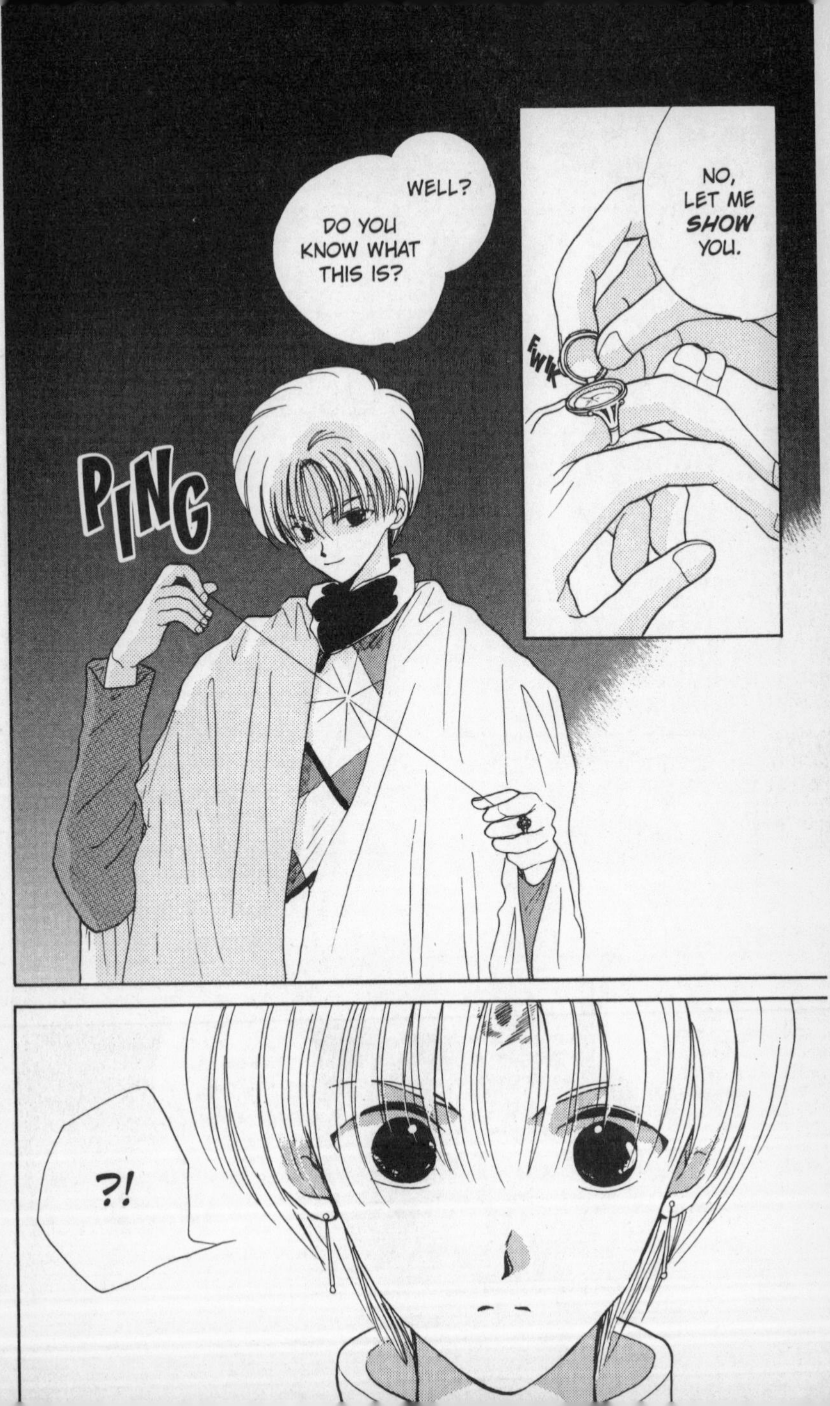
NO, LET ME SHOW YOU.
FWIK
WELL?
DO YOU KNOW WHAT THIS IS?
PING
?!

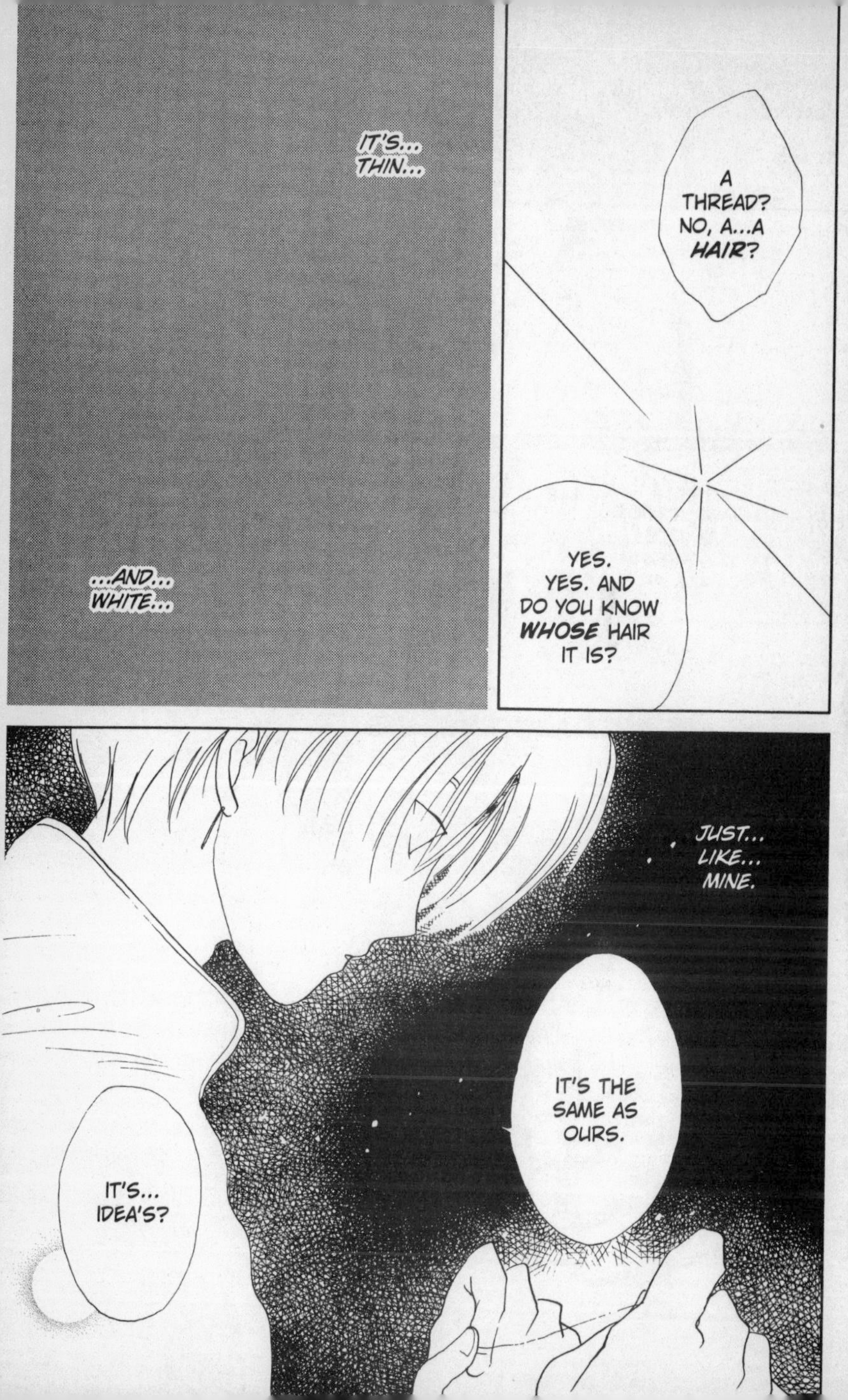
A THREAD? NO, A...A *HAIR*?
YES. YES. AND DO YOU KNOW *WHOSE* HAIR IT IS?
IT'S... THIN...
...AND... WHITE...
JUST... LIKE... MINE.
IT'S THE SAME AS OURS.
IT'S... IDEA'S?

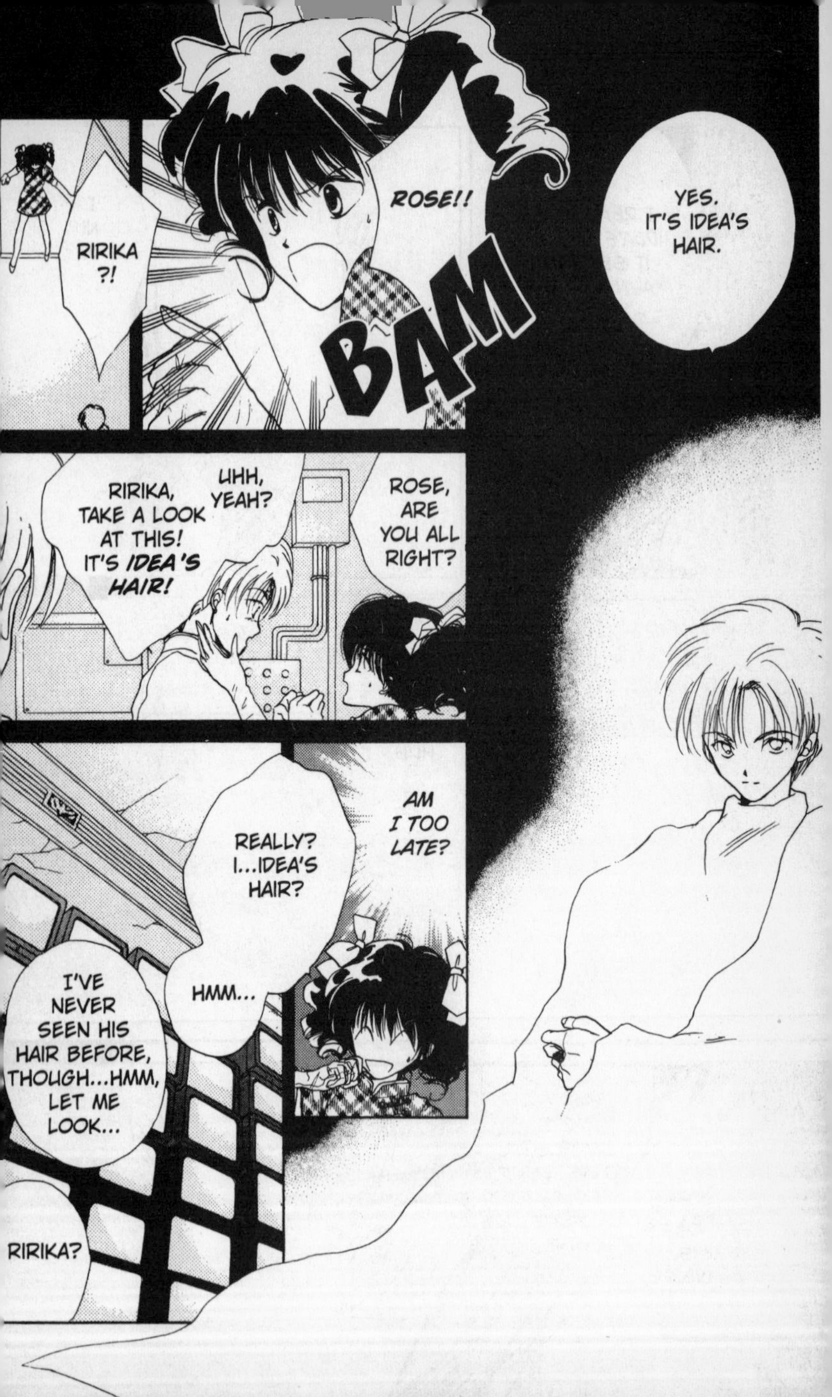
YES. IT'S IDEA'S HAIR.
ROSE!!
BAM
RIRIKA ?!
ROSE, ARE YOU ALL RIGHT?
UHH, YEAH?
RIRIKA, TAKE A LOOK AT THIS! IT'S *IDEA'S HAIR!*
AM I TOO LATE?
REALLY? I...IDEA'S HAIR?
HMM...
I'VE NEVER SEEN HIS HAIR BEFORE, THOUGH...HMM, LET ME LOOK...
RIRIKA?

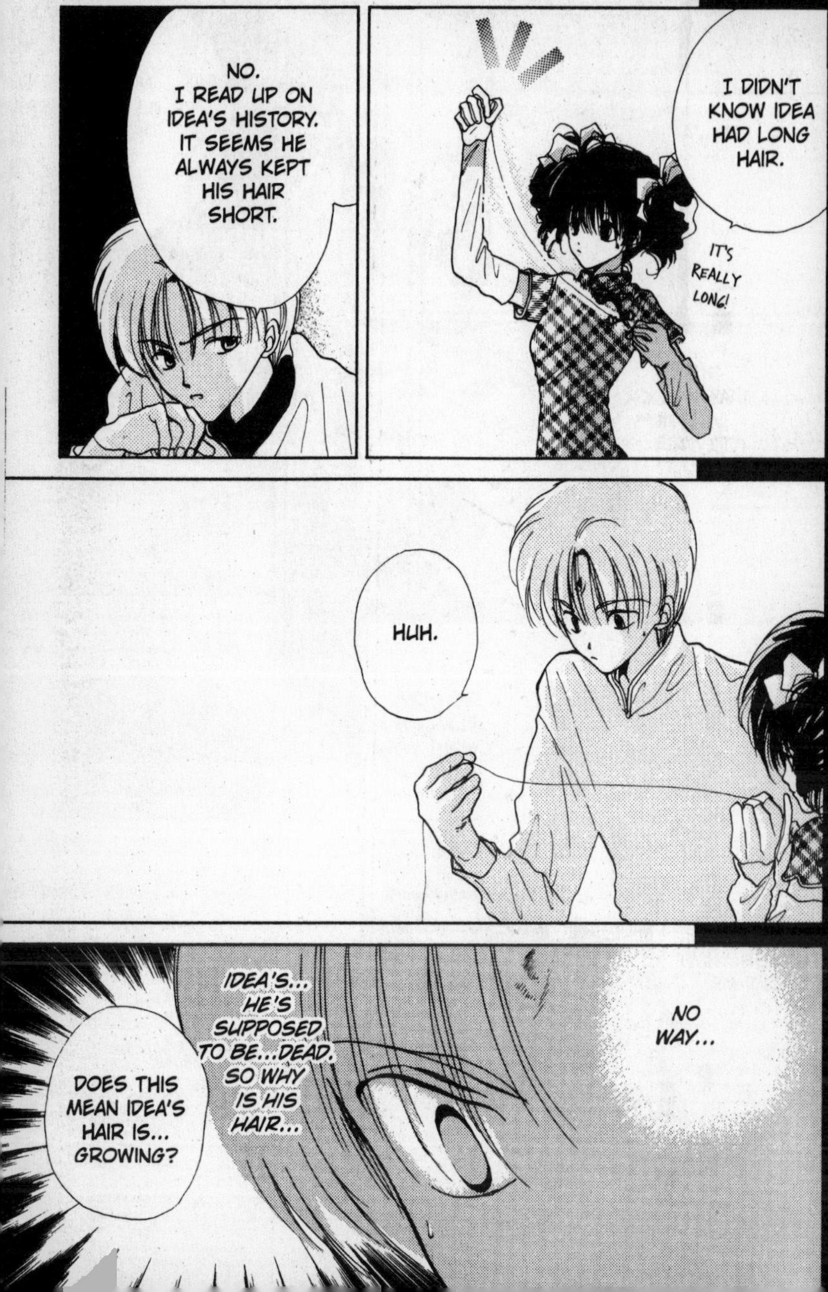
I DIDN'T KNOW IDEA HAD LONG HAIR.
IT'S REALLY LONG!
NO. I READ UP ON IDEA'S HISTORY. IT SEEMS HE ALWAYS KEPT HIS HAIR SHORT.
HUH.
NO WAY...
IDEA'S... HE'S SUPPOSED TO BE...DEAD. SO WHY IS HIS HAIR...
DOES THIS MEAN IDEA'S HAIR IS... GROWING?

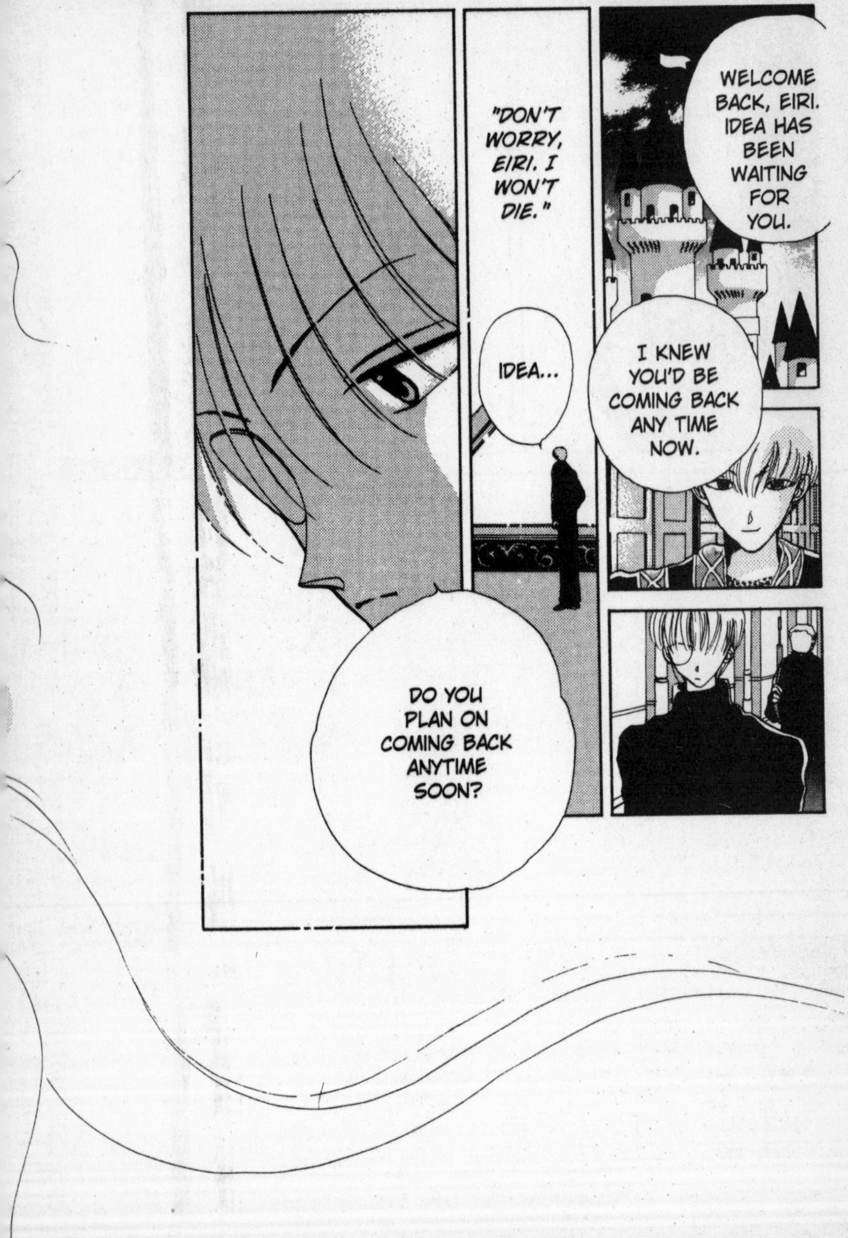
WELCOME BACK, EIRI. IDEA HAS BEEN WAITING FOR YOU.
I KNEW YOU'D BE COMING BACK ANY TIME NOW.
"DON'T WORRY, EIRI. I WON'T DIE."
IDEA...
DO YOU PLAN ON COMING BACK ANYTIME SOON?

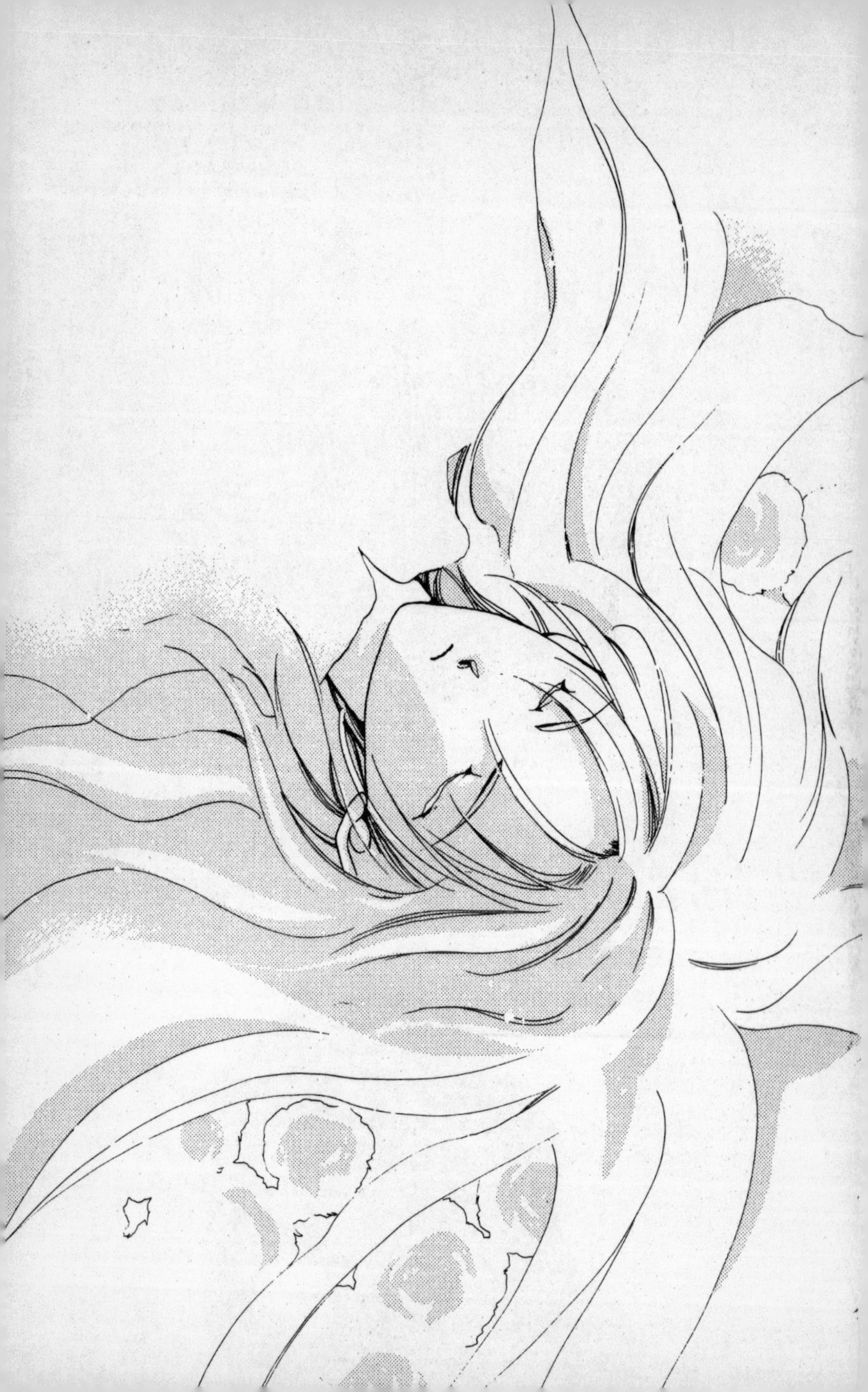

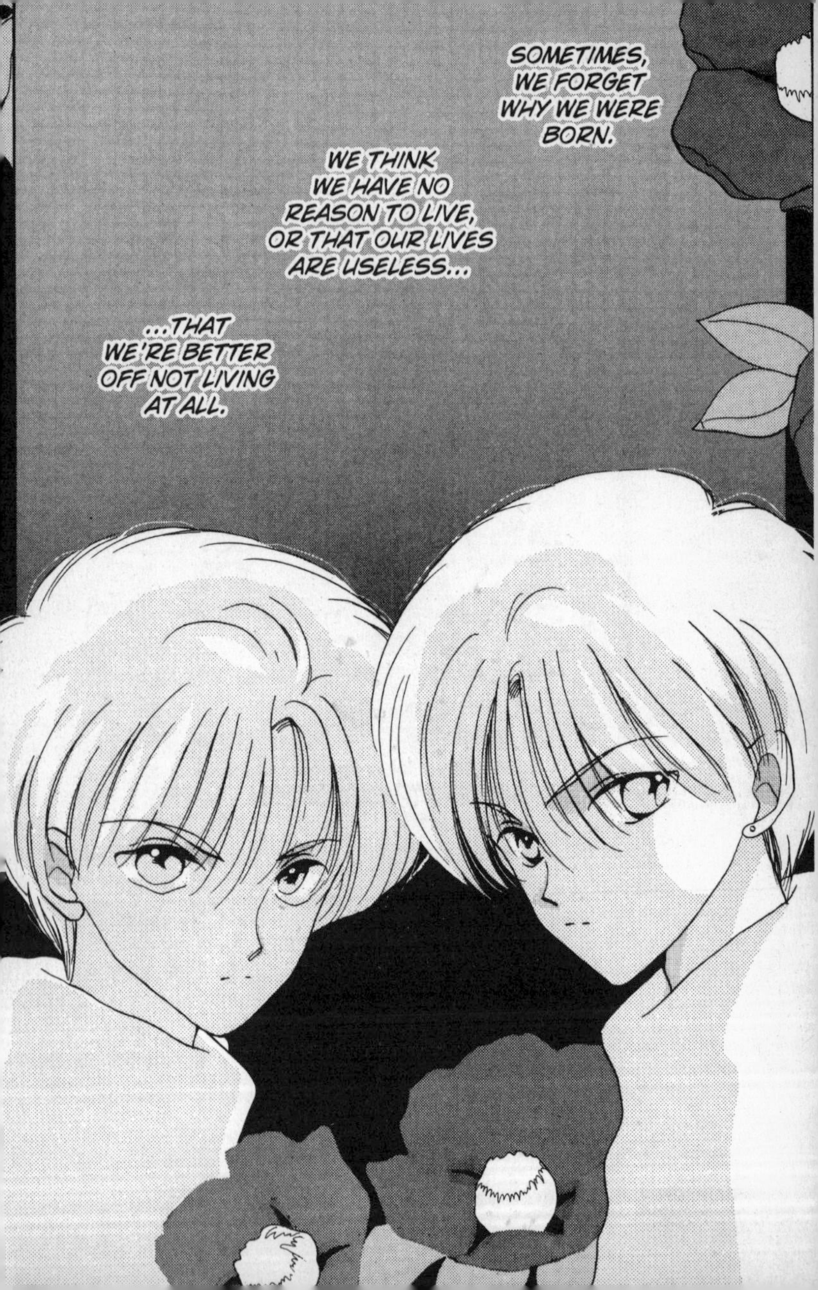
SOMETIMES, WE FORGET WHY WE WERE BORN.
WE THINK WE HAVE NO REASON TO LIVE, OR THAT OUR LIVES ARE USELESS...
...THAT WE'RE BETTER OFF NOT LIVING AT ALL.

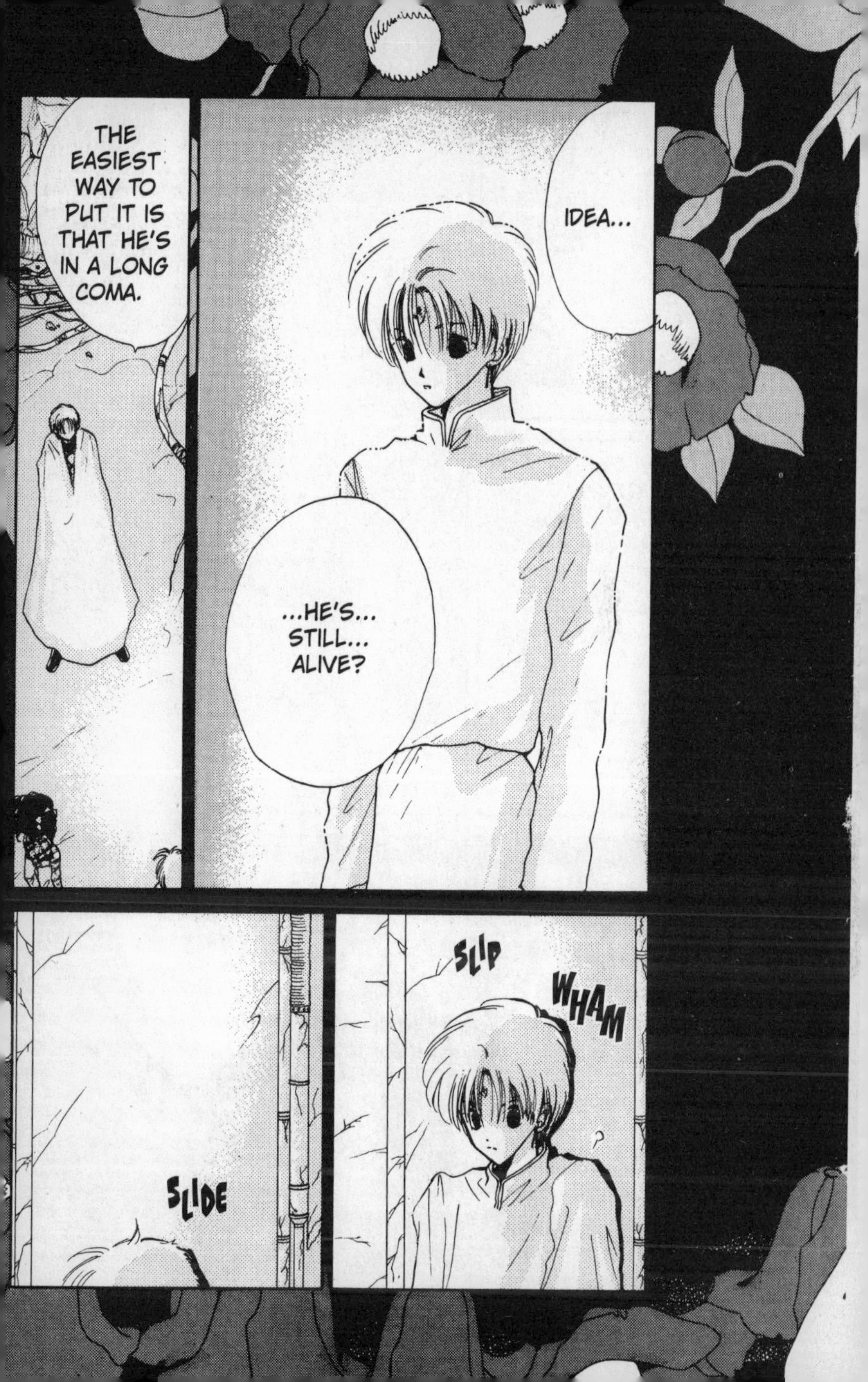
IDEA...
...HE'S... STILL... ALIVE?
THE EASIEST WAY TO PUT IT IS THAT HE'S IN A LONG COMA.
SLIP
WHAM
SLIDE

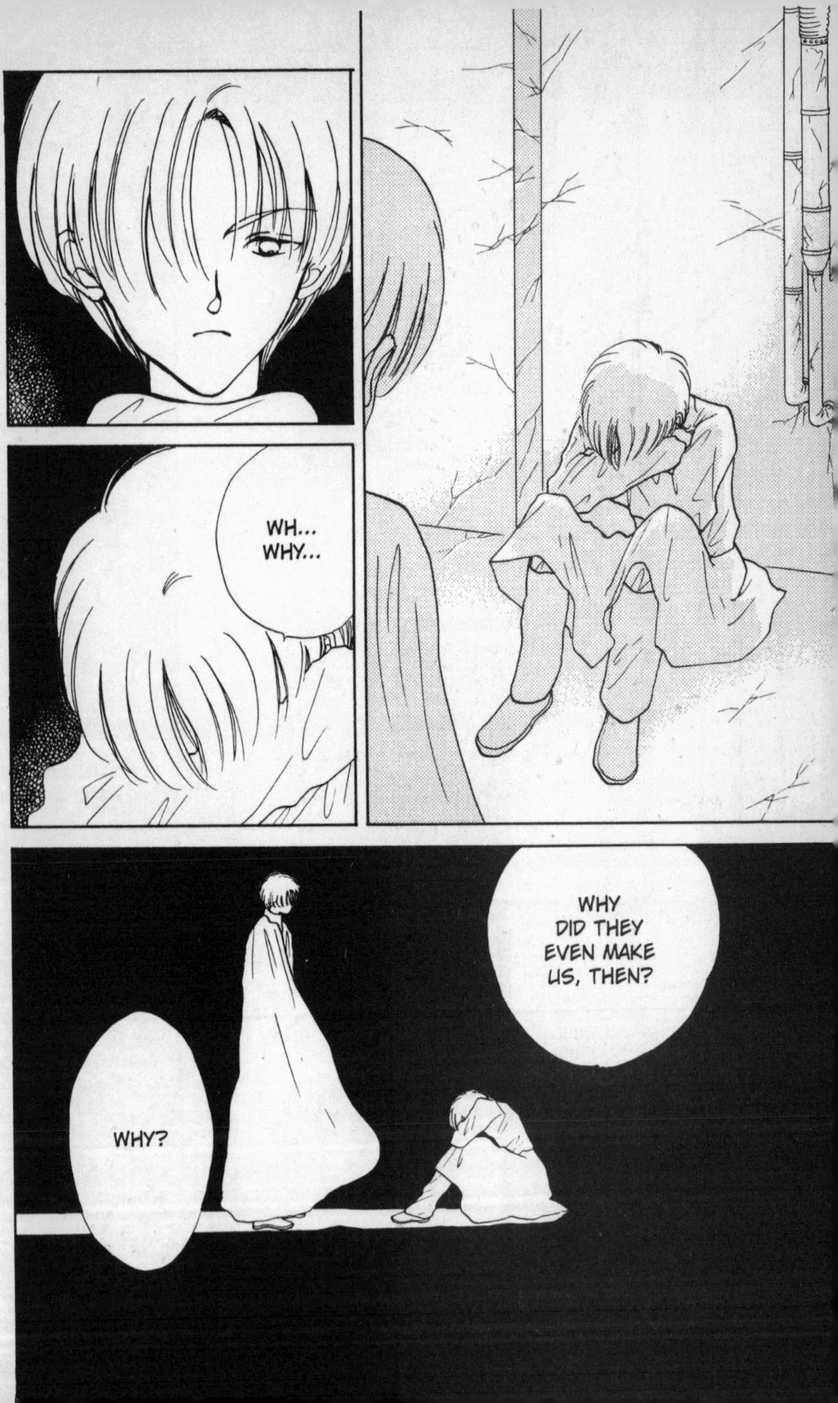
WH... WHY...
WHY DID THEY EVEN MAKE US, THEN?
WHY?

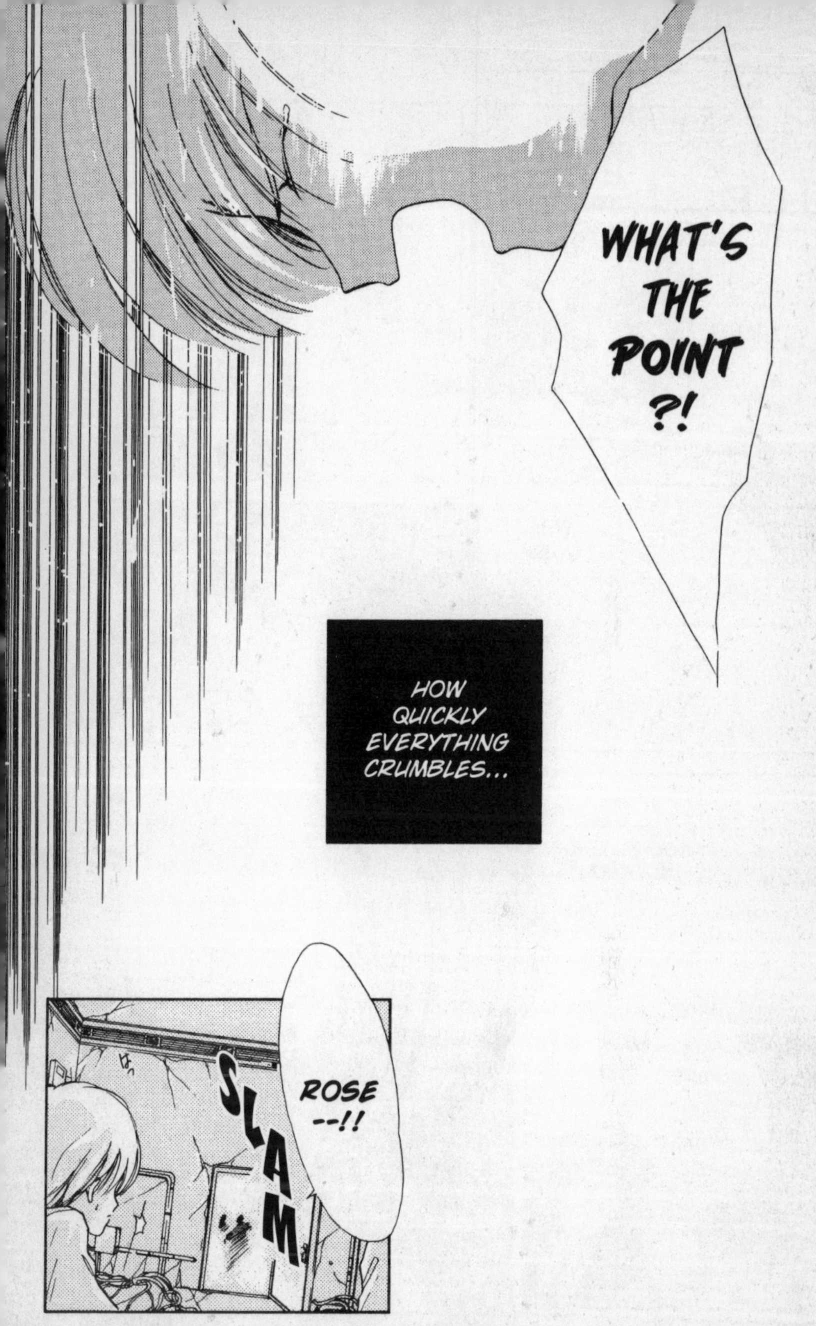
WHAT'S THE POINT ?!
HOW QUICKLY EVERYTHING CRUMBLES...
ROSE --!!
SLAM

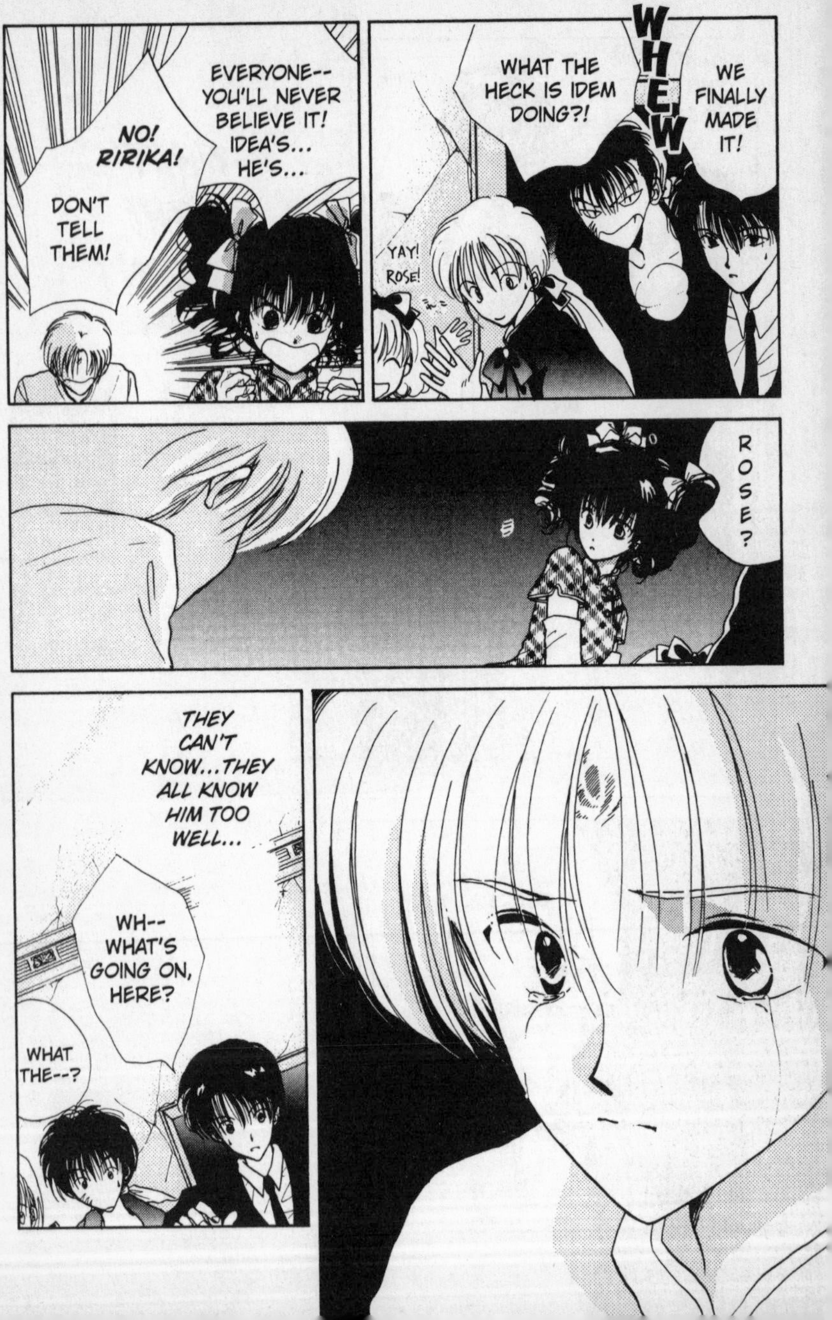
WE FINALLY MADE IT!
WHEW
WHAT THE HECK IS IDEM DOING?!
YAY! ROSE!
EVERYONE-- YOU'LL NEVER BELIEVE IT! IDEA'S... HE'S...
NO! RIRIKA!
DON'T TELL THEM!
ROSE?
THEY CAN'T KNOW...THEY ALL KNOW HIM TOO WELL...
WH-- WHAT'S GOING ON, HERE?
WHAT THE--?

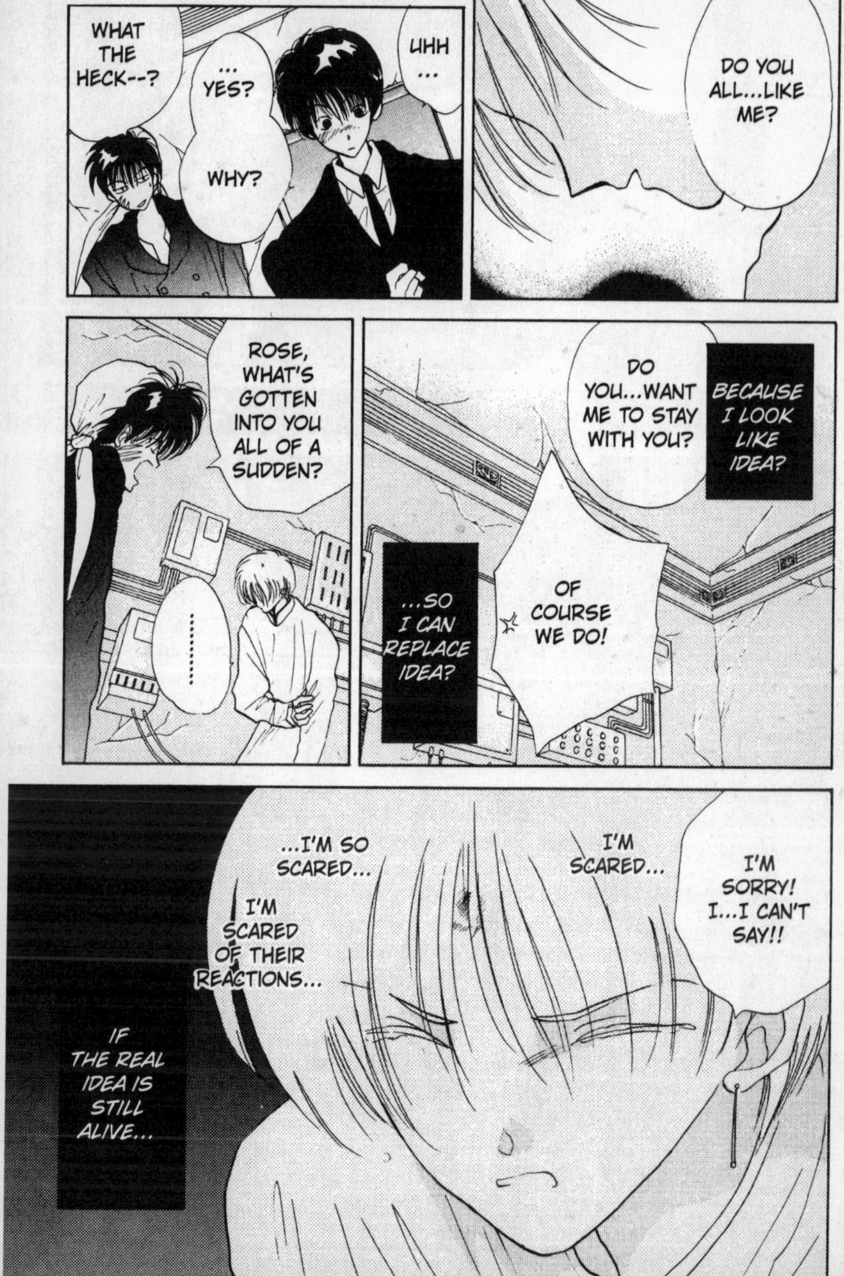
DO YOU ALL...LIKE ME?
UHH ...
... YES?
WHAT THE HECK--?
WHY?
BECAUSE I LOOK LIKE IDEA?
DO YOU...WANT ME TO STAY WITH YOU?
OF COURSE WE DO!
...SO I CAN REPLACE IDEA?
ROSE, WHAT'S GOTTEN INTO YOU ALL OF A SUDDEN?
......
I'M SORRY! I...I CAN'T SAY!!
I'M SCARED...
...I'M SO SCARED...
I'M SCARED OF THEIR REACTIONS...
IF THE REAL IDEA IS STILL ALIVE...

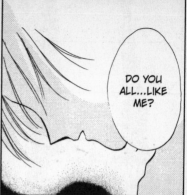

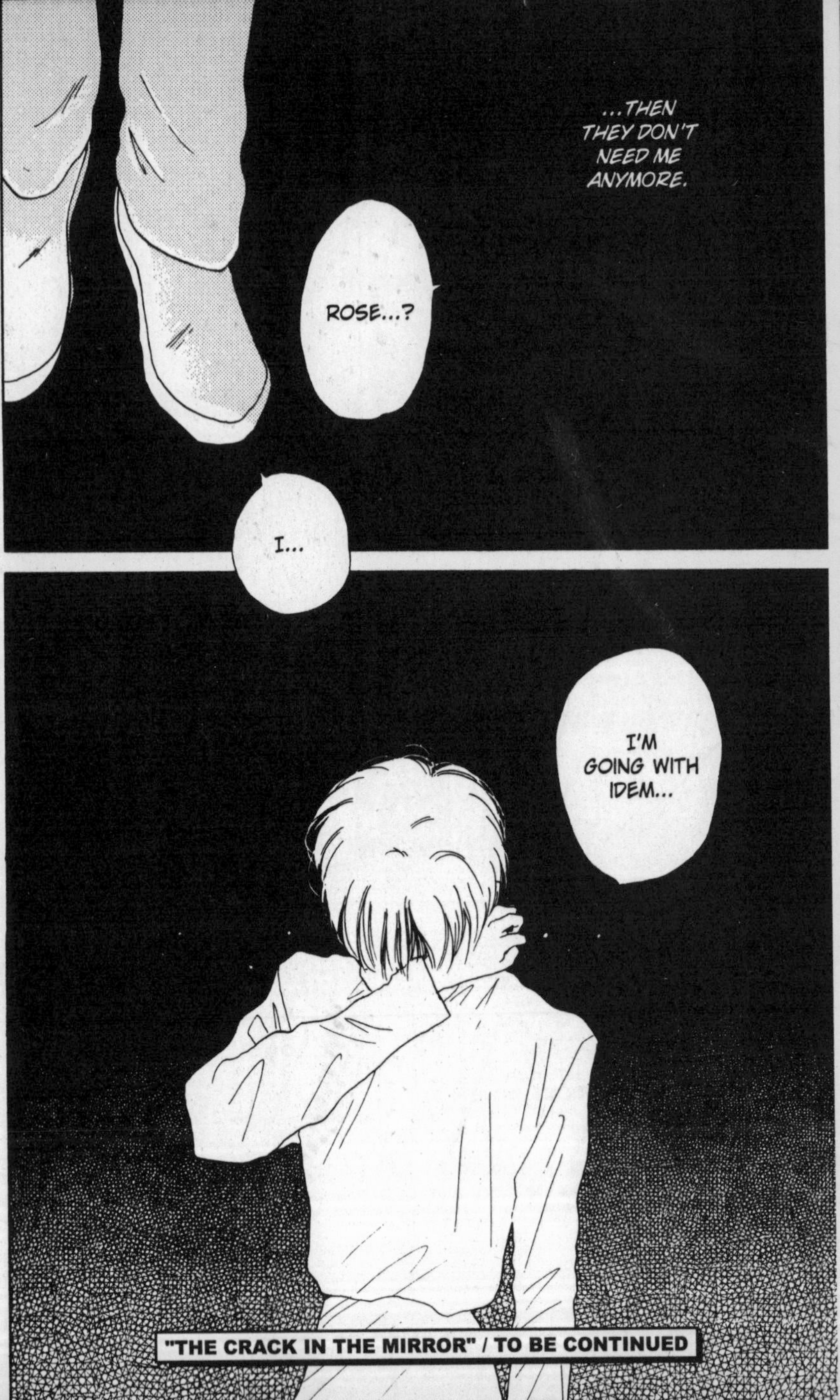
...THEN THEY DON'T NEED ME ANYMORE.
ROSE...?
I...
I'M GOING WITH IDEM...
"THE CRACK IN THE MIRROR" / TO BE CONTINUED

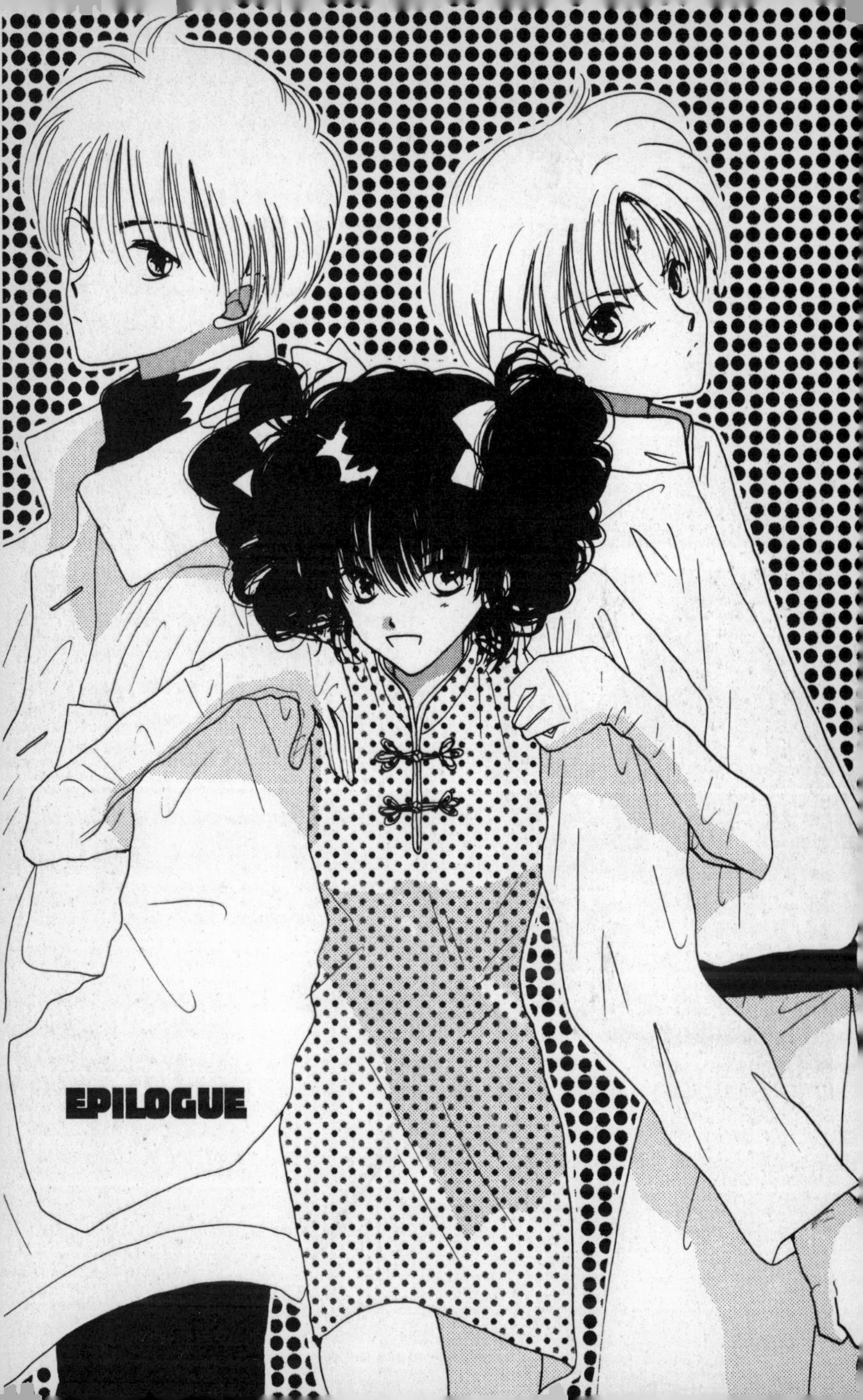
EPILOGUE

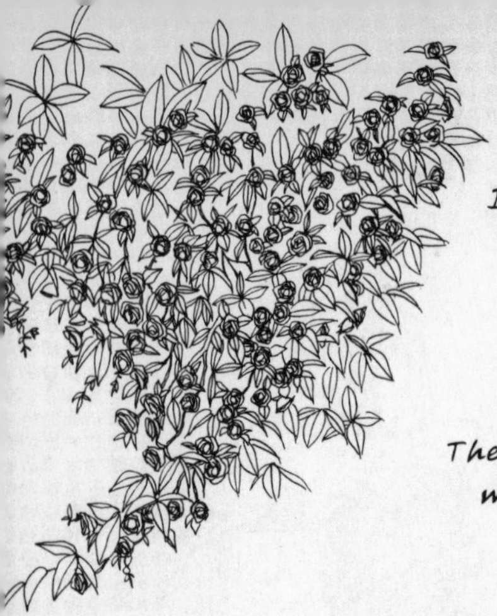

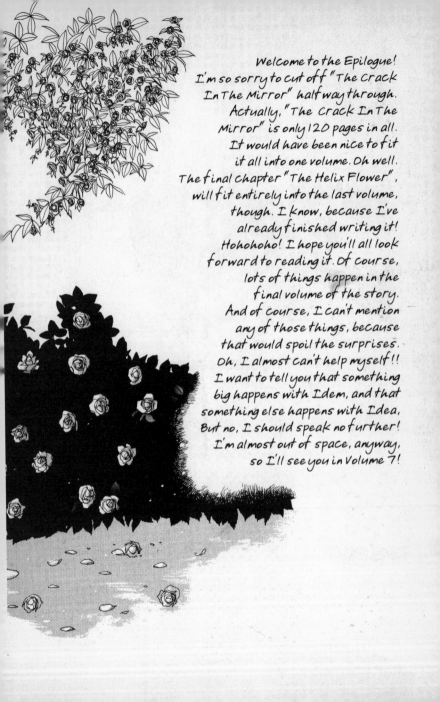

Welcome to the Epilogue! I'm so sorry to cut off "The Crack In The Mirror" halfway through. Actually, "The Crack In The Mirror" is only 120 pages in all. It would have been nice to fit it all into one volume. Oh well. The final chapter "The Helix Flower", will fit entirely into the last volume, though. I know, because I've already finished writing it! Hohohoho! I hope you'll all look forward to reading it. Of course, lots of things happen in the final volume of the story. And of course, I can't mention any of those things, because that would spoil the surprises. Oh, I almost can't help myself!! I want to tell you that something big happens with Idem, and that something else happens with Idea, But no, I should speak no further! I'm almost out of space, anyway, so I'll see you in Volume 7!

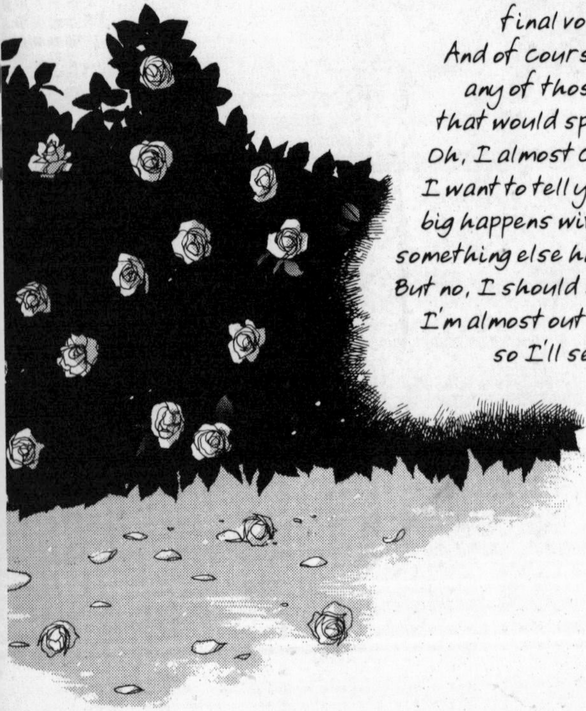

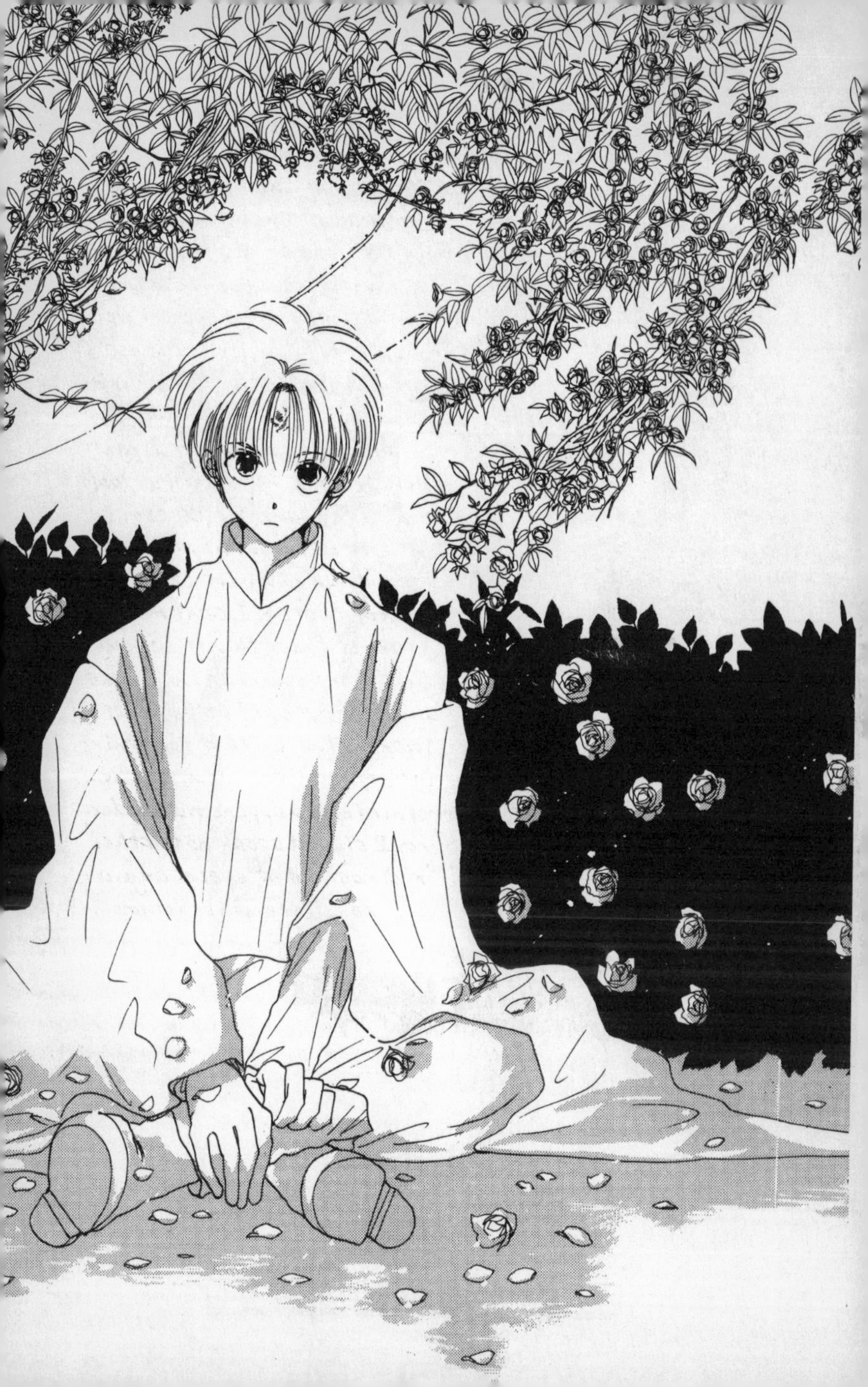

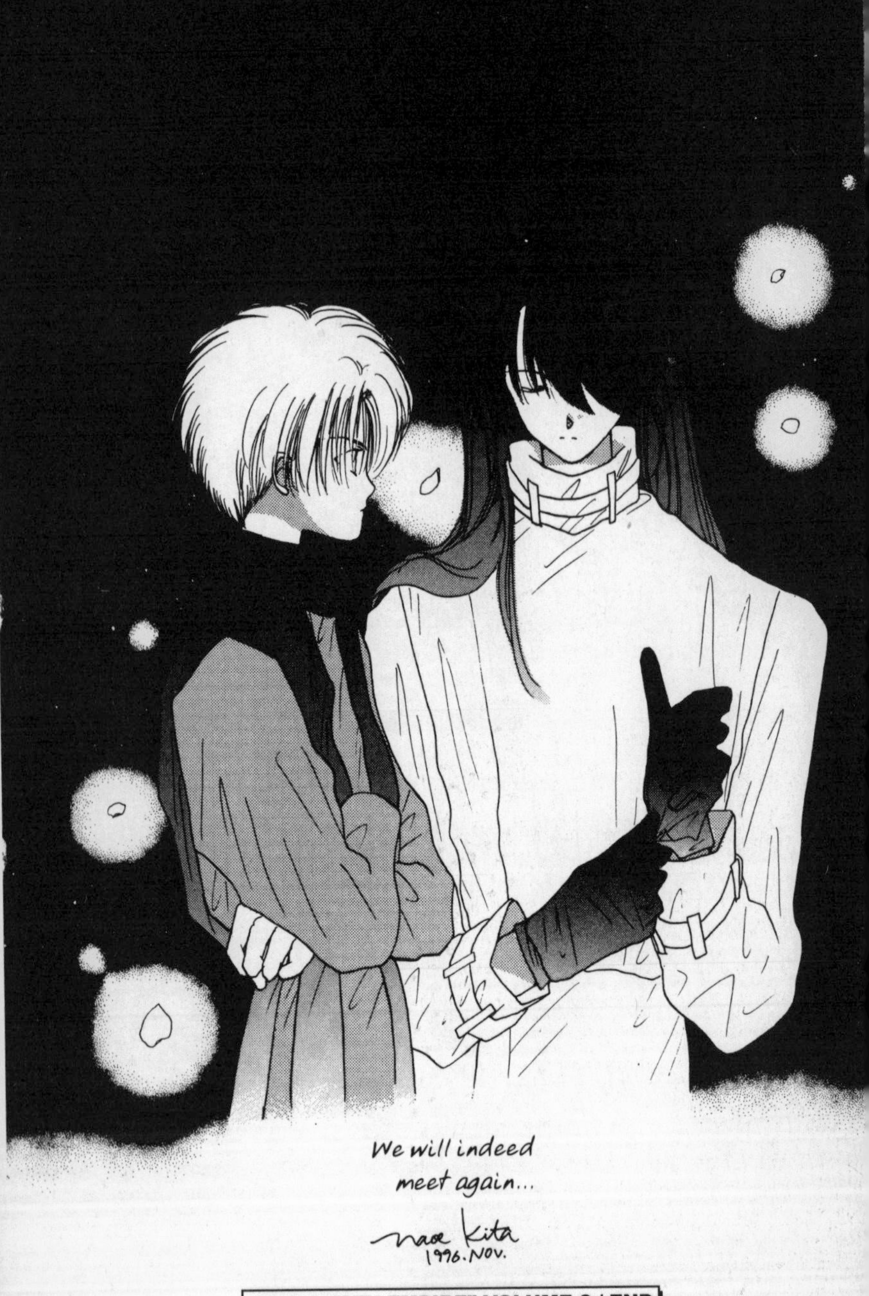
We will indeed
meet again...
naoe kita
1996. NOV.

"THE EMPTY EMPIRE" VOLUME 6 / END

KARA NO TEIKOKU Volume 6 © 1996 Naoe Kita.
All Rights Reserved. First published in Japan in 1996
by HAKUSENSHA, INC., Tokyo.

THE EMPTY EMPIRE Volume 6, published by WildStorm
Productions, an imprint of DC Comics, 888 Prospect St.
#240, La Jolla, CA 92037. English Translation © 2008. All
Rights Reserved. English translation rights in U.S.A. and
Canada arranged by HAKUSENSHA, INC., through Tuttle-
Mori Agency Inc., Tokyo. CMX is a trademark of DC Comics.
The stories, characters, and incidents mentioned in this
magazine are entirely fictional. Printed on recyclable paper.
WildStorm does not read or accept unsolicited submissions
of ideas, stories or artwork. Printed in Canada.

DC Comics, A Warner Bros. Entertainment Company.

Tim Rogers – Translation and Adaptation

Wilson Ramos – Lettering

Larry Berry – Design

Jim Chadwick – Editor

CMX

ISBN: 1-4012-1437-1
ISBN-13: 978-1-4012-1437-1

KARA NO TEIKOKU
THE EMPTY EMPIRE

Volume 7

By Naoe Kita. Almost from the time his existence was revealed, Rose became the target of Idem, the other clone of Idea who currently occupies the throne. Now the two are teaming up together…to find and confront Idea. Are the rumors true? Is the beloved Emperor from whom they were both cloned really still alive? If so, where has he been and what possible explanation can there be for the public story of his alleged death? The answers will all be

All the pages in this book were created—and are printed here—in Japanese RIGHT-to-LEFT format. No artwork has been reversed or altered, so you can read the stories the way the creators meant for them to be read.

RIGHT TO LEFT?!

Traditional Japanese manga starts at the upper right-hand corner, and moves right-to-left as it goes down the page. Follow this guide for an easy understanding.

For more information and sneak previews, visit cmxmanga.com. Call 1-888-COMIC BOOK for the nearest comics shop or head to your local book store.

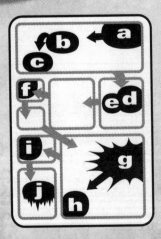